Linguistics and New Testament Interpretation

Essays on
Discourse
Analysis

Contributors

DAVID ALAN BLACK is adjunct professor of New Testament at Talbot School of Theology.

RANDALL BUTH is a translation consultant with the United Bible Societies.

JOHN C. CALLOW is an international linguistic consultant with the Summer Institute of Linguistics and Wycliffe Bible Translators.

KATHLEEN CALLOW is an international translation consultant with the Summer Institute of Linguistics and Wycliffe Bible Translators.

STEPHEN H. LEVINSOHN is an international linguistic consultant with the Summer Institute of Linguistics and Wycliffe Bible Translators.

ROBERT LONGACRE is professor of Linguistics at the University of Texas at Arlington.

J. P. LOUW is professor of Greek at the University of Pretoria.

NEVA F. MILLER is an international translation consultant with the Summer Institute of Linguistics and Wycliffe Bible Translators.

CARROLL D. OSBURN is professor of New Testament at Abilene Christian University.

H. VAN DYKE PARUNAK is a scientific fellow at the Industry Technology Institute.

KERMIT TITRUD is a translation consultant with the Summer Institute of Linguistics and Wycliffe Bible Translators.

JOHN C. TUGGY is an international translation consultant with the Summer Institute of Linguistics and Wycliffe Bible Translators.

ERNST R. WENDLAND is a translation consultant with the United Bible Societies.

LINGUISTICS AND NEW TESTAMENT INTERPRETATION

ESSAYS ON DISCOURSE ANALYSIS

EDITED BY

DAVID ALAN BLACK

WITH KATHARINE BARNWELL AND STEPHEN LEVINSOHN

FOREWORD BY EUGENE A. NIDA

BROADMAN PRESS
NASHVILLE, TENNESSEE

© Copyright 1992 • Broadman Press
All rights reserved

225,48
L755 b

4215-09
ISBN: 0-8054-1509-2

Dewey Decimal Classification: 225.6
Subject Heading: Bible N.T.—Criticism, Interpretation, etc. // Linguistics
Library of Congress Catalog Card Number: 92-25320
Printed in the United States of America

Library of Congress Cataloging-in-Publication Data

Linguistics and New Testament interpretation / David Alan Black, editor.
    p. cm.
    Selected papers from a conference held in 1991, sponsored by
Wycliffe Bible Translators.
    Includes bibliographical references.
    ISBN 0-8054-1509-2
    1. Bible. N.T.—Language, style—Congresses. 2. Bible. N.T.—
Criticism, interpretation, etc.—Congresses. 3. Bible. N.T.—
Translating—Congresses. I. Black, David Alan, 1952   .
II. Wycliffe Bible Translators.
BS2316.L56   1992
225.4'8—dc20   92-25320
                                                                      CIP

Al profesor Jesús Peláez

*Un recuerdo como
expresión de gratitud
para un estimado
amigo y colega*

Contents

Forward   9
Eugene A. Nida
Introduction   10
David Alan Black

Part I   New Methodological Approaches

1   Reading a Text as Discourse   17
J. P. Louw
2   Participant Reference in Koine Greek Narrative   31
Stephen H. Levinsohn
3   Semantic Paragraph Patterns: A Fundamental
Communication Concept and Interpretive Tool   45
John C. Tuggy
4   Constituent Order in Copula Clauses: A Partial Study   68
John C. Callow
5   Discourse Analysis, Synoptic Criticism, and Markan Grammar:
Some Methodological Considerations   90
David Alan Black

Part II   Applications to Specific Texts

6   A Tale of Two Debtors: On the Interaction of Text, Cotext, and
Context in a New Testament Dramatic Narrative (Luke 7:36–50)   101
Ernst R. Wendland
7   Οὖν, Δέ, Καί, and Asyndeton in John's Gospel   144
Randall Buth
8   The Imperativals of Romans 12   162
Neva F. Miller
9   The Disappearing Δέ in 1 Corinthians   183
Kathleen Callow
10   Patterns of Thematic Development in 1 Corinthians 5:1–13   194
Kathleen Callow
11   Dimensions of Discourse Structure:
A Multidimensional Analysis of the Components and
Transitions of Paul's Epistle to the Galatians   207
H. Van Dyke Parunak
12   The Function of Καί in the Greek New Testament
and an Application to 2 Peter   240
Kermit Titrud
13   Towards an Exegesis of 1 John Based on the Discourse
Analysis of the Greek Text   271
Robert Longacre
14   Discourse Analysis and Jewish Apocalyptic in the Epistle of Jude   287
Carroll D. Osburn

Foreword

Linguistics and New Testament Interpretation: Essays on Discourse Analysis represents a diverse set of articles by persons with quite different backgrounds: linguists, Bible scholars, and Bible translators. The subjects discussed and the viewpoints expressed reflect a wide range of interest and concern. This volume is the first of what is hoped will be a series of publications designed to combine linguistic insights, findings in biblical scholarship, and field experience by Bible translators working in very different types of languages and cultures. For the most part, specialists representing these three fields of endeavor have had few opportunities to interact in an academic context. In order to remedy this situation, the Summer Institute of Linguistics hosted a consultation at which a number of papers were given. Some of the more insightful and helpful of these contributions were chosen for this publication. They are clearly quite diverse in both content and methodology, but this is significant in that it reflects the many diverse areas in which linguistics, biblical studies, and Bible translating intersect; and it provides some idea of the wide range of topics which need to be investigated from this three-way perspective.

The papers also differ greatly in the extent of technical vocabulary, an increasingly typical aspect of academic specialization. Meaningful communication between diverse disciples must constantly grapple with this problem, and perhaps the exposure to papers reflecting these differences can be a positive, although sometimes difficult, learning experience.

Perhaps the most important aspect of these papers is the fact that they represent the thinking of persons who have had concrete experience in attempting to communicate the truths of the gospel in a wide range of languages in many different parts of the world. This provides a sense of realism that many compilations of academic papers lack, and it may also provide a context in which intricately related disciplines can find a large area of common ground.

Eugene A. Nida

Introduction

"It is the task and duty of the N.T. student to apply the results of linguistic research to the Greek of the N.T." (Robertson 1914:3). These words of A. T. Robertson, "that towering genius and masterful scholar" (Dana 1927:vi), are as true today as when they were first published in 1914. Robertson's *A Grammar of the Greek New Testament in the Light of Historical Research* was nothing short of epoch-making in its use of linguistic principles, as far as these principles were known and understood. The best modern textbooks on Greek grammar gladly acknowledge their debt to Robertson's pioneering work. Other scholars may place in the hands of Greek students their own contributions, but no book can ever replace the immense learning of Robertson's "Big Grammar."

In one sense, however, what Robertson (1914:4) wrote in his preface about his predecessor, Johann Winer, was true of Robertson himself: "he was a pathfinder." Robertson's grammar, though employing a linguistic approach, went little beyond the study of comparative philology. Robertson is not, of course, to be blamed for this, for linguistics was at that time almost totally confined to questions of grammatical history. The descriptive and historical grammars produced by Robertson and his followers still provide invaluable material for students of New Testament Greek. Yet as linguistics continued to develop as a science in the mid- and late-twentieth century, Greek grammar remained curiously stagnant.

It is not possible here to discuss the post-Robertson era in any detail.[1] The traditional approach is still found in the grammars of

---

[1] For a more complete discussion, reference may be made to Black (1991:377–406).

Machen, Dana and Mantey, and Davis, to name but a few. The same perspective, though with a modern twist, is found in the textbooks of Mueller and Larson. However, we see a distinct transition toward the new era in the works of Goetchius, Funk, LaSor, and Powers. The present writer's *Linguistics for Students of New Testament Greek* attempted to give this new knowledge a succinct form. Enough linguistic ink has now been spilled to suggest that a revolution of sorts has occurred in the study of the language. Today any work on New Testament Greek that ignores these new findings will not easily escape the charge of obscurantism.

The most abundant source of new light for the grammar of New Testament Greek is found in specialized monographs and scholarly articles appearing in journals and *Festschriften.* The serious student of the New Testament can only rejoice at the wealth of material now available. There is now even a journal devoted entirely to the study of New Testament Greek in the light of modern linguistics.[2] These are all helpful, but Richard Erickson (1983:263) is right in arguing that we need textbooks that deal with the Greek of the New Testament "from points of view informed by modern linguistic theory." It can hardly be denied that books integrating New Testament Greek grammar with contemporary linguistics are still very desirable.

It is just here that the present collection of essays may have its greatest value. A new "Robertson" it certainly is not, though we may hope that new Robertsons and Dana and Manteys will soon pass on the modern learning to a new generation of intermediate and advanced Greek students. This symposium has a less ambitious—and more focused—aim. With an eye on the beginning student, the contributors have attempted to show how one linguistic methodology—discourse analysis—contributes directly to the overriding aim of understanding the message of the New Testament. The papers grew out of a conference of linguists and biblical scholars held at the Summer Institute of Linguistics Center in Dallas, Texas, under the auspices of the International Translation Department of Wycliffe Bible Translators. In a series of fifty seminars during a two-week period in May, 1991, participants discussed various aspects of discourse analysis with special reference to the Greek of the New Testament. Their purpose was to determine the relevance of discourse analysis for biblical exegesis as well as its implications for the theory and practice of Bible translation.

---

[2] The journal, entitled *Filologia Neotestamentaria* (Journal of New Testament Philology), is published under the auspices of the University of Córdoba, Spain.

The seminars were organized by Dr. Katherine Barnwell of the International Translation Department and led by Dr. Stephen Levinsohn, an SIL linguist currently working in Colombia, South America. At the conclusion of the conference, the editor, at the behest of Broadman Press and in consultation with Drs. Barnwell and Levinsohn, selected several of the seminar papers for inclusion in the present volume. The editor also invited several non-participants, all experts in Greek linguistics, to be involved in the book by contributing an essay on a specific aspect of the subject. The present collection of papers may therefore be considered a synopsis of current thinking on the topic of Greek discourse analysis as presently reflected in the work of a broad range of Bible translators, linguists, and biblical scholars.

The resultant book, *Linguistics and New Testament Interpretation: Essays on Discourse Analysis,* is intended as an introduction to Greek discourse analysis with special emphasis on its practical application to the language of the New Testament. Generally speaking, discourse analysis is the attempt to study the organization of language above the sentence level. It is the study of larger linguistic units such as entire conversations or written texts. Discourse analysis is also concerned with language as it is used in social contexts, the belief being that language and situation are inseparable. In fact, much of the work in discourse analysis is directed toward investigating the relationships between language, action, thought, and situation.

Chief among the concerns of discourse analysis is to show the internal coherence or unity of a particular text. Discourse analysis involves a *wholistic* study of the text. It is not simply "verse by verse analysis" (the method usually taught in seminaries and employed in most commentaries), but rather an analysis of how verses fit into the structural unity of the entire text. It is critical to realize that discourse analysis is not merely an investigation into the flow of thought of a text, but is at heart an investigation into how the text *produces* flow of thought. Hence "text" and "discourse" are synonymous terms. This means, for example, that a section of text such as the Christ-hymn of Philippians 2:6–11 cannot be studied independently of the discourse as a whole (here, the Book of Philippians). The hymn bears an important relationship to its surrounding co-text, and how one understands this relationship will determine to a significant degree how one understands such matters as the hymn's authorship, purpose, literary form, and so on. Discourse analysis, then, is an attempt to see how a text coheres, how it fits together as a unified whole, and how the relationship between its sentences constitutes the "text." This volume examines in greater detail the place of discourse analysis in biblical exegetics.

A word on the contents of the book. Part I introduces several fundamental methodological principles of discourse analysis. Here the contribution of J. P. Louw, "Reading a Text as Discourse," is foundational and should be read prior to the other essays in the book. It is fitting that the opening essay should have been contributed by Professor Louw, whose classic 1973 article in *The Bible Translator* entitled "Discourse Analysis and the Greek New Testament" set the stage for much of the subsequent discussion. Part II analyzes the discourse features of selected New Testament texts, offering original, provocative interpretations of significant passages. These essays attempt to show how a text's macrostructure is normally marked on the surface level by various linguistic signals provided to the reader by the author. It is the editor's hope that, taken together, these essays will serve, not only as an overview of current scholarship on Greek discourse analysis, but also—and perhaps especially so—as a tool for all students of the Bible, calling them to recognize the significance of the larger discourse as an imperative component in any theory and practice of New Testament interpretation.

It is not our desire to imply that the final word on Greek discourse analysis has now been said. The essays in this volume offer many insights for students of the New Testament, but more refinements of the method are to be expected and welcomed. To do discourse analysis is to recognize that the interpreter is no longer analyzing mere words and sentences but moving beyond this level of language and asking important questions about the text as a whole. It is to be hoped that the present volume, as a contribution to such study, will be an impetus to other scholars and scholars-in-the-making to expand on and refine this developing field of linguistics.

The editor wishes to express his profound appreciation to the contributors for their essays, to his friend and colleague David Dockery for his enthusiastic support of this venture from beginning to end, and to Katy Barnwell for her assistance in the planning and implementation of this volume at every stage of its journey into print. As a token of thanks for kindness beyond measure during a week of lectures on Spain's Costa del Sol in August, 1990, and in recognition of his contribution to the founding of *Filología Neotestamentaria*, this volume is gratefully and joyfully dedicated to Professor Jesús Peláez of the University of Córdoba, Spain.

David Alan Black

References

Black, David Alan. 1988. *Linguistics for Students of New Testament Greek.* Grand Rapids: Baker.

_____. 1991. "The Study of New Testament Greek in the Light of Ancient and Modern Linguistics." *New Testament Criticism and Interpretation: Essays on Methods and Issues,* ed. by D. A. Black and D. S. Dockery. Grand Rapids: Zondervan.

Dana, H. E. and Julius R. Mantey. 1927. *A Manual Grammar of the Greek New Testament.* Toronto: Macmillan.

Erickson, Richard J. 1983. "Linguistics and Biblical Language: A Wide Open Field." *Journal of the Evangelical Theological Society* 26.

Robertson, A. T. 1914. *A Grammar of the Greek New Testament in the Light of Historical Research.* Nashville: Broadman.

Part I

New Methodological Approaches

1

Reading a Text as Discourse

J. P. Louw

People living in societies where reading is part of daily life often tend to think of reading a text as a fairly uncomplicated procedure. Once a person has accomplished the basic skills of literacy, it seems natural for many that the only further impediment to a proper understanding of a text is knowing the meaning of all the words and having a good dictionary at hand. Popular appeals to "what the Bible really says" are usually comments on word meanings. Even Bible commentaries and sermons focus to a large extent on word meanings. Except for occasional references to historical or cultural issues, words and "what they mean" have become the beginning and end of most attempts to arrive at a proper understanding of a passage.

There is yet another popular aspect to reading a text, especially Scripture. All people have their own cultural, political, religious, and psycho-personal convictions. These convictions reinforce each other to impose a set of presuppositions so deeply rooted that we hardly question their validity. Our understanding of a text is thus enlarged beyond the word level by reading a text from preconceived perspectives. Even though people may agree that it is important to be aware of not being misled by their subjective opinions, sociological, marxist, capitalist, catholic, calvinistic, pentecostal, evangelical, and other orientations do offer a framework for reading a Bible text. Such a reading may be called a secondary reading of a text since it entails a semantic reinterpretation of the vocabulary, the discourse structure, and the pragmatics of the text (Louw 1984, 1986).

Readers who try to be objective often insist that presuppositions can be controlled or at least moderated by strict adherence to the exact wording of the text, that is, by reading it "just as it stands"—a primary reading. It usually comes as a surprise to learn that there are various levels of meaning: word meanings (whether lexical or contextual), phrase meanings, sentence meanings, and discourse meanings. The worst comes when linguists insist that the meaning of a sentence is not merely the sum total of the meanings of the words comprising the sentence and, similarly, that discourses are not a matter of sentence meanings strung together. Reading a text involves far more than reading words and sentences. This implies that a primary reading of a text is not necessarily the "correct" reading in terms of the original author's intention. It is merely a reading that corresponds to what the syntactic (including micro and macro structures) and semantic features (extending to all possible semiotic signs) of the text allow within a particular setting. At least three major sets of features condition the reading: *extra-linguistic features* such as time and place, typography, format, medium of presentation, and background and history of a text; *para-linguistic features* such as punctuation, intonation, pause, speech acts, genre (e.g., epic, lyric, drama, conversation, parable), discourse types (narrative, exposition, description, dialogue, lists), communication functions (informative, imperative, emotive, phatic, etc.); and *linguistic features* such as word order, embedding, nominalization, levels of language, style, and, in particular, the discrepancy between syntax and semantics. All these features are but part of the structure of a text.

Reading is, in fact, a very complex process. It is precisely here where discourse analysis as a conscious procedure reveals how we read and understand a text. Discourse analysis is not a recipe that can be applied to ensure a final reading of a passage, void of any subjective notions. It is rather a demonstration, a displaying or showing, first of all to oneself, how the text is being read, then giving account to others how the text is read and used to eventually come to an understanding of the text. In short, it is revealed reading; it charts the course of the reading process. Since reading a text begins with what has been written in a natural language, it is a linguistic procedure in the widest sense. It gives an account of how a person understands the syntax and semantics of a text. It shows how and what one compares or contrasts in recognizing the various semantic aspects of the text that are used in putting together the argument developed in the text.

Discourse analysis should never be anything else other than an analysis of the discourse. A so-called structural reading may be an analysis of how the text is structured and as such would be part of discourse analysis. If a structural reading is an application of a literary theory of structuralism applied to a text, we no longer have an analysis of the structure of a text, but rather a critique of a text in terms of such a theory. More so, an ideological reading of a text, whether political or theological, is not a discourse analysis of the text but a reading using the text as illustrative material to substantiate such a reading. The text is then decontextualized and used as a token in itself.

The past two decades have produced extensive literature on discourse analysis dealing with various aspects of a text. One may even refer to a grammar of texts. Some of these studies focus on the syntax of a text and deal with issues such as cohesion, anaphora, hierarchy of syntactic strata, sequences and levels, ellipsis, the function of pronouns, particles, etc., in discourses. Others focus on the semantics texts by looking at the paragraph as a basic unit, or how semantic relations are textually marked, or the structure of information in a text, or how reference and coherence function as semantic indicators, or plot structure and the interplay of participants in a text. Then there are studies on presuppostion and inference in texts, on speech acts, on the relevance of utterances—in short, on the pragmatics of a text. Another trend is to look at the typology of texts (written, spoken, expository, narrative, scientific, conversational) or the psychology of processing information with attention to cognitive processes of comprehension and recall. Many studies have been undertaken to explain the stylistic devices of discourse, especially rhetorical choices and theme dynamics.

All these studies indicate how extensive the field of discourse analysis is. Reading a text is indeed a complex procedure. There are numerous aspects to be recognized if one intends to read closely. Many readers, however, though they may think they read closely, will rarely stop and check whether all discourse features have been considered. Yet the more one considers, the more one can expect to infer from a text. What is important, however, is to be able to give account of the inferences. There are so many pitfalls that it may be asked whether a complete reading is at all possible. Yet, all people do read and understand texts. The final question is not so much a matter of the extent of understanding but rather of being able to justify *what* is being understood, and especially to be sensitive to over-intepretation. This is one of the main sins of biblical scholarship.

Since any analysis, by necessity, is in danger of "reading into" a text, it is important to be alert of not going beyond the text. This is not the same as going behind the text. Many discourse considerations, especially para-linguistic and extra-linguistic concerns, can enable a reader to go behind a text. Going *beyond* a text involves a refusal to recognize the discourse constraints of a text. The closest one can get to this ideal is to take the linguistic syntax, which is perhaps the most objective feature of a text, as the point of departure that will constrain the overall process of discourse analysis. This contention rests on the assumption that the linguistic syntax of a text shows how the author (or the redactor if one wishes) composed the text. Naturally, the question comes to mind whether the text was so well composed that it perfectly reflects what the author intended to communicate. This question, however, is largely irrelevant since discourse analysis is not analyzing the author's intent; it can merely analyze the text. Pressing issues like these to absurdity would make all communication irrelevant; nevertheless, they may serve as a cautioning device.

Starting with the syntax of the text involves the semantic flow of the argument. This sets the constraints for all further inferences. The more a reader becomes competent in handling discourses, the more readily the flow of a text will become apparent. A text such as Matthew 19:13–15 may illustrate the point. The flow of the argument is linear, with one incident following another. One hardly needs to map the sentence units. Nevertheless, it is important to recognize that there are four syntactic constructions to be charted as follows:

Matthew 19:13–15

1. τότε προσηνέχθησαν αὐτῷ παιδία

purpose └─▸ ἵνα

           ├─▸ τὰς χεῖρας ἐπιθῇ αὐτοῖς
           └─▸ καὶ προσεύξηται

2. οἱ δὲ μαθηταὶ ἐπετίμησαν αὐτοῖς

3. ὁ δὲ Ἰησοῦς εἶπεν

    content ├─▸ ἄφετε τὰ παιδία
            ├─▸ καὶ μὴ κωλύετε αὐτὰ ἐλθεῖν πρός με
    reason └─▸ τῶν γὰρ τοιούτων ἐστὶν ἡ βασιλεία τῶν οὐρανῶν

4. καὶ ἐπιθεὶς τὰς χεῖρας αὐτοῖς

    └───── ἐπορεύθη ἐκεῖθεν

Here are four participants, of which the first (those who brought the children) are unidentified and, in fact, unimportant to the events. The other three are the children, the disciples, and Jesus. The children are referred to in all four syntactic units. They are the protagonists evaluated by the disciples and by Jesus. Only the reason, that is, the basis for their evaluation by Jesus, is made explicit: children portray those who belong to God's kingdom. (Mark 10:15 and Luke 18:17 enlarge upon the nature of the portrayal.) Thus the discourse structure of Matthew 19:13–15 points to "children portray the kingdom of God" as the maxim of the incident and the pivot point of the discourse.

Narrative texts such as Matthew 19:13–15 hardly need to be mapped on paper. They are uncomplicated; one can immediately see what is involved. The sentences are short with very little embedding. Most competent readers will follow the argument without any difficulty. Nevertheless, the charting of the syntactic units is an aid to sense the gist of the narration. All further inferences or comments on the text as well as all further applications of the text that may be exegetically relevant need to be made within this frame of reference in order to avoid overinterpretation of the text. Discourse analysis should never be an aid to overinterpreting a passage. It is rather a type of translation. Its real value lies in letting the reader see the communication in its full extent—not merely verse by verse—so that the subsequent detail comments may not violate the overall message.

The custom of dividing biblical texts into chapters and verses helps locate a particular word or statement. However, it has been extremely misleading in destroying the cohesion of a text by luring readers into exegeting verses. This has been one of the main reasons for the popular word-oriented explanations of what the Bible "really says."

The following discourse outline of John 3:1–21 is a stretch of language without any artificially numbered divisions imposed on the text and may prove the point. The total discourse is outlined in terms of the constituent syntactic units of the text as such and highlights its real clusters of communication. Note how such an outline immediately displays the flow of the text.

John 3:1–21

ἦν δὲ ἄνθρωπος

    ἐκ τῶν Φαρισαίων
    Νικόδημος ὄνομα αὐτῷ
    ἄρχων τῶν Ἰουδαίων

οὗτος ἦλθεν πρὸς αὐτὸν νυκτὸς καὶ εἶπεν αὐτῷ

    Ῥαββί, οἴδαμεν ὅτι ἀπὸ θεοῦ ἐλήλυθας διδάσκαλος

      οὐδεὶς γὰρ δύναται ταῦτα τὰ σημεῖα ποιεῖν

        ἃ σὺ ποιεῖς

      ἐὰν μὴ ᾖ ὁ θεὸς μετ' αὐτοῦ

ἀπεκρίθη Ἰησοῦς καὶ εἶπεν αὐτῷ
└► ἀμὴν ἀμὴν λέγω σοι
    └► ἐὰν μή τις γεννηθῇ ἄνωθεν
       └► οὐ δύναται ἰδεῖν τὴν βασιλείαν τοῦ θεοῦ
λέγει πρὸς αὐτὸν ὁ Νικόδημος
  ├► πῶς δύναται ἄνθρωπος γεννηθῆναι γέρων ὤν
  └► μὴ δύναται εἰς τὴν κοιλίαν τῆς μητρὸς αὐτοῦ δεύτερον
    εἰσελθεῖν καὶ γεννηθῆναι
ἀπεκρίθη Ἰησοῦς
└►ἀμὴν ἀμὴν λέγω σοι

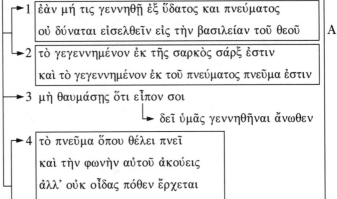

A

ἀπεκρίθη Νικόδημος καὶ εἶπεν αὐτῷ
└► πῶς δύναται ταῦτα γενέσθαι
ἀπεκρίθη Ἰησοῦς καὶ εἶπεν αὐτῷ
├► σὺ εἶ ὁ διδάσκαλος τοῦ Ἰσραὴλ καὶ ταῦτα οὐ γινώσκεις
└► ἀμὴν ἀμὴν λέγω σοι ὅτι

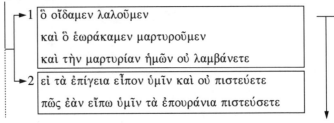

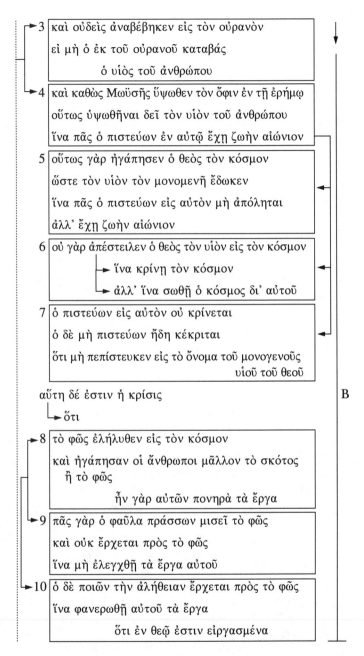

3 καὶ οὐδεὶς ἀναβέβηκεν εἰς τὸν οὐρανὸν
  εἰ μὴ ὁ ἐκ τοῦ οὐρανοῦ καταβάς
      ὁ υἱὸς τοῦ ἀνθρώπου

4 καὶ καθὼς Μωϋσῆς ὕψωθεν τὸν ὄφιν ἐν τῇ ἐρήμῳ
  οὕτως ὑψωθῆναι δεῖ τὸν υἱὸν τοῦ ἀνθρώπου
  ἵνα πᾶς ὁ πιστεύων ἐν αὐτῷ ἔχῃ ζωὴν αἰώνιον

5 οὕτως γὰρ ἠγάπησεν ὁ θεὸς τὸν κόσμον
  ὥστε τὸν υἱὸν τὸν μονομενῆ ἔδωκεν
  ἵνα πᾶς ὁ πιστεύων εἰς αὐτὸν μὴ ἀπόληται
  ἀλλ᾽ ἔχῃ ζωὴν αἰώνιον

6 οὐ γὰρ ἀπέστειλεν ὁ θεὸς τὸν υἱὸν εἰς τὸν κόσμον
      ἵνα κρίνῃ τὸν κόσμον
      ἀλλ᾽ ἵνα σωθῇ ὁ κόσμος δι᾽ αὐτοῦ

7 ὁ πιστεύων εἰς αὐτὸν οὐ κρίνεται
  ὁ δὲ μὴ πιστεύων ἤδη κέκριται
  ὅτι μὴ πεπίστευκεν εἰς τὸ ὄνομα τοῦ μονογενοῦς
                        υἱοῦ τοῦ θεοῦ

αὕτη δέ ἐστιν ἡ κρίσις   B
      ὅτι

8 τὸ φῶς ἐλήλυθεν εἰς τὸν κόσμον
  καὶ ἠγάπησαν οἱ ἄνθρωποι μᾶλλον τὸ σκότος
      ἢ τὸ φῶς
          ἦν γὰρ αὐτῶν πονηρὰ τὰ ἔργα

9 πᾶς γὰρ ὁ φαῦλα πράσσων μισεῖ τὸ φῶς
  καὶ οὐκ ἔρχεται πρὸς τὸ φῶς
  ἵνα μὴ ἐλεγχθῇ τὰ ἔργα αὐτοῦ

10 ὁ δὲ ποιῶν τὴν ἀλήθειαν ἔρχεται πρὸς τὸ φῶς
   ἵνα φανερωθῇ αὐτοῦ τὰ ἔργα
       ὅτι ἐν θεῷ ἐστιν εἰργασμένα

The discourse starts by introducing the two participants, Nicodemus and Jesus (Νικόδημος and αὐτὸν, Ῥαββί), stating the credentials of Nicodemus as a Pharisee and Jewish leader who accepted the authority of Jesus as one sent by God. It is quite remarkable that the narration then skips the preliminaries by moving directly to the issue of γεννηθῆναι ἄν-ωθεν and εἰσελθεῖν εἰς τὴν βασιλείαν τοῦ θεοῦ. How the conversation started and proceeded up to this point is of no concern to the author. The total discourse shows that the historic encounter is merely used as a setting to explain this important issue and to comment on the significant implications involved. The explanation is given in the section marked A (vv. 3–8) and the implications follow in the section marked B (vv. 11–21). In the A section the words spoken by Jesus are clearly discernable, while in the B section only the first part of the implications (marked by the four syntactic units indicated as 1 + 2 and 3 + 4, comprising vv. 11–15) can be undoubtedly assigned to Jesus. The second set (marked by the three syntactic units indicated as 5, 6, and 7, comprising vv. 16–18) contains in itself a comment on the ἵνα clause in unit 4, each taking the argument a step further. These comments may be assigned to Jesus as part of His reply to Nicodemus, but they could also be understood as John's reflection; the discourse structure is not that explicit. The final section (marked by the three syntactic units indicated as 8, 9, and 10, comprising vv. 19–21) seems to be John's comment. It is a feature of John's style to interweave theological reflection with actual conversation.

The discourse outline given above shows how Nicodemus understood ἄνωθεν as a time designation denoting a repeated subsequent event: being physically born again. Jesus' reply is significant. It consists of five sentence units, of which the third ("do not marvel that I said, you must be born ἄνωθεν") repeats the issue. The preceding two units explain the means of ἄνωθεν as a spiritual birth ("be born from above"). The second of the two units states the issue unambiguously: "what is born of a human is physical, what is born of the Spirit is spiritual" (v. 6). This explains the expression ἐξ ὕδατος καὶ πνεύματος in the first unit. The grammatical construction of the first unit is condensed and reflects what ancient rhetoricians referred to as brevity (βραχύτης). In reply to the objection by Nicodemus that a person cannot re-enter the mother's womb, Jesus says in effect: yes, that is true; there is physical birth, but there is also spiritual birth—without which no one can enter the kingdom of God. The fourth and fifth units enlarge upon the explanation by defining spiritual birth as, in a way, comparable to the wind: it is not in itself physically discernable, yet its activity and effect are clear. Thus it is with anyone born of the Spirit of God. The discourse style is elegant in being concise and forceful.

The implications of what "being born of the Spirit" entails are then spelled out in ten sentence units (section B), of which the first two stress the fact that while Nicodemus and the people find it hard to accept what Jesus is teaching on everyday matters (τὰ ἐπίγεια, unit 2), it stands to reason that heavenly matters (τὰ ἐπουράνια) should be even more difficult to comprehend. Yet they can be assured that Jesus knows what He is talking about (unit 1). Units 3 and 4 form another semantic cluster: heavenly matters are indeed difficult to grasp. In fact, no one has ever gone up to heaven to see what is involved. However, there is one who can truly explain such matters—the one who came from heaven, the Son of Man. As Moses in the desert lifted up the (bronze) snake for the people to look up to and be healed, so the Son of Man, Jesus Himself, is the one to look up to in order to experience eternal life. This very expression (ἵνα πᾶς ὁ πιστεύων ἐν αὐτῷ ἔχῃ ζωὴν αἰώνιον) is then enlarged upon in the following three (5–7) sentence units: item 5 takes up this statement almost verbally except for adding μὴ ἀπολήται, which is echoed in 6 by κρίνη, while σωθῇ in 6 takes up ἔχῃ ζωὴν αἰώνιον in 5 as semantically equivalent in effect. Unit 7 takes up κρίνη again, linking it to πιστεύων in 5 and also to μὴ ἀπόληται. The final three units (9–10) are introduced by αὕτη δέ ἐστιν ἡ κρίσις, "this is the basis for deciding," that is, this is the essence of understanding "believe—being saved" and "disbelief—being judged and condemned." It is a matter of light and darkness, that is, of doing evil and doing what God requires.

The twofold meaning of ἄνωθεν in Greek (usually translated as "from above" and "again") is highlighted as the crucial issue, not only in the understanding of γεννηθῆναι ἄνωθεν by Nicodemus but also as vital to the essence of the total discourse as explained in the section marked B, especially in units 5–10. This demarcates John 3:1–21 as a major semantic unit that needs to be read as a single stretch of communication. The statement in verse 3, namely, ἀμὴν ἀμὴν λέγω σοι ἐὰν μή τις γεννηθῇ ἄνωθεν, οὐ δύναται ἰδεῖν τὴν βασιλείαν τοῦ θεοῦ (and its partial restatement in verse 7) is the pivot point of the discourse.

The above outline charts the flow of the argument in John 3:1–21. As such, discourse analysis is a type of translation pointing to the gist of the argument developed in the text. It offers a reading of the text that can be justified by the constrains of the text and can now serve as a framework to look into more detailed matters of exegesis, including comments on single words and phrases. For example, ὕψωσεν and ὑψωθῆναι in verse 14 involve a semantic play on the two lexical meanings of ὑψόω, namely, "to lift up" as causing a spatial position and "to exalt" as causing a high position of status. On the level of the first meaning (comparable to how Moses lifted up the bronze snake) Jesus must be lifted up, figuratively speaking, so that people can look up to Him as Savior. Yet the "lifting up" of Jesus is, in essence, recognizing that He is the one to be exalted as the real Savior so that whoever believes in Him may have eternal life. Such a play on words is typical of Johannine style. In Acts 5:30, 31, Peter voiced the same confession by pointing out that God raised Jesus and exalted (ὕψωσεν) Him as Leader and Savior. The discourse structure on John 3:16–18 (units 5, 6, and 7 of section B of the discourse outline) validates the semantic play of the meanings of ὑψόω as a legitimate inference.

A competent reader may not always find it necessary to go to such great lengths to understand the argument of a text. Many, or at least some, of the issues displayed above may be comprehended offhand while reading the text. It all depends on the reader's familiarity with the subject matter. One should be careful not to be overconfident. It usually pays to graph the discourse structure carefully.

As soon as discourses become more complex, the need for closer scrutiny becomes vital. The more competent a reader is, the further such a reader can move up the line of complexity before it becomes imperative to map all the features of a text. The moment one doubts whether one understands the argument of a text is the exact point where a more detailed discourse analysis is required. It is a matter of evaluating one's uncertainties.

Reasoned texts are usually more complicated. They tend not to be linear but to look forward and backward, to debate by inference and logic arranged in dependent and main arguments. One has to read slower and pay careful attention to the variety of items brought into the argument and how they are interrelated. A text such as Colossians 2:20–3:4 may illustrate the point.

The grammatical syntax of Colossians 2:20–23 clearly shows one construction unit having as its matrix a question τί δογματίζεσθε ("why do you obey rules?") (Louw and Nida 1989). The content of these rules are given in the phrase μὴ ἅψῃ μηδὲ γεύσῃ μηδὲ θίγῃς ("don't handle, don't taste, don't touch"). The matrix and its content are enlarged by a number of clauses. The matrix follows a conditional clause (εἰ ἀπεθάνετε σὺν Χριστῷ) linking the question (τί) by constituting (syntactically) the statement "if . . . why?" which functions (semantically) as a speech act to emphasize that the condition is a claimed fact. This is a popular strategy in Pauline style, saying literally "if . . . why?" but actually meaning "since . . . why?", implying that for those who have really "died with Christ" (a figurative expression meaning having completely associated themselves with Christ by severing [ἀπό] all ties to the basic principles that underlie the concepts and aspirations of the world) it stands to reason that they could not practice their religion as essentially a set of forbearance rules. The phrases ἀπὸ τῶν στοιχείων τοῦ κόσμου and ὡς ζῶντες ἐν κόσμῳ are semantically synonymous, the first stating the issue negatively (ἀπό),

Colossians 2:20–3:4

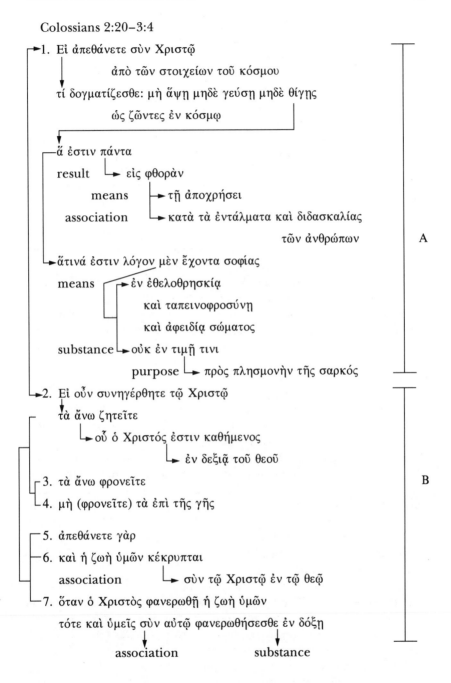

1. Εἰ ἀπεθάνετε σὺν Χριστῷ

        ἀπὸ τῶν στοιχείων τοῦ κόσμου

τί δογματίζεσθε: μὴ ἅψῃ μηδὲ γεύσῃ μηδὲ θίγῃς

        ὡς ζῶντες ἐν κόσμῳ

ἅ ἐστιν πάντα

result   εἰς φθορὰν

      means   τῇ ἀποχρήσει

      association   κατὰ τὰ ἐντάλματα καὶ διδασκαλίας

                        τῶν ἀνθρώπων   A

ἅτινά ἐστιν λόγον μὲν ἔχοντα σοφίας

means   ἐν ἐθελοθρησκίᾳ

           καὶ ταπεινοφροσύνῃ

           καὶ ἀφειδίᾳ σώματος

substance   οὐκ ἐν τιμῇ τινι

      purpose   πρὸς πλησμονὴν τῆς σαρκός

2. Εἰ οὖν συνηγέρθητε τῷ Χριστῷ

τὰ ἄνω ζητεῖτε

      οὗ ὁ Χριστός ἐστιν καθήμενος

           ἐν δεξιᾷ τοῦ θεοῦ

3. τὰ ἄνω φρονεῖτε   B

4. μὴ (φρονεῖτε) τὰ ἐπὶ τῆς γῆς

5. ἀπεθάνετε γὰρ

6. καὶ ἡ ζωὴ ὑμῶν κέκρυπται

association   σὺν τῷ Χριστῷ ἐν τῷ θεῷ

7. ὅταν ὁ Χριστὸς φανερωθῇ ἡ ζωὴ ὑμῶν

τότε καὶ ὑμεῖς σὺν αὐτῷ φανερωθήσεσθε ἐν δόξῃ

      association   substance

the second positively (ζῶντες ἐν, "living in union with"). This repetition is an emphatic device to say: "You have become followers of Jesus Christ, and, as such, you have indeed turned away from the tenets of the world. How can you then continue to see religion as merely a set of rules, that is—by implication—still thinking that complying to the letter of the Mosaic law within a Christian framework is real Christianity?"

These inferences derived from a number of presumed paralinguistic features are closely linked to the lexical and syntactical features of the text. The outlay of the linguistic elements of the text highlights relationships between the constituent units. The enlargements on the content phrase (μὴ ἅψῃ μηδὲ γεύσῃ μηδὲ θίγῃς) illustrate these notions even more clearly. Two relative clauses introduced by ἅ and ἅτινα explain fully what the "if . . . why?" matrix involves. Mapping the elements and their markers (mostly the grammatical cases and prepositions) almost impels the reader to account for the relationship between the units. These relationships are perhaps the most crucial indicators of how the text is read and understood. In the above outline these are defined by the terms "result, means, association, substance, and purpose"—and these are mostly the lexical meanings designated by the prepositions (εἰς, κατά, ἐν, πρός). Correlating this information with the semantic analysis of the many noun forms of the vocabulary (of which the majority pertains semantically to events) provides one with the data to determine the flow of the discourse argument.

The argument of the two relative clauses can now be rephrased. The term πάντα shows that the three "don'ts" are merely illustrative examples of obeying various rules. A religion based on rules results (εἰς) in a state of ruin (φθοράν), implying that the precepts are bound to disintegrate. This is a natural inference from human experience, since people are ingenious to rationalize ways of side-stepping rules and regulations. The Jewish teachers of the Law were noted for comments to this effect. The text then states the means (dative case) by which the ruin is accomplished, namely, by sheer use (τῇ ἀποχρήσει), especially when it involves (κατά marking an associative relation) rules and teachings devised by people.

The ἅ is now presumed by the ἅτινα, taking the same line of argument a little farther. Such rules, of course, appear to be based on wisdom since they are brought about by (ἐν) a set of religious practices resulting from one's own desires and initiatives (ἐθελοθρησκία), by a desire to demonstrate one's ethical humility (ταπεινοφροσύνη), and by severe self-control of one's natural desires (ἀφειδίᾳ σώματος). These means are in themselves laudable, though they are all man-made. They claim to be based on wisdom, but they have no real value (ἐν marking substance), that is, they are not helpful to attend to (πρός) the problem of sensual indulgence (πλησμονὴ τῆς σαρκός) or, stated positively, of controlling sensual desires.

The argument put forward in this first full sentence (section A) of our discourse (Col. 2:20–23) can now be summarized as follows: true religion is not a matter of devising and complying to a set of ethical rules. A person who has experienced a complete turning away from the concepts and aspirations of human principles and procedures by partaking in the new life in union with Christ (ἀπεθάνετε σὺν Χριστῷ) has a different orientation. The next section (B) of the discourse explains the details. It is linguistically phrased by means of six grammatical sentence units (marked as 2–7 in the above discourse outline comprising Col. 3:1–4). These six units, however, are closely linked, as will be shown in the subsequent discussion. In fact, they constitute a major semantic unit (B) that is the counterpart of the first major unit (A). Note that both units are introduced by a conditional clause: εἰ ἀπεθάνετε, εἰ συνηγέρθητε, echoing a similar argument expounded especially in Romans 6:1–14. The same speech act is semantically relevant: you did die with Christ/you were indeed resurrected with Christ—now then. . . . This implies that if the first (death/resurrection) is a reality in the believer's life, the second (the enlargments) should, of necessity, also be a reality.

The second syntactic unit introducing the B section of the discourse has as its matrix τὰ ἄνω ζητεῖτε ("desire to experience the things above"). Then τὰ ἄνω is explained by οὗ ὁ Χριστός ἐστιν καθήμενος and specified as ἐν δεξιᾷ τοῦ θεοῦ. That is to say, if indeed you are raised to a new life sharing in the death and resurrection of Christ, your desires must then, of necessity, be at one with Christ and God the Father.

The third and fourth units repeat the same: your minds should be where Christ is. Or stated negatively: your minds should not be focused on what pertains to the world. In a sense this echoes the ἀπὸ τῶν στοιχείων τοῦ κόσμου at the beginning of section A.

The content of sentence units 2, 3, and 4 is now restated in terms of both conditional clauses (in A and B) by a very neatly structured group of sentences (5, 6, and 7) in which themes are chiastically arranged with ἐν τῷ θεῷ as a turning point to emphasize the key elements:

ἀπεθάνετε	ζωὴ ὑμῶν			κέκρυπται	Χριστῷ
1	2			3	4
		θεῷ			
Χριστός	φανερωθῇ		ζωὴ ὑμῶν	φανερωθήσεσθε	
4	3		2	1	

In a sense we have a summary of the total argument: you died which means that your life is hidden with Christ/when Christ becomes manifest as being your life, you will become manifest (as sharing) in (His) glory. All these counterparts culminate in your union with God.

The discourse, however, continues from Colossians 3:5 onwards by listing and discussing various features of practical Christian conduct, similar in essence to giving rules and teachings. Does this now contradict the argument proposed by the relative clauses of section A (Col. 2:22–23)? Not at all. Section B is the catalyst. The total argument can now be restated as follows: true Christianity is not a matter of obeying rules and regulations; it is a personal, associative relationship with God in union with Christ Jesus, so radical that one can even talk of a death and resurrection resulting in a new way of life in which ethical conduct is a product of this new relationship, not a precondition. This reminds one of Jesus' saying: οὐκ ἦλθον καταλῦσαι ἀλλὰ πληρῶσαι, "I did not come to do away [with the law and the teachings of the prophets], but to give them true meaning" (Matt. 5:17).

References

Louw, J. P. 1986. "Macro Levels of Meaning in Lk 7.36–50." *A South African Perspective on the New Testament*. Leiden: Brill.

_____. 1984. "Primary and Secondary Reading of a Text." *Neotestamentica* 18.18–25.

Louw, J. P. and Nida, E. A. 1989. *Greek-English Lexicon of the New Testament based on Semantic Domains*. New York: United Bible Studies.

2

Participant Reference in Koine Greek Narrative[1]

Stephen H. Levinsohn

Greek, like all languages, has a fairly extensive range of means of referring to participants in a story, from "zero anaphora," or implicit reference reflected only in the appropriate person affix in the verb, to sets of pronouns (articular and demonstrative), to a full noun phrase. In this paper, I look at factors which determine which is to be used. From an understanding of these factors, more can be discerned about the author's intentions as to the status of the participants in the story, whether or not certain events or speeches are highlighted, and whether or not successive incidents are closely associated.

I describe on pages 31–34 how major and minor participants are distinguished. I then consider Givón's (1983:18) "Iconicity Principle" for further reference to participants who have been introduced to a story and note areas in which the principle is inadequate (pp. 34–35). On pages 35–40, I discuss further reference to participants in terms of default and marked encoding. Finally, on pages 41–43, I look at the system of reference to Jesus as central character in the Gospels and its implications for identifying major divisions in the narrative and highlighted speeches or actions.

The Status of Participants and Their Introduction

Languages commonly make a distinction between *major* and *minor* participants,[2] a distinction which also is required by default rules for encoding references to participants which I propose for Koine Greek

---

[1] This paper is adapted from chapter 8 of Levinsohn forthcoming.

[2] For a fuller discussion of the difference between major and minor participants, together with references to literature on the distinction, see Levinsohn 1987:18.

(pp. 35–40). One difference between the two categories of participants is that minor participants just appear and disappear, without
any formal introduction. In addition, they are often referred to in
full, each time they are involved in the story. Major participants, in
contrast, are introduced formally in some way, and typically are involved in a series of events.

Major participants in Koine Greek narrative are introduced in three
typical ways: (a) in a non-active way in a clause with a non-event verb
like εἰμί "be," and/or (b) with τις attributive to a noun phrase; (c) in an
active way to an existing scene in connection with ἰδού "behold."

(a) It is common for a major participant to be introduced in a *non-
active* way in a non-event clause, then be involved in the event described in the next clause. This is how the prodigal son is introduced
in Luke 15:11–12a:

(15:11)   ἄνθρωπός τις εἶχεν δύο υἱούς
           man certain 3S-had two sons
(15:12a)   καὶ εἶπεν ὁ νεώτερος αὐτῶν τῷ πατρί . . .
           and 3S-said the younger of-them to-the father

The non-event clause may posit the existence of the participant
who is being introduced, as in Acts 9:10a:

(9:10a)   ἦν δέ τις μαθητὴς ἐν Δαμασκῷ ὀνόματι Ἀνανίας
           3S-was now certain disciple in Damascus by-name Ananias
(9:10b)   καὶ εἶπεν πρὸς αὐτὸν ἐν ὁράματι ὁ κύριος Ἀνανία
           and 3S-said to him in vision the Lord Ananias

(b) Another common way for major participants to be introduced is
with a noun phrase to which τις is attributive. In both Luke 15:11 (ἄνθρωπός τις "a certain man") and Acts 9:10a (τις μαθητής "a certain disci-
ple"), τις is used in connection with the introduction of a major
participant in a non-event clause. A participant may also be introduced in a more active role, as is the case with Cornelius in Acts 10:1ff:

(10:1)   ἀνὴρ δέ τις ἐν Καισαρείᾳ ὀνόματι Κορνήλιος . . .
           man now certain in Caesarea by-name Cornelius
(10:3)   εἶδεν ἐν ὁράματι . . . ἄγγελον τοῦ θεοῦ εἰσελθόντα . . .
           3S-saw in vision angel of-the God entering

Note that τις by itself (i.e., not attributive to a noun phrase), is
used to introduce minor participants as "someone." See, for example, Acts 5:25.

(c) ἰδού "behold," followed immediately by reference to a new participant, is used to introduce major participants in an *active* to an *existing* scene. Van Otterloo (1988:34) says that ἰδού is used in this way
"to focus special attention on a major . . . participant as he/she/it is

introduced onto the event line of an episode." Matthew 2:1 illustrates this usage.[3]

(2:1a) τοῦ δὲ Ἰησοῦ γεννηθέντος ἐν Βηθλεὲμ τῆς Ἰουδαίας ἐν ἡμέραις Ἡρῴδου τοῦ βασιλέως
of-the now Jesus having-been-born in Bethlehem of-the Judaea in days of-Herod the king
(2:1b) ἰδοὺ μάγοι ἀνατολῶν παρεγένοντο εἰς Ἰεροσόλυμα
behold magi from east 3P-arrived in Jerusalem

I have not yet discussed the status of supernatural participants. Sometimes they are treated as minor participants and sometimes as major ones, depending on the passage. However, it is generally the case (Levinsohn 1987:18f) that supernatural participants "may be thought of as 'external' to the central scenes of the narrative . . . as the interactions between human participants unfold. Like minor participants, supernatural participants often just appear and act, then disappear from the scene, leaving the human interactions to continue."

Acts 5:19 is an example of a supernatural participant occupying a minor role, just appearing and disappearing (the major participants are the apostles and the authorities, the latter being reintroduced in v. 21b):

(5:17–18) But the high priest rose up and all who were with him . . . filled with jealousy, they arrested the apostles and put them in the common prison.
(5:19) ἄγγελος δὲ κυρίου διὰ νυκτὸς ἤνοιξε τὰς θύρας . . .
angel but of-Lord during night 3S-opened the doors

In Matthew 1:20, in contrast, the angel is introduced in an active role to an existing scene, just like any other major participant.

(1:20a) ταῦτα δὲ αὐτοῦ ἐνθυμηθέντος
these but his thinking-on

---

[3] Van Otterloo (1988) fails to distinguish between instances of ἰδού in which the reference to the new participant occurs immediately after ἰδού, and those in which ἰδού is followed by a verb. If this distinction is made, it turns out that a participant introduced immediately following ἰδού typically comes into the scene in an active way. When ἰδού is followed by a verb, in contrast, it is a significant *act* that is introduced to the existing scene, and any participant involved is cast in a *non-active* role. Examples of ἰδού followed by a verb include Matt. 3:16b [καὶ ἰδοὺ ἠνεῴχθησαν [αὐτῷ] οἱ οὐρανοί "and behold, the heavens were opened [to him]"] and Matt. 9:2 [καὶ ἰδοὺ προσέφερον αὐτῷ παραλυτικόν "and behold, they (unspecified) brought to him a paralytic"].

Groce points out (1991:128) that many participants introduced by ἰδού are "accorded only obscure reference, without a given name in most cases." Such participants might well not have been perceived to have a major role to play in the incident into which they were introduced, had ἰδού not been used.

(1:20b) ἰδοὺ ἄγγελος κυρίου κατ' ὄναρ ἐφάνη αὐτῷ . . .
         behold angel of-Lord by dream 3S-appeared to-him

Givón's "Iconicity Principle" for Participant Reference

Once a participant has been introduced to the story, the way he or
she is referred to again depends on a number of factors. Primary
among these is what Givón (1983) calls "topic continuity": whether
the participant is already on stage or is being reintroduced after an
absence, and whether his or her role remains the same or changes.
Other factors which affect participant reference include the number
of participants on stage, the status of the participant, and whether
the sentence concerned is highlighted or not.

Givón's "Iconicity Principle" (1983:18) states, "The more disruptive, surprising, discontinuous or hard to process a topic is, the more
coding material must be assigned to it." In the case of Koine Greek,
encoding is on the scale:

zero anaphora
articular pronouns
independent pronouns
full noun phrases (including proper nouns).

My experience is that Givón's Iconicity Principle works up to a
point. For example, the principle correctly predicts that, when there
is "topic" discontinuity because a participant is being reintroduced
after an absence, it is normal to refer to him or her with a full noun
phrase. Similarly, it is normal to use a full noun phrase when a sentence is highlighted because the event described is "disruptive, surprising" (Ibid.). However, sentences may be highlighted and a full
noun phrase employed when the information concerned is important but neither disruptive nor surprising (e.g., a key speech). Also, it
is not clear whether the principle covers the use of full noun phrases
at the beginning of new "narrative units" (Fox 1987:168), when the
participants remain the same and occupy the same roles in successive paragraphs of a narrative.

One factor that is not covered by Givón's principle is that of the *status* of the participant. As I show on pages 35–40, the form of reference
chosen depends on whether two major participants are interacting, or
whether the interacting participants are one major and one minor.[4]

---

[4] A further factor not covered by Givón's principle is that of the local *salience* of the
participant. "Salience relates to the way in which certain actants present in a situation
are seized on by humans as foci of attention" (Comrie 1989:199). In Levinsohn forthcoming, I argue that, in the Acts of the Apostles, the anarthrous versus arthrous reintro-
duction of participants by name depends on whether they are respectively salient or not.

Given the above reservations about Givón's Iconicity Principle, I now propose an alternative approach to the encoding of further reference to participants, which incorporates the insights offered by the principle, but identifies when default encoding has been used, and explains the significance of marked forms of encoding.

Default and Marked Encoding of Participant Reference

I approach the analysis of further reference to participants who have already been introduced to a story in terms of default and marked encoding. First, I specify default encoding for various situations in which, in Givón's terms, there is no great discontinuity or surprise. Marked forms of encoding are those which are other than the default value for a specific situation. Marked forms occur in specific contexts, in particular at the beginning of narrative units such as paragraphs and in highlighted sentences.

Default encoding for Koine Greek narrative includes the following rules for subjects:

(1) If the subject is the same as in the previous clause,[5] no overt reference is made to the subject.[6]

(2) If the subject was the addressee of an immediately preceding speech, an articular pronoun is used, unless the subject addresses someone other than the previous speaker.

(3) If a non-subject in one clause becomes the subject of the next, and a major participant is interacting with a minor participant or is alone, no reference is made to the subject.[7]

(4) In all other occasions in which there is a change of subject, a full noun phrase is used to refer to the subject. (These include occasions in which a participant is reintroduced and those in which two major participants are interacting.)

(5) If the genitival subject of a genitive absolute is the same as that of the previous clause, an independent pronoun is used. (This is because, in genitives absolute, the subject generally is obligatory.[8])

---

[5] If the subject is the same as in the last independent clause describing an event of the story, no overt reference is made to it, even if an intervening non-event clause has a different subject. This proviso is illustrated in Acts 5:2c (passage 2 below), Luke 20:20 (passage 4), and Matthew 4:19 (passage 5).

[6] When the subject of the previous clause is included in a plural subject in the next clause, this is usually treated as the same subject, for the purposes of participant reference encoding. See Luke 15:24b (passage 1 below).

[7] See pp. 41–43 for a modification of this rule, when the "central character" becomes subject after being non-subject.

[8] Genitives absolute occur without overt subjects in Luke 12:36 and Acts 12:31, plus as variants in other passages. If no overt reference were considered to be the default

The most frequent instances of *marked* encoding of subjects involve occasions when the subject remains the same between sentences (see default rule 1) or the previous addressee becomes the subject (default rule 2), yet a full noun phrase or, more rarely, an independent pronoun is used.

I now illustrate the five default encoding rules given above from the parable of the Prodigal Son (Luke 15:11–32). Passage 1 displays how the participants are referred to and which default rule is operating. (I do not indicate how the participants are referred to within the reported speeches, as these are embedded in the overall narrative.)

I use the following *abbreviations*: art "articular pronoun"; GA "genitive absolute"; intro "introduction"; NP "full noun phrase"; pn "independent pronoun"; Ø "no overt reference, zero anaphora."

The *numbers* in parentheses refer to the referents: (1) is the father; (2) the younger son; (3) the older son; (4) the citizen of verse 15; (5) the slaves of verse 22; and (6) the lad of verse 26. The first three are major participants; the other three are minor ones.

The *default* column numbers indicate which of the five default encoding rules for subject is operating. The absence of a number indicates that the encoding is not a default value.

Passage 1: Luke 15:11–32

(v)	(subject)	(non-subject)	(default)	(summary of contents)
(11)	NP (1)	NP (2 + 3)	intro	(man had two sons)
(12a)	NP (2)	NP (1)	4	(said, "Give me share")
(12b)	art[a] (1)	pn (2 +3)	2	(divided living)
(13a)	NP (2)		4	(departed to far country)
(13b)	Ø (2)		1	(squandered property)
(14a)	pn (2)		5	(when spent everything; GA)
(14b)	famine		intro	(arose in that country)
(14c)	pn (2)		—	(began to be in want)
(15a)	Ø (2)	NP (4)	1	(joined himself to)
(15b)	Ø (4)	pn (2)	3	(sent into his fields)

---

encoding for genitives absolute with the same subject as the previous clause, the presence of the independent pronoun could readily be explained in terms of new narrative units or of highlighting the event described in the following independent clause.

(v)	(subject)	(non-subject)	(default)	(summary of contents)
(16a)	Ø (2)		3	(longed to feed on pods)
(16b)	no-one	pn (2)	4	(gave anything)
(17)	Ø (2)		3	(coming to himself, said)
(20a)	Ø (2)	NP (1)	1	(rising up, came to)
(20b)	pn (2)		5	(while yet at a distance; GA)
(20c)	NP (1)	pn (2)	4	(saw)
(20d)	Ø (1)		1	(had compassion)
(20e)	Ø (1)	pn (2)	1	(running, embraced)
(20f)	Ø (1)	pn (2)	1	(kissed)
(21)	NP (2)	pn (1)	4	(said to)
(22)	NP (1)	NP (5)	4	(said to)
(24b)	Ø (1 +)		1 note	(began to make merry)
(25a)	NP (3)		4	(was in the field)
(25b)	Ø (3)		1	(as drew near, heard music)
(26)	Ø (3)	NP (6)	1	(calling, asked what meant)
(27)	art (6)	pn (3)	2	(said, "Your brother came")
(28a)	Ø (3)		3	(was angry)
(28b)	Ø (3)		1	(refused to go in)
(28c)	NP (1)	pn (3)	4	(coming out, besought)
(29)	art (3)	NP (1)	2	(answering, said)
(31)	art (1)	pn (3)	2	(said)

a. Some MSS have no overt reference to the father in v. 12b, perhaps implying that he is the "central character" of the story; see "References to Jesus as central character in the Gospels."

The above passage shows that the status of the participants must be taken into account, in order to explain why no overt subject occurs in connection with some changes of subject, but a full noun

phrase is used in other instances. No overt subject occurs in verses
15b, 16a, or 28a (default rule 3), as only one major participant is on
stage. In verses 21 and 22, in contrast, a full noun phrase is used,
since two major participants are on stage (default rule 4). Note that,
in verse 22, although the father was the addressee of the previous
speech, he speaks to the servants, not to his son. Consequently, default rule 4 applies, rather than rule 2.

In only one clause in the above passage does the participant reference encoding deviate from the default rules. This is in verse 14c,
where an independent pronoun is used. The referent is the only major participant on stage, so the default encoding would have been no
overt reference (rule 3). However, verse 14a would appear to begin a
new narrative unit, so more marked encoding is employed.

Passage 2 illustrates the use of a full noun phrase, in connection
with the climactic event of an incident. In Acts 5:5, the default encoding of reference to Ananias would have been an articular pronoun, as he was the addressee of the previous speech. The marked
encoding contributes to the highlighting of this climactic event. ((A)
refers to Ananias; (P) to Peter; and (Y) to the youths of v. 6a.)

Passage 2: Acts 5:1–6.

(v)	(subject)	(non-subject)	(default)	(summary of contents)
(1)	NP (A)	NP (wife)	intro	(sold property with)
(2a)	Ø (A)		1	(appropriated part of price)
(2b)	NP (wife)		4	(being aware of it; GA)
(2c)	Ø (A)	NP (apostles)	1[a]	(bringing, placed at feet of)
(3)	NP (P)	Ø (A)	4	(said)
(5)	NP (A)		—	(hearing, died)
(6a)	NP (Y)	pn (A)	intro	(arising, wrapped)
(6b)	Ø	Ø (A)	1	(carrying out, buried)

a. The subject of v. 2c is the same as that of the last independent clause, viz. v. 2a.

In the following conversation (passage 3) between the Lord and
(another) Ananias, several of the speeches are introduced with
marked encoding of the subject. The Lord's (L) instructions to Ana-

nias (A; Acts 9:11, 15) may both be viewed as key speeches. Ananias's objection of verse 13 is also introduced with a full noun phrase; this is the norm when the previous addressee seizes the initiative (see Levinsohn forthcoming, chapter 9). Finally, following the conversation, a full noun phrase is used to refer to Ananias in verse 17a, even though he is the addressee of the last speech (see default rule 2), because verse 17a begins a new narrative unit. (See below on the lack of overt reference to Saul (S) in many MSS in v. 19b.)

Passage 3: Acts 9:10–20.

(v)	(subject)	(non-subject)	(default)	(summary of contents)
(10a)	NP (A)		intro	(there was in Damascus)
(10b)	NP (L)	pn (A)	intro	(said to)
(10c)	art (A)	Ø (L)	2	(said)
(11)	NP (L)	pn (A)	—	([said] to)
(13)	NP (A)	Ø (L)	—	(answered)
(15)	NP (L)	pn (A)	—	(said to)
(17a)	NP (A)		—	(went away)
(17b)	Ø (A)		1	(entered the house)
(17c)	Ø (A)	Ø (S)	1	(putting hands on, said)
(18a)	NP (as scales)	pn (S)	4	(fell away from eyes of)
(18b)	Ø (S)		3[a]	(saw again)
(18c)	Ø (S)		1	(rising up, was baptized)
(19a)	Ø (S)		1	(taking food, was strengthened)
(19b)	Ø[b] (S)	NP (disciples)	1	(was with some days)
(20	Ø (S)		1	(proclaimed Jesus in synagogues)

a. In v. 18b, Ananias seems to have faded out of the scene, leaving Saul as the only (major) participant on stage.

b. Some MSS refer to Saul in v. 19b with a full noun phrase, implying that they discern a new narrative unit at this point.

The above passages have illustrated that, if more coding material is used than that predicted by the default rules, either a new narrative unit has begun, or else an action or speech has been highlighted. In the case of speeches which are introduced with a full noun phrase rather than an articular pronoun, either the speech is a key one, or else it represents a new initiative on the part of the speaker (Levinsohn forthcoming, chapter 9).

If *less* coding material is used than might have been anticipated, as when no overt reference to the subject occurs at what appears to be the beginning of a new narrative unit, this may imply that the writer perceived the passages concerned to be united by a common overall theme. This is illustrated in Acts 9:19b (passage 3 above); most MSS make no overt reference to Saul, though many versions begin a new narrative unit at this point. The absence of overt reference to Saul implies that the incidents before and after verse 19b should be perceived as dealing with a single overall theme, such as part one of the story of Saul's Christian life.

In other instances in which less coding material is used than might have been anticipated, the expectation of the analyst may need to be questioned. For example, some versions consider that Luke 20:20 (passage 4 below) begins a new narrative unit. However, there is no overt reference in this verse to the scribes (S) who were reintroduced in verse 19. This is consistent with default rule 1, but not with the expectation that new narrative units begin with more encoding. In fact, the new narrative unit begins at verse 19, as the marked encoding of reference to the previous addresses implies (see default rule 2). (For further discussion of this passage, see Levinsohn forthcoming, ch. 13.) (J) in passage 4 refers to Jesus.

Passage 4: Luke 20:17–21.

(v)	(subject)	(non-subject)	(default)	(summary of contents)
(17f)	art (J)	pn (S)	2	(looking at, said)
(19a)	NP (S)	pn (J)	4	(sought to lay hands on)
(19b)	Ø (S)	NP (people)	1	(feared)
(19c)	Ø (S)		1	(for knew that)
(19d)	Ø (J)	pn (S)	(see sec. 4)	(had told parable against)
(20)	Ø (S)	NP (spies)	1[a]	(watching, sent)
(21)	Ø (S)	pn (J)	1	(questioned, saying)

a. The subject of v. 20 is the same as in the last event clause, viz. v. 19b.

References to Jesus as Central Character in the Gospels

It is often necessary to recognize, among the cast of major participants, a central character for all or part of a story (Levinsohn 1987:18). Once formally introduced, reference to this character typically is minimal (see Marchese 1984:234f).

In the Gospels, Jesus is the central character and, at the beginning of new narrative units,[9] the norm is for reference to Him to be zero (or, in genitives absolute, an independent pronoun), even when He was not the subject of the previous clause. In other words, default encoding for the central character as subject, when He was in a non-subject role in the previous clause, is no overt reference (contrast default rule 3). Examples include Matthew 4:12, 23 (most MSS), and 5:1 (passage 5 below). In such instances, the author perceives a continuity of overall theme between the incidents concerned.

If the default encoding for the central character as subject is no overt reference, this implies that any overt reference to Jesus as subject, when He is already on stage, is marked encoding. Overt reference (typically, a full noun phrase) is indicative of one of two situations:

- a perceived change of overall theme;
- a key speech or action.

Passage 5 illustrates default and marked encoding of reference to Jesus as central character. Read over the passage, noting especially those clauses I have marked as not conforming to the default encoding rules of section 3. I will then comment on how the participants are referred to in the passage.

Abbreviations are as follows: (A) Andrew; (An) angels; (CC) central character; (D) the devil; (J) Jesus; (Ja) James; (Jo) John; (P) Peter.

Passage 5: Matthew 4:1–5:1.

(v)	(subject)	(non-subject)	(default)	(summary of contents)
(1)	NP (J)	NP (Spirit)	— (CC)	(was led into wilderness by)
		NP (D)		(to be tempted by)
(2)	Ø (J)		1	(after 40 days, hungered)
(3)	NP (D)	pn (J)	4	(approaching, said)
(4)	art (J)		2	(answering, said)
(5a)	NP (D)	pn (J)	—	(takes into the holy city)

---

[9] I have generally taken the paragraphing in Brown, Comfort, and Douglas (1990) as the basis of my discussion of new narrative units in the Gospels.

(v)	(subject)	(non-subject)	(default)	(summary of contents)
(5b)	Ø (D)	pn (J)	1	(stood on wing of temple)
(6)	Ø (D)	pn (J)	1	(says to)
(7)	NP (J)	pn (D)	— (CC)	(said to)
(8a)	NP (D)	pn (J)	—	(takes to high mountain)
(8b)	Ø (D)	pn (J)	1	(shows all kingdoms, glory)
(9)	Ø (D)	pn (J)	1	(said to)
(10)	NP (J)	pn (D)	— (CC)	(says to)
(11a)	NP (D)	pn (J)	—	(leaves)
(11b)	NP (An)		intro	(approached)
(11c)	Ø (An)	pn (J)	1	(ministered to)
(12)	Øª (J)		3 (CC)	(hearing, departed to Gal.)
(13)	Ø (J)		1	(leaving, dwelt in Caper.)
(14–16)	the spoken through Isaiah		4	(that might be fulfilled)
(17)	NP (J)		—	(began to proclaim & say)
(18a)	Ø (J)	NP (P, A)	1	(walking, saw)
(18b)	Ø (P, A)		3	(for were fishermen)
(19)	Ø (J)	pn (P, A)	1ᵇ	(says to)
(20)	art (P, A)	pn (J)	2	(leaving nets, followed)
(21a)	Ø (J)	NP (Ja, Jo)	3 (CC)	(going on, saw)
(21b)	Ø (J)	pn (Ja, Jo)	1	(called)
(22)	art (Ja, Jo)	pn (J)	2	(leaving boat, followed)
(23)	Øª (J)		3 (CC)	(went about teaching)
. . .				
(5:1)	Ø (J)	NP (crowds)	3 (CC)	(seeing, went up mount)

a. Some MSS refer to Jesus in vv. 12 and 23 with a full noun phrase, implying that they discern a new narrative unit at these points.

b. The subject of v. 19 is the same as in the last event clause, viz. v. 18a.

In the above passage, reference to Jesus at the beginning of a new narrative unit is overt only in 4:1, 17 (but see footnote 9). The implication is that the events of 4:1–16 and of verses 17ff are associated together, with verses 1 and 17 representing the beginning of units with new overall themes. (On v. 17, Schooling [1985:21] observes that, in Matthew's Gospel, ἀπὸ τότε "from that time" occurs at the beginning of major units.)

In contrast, reference to the devil (D) is overt at the beginning of each new narrative unit (4:5a, 8a, 11a). In each instance, he was the addressee of the previous speech, so the articular pronoun would have been the default encoding (rule; compare vv. 20, 22).

In Matthew 4:7, 10, reference to Jesus is overt, in connection with the introduction to a key speech which concludes the narrative unit.

To conclude, I have argued that further reference to participants who have already been introduced to a story in Koine Greek may be described in terms of default encoding rules together with marked forms of encoding. The default rules require a distinction to be made between major and minor participants and, among the cast of major participants, the identification of a central character. Marked forms of encoding occur at the beginning of narrative units and in highlighted sentences. The absence of a marked form of encoding at the apparent beginning of a narrative unit implies that the writer perceived an overall theme which united the passages concerned.

References

Brown, Robert K., Philip W. Comfort, and J. D. Douglas. 1990. *The New Greek-English Interlinear New Testament.* Wheaton, IL: Tyndale.

Comrie, Bernard. 1989. *Language Universals and Linguistic Typology.* Chicago: University of Chicago Press.

Fox, Barbara. 1987. *Anaphora in Popular Written English Narratives. Coherence and Grounding in Discourse.*, ed. by R. S. Tomlin. Amsterdam: Benjamins. Pp. 157–74.

Givón, Tammy, 1983. *Topic Continuity in Discourse.* Amsterdam: Benjamins.

Groce, William W., Jr. 1991. "A Salience Scheme Approach to the Narrative of Matthew in the Greek New Testament." M.A. diss., University of Texas at Arlington.

Levinsohn, Stephen H. 1987. *Textual Connections in Acts.* Atlanta, GA: Scholars Press.

———. Forthcoming. *Discourse Features of New Testament Greek: A Coursebook.* Dallas: Summer Institute of Linguistics.

Marchese, Lynell. 1984. "Pronouns and Full Nouns: A Case of Mis-representation." *The Bible Translator* 35. 2.234–35.

Schooling, Stephen. 1985. "More on Matthew's Brackets: A Study of the Function of Time References in Matthew's Gospel." *Selected Technical Articles Related to Translation* 13. Dallas: Summer Institute of Linguistics. Pp. 14–27.

Van Otterloo, Roger. 1988. "Towards An Understanding of 'Lo' and 'Behold': Functions of ἰδού and ἴδε in the Greek New Testament." Dallas: *Occasional Papers in Translation and Textlinguistics* 2. 1.34–64.

3

Semantic Paragraph Patterns: A Fundamental Communication Concept and Interpretive Tool

John C. Tuggy

Whoever speaks or writes must assume that the audience shares innate human mental capabilities and a large amount of language and cultural experience. If these are not presupposed or shared, the communicative attempt will essentially fail.

There seem to be some basic cognitive processes[1] which are innate in humans, i.e., processes by which we categorize our experience of the universe around us which are, in turn, modified by our culture. These processes are inherent in our humanity (experiencing the world around us by means of our sensory systems and our interpretation of the experiences). These processes are the basis upon which we learn. We have the ability to perceive the universe in identifiable units[2] and relate[3] these units to other entities, resulting in a categorization of our experience. For instance, we experience a dog, a cat, and a canary, and relate them to each other as household pets. We are also able to communicate our experience and categorizations in ways which will accomplish our purpose for communicating them.[4]

[1] Much of what is presented here corroborates with Lakoff's (1985) expert presentation of the present state of cognitive science. Both Callow (1989) and Lakoff agree that we as human-beings are central to cognition and communication. Neither of these phenomena can be separated from the person. The world out there does not have inherent categories aside from our perception of it.

[2] These identifiable units are Lakoff's cognitive prototypes.

[3] I very much like the various forms of relations between the prototypical entities presented by Lakoff (1985:113–14, 153–54). Even our attempt to categorize semantic rhetorical patterns primarily presents the prototypical forms as a recognizable starting point. Much more study will have to be done to demonstrate the specific types of extensions and overlaps.

[4] The theoretical framework behind this application of innate abilities or processes has been discussed by Callow (1989).

I will show that we pattern discourse according to our cognitive processes. These processes function at the semantic paragraph level of discourse to categorize a set of *paragraph patterns*. We shall limit the discussion to written monologue. We shall a) consider what paragraphs patterns are, and b) attempt to define the various paragraph patterns and show the relationships of the various units which make up these patterns in differing semantic genres.

Paragraph Patterns

Paragraph patterns are a set of semantic structures which communicators use to organize messages in a way that will accomplish the purpose of communication.

Any particular semantic paragraph pattern is the intersection of the following cognitive processes: (1) communicator's intended effect on his audience, (2) time or space sequentiality, (3) deductive perception of reality, and (4) message organization. We shall consider each of these processes demonstrating how each process in turn intersects with the other processes.

Communicator's Intended Effect on the Audience

As has been demonstrated by Callow (1989), all verbal or written communicative attempts are for the primary purposes[5] of: (1) affecting the *emotions* of the audience, (2) affecting the *ideas* of the audience, or (3) affecting the *behavior* of the audience. There can be no meaningful communication without the communicator choosing one of these three purposes[6] or a combination[7] of them. One can affect the hearer's emotions by describing one's own emotional experience (like describing a sunset). One can affect the hearer's ideas by sharing information with him (like explaining why Washington confessed to cutting down the cherry tree). Affecting the ideas includes the request for information. One can affect the hearer's behavior by appealing to him to behave in a specific manner (like requesting someone to close the door).

These three intents are the most basic characteristics of the primary semantic genres of discourse.

Time and Space Sequentiality Cognition

Although a person speaks in a sequential string because of the very nature of language, the communicator has the choice of expressing

---

[5] This is necessarily a very generalized concept of communicative intend. English has many lexemes which identify the more prototypical grammatical genre.

[6] Callow uses the term "imports" for purpose or intent.

[7] This does not present paragraph patterns in water-tight compartments, because that is not the nature of cognitive processes and this is evidenced especially at this level and higher levels of discourse.

his or her intent with or without a focus on time or space sequentiality. For example, he or she can affect the emotions, or the ideas, or the behavior of the addressee by narrating an experience following a temporal line or by explaining the experience without a temporal focus.

Example 1: All four Gospels[8] are quite explicit in recounting the death and resurrection of Jesus Christ following a temporal sequence. See Matthew 27:32–28:20.

Example 2: 1 Corinthians 15:3–5—"1 What I received I passed on to you as of first importance: 2 that Christ died for our sins according to the Scriptures, 3 that he was buried, 4 that he was raised on the third day according to the Scriptures, and 5 that he appeared to Peter, and then to the Twelve."

Comparing examples 1 and 2 we observe that the first focuses on a temporal sequential ordering to narrate the various episodes and incidents involved in the death and resurrection of Christ. However, in the second example the focus is explicitly on the importance of certain incidents as fulfillment of Old Testament Scripture and on their concomitant significance. The ordering of the events in units 25 is the same as in the narration by Matthew, but the focus is on their importance and meaning as expressed in unit 1.

This temporal and spatial sequence is an innate observation that we make of the universe in which we live. Time sequence relations are observations that one event occurs after another. We also readily observe spatial sequence relations by choosing a focal point of a location and describing all other objects as they relate to the focal point.

Example 3: Luke 5:12–14—"1 While Jesus was in one of the towns, a man came along who was covered with leprosy. 2 When he saw Jesus, he fell with his face to the ground and begged him, 'Lord, if you are willing, you can make me clean.' 3 Jesus reached out his hand and touched the man. 'I am willing,' he said. 4 And immediately the leprosy left him. 5 Then Jesus ordered him. . . . "

Example 4: notice Revelation chapter 4, where the Apostle John describes, first of all, the focal point of the heavenly scene, the throne, and then in succession, all the other participants as they are spatially related to the throne.

Note: each unit, units 1–5, in example 3 is ordered in a temporal sequence; i.e., the author is focusing on the events in the temporal order in which they actually occurred. However, in example 4 the

---

[8] Practically all the examples presented are taken from the Bible. This has been done because of the audience which I am addressing. Nevertheless, I have used in lectures examples from other sources, primarily short stories, essays, advertisements, etc., from *Reader's Digest*, February, 1985.

author is not focusing on any time sequence but rather on the spatial relation radiating out from a central point of reference.

We express our internal emotions as we react to the world around us without a focus of time and space, but we frequently express something of beauty with a focus on space.

> Example 5: John 12:27–28a—"1 Now my heart is troubled, and what shall I say? '2 Father, save me from this hour'? 3 No, it was for this very reason I came to this hour. 4 Father, glorify your name!"

Note: there is no temporal or spatial sequentiality in focus.

Compare example 5 with example 4. In the first example the author is focusing on Jesus' emotional reaction to the pain and anguish which He knew He was about to suffer. The focus is on an expression of His mixed emotions without time or space sequencing being of any significance. However, in example 4, the author is expressing the beauty of the heavenly scene focusing on the central figure of the throne and extending the description in a spatial succession away from the central figure.

We can express ideas narrating them with a temporal focus (see example 3 on page 47), or we can express ideas without a temporal focus (see next example), but with a focus such as cause-effect.

> Example 6: John 3:31–32—"1 ... the one who is from the earth belongs to the earth, 2 and speaks as one from the earth. 3 The one who comes from heaven is above all. 4 He testifies to what he has seen and heard . . ."

We can appeal to the addressee without a temporal or spatial focus but possibly with a motivational focus (see the next example), but when we instruct someone to carry out a sequence of actions the focus would normally be a temporal or spatial sequence (see example 8).

> Example 7: Revelation 2:5—"1 Repent and do the things you did at first. 2 If you do not repent, I will come to you and remove your lampstand from its place."

Note: the appeal is to repent, but the motivation for that action comes in the speaker's assumption that the hearers consider their position among the lampstands of great value.

> Example 8: Luke 19:30–31—"1 Go to the village ahead of you, and as you enter it, you will find a colt tied there, which no one has ever ridden. 2 Untie it 3 and bring it here. 4 If anyone asks you, 'Why are you untying it?' tell him, 'The Lord needs it.'"

Note: the actions involved in units 1–3 are actions which must be taken in the order stated in order to make the donkey available for Jesus to ride.

We can now consider the various semantic genres caused by the intersection of the communicator's intent on the audience and the focus of plus or minus temporal and spatial sequentiality.

Intersection of Intent with Sequentiality are the Characteristics of the Primary Semantic Genre

The matrix of Primary Semantic Genre, table 1, demonstrates the intersection of the communicator's intent and sequentiality and how these are the main constituent processes involved in the various primary semantic genres as shown in the following table 1:

Table 1: Primary Semantic Genres

	–sequentiality	+sequentiality
To Affect Behavior	Hortatory	Procedural
To Affect Ideas	Expository	Narrative
To Affect Emotions	Emotional	Descriptive

Here we observe that there are six primary semantic genres. These primary genres are different from the various grammatical genres. Semantic genres are characterized by the two cognitive processes of author's intent and sequentiality as mentioned above. Grammatical genre are characterized by certain surface forms which are language specific and very frequently reflect the author's intent and sequentiality. Furthermore, there can be mismatching between the semantic genres and grammatical genres. For instance, the Gospels are primarily narrative surface genre but have an underlying hortatory intent by showing the addressee how he should or should not react to the message. Another example: although the communicator intends to affect the behavior of the addressee, he can use an expository grammatical genre to accomplish his purpose, thus softening the tone of his demands. Consider, "if we confess our sins, he . . . forgives us our sins," meaning, "confess your sins to God, since he forgives us our sins if we confess them to him."

The three intents have an ascending impact on the addressee from affecting the emotions to affecting the ideas and actions. The addressee is constantly anticipating the greater impact intended by the communicator. (For example: When my father used to say, "How would you like to feed the dog?" I knew well the answer should not be, "No, not just now." His intent was a mitigated command, "Please, feed the dog." The grammatical request for information affecting ideas was intended and understood as affecting actions.)

Because of the mismatching between the semantics and the grammar, and because of the principle of ascending addressee impact, the communicator has various rhetorical devices for achieving his intention on the addressee. He can use this mismatching as a communicative strategy.

The six primary semantic genres are as follows:

1) Hortatory: The intersection of the communicator intending to affect the behavior of the addressee without focusing on temporal sequence.

> Example 9: 1 John 2:15–17—"**1** Do not love the world or anything in the world. . . . **2** For everything in the world . . . come not from the Father but from the world. . . . **3** The world and its desires pass away, but the man who does the will of God lives forever."

Note: there is no temporal sequentiality in focus between units 1 and 2; the focus is of a deductive nature.

2) Procedural: The intersection of the communicator intending to affect the behavior of the addressee focusing on temporal or spatial sequence. Example 8 on page 48 demonstrates a procedural semantic paragraph. Note: units 1–3 present the steps in a temporal sequence that were to be taken in order that Jesus could make use of the donkey.

3) Expository: The intersection of the communicator intending to affect the ideas of the addressee without focusing on temporal sequence.

> Example 10: 1 John 1:5—"**1** This is the message we have heard from him and declare to you: **2** God is light; in him there is no darkness at all."

Note: although there is a sequential focus within unit 1, there is no such relationship between units 1 and 2.

4) Narrative: The intersection of the communicator intending to affect the ideas of the addressee focusing on temporal sequence.

> Example 11: Mark 1:21–28—"**1** . . . Jesus went into the synagogue and began to teach. . . . **2** Just then a man . . . possessed by an evil spirit cried out. . . . **3** 'Be quiet!' said Jesus sternly. 'Come out of him.' **4** The evil spirit shook the man violently and came out of him with a shriek. . . . "

Notice the temporal sequence established between each succeeding unit.

5) Emotional: The intersection of the communicator intending to affect the emotions of the addressee without focusing on spatial sequence. See example 5 on page 48. Note: the progression from units 1 through 4 do not focus on a temporal frame but rather on a reason-result relationship.

6) Descriptive: The intersection of the communicator intending to affect the emotions of the addressee focusing on spatial sequence.

Example 12: 1 John 1:1–3—"**1** That which was from the beginning, **2** which we have heard, **3** which we have seen with our eyes, which we have looked at **4** and our hands have touched . . . **5** we have seen it **6** and testify to it, and we proclaim to you the eternal life . . . "

Notice the spatial sequencing in focus: First is the topic third person; then the first person plural eyes, ears, and hands; finally, the second person plural. A question may arise as to why this has not been considered as an expository paragraph where John is giving evidence for this authority to write about these matters. Certainly this would be the tendency caused by the principle of the hearer anticipating a higher impact; i.e., the hearer might assume that an emotional paragraph would have an affect on the ideas. However, there are no characteristic features of an expository paragraph defending a thesis or claim. John does not make any explicit defence of his authority in this paragraph, although he does so later in the epistle. Also observe Revelation 9:7–10; 17:4–6; 19:11–16.

As previously mentioned, one has the choice of affecting a person's *behavior* by either using a hortatory or procedural genre. To affect a person's *ideas*, one can choose to use either an expository or narrative genre. In the same way, one has the choice of affecting a person's *emotions* by using an emotional or descriptive genre.

We can now proceed to consider the semantic element of our deductive perception of reality.

Deductive Perception

As we observe ourselves and the universe around us, we innately interpret events as related to each other or related to us in some way; i.e., we perceive events as being in either a *problem-solution, cause-effect,* or *volition-accomplishment* relationship. These three perceptive relationships are involved in everything we interpret and say about our universe.

1) We understand some events as problematic, upsetting the balance of other events around, which require still other events to solve the imbalance. These imbalances create tensions which remain until resolved; these need to be brought back to normalcy. We shall refer to this deductive perception as *solutionality*.

Example 13: Luke 18:15–16—"**1** People were also bringing babies to Jesus to have him touch them. **2** When the disciples saw this, they rebuked them. **3** But Jesus called the children to him and said, 'Let the little children come to me. . . . ' "

Note: the problematic event was that the disciples were hindering the people in bringing the babies. The imbalance is resolved by Jesus commanding them to allow the children to go to Him.

2) We understand some observed events as the cause[9] for other events. We shall refer to this deductive perception as *causality*. Example 6 on page 48 demonstrates this type of causality. Note: the fact presented in unit 1 causes the event in unit 2, and the fact presented in unit 3 causes the event in unit 4.

3) We observe some events which neither are in a cause-effect nor problem-solution relationship but we recognize their relationship to each other as a process toward fulfilling someone's desire. When there is no immediate causality nor solutionality relationship between events, we attribute personal volitionality as the directive of the events. This could be called "indirect cause,"[10] but lacks the volition feature that we attribute to such acts. We shall refer to this deductive perception as *volitionality*.

> Example 14: Mark 1:35–39—"1 . . . Jesus got up, left the house and went off to a solitary place, where he prayed. 2 Simon and his companions . . . found him, (and) they exclaimed: 'Everyone is looking for you!' 3 Jesus replied, 'Let us go somewhere else . . . ' 4 So he traveled throughout Galilee, preaching. . . . "

Note: all the principle events in each unit were directed by Jesus' desire to preach in other parts of Galilee.

The intersection of these perceptions of reality with the primary semantic genres produces a matrix with eighteen slots filled by the semantic paragraph patterns. Each pattern is structured around characteristic semantic relations which organize the text. Semantic paragraphs consist of one of these eighteen patterns. This intersection of semantic genres, deductive perception, and organization can be observed in Table 2: Semantic Paragraph Patterns and Their Organizations.

Organization of Unit Relations—Semantic Syntax

Every communication unit must be organized. It is not haphazard but constrained by certain characteristic elements, some of which are usually required and others optional. At the semantic level of language, the ordering of the elements is not of primary importance but certain characteristic units (usually required elements) must be present. These units are like signposts advising the addressee regarding the progress of the communication. The characteristic units

---

[9] Lakoff (1985:54–55) has an interesting discussion on prototypical causation. The type of causation to which I am referring is tagged as "involuntary causation" in his discussion.

[10] Lakoff (1985:55) views this as the more representative form of prototypical causality. However, Mann and Thompson (1987) refer to this as "indirect cause."

function to bring about completeness and closure to the communication. The addressee is assured that closure has been accomplished when the characteristic units are present. (Example: notice especially the clues that a person's discourse is complete in the conversational exchange in John 6:25–34ff.) This constraint or predictability of elements within a communication unit is what we are calling "semantic paragraph pattern." We consider this organization of semantic units to be the *semantic syntax* of a semantic paragraph.

By asserting that there are some characteristic units, we also recognize that there are some optional units in a communication pattern. These optional pattern elements function to support, enhance, clarify, increase impact, shift focus, and so on, within the communication pattern.

Semantic paragraph patterns are used to organize the semantic elements by the communicator, and to identify the same (semantic syntax) by the addressee. Thus, semantic paragraph patterns are a fundamental linguistic tool for both communicating and for interpreting communication.

These semantic patterns are only relevant in the semantic paragraph (minimal communication unit) and some larger units. One must also be aware of embedding of semantic paragraphs and their patterns.

Intersection of Semantic Genres with Deductive Perception and Organization

Bringing together the intersection of the semantic elements of author's intent, sequentiality, perception, and organization, we see how each semantic paragraph pattern contrasts with the others. Observe table 2: Semantic Paragraph Patterns and Their Organizations. The vertical columns refer to the perception of reality; the horizontal columns refer to the six semantic genres; and the matrix intersections refer to the semantic paragraph patterns. There are no name-tags for each pattern, but the structure of each is shown by the characteristic (+) and the optional (±) components.

The details regarding table 2 will be discussed under the section "Definition of Relationships."

Definition of Relationships

The semantic features that make up each of the patterns are identified by names which attempt to show their function, which we shall call "role." Frequently, these units are paired evidencing a particular relationship between them. Instead of attempting to tag the relationship of these paired units, we refer to the relationships by the combined roles. For instance, instead of saying that in a narrative there is

Table 2: Semantic Paragraph Patterns and their Organizations

	SOLUTIONALITY	CAUSALITY	VOLITIONALITY
HORTATORY	+change ±evidence(n) +APPEAL ±resistance+PERSUADE	+basis(n)+APPEAL	+motivation+ENABLEMENT(n)
PROCEDURAL	+need+step(n) +ACCOMPLISHMENT ±hindrance+RESOLUTION	+APPEAL(n)+outcome(n)	+STEP(n)+accomplishment
EXPOSITORY	+hypothesis ±evidence(n)+THESIS ±objection +REFUTATION/REJECTION	+evidence(n)+IMPLICATION or +evidence+INFERENCE(n)	+justification(n)+CLAIM
NARRATIVE	+problem+RESOLUTION +resolving-incident(n) ±complication+RESOLUTION	+occasion+OUTCOME	+step(n)+GOAL
EMOTIONAL	+mixed-emotions±seeking +EMOTIONAL-RECONCILIATION ±intensify+RECONCILE	+situation(n)+REACTION ±belief	+belief(n)+CONTROL
DESCRIPTIVE	+expectancy+FULFILLMENT. ±experience(n) ±frustrative+ENCOURAGE	+situation(n)+REACTION	+description(n)+DECLARATION

a "complication" relationship, we refer to this by "complication-RESOLUTION." Notice that this tagging also makes explicit that the capitalized role is the prominent (nuclear), while the lower-case is the supportive role. Not all relationships are binary (like problem-RESOLUTION), but can have several elements (like need-step(n)-ACCOMPLISHMENT).

As we attempt to define each of these relationships, we will mention: a) the name of the relationship, b) what is its structural function within the paragraph pattern, c) what is the function of each role in the relationship, and d) what is the expected reaction of the addressee to the relationship.

Terms for Units in HORTATORY Semantic Genre

The roles in HORTATORY paragraph pattern are defined as:

a) **change-APPEAL** relationship is the core of the solutionality pattern of hortatory discourse producing a struggle or tension. The *change* is the behavioral problem that the author wants solved. The *APPEAL* is the central role whereby the communicator attempts to change the problematic actions of the hearer by various appeal strategies realized in the surface, e.g., commands, suggestions, rhetorical questions, harangue, or other mitigated forms of appeal. The communicator expects the addressee to recognize the command(s) in the appeal as the solution to the problematic behavior.

> Example 15: Ephesians 6:10–18—"1 Finally, be strong in the Lord and in his mighty power. Put on the full armor of God 2 so that you can take your stand against the devil's schemes. 3 For our struggle is not against flesh and blood, but against the rulers, against the authorities, against the powers of this dark world and against the spiritual forces of evil in the heavenly realms. 4 Therefore put on the full armor of God, 5 so that when the day of evil comes, you may be able to stand your ground, and after you have done everything, to stand . . . 6 And pray in the Spirit on all occasions with all kinds of prayers and requests. . . . "

Note: units 2 and 5 are the desired results of the behavior that needs to be changed; the problematic behavior is implied. Units 1 and 4 are the appeal, first presented in a generic form, then a specific, which is repeated in unit 4. Units 1–5 are an embedded paragraph within paragraph 1–6.

b) **evidence(n)** are the reasons, acceptable to the addressee, presented to support the appeal (the action that should be taken). The *evidence* can be: *axiomatic, intellectual, authoritative, emotional, harangue,* and others. The communicator expects an increasing acceptance of the appeal by the audience.

See example 15 above. Note: unit 3 presents specific evidence that we are in a battle, though not a physical one. Our adversaries are not other human entities but evil spiritual powers. So, the appeal to put on God's full armor becomes more acceptable.

c) **resistance-PERSUADE** are roles embedded in the change-APPEAL relationship. This relationship would block the addressee from accepting the appeal until the matter is brought to normalcy. The *resistance* role states either the known or imagined problem that the addressee would have for accepting the appeal. The *persuade* role solves the *resistance* by persuading the hearer that the resistance is not valid. The addressee's disposition to accept the appeal is increased.

> Example 16: Exodus 3:10–4:20—1 "So now, go. I am sending you to Pharaoh to bring my people the Israelites out of Egypt." 2 But Moses said to God, "Who am I? . . . " 3 And God said, "I will be with you. . . . " 4 Moses said to God, "Suppose I go to the Israelites . . . and they as me, 'What is his name?' then what shall I tell them?" 5 God said to Moses, "I am who I am. . . . " 6 Moses answered, "What if they do not believe me? . . . " 7 . . . The Lord said, "Throw it [the staff] on the ground." 8 Moses said to the Lord, "O Lord, I have never been eloquent. . . . " 9 The Lord said to him, "Who gave man his mouth? . . . Is it not I? . . . " 10 But Moses said, "O Lord, please send someone else to do it." 11 Then the Lord's anger burned against Moses and he said, "What about your brother, Aaron the Levite? . . . He will speak to the people for you, and it will be as if he were your mouth and as if you were God to him. . . . " . . . 12 So Moses took his wife and sons, put them on a donkey and started back to Egypt.

Note: this whole repartee is embedded in a narrative about God taking the Israelites out of Egyptian bondage. In unit 1 the appeal to Moses is presented. All the other units are paired in the example to show each resistance (even numbers) and the persuasion (odd numbers) until all is resolved in unit 12.

d) **basis(n)-APPEAL** relationship is the core of the causality pattern of hortatory discourse without a struggle or tension. The *basis* role presents the hearer with a basis which would increase his acceptability of the *appeal*. The *basis* can be: *motivational* (of value to the hearer), *warning, trust, emotional, authoritative, axiomatic,* and so on.

See example 9 on page 50. Note: units 2 and 3 are the bases for the appeal in unit 1.

e) **motivation-ENABLEMENT(n)** relationship is the core of the volitionality pattern of hortatory discourse. In the *motivation* role the communicator presents the addressee with a desired but unrealized situation. The communicator presents in the *enablement* one or more actions that will result in the desired situation. The addressee is expected to have an increased desire to perform the actions presented according to how he values the ultimate situation.

See example 15 on page 55. Note: units 1–5 present the motivation, and unit 6 the enablement. In effect, Paul is saying, "Be strong in the Lord, and pray in the Spirit in order to do so." Here is an example of paragraph embedding. Embedded within units 1–6 are units 1–5 which are of the solutionality type internally but function here as the motivation for unit 6.

Terms for Units in PROCEDURAL Semantic Genre

The roles in **PROCEDURAL** paragraph patterns are defined as:

a) **need-ACCOMPLISHMENT** relationship is the core of the solutionality pattern of procedural discourse producing a struggle or tension. The *need* role presents the problem that should be solved by performing various actions. The *accomplishment* is the primary or ultimate action the communicator intends that the addressee perform. The communicator expects the addressee to recognize the action(s) in the appeal as the solution to the expressed need.

> Example 17: This is the most common type of procedural text used by the Candoshi[11] (which goes like this): **1** After we got married, my wife and I needed a house. **2** First one gets enough food for a week. **3** Then one invites one's neighbors to help with the building. **4** We all cut the poles we need, dig holes, put in the poles, and build the roof frame. **5** After working hard for a whole week, one runs out of food and is tired. **6** One has to rest by getting more food from the jungle. **7** One will finally build the beds, shelves, and hangars. **8** Then one moves in. **9** That's what one needs to do to make a house.

Note: unit 1 presents the need while unit 9 is the accomplishment telling the listener that he should do the same in order to build a house.

b) The **step(n)** roles are the events that move the discourse toward the accomplishment of the stated need. The communicator expects the addressee to perform the same steps.

See the above example 17. Note: units 2, 3, 4, 7, and 8 are the steps to be taken.

c) **hindrance-RESOLUTION** are roles embedded in the need-ACCOMPLISHMENT relationship. This relationship would block the addressee from the desired accomplishment until the imbalance is resolved. The *hindrance* role states a potential problem that the addressee would have in performing the steps that will fill his need. The *resolution* role solves the hindrance. The addressee is better prepared to accomplish what is desired.

---

[11] My wife and I worked for over twenty years with a Peruvian aboriginal group learning their language and culture, preparing educational materials, and translating the New Testament.

See example 17 on page 57. Note: unit 5 presents a hindrance to completing the house, but unit 6 presents the resolution to that hindrance.

d) **APPEAL(n)-outcome** relationship is the core of the causality frame of procedural discourse which is without struggle or tension. The *appeal(s)* role presents the addressee with what should be done to produce the intended *outcome.* The addressee is expected to perform what is requested because the outcome is already accepted to be of value.

> Example 18: 1 Peter 2:11–12—"**1** Dear friends, I urge you, as aliens and strangers in the world, to abstain from sinful desires, which war against your soul. **2** Live such good lives among the pagans that, **3** though they accuse you of doing wrong, they may see your good deeds and glorify God on the day he visits us."

Note: units 1 and 2 are the appeals, while unit 3 is the outcome if the appeals are obeyed. This outcome of glorifying God on the great day is to be accepted by the hearers as of great value.

e) **STEP(n)-accomplishment** relationship is the core of the volitionality pattern of procedural discourse. The *step(n)* roles lead to a goal which the hearer accepts as of value. In the *accomplishment* role the communicator presents the unrealized desired goal of the ordered action(s). The addressee is expected to recognize that the action(s) presented in the step(s) will accomplish the intended goal.

See example 8 on page 48. Note: units 1–2 present the steps to accomplish the goal presented in unit 3.

There are specific kinds of steps, as follows:

1) **evaluation** is the role which describes the test to be performed to determine whether the previous step role(s) has been performed successfully or not.

2) **option** is the role which presents alternate step role(s) when certain *conditions* are met in a procedure. (Observe unit 4 in example 8 on page 48.)

3) **parallel** is the role which presents an action which must be performed simultaneously with the step in question.

4) **recursion** is the role which presents information that certain steps must be *repeated until* a specified *condition* has been met.

5) **regression** is the role which presents information that certain steps must be repeated in inverse sequence in order to get a second desired *accomplishment.*

Terms for Units in EXPOSITORY Semantic Genre

The roles in EXPOSITORY paragraph patterns are defined as:

a) **hypothesis-THESIS** relationship is the core of the solutionality paragraph pattern of expository discourse producing a struggle or tension argument. The hypothesis is the major premise that the author has for the argument, i.e., *thesis*. If the hypothesis is credible, the thesis will then also be credible. The addressee is expected to accept the truth of the thesis on the basis of the truth of the *hypothesis*.

Example 19: 1 Timothy 6:6–8—"**1** Godliness with contentment is great gain. **2** For we brought nothing into the world, and we can take nothing out of it. **3** But if we have food and clothing, we will be content with that."

Note: unit 1 is the thesis. Unit 3 is the hypothesis or major premise supporting unit 1.

b) **evidence(n)** role is the minor premise which supports both the *hypothesis* and the *thesis*. The addressee finds the evidence more credible than the hypothesis or thesis. These evidences will increase credibility in the truth value of the thesis presenting various kinds of evidence like: *axiomatic, illustrative, emotional, intellectual, physical, refutational, absurdity*, etc.

See example 19 above. Note: unit 2 (evidence) supports unit 3 (the hypothesis), and both together support unit 1 (the thesis).

c) **objection-REFUTATION** are roles embedded in the hypothesis-THESIS relationship. This relationship blocks the truth value of the thesis until the objection is solved as invalid by refutation or rejection. The *objection* role states either a known or imagined problem that the addressee would have in accepting the *thesis*. The addressee's disposition to accept the thesis is increased.

Example 20: Romans 6:1–2 which is part of a large argument. "**1** What shall we say, then? Shall we go on sinning so that grace may increase? **2** By no means! We died to sin; how can we live in it any longer?"

Note: unit 1 is the objection and unit 2 refutes the objection by rejecting it as invalid.

d) **evidence(n)-IMPLICATION** relationship is the core of the causality paragraph pattern of expository discourse without a struggle or tension. The *evidence* role presents the hearer with all the information which will support the credibility of the *implication*. The addressee is expected to accept the implication.

See example 6 on page 48. Note: units 1, 2, and 3 present two evidences for the implication in unit 4.

e) **evidence-INFERENCE(n)** relationship is an alternate core of the causality paragraph pattern of expository discourse without a struggle or tension. The *evidence* role presents the hearer with the single basis which supports one or various *inferences*. The addressee is expected to accept the inferences in accord with the truth value of the evidence.

Example 21: Romans 3:21–31—"**1** But now a righteousness from God, apart from law, has been made known, to which the Law and Prophets testify. **2** This righteousness from God comes through faith in Jesus Christ to all who believe. **3** There is no difference, for all have sinned and fall short of the glory of God, and are justified freely by his grace through the redemption that came by Christ Jesus. **4** God presented him as a sacrifice of atonement, through faith in his blood. **5** He did this to demonstrate his justice. . . . **6** Where, then is boasting? It is excluded. . . . **7** Is God the God of Jews only? Is he not the God of Gentiles too? Yes, of Gentiles too. . . . **8** Do we, then nullify the law by this faith? Not at all! Rather, we uphold the law."

Note: units 1 and 2 state the evidence or basis upon which all the rest of the units (3–8) inferred. The evidence stated in units 1 and 2 are not defended at this point; that is for later development in the book. Paul expects the audience to accept the truth value of the evidence "at face value" for just now. That is, if the evidence is true, then all the inferences which follow are also true.

f) **justification(n)-CLAIM** relationship is the core of the volitionality paragraph pattern of expository discourse. The *justification* roles present the evidence which the author knows will enhance the credibility of the claim to the addressee. The addressee is expected to increasingly credit the claim.

Example 22: John 2:18–22—"**1** Then the Jews demanded of him, 'What miraculous sign can you show us to prove your authority to do all this?' **2** Jesus answered them, 'Destroy this temple, and I will raise it again in three days.' **3** The Jews replied, 'It has taken forty-six years to build this temple, and you are going to raise it in three days?' **4** But the temple he had spoken of was his body. **5** After he was raised from the dead, his disciples recalled what he had said. **6** Then they believed. . . . "

Note: units 4–6 are justifications that enhance the credibility of unit 2. Also see example 10 on page 50.

Terms for Units in NARRATIVE Semantic Genre

In narrative the paragraph pattern is called **PLOT**. The plot roles are defined as follows:

a) **problem-RESOLUTION** relationship is the core of the solutionality plot[12] of narrative discourse producing a struggle or tension. The

---

[12] Narrative plot structure was the concept that sparked the whole concept of semantic paragraph patterns. The three basic plots of solutionality, occasion-outcome, and step(n)-GOAL were extended by analogy to other genre. Narrative plot has been recognized since antiquity, as have various other rhetorical forms, but the question has been, how are these similar and why are they recognizable forms? I think we now have a good initial accounting of these through cognitive and communication theory.

problem is the imbalance in the narrative on which the rest hangs until the imbalance is resolved. The *resolution* is the central role where the communicator will eliminate the tension. The addressee is expected to recognize the solution and the end of the struggle.

> Example 23: Mark 1:29–31—"1 . . . they went with James and John to the home of Simon and Andrew. **2** Simon's mother-in-law was in bed with a fever, **3** and they told Jesus about her. **4** So he went to her, took her hand and helped her up. **5** The fever left her and she began to wait on them."

Note: unit 2 presents the problem of the narrative while unit 5 presents the resolution.

b) **resolving incident(n)-RESOLUTION** relationship is a group of events that *respond* to the story problem and lead toward a solution of the story. The communicator expects the addressee to increase his expectancy of the story *resolution*.

See example 23 above. Note: units 3 and 4 are groups of actions in response to the problem stated in unit 2. These incidents lead toward the resolution in unit 5.

c) **complication-RESOLUTION** is an embedded problem-resolution within the whole narrative which blocks the story resolution. The *complication* must be resolved (in some cases both the complication and the main problem are resolved by a single action performed by the main participant) before the story can be brought to completion. The addressee is expected to react with heightened interest.

> Example 24: Mark 2:1–12—"1 . . . Some men came, bringing to him a paralytic, carried by four of them. **2** Since they could not get him to Jesus because of the crowd, **3** they made an opening in the roof above Jesus and, . . . lowered the mat the paralyzed man was lying on."

Note: unit 2 is a complication which blocks the resolution to the problem of getting the man to Jesus so He could heal him, while unit 3 resolves the complication. There is another complication in verses 5–11.

d) **occasion-OUTCOME** relationship is the core of the causality plot of narrative discourse without a struggle or tension. The essential relation between events is that of stimulus-response. The first in sequence is the *stimulus* for the second which is the *response* to that stimulus. Frequently, the outcome will, in turn, become the occasion for another event. The addressee is expected to recognize the occasion as a cause for the outcome, and to increase his or her anticipation for the outcome.

See example 11 on page 50. Note: unit 2 is the occasion for the outcome in unit 3, which in turn becomes the occasion for the outcome in unit 4.

e) **episode-SEQUEL** relation is similar to occasion-OUTCOME except that it refers to high-level structures, i.e., the story or episode is the occasion for the events that follow: the moral of the story, the purpose of the story, the final result of the story, etc.

> Example 25: the narrative of Mark 1:21–28 has its sequel in verses 27–28—"The people were all so amazed that they asked each other, 'What is this? A new teaching—and with authority! He gives orders to evil spirits and they obey him.' "

Note: the occasion for what is presented in verses 27–28 is the whole episode of Jesus teaching in the synagogue and expelling the evil spirit from a man as presented in verses 21–26. The sequel or outcome of the whole episode is presented in verses 27–28.

f) **move(n)-GOAL** relationship is the core of the volitionality plot of narrative discourse. The *move* role is a progression of events that lead toward the *goal* (accomplishing a final volitional event); there is no struggle or tension nor a stimulus and a response. The communicator expects the addressee to recognize the move(s) as volitionally directed causes for the desired goal.

Example 14 on page 52 demonstrates this pattern. Note: Jesus' final intent is presented in unit 4, which is the goal of the volitional causes in the events in units 1–3.

g) **setting** is a role in narrative in which the participants, location, and/or time orientation of the story is stated. The communicator expects the addressee to use the information for interpreting the events of the narrative.

See example 11 on page 50. Note: unit 1 of this narrative presents the location, main participant, and background actions for the narrative.

h) **preliminary incident** role occurs occasionally when the action of the narrative gets underway before the problem is stated in a solutionality plot. The event is not a stimulus for the succeeding narrative. The addressee is expected to heighten attention for the forthcoming problem.

> Example 26: Mark 5:21–43—Before Jairus stated the problem of his dying daughter, the text says, "a large crowd gathered around him [Jesus] while he was by the lake. Then one of the synagogue rulers . . . came there."

Note: the action of the large crowd gathering is part of the setting, while the action of Jairus coming to Jesus actually gets the events of the story underway. But the problem has not been stated yet; it is stated in the next event.

Terms for Units in EMOTIONAL Semantic Genre

a) **mixed-emotions-EMOTIONAL-RECONCILIATION** relationship is the core of the solutionality paragraph pattern of emotional discourse producing a struggle or tension. The *mixed-emotions* is the problem that the communicator must resolve and on which the communication hangs until the imbalance is resolved. The *emotional-reconciliation* is the role whereby the communicator resolves the tension by acceptance or rejection of the problem. The addressee is expected to recognize the *emotional reconciliation* as the solution to the problem, and to react emotionally similar to the emotions of the communicator.

See example 5 on page 48. Note: units 1–3 present conflicting emotions which are resolved or reconciled in unit 4.

b) **seeking(n)** role is the emotional responses to the mixed-emotions leading to a reconciliation. The communicator expects the addressee to respond with sympathetic emotions.

See example 5 on page 48. Note: units 2 and 3 present alternate means of seeking a response to the mixed emotions. Here the alternate in unit 2 is unacceptable.

c) **intensify-RECONCILE** is an embedded problem-solution within the mixed-emotions-EMOTIONAL-RECONCILIATION relationship which blocks the solution. The *intensify* role augments the emotional problem and must be resolved before the main problem can be solved. The addressee is expected to react with heightened emotions.

Example 27: Psalm 73—"**1** Surely God is good to Israel,/ to those who are pure in heart./ **2** But as for me, my feet had almost slipped;/ I had nearly lost my foothold./ **3** For I envied the arrogant when I saw the prosperity of the wicked./ . . . This is what the wicked are like—/ always carefree, they increase in wealth./ **4** Surely in vain have I kept my heart pure;/ . . . When I tried to understand all this,/ it was oppressive to me/ **5** till I entered the sanctuary of God;/ then I understood their final destiny./ . . . **6** But as for me, it is good to be near God./ I have made the Sovereign Lord my refuge;/ I will tell of all your deeds."

Note: unit 4 intensifies the problem that the writer expressed in units 2 and 3. This intensification must be resolved, and is resolved together with the main problem in unit 5.

d) **situation(n)-REACTION**[13] relationship is the core of the causality paragraph pattern of emotional discourse without a struggle or tension. The *situation* is made up of factors outside of the communi-

---

[13] The whole matter of emotional genre and corresponding patterns is, as far as I know, essentially an unexplored semantic area. I was made aware of this by Callow's (1985) work. What is presented here is an extension by analogy of the other semantic paragraph patterns. The emotional causality pattern has already proved itself useful by explaining certain discourse phenomena that presented many intentional difficulties. The labels in this area might well be improved to be more descriptive, but the central concepts are consistent with the rest of what has been presented.

cator to which he or she will *react emotionally*. The addressee is expected to recognize the situation as a cause for the reaction, and to react in the same manner as the communicator.

> Example 28: Psalm 13—"1 How long, O Lord? Will you forget me forever?/ How long will you hide your face from me?/ 2 How long must I wrestle with my thoughts and every day have sorrow in my heart?/ 3 How long will my enemy triumph over me?/ 4 Look on me and answer, O Lord my God./ Give light to my eyes, or I will sleep in death;/ my enemy will say, 'I have overcome them,'/ and my foes will rejoice when I fall./ 5 But I trust in your unfailing love;/ 6 my heart rejoices in your salvation./ I will sing to the Lord, for he has been good to me."

Note: units 1–4 are the situation to which the communicator would react, and unit 6 is the reaction.

e) **belief** is the role in which the communicator can express his or her belief system, which interprets and determines his or her reaction to a particular situation. The addressee is expected to recognize that the belief system interprets the reaction, and to increase sympathetic reaction to the communicators expressed emotions in the *reaction*.

See example 28 above. Note: unit 5 is the expressed belief system that causes the reaction of unit 6.

f) **belief(n)-CONTROL** relationship is the core of the volitionality paragraph pattern of emotional discourse. The *belief* role is a progression of communicator beliefs that leads toward the *control* of his or her emotions. The communicator expects the addressee to recognize that the belief system leads to emotional control, and to increasingly understand that his or her beliefs lead to the desired emotional control.

> Example 29: Romans 8:23–38—"1 No, in all these things we are more than conquerors through him who loved us. 2 For I am convinced that neither death nor life, neither angels nor demons, neither the present nor the future, nor any powers, neither height nor depth, nor anything else in all creation, will be able to separate us from the love of God that is in Christ Jesus our Lord."

Note: this is an embedded paragraph of a larger complex paragraph. Unit 2 presents the belief system which is the indirect volitional cause of the reaction in unit 1.

Terms for Units in DESCRIPTIVE Semantic Genre

The roles in **DESCRIPTIVE** paragraph patterns are defined as:

a) **expectancy-FULFILLMENT** relationship is the core of the solutionality paragraph pattern of descriptive discourse producing a struggle or tension. The *expectancy* is the problem that the communicator must solve and on which the communication hangs until the imbalance is solved. The *fulfillment* is the role whereby the communicator resolves the tension. The addressee is expected to recognize that the fulfillment resolves the tension stated in the expectancy, and to react to the tension with a certain degree or type of emotion.

Example 30: Luke 24:19–32—"'1 About Jesus of Nazareth,' they replied. 'He was a prophet, powerful in word and deed before God and all the people. **2** The chief priests and our rulers handed him over to be sentenced to death, and they crucified him; **3** but we had hoped that he was the one who was going to redeem Israel. . . . ' He said to them, '**4** How foolish you are, and how slow of heart to believe all the prophets have spoken! Did not the Christ have to suffer these things and then enter his glory?' . . . They asked each other, '**5** Were not our hearts burning within us while he talked with us on the road and opened the Scriptures to us?' "

Note: unit 3 presents an expectancy imbalance which must be fulfilled in unit 5.

b) **experience(n)** role is a group of experiences that are a *response* to the expectancy and lead toward a fulfillment of the description. The communicator expects the addressee to react positively from the same shared experience.

See example 30 above. Note: unit 1 is an experience event that leads toward the fulfillment in unit 5.

c) **frustrative-ENCOURAGE** is an embedded problem-solution within the description which blocks the fulfillment by frustrating the expectancy. The *frustrative* role increases the expectancy until it is solved. The addressee is expected to react with increased expectancy.

Note: in example 30, unit 1–2 frustrates the expectancy of unit 3, but unit 4 encourages the listener contrary to his or her frustration.

d) **situation(n)-REACTION** relationship is the core of the causality paragraph pattern of the descriptive discourse. The *situation* is made up of factors in the communicator's environment to which he or she will *react* emotionally. The relation between *situations* is that the first in sequence is the *stimulus* for the second, which is the *response* to that stimulus. The addressee is expected to recognize that the situations are the cause for the reaction, and to react in the same manner as the communicator.

Example 31: Galatians 1:6—"**1** I am astonished **2** that you are so quickly deserting the one who called you by the grace of Christ and are turning to a different gospel. . . . "

Note: the whole paragraph from verse 6 to verse 10 is built on the nucleus of units 1 and 2. Unit 1 is Paul's reaction to the situation described in unit 2. Verses 7–10 is an amplification of "a different gospel" mentioned in unit 2.

e) **description(n)-DECLARATION** relationship is the core of the volitionality paragraph pattern of descriptive discourse. The *description* is the progression mainly of stative type propositions that lead toward a final declaration about the reality as viewed by the communicator. The communicator expects the addressee to recognize that the descriptions are the interpretational basis for the declaration, and to increasingly accept his declaration about the experience.

See example 12 on page 51. Note: units 1–4 are a description leading to the declaration presented in units 5 and 6 regarding the description. See note under this example on page 51 for a defence as to why I do not consider this an expository paragraph in which John defends his authority to declare the message.

Summary

We have observed in the examples presented that the author primarily focuses on one of the six basic semantic genre; hortatory, procedural, expository, narrative, emotional, and descriptive. We have also observed what the main semantic paragraph patterns are in monologue discourse. We have observed that these patterns reflect the author's intended effect on the audience and his or her perception as to whether solutionality, causality, or volitionality is involved.

These categorizations and patterns are not presented as watertight concepts, but rather as prototypical concepts. There are fuzzy areas, extensions, and maybe gradations. However, with this view of semantic paragraphs, we have a solid starting point.

Since these patterns are grounded on our human cognitive ability, we conclude that they are basic to human communication and its interpretation.

One very specific application which has arisen from understanding text through these communicative perspectives has been a productive translational procedure. The procedure has essentially six steps: (1) determine the boundaries of a particular semantic paragraph; (2) determine the focal genre and pattern; (3) understand the details within this context; (4) translate the characteristic or nuclear part of the paragraph first; (5) translate the supportive material; and (6) make sure this paragraph is correctly joined to the previous context.

Bibliography

Beekman, John and John C. Callow. 1974. *Translating the Word of God.* Grand Rapids: Zondervan Publishing House.

Beekman, John, John C. Callow, and Michael Kopesec. 1981. *The Semantic Structure of Written Communication*, 5th revision. Dallas: Summer Institute of Linguistics.

Callow, Kathleen. 1989. *Meaning and the Analysis of Texts.* (Prepublication Draft) Dallas: Summer Institute of Linguistics.

Grimes, J. E. 1975. *The Thread of Discourse.* The Hague.

Halliday, M. A. K. and R. Hasan. 1976. *Cohesion in English.* London: Longman. English Language Series, Title No. 9.

Holy Bible. New International Version. 1984. Grand Rapids: Zondervan.

Lakoff, George. 1987. *Women, Fire, and Dangerous Things.* Chicago/London: University of Chicago Press.

Longacre, Robert E. 1983. "Exhortation and Mitigation in First John." *Selected Technical Articles Related to Translation.* Vol. 9, 12–83. Dallas: Summer Institute of Linguistics. Pp. 3–44.

_____. 1983. *The Grammar of Discourse: Notional and Surface Structures.* New York: Plenum.

Mann, William C. and Sandra A. Thompson. 1987. "Rhetorical Structure Theory: A Theory of Text Organization." Reprinted from *The Structure of Discourse.* Marina del Rey, California: Information Sciences Institute.

4

Constituent Order in Copula Clauses: A Partial Study

John C. Callow

Introduction

The data base for this paper consists of the copula clauses found in 1 Corinthians, about two hundred in all. A "copula clause" is any clause in which the verb is some form of εἶναι, γίνεσθαι, or ὑπάρχειν (verbs with the meaning "to be" or "to become") and which has one or both of the two further elements of subject (S) and complement (C). (There are copula-type clauses, such as πιστὸς ὁ θεός in 1:9, which is readily analysed as having the structure CS, but which has no verb (V). Such verbless copula clauses would be an interesting study, particularly as to what motivates the author to use a verbless form rather than one with a verb.)

This paper is entitled "a partial study" for two reasons. One is that the data base is considerably less than the whole New Testament. As stated above, it is based on all the copula clauses identified in 1 Corinthians. This has been supplemented by a quick inventory of copula clauses in Romans, about 130 in all. The other reason is that the analysis presented is also partial. It became clear, as the work progressed, that a complete study would have to say a lot more about the placing of the subject phrase in copula clauses than this study does. It is hoped, however, that even this partial study will prove to be a stimulus to further research in these very interesting clauses and that what is unresolved in this paper will be resolved by others in due course.

Subject-initial Copula Clauses

In presenting the analysis of a complex mass of data, it is always difficult to know just where to begin. In particular, there is the question of whether to make the various *factors* affecting constituent order the framework of the presentation, or to divide the presentation up in accordance with the different *constituent orders*. For this paper, I have decided to follow the latter course. I will discuss the subject-initial patterns first, since there are more of them and so the factors affecting their order are more readily exemplified. There are two subject-initial patterns, SCV and SVC, which will be discussed in turn. Then complement-initial patterns (CVS and CSV) and verb-initial patterns (VSC and VCS) will also be presented.

The SCV Pattern

As already stated, this is the most common individual pattern, with about fifty examples in 1 Corinthians (about 25% of the total number of copula clauses in 1 Corinthians) and about thirty in Romans (about 22% of the total number of copula clauses in Romans). For this particular study, it is assumed, following Levinsohn (1991:ch. 1), that the subject is the "local topic" and that that is also why it is initial (disregarding other constituents of the clause such as conjunctions and adverbs which occur before the subject and lie outside the scope of this paper).[1] The discussion will therefore focus on the order C before V, as opposed to the order C after V, with S regarded as a given. (In both of these patterns, the fact that the subject precedes the complement is regarded as a case of the topic preceding the comment.)

In this paper, I am taking the neutral stance of not referring to C as "forefronted" since that would imply that either SVC or VSC was the basic pattern. Rather, I am looking for factors to account for every pattern in its own right, without assuming that there is a basic pattern from which the others can be derived.

The factor of contrast. By "contrast," in the context of copula clauses in 1 Corinthians, I am referring to two complements which have antonyms or which are in contrast in the context, although not with antonyms. So I am speaking here of contrasted complements being found *before* the verb.

---

[1] The only monograph on copula clauses in the New Testament that I know of is Lane C. McGaughy's (1972) work. One major matter to which McGaughy addresses himself is how to distinguish between the Subject and the Complement. In this connection, he gives a series of ordered rules of which the following are of particular interest: "Rule 3c. The word or word cluster determined by an article is the subject" (p. 49). "Rule 3d. If both words or word clusters are determined by an article, *the first one is the subject*" (p. 53) (emphasis mine). He then comments that "there are 22 examples of two articular clusters connected by the third singular present verb, ἐστίν, in the New Testament. An analysis of . . . the discourse structure revealed that the subject precedes the predicate nominative in all 22 cases" (p. 53).

When it comes to the examples, there are inevitably certain complications. One is that when the complements are in contrast, and the subject is the same, the subject is omitted in the second clause, giving a CV pattern:

7:14a   ἐπεὶ ἄρα τὰ τέκνα ὑμῶν ἀκάθαρτά ἐστιν,
7:14b   νῦν δὲ   ἅγιά ἐστιν.
"If that were the case, then your children would be 'unclean'; but in fact they are 'holy.'"[2]

A more complex case is found in 1:18, in which the peripheral elements of the complement are in contrast with each other, as well as the core or nuclear elements:

1:18   ὁ λόγος γὰρ ὁ τοῦ σταυροῦ τοῖς μὲν ἀπολλυμένοις μωρία ἐστίν,
1:18b   τοῖς δὲ σῳζομένοις ἡμῖν δύναμις
                                  θεοῦ ἐστιν.
"For the message of the cross is foolishness to those who are perishing, but it is the power of God to those who are being saved, that is, us."

Occasionally, the first clause has the verb in participle form, the second in finite form:

12:12   πάντα δὲ τὰ μέλη τοῦ σώματος, πολλὰ ὄντα ἕν ἐστιν σῶμα
"all the parts of the body, although many, constitute (= are) only one body"

There are other variations also. For example, in 3:18, the common subject is expressed as the subject of an orienter, and the second clause is in the form of a third person command:

3:18a   εἴ τις δοκεῖ σοφὸς εἶναι . . .
3:18b   μωρὸς γενέσθω
"If anyone thinks he is wise, let him become foolish."

As noted above, in the cases where there is a common subject, one of the two clauses occurs in the form CV only, with no overt subject phrase. In those cases in which the verb is first or second person, the pattern is also commonly CV, the subject being expressed in the verb. This again applies equally to statements and commands.

14:20a Ἀδελφοί, μὴ παιδία γίνεσθε ταῖς φρεσίν . . .
14:20c ταῖς δὲ φρεσὶν τέλειοι γίνεσθε.
"Brothers, stop being children in the way you think . . . be adults in the way you think."

---

[2] The translations given of the examples are my own.

9:22b τοῖς πᾶσιν γέγονα πάντα,
9:22c ἵνα πάντως τινὰς σώσω.
"I have become all things to all people, so that I might, in every way, save some."

In this latter example, only the first clause is a copula cause, and it is the periphery of the complement, τοῖς πᾶσιν "to all people"; that is in contrast with τινάς "some people." Where only the periphery of the complement precedes the verb, it is still analysed as having the pattern (S)CV; see also ἕν ἐστιν σῶμα in 12:12 above.

At this point, it is worth drawing attention to the fact that, in 1 Corinthians, the subject is sometimes found contrasted as well as the complement. This has no effect on the order SCV. For example:

6:16 οὐκ οἴδατε ὅτι ὁ κολλώμενος τῇ πόρνῃ ἕν σῶμά ἐστιν . . .
6:17 ὁ δὲ κολλώμενος τῷ κυρίῳ ἕν πνεῦμά ἐστιν.
"Don't you know that he who is joined to a prostitute is one body with her? But he who is joined to the Lord is one spirit with him."

11:7a ἀνὴρ μὲν . . . εἰκὼν καὶ δόξα θεοῦ ὑπάρχων·
11:7b ἡ γυνὴ δὲ   δόξα ἀνδρός ἐστιν
"a man . . . is the image and glory of God; but a woman is the glory of man."

And, as was the case with a common subject, one of the clauses is not necessarily a copula clause.

14:14b τὸ πνεῦμά μου προσεύχεται,
14:14c ὁ δὲ νοῦς μου ἄκαρπός ἐστιν.
"my spirit is praying, but my mind is inactive"

Finally, there are a few cases in which the contrasted constituents *are* internal to the clause, that is, part or all of the subject is in contrast with part of all of the complement.

1:25a ὅτι τὸ μωρὸν τοῦ θεοῦ σοφώτερον τῶν ἀνθρώπων ἐστίν
"because the folly of God is wiser than men"

7:29 ἵνα καὶ οἱ ἔχοντες γυναῖκας ὡς μὴ ἔχοντες ὦσιν
"so that those who have wives be like those who haven't"

The factor of emphasis. Kathleen Callow (1974:73) defines "emphasis" as follows: "normally involves the speaker-hearer relationship in some way." She also states that emphasis highlights information that is "of particular interest or significance" or "which will be surprising to the hearer."

I think it is fair to say that while it is inherently likely that there will be examples of emphasis in this sense in such an I-you document as a letter, they are not going to be easy to define in any more precise way. The examples presented here as illustrating the factor of emphasis fall, broadly speaking, into two groups:

(a) those in which the writer gives an evaluation of the readers or himself;

(b) those in which a personal-type comment, I-oriented, closes a semantic unit which is not in itself an I-oriented unit.

Some examples of evaluative comments are given below:

5:2   καὶ ὑμεῖς πεφυσιωμένοι ἐστέ
"and yet you are full of yourselves!"

4:8   ἤδη κεκορεσμένοι ἐστέ
"already you have eaten your fill!"

4:9   ὅτι θέατρον ἐγενήθημεν τῷ κόσμῳ καὶ ἀγγέλοις καὶ ἀνθρώποις
"because we have become a public spectacle to the world and to angels and to mankind"

4:13   ὡς περικαθάρματα τοῦ κόσμου ἐγενήθημεν
"we are like the world's rubbish"

15:19 ἐλεεινότεροι πάντων ἀνθρώπων ἐσμέν
"then we are more to be pitied than anyone else!"

Note that, as with the examples of contrast, the subject is not usually expressed apart from the verb-ending. Since these examples of emphasis are reflecting the "speaker-hearer relationship," they are all first and second person, and the absence of a free subject is much more common.

Some examples of personal-type comments at the end of a unit are now given.

9:27   μή πως, ἄλλοις κηρύξας, αὐτὸς ἀδόκιμος γένωμαι
"lest, after having preached to others, I myself be rejected"

(It could well be argued that this is evaluative, as shown by the use of ἀδόκιμος "rejected." The "personal-type" comment is, in this case, evaluative, so it could also be grouped with the first set of examples. The distinction is a convenient one, but hardly a rigid one.)

14:37 ἐπιγινωσκέτω ἃ γράφω ὑμῖν ὅτι κυρίου ἐστὶν ἐντολή.
"then let him acknowledge that what I am writing to you is a commandment from the Lord"

(This could also be analysed as an implicit contrast between "the Lord" and "me"—the commandment is not from me, but from the Lord.)

10:22 μὴ ἰσχυρότεροι αὐτοῦ ἐσμεν;
"We aren't stronger than him, are we?"

Note that 15:19, cited in the first group, is also unit-final.

The factor of focus. Focus is defined by K. Callow (1974) as "spotlighting items of particular interest." In this paper, a focussed concept, either the complement or part of it, is a significant concept for the following material.

In the following examples, it is hardly possible to give a detailed exegesis of the material following each example, but I will try to say enough so that the grounds for the analysis are reasonably clear.

3:13 ἑκάστου τὸ ἔργον φανερὸν γενήσεται
"the quality of each person's work will be made clear"

This example is followed by what I am calling a "γάρ unit" consisting of the rest of verse 13 and verses 14 and 15. Note the occurrence of δηλώσει "will make obvious," ἀποκαλύπτεται "will be revealed," ὁποῖον "what sort it is," δοκιμάσει "will test," μένει "remains = survives the fire," and κατακαήσεται "will be burned up."

4:4 ὁ δὲ ἀνακρίνων με κύριός ἐστιν
"the one who will assess me is the Lord"

This is followed by a ὥστε unit urging the Corinthians to leave all judgment to the Lord, when He comes; His judgment is then described.

6:15 οὐκ οἴδατε ὅτι τὰ σώματα ὑμῶν μέλη Χριστοῦ ἐστιν;
"Don't you realise that your bodies are parts of Christ?"

This verse is one point in Paul's argument here, verse 16 being a second point. The rest of verse 15 is a rhetorical question making central use of the complement concept μέλη Χριστοῦ and its rejection with μὴ γένοιτο.

8:9 βλέπετε δὲ μή πως ἡ ἐξουσία ὑμῶν αὕτη πρόσκομμα γένηται τοῖς
      ἀσθενέσιν/ἀσθενοῦσιν
"Make sure that this 'authority' of yours doesn't become
a 'stumbling-block' to those who are weak"

Verses 10 and 11 are a γάρ unit which follows through on what is likely to happen if the "authority" referred to is in fact misused and causes problems to others.

10:6 ταῦτα δὲ τύποι ἡμῶν ἐγενήθησαν
"These events are examples to us."

This statement is followed by a negative purpose "that we may not desire evil as they did" and a series of negative exhortations each followed by a καθώς statement drawing a comparison with what happened to the Israelites in the wilderness when they committed that particular sin.

7:32 θέλω δὲ ὑμᾶς ἀμερίμνους εἶναι
"I want you to be free from worry."

This statement leads into a discussion of worry or concern in the context of married life, which closes with verse 35; note the final synonymous term ἀπερισπάστως "free from distraction."

As with the previous factors of contrast and emphasis, there are examples with no free subject phrase.

3:16 οὐκ οἴδατε ὅτι ναὸς θεοῦ ἐστε;
"Don't you realise that you are the temple of God?"

This leads into a short unit, consisting only of verse 17, centering on the concept ναὸς Θεοῦ.

7:25 γνώμην δὲ δίδωμι ὡς ἠλεημένος ὑπὸ κυρίου πιστὸς εἶναι
"However, I am giving you my advice as someone who, as a result of the Lord's mercy, can be relied on."

This differs somewhat from the examples above in that verses 26ff are Paul's advice, not a discussion of his reliability. This could in fact be considered an evaluation, but the context is obviously different from the examples given above of emphasis. Rather, Paul is validating his advice on the basis of his character. Without a character reference, so to speak, who was going to listen to his advice? Hence, it can be considered a key concept in persuading the Corinthians to listen carefully to what he has to say.

All the above examples are considered to be cases of *cataphoric* focus, in which a key concept for the following material is signalled as such by the order complement before the verb. But this obviously raises the question of whether there is such a phenomenon as anaphoric focus; if so, what does it look like?

The answer appears to be that there is, though rather less common than cataphoric focus, and not always so straightforward to analyse. It seems to me that the data about to be described is similar enough to cataphoric focus to be considered a corresponding anaphoric focus.

An example will help clarify the situation I am trying to describe:

2:14 μωρία γὰρ αὐτῷ ἐστιν
"for they are foolishness to him"

This clause gives a reason to the statement immediately preceding that "a natural man does not receive the things of God's Spirit." It is not cataphoric—the remaining verses in chapter 2 (14–16) deal with the "natural/spiritual" contrast. It is concluded, therefore, that μωρία "foolishness" is a focussed key concept in the γάρ clause, referring *back* to the preceding clause, i.e., anaphorically.

Some other examples which seem best explained in this way are:

3:17 ὁ γὰρ ναὸς τοῦ θεοῦ ἅγιός ἐστιν
"for God's temple is holy"

This is the explanation for the preceding statement that "God will destroy anyone who destroys his temple," the key concept in the explanation being ἅγιος.

3:19 ἡ γὰρ σοφία τοῦ κόσμου τούτου μωρία παρὰ τῷ θεῷ ἐστιν
"for the world's wisdom is foolishness in God's estimation"

This is the opening statement in a γάρ unit which consists of Old Testament quotes supporting the above claim. At the same time the complement, μωρία παρὰ τῷ θεῷ, is the key concept in the support for the exhortation immediately preceding it. However, while it appears to have the same anaphoric focus and function as 3:17, it differs in that (a) it does pick up preceding vocabulary; (b) it could also be considered cataphoric relative to the γάρ unit (note that the final quote ends with μάταιοι "foolish"); and (c) it also exhibits internal contrast. It might be better to consider the complement here a "hinge" concept, both anaphoric and cataphoric, rather than purely one or the other.

In 11:27 there seems to be a similar example to 3:19:

11:27 ὥστε, ὅς ἂν ἐσθίῃ τὸν ἄρτον ἢ πίνῃ τὸ ποτήριον τοῦ κυρίου
        ἀναξίως ἔνοχος ἔσται τοῦ σώματος καὶ αἵματος τοῦ κυρίου
"Consequently, anyone who eats the bread or drinks the cup
of the Lord in an unworthy manner will be guilty with regard
to the body and blood of the Lord."

In the conclusion introduced by ὥστε, the crucial concept is ἔνοχος "guilty." In that sense, it looks back to the preceding statements about the Lord's Supper and their behaviour at it (vv. 17–26). Yet the following exhortations are also based on it; note in particular, δοκιμαζέτω ἄνθρωπος ἑαυτόν "let a person test himself," κρίμα "judgment," and various compounds of κρίνω "to judge" (vv. 31 and 32). Hence, it is an anaphoric key concept in the conclusion to the preceding argument, but also a cataphoric key concept for the following exhortation.

Two special cases need to be considered. The first is those in which the phrase ἐν ὑμῖν "in/among you" occurs as the complement before the verb. This is found three times in three very similar examples:

1:11 ἐδηλώθη γάρ μοι . . . ὅτι ἔριδες ἐν ὑμῖν εἰσιν
"I have been informed . . . that there are factions among you."

11:18 πρῶτον μὲν γὰρ . . . ἀκούω σχίσματα ἐν ὑμῖν εἶναι
"For first of all . . . I hear that there are divisions among you."

11:19 δεῖ γὰρ καὶ αἱρέσεις ἐν ὑμῖν ὑπάρχειν
"For there must be different parties among you."

The first example initiates a γάρ unit (vv. 11 and 12) which follows a threefold command to be united and not divided in verse 10. The other two examples follow a rebuke in verse 17 about their behaviour when they assembled to celebrate the Lord's Supper. In both contexts factions and divisions are very much in focus; but the factions and divisions are among *them*, the recipients of the letter, not others, and they are the ones who are being exhorted and rebuked. Hence the position before the verb is considered a focussed one.

The second special case consists of second person plural commands in the form CV. They are the following:

4:16 παρακαλῶ οὖν ὑμᾶς, μιμηταί μου γίνεσθε.
"I urge you, therefore, be imitators of me."

10:7 μηδὲ εἰδωλολάτραι γίνεσθε
"Do not be idolaters."

10:32 ἀπρόσκοποι καὶ Ἰουδαίοις γίνεσθε καὶ Ἕλλησιν
"Do not cause offence to Jews or Gentiles."

11:1 μιμηταί μου γίνεσθε
"Be imitators of me."

15:58 ὥστε . . . ἑδραῖοι γίνεσθε, ἀμετακίνητοι
"So then . . . be firm, unshakable."

All of these examples, except the first, appear to function anaphorically: 10:32, 11:1, and 15:58 are, in fact, closing exhortations for units of varying sizes; 10:7 is the first of a series of negative commands, each of which, however, is based on the (bad) example of the forefathers referred to in 10:1–6. 4:16 can be considered to be both anaphoric, referring back to verses 14 and 15 in which Paul speaks of himself as the Corinthians' "father" (note, too, the οὖν), and cataphoric, as in the following verses Paul tells them that he is sending Timothy to them, whom he refers to as τέκνον μου "my child" and who will remind them of "my ways in Christ."

While, as always in such analyses, there is a residue of puzzling cases, so far as I am able to judge, the three factors of contrast, emphasis, and focus account for all the cases of (S)CV in 1 Corinthians. From a theoretical perspective, I would like to see if these factors could be united in a theoretical approach that draws more obviously on what could perhaps be called "larger scale" thinking. My anticipation is that something along the line of "theme development" will prove, in the short or long run, to unite the above insights into a comprehensive discourse theory of New Testament Greek.

The SVC Pattern

In seeking explanations for this pattern, i.e., why the complement should follow the verb, three possible approaches are available. One is to regard this pattern as "basic," and so not needing any particular explanation. A second is to establish the absence of the factors that give rise to the pattern (S)CV—no contrast, no emphasis, and no focus. The third is to look for positive reasons, so to speak, for the occurrence of the complement after the verb.

Let us take this last approach first. One factor that can cause a constituent to be placed at the end of a clause is its length, and there does appear to be one example where the length of the complement might well account for its following the verb:

5:11 ἐάν τις ἀδελφὸς ὀνομαζόμενος ᾖ πόρνος ἢ πλεονέκτης ἢ εἰδωλολάτρης ἢ λοίδορος ἢ μέθυσος ἢ ἅρπαξ
"if anyone who bears the name of 'brother' should be an immoral person or a 'money-grubber' or an idolater or foul-mouthed or a drunkard or a swindler"

In seeking a general solution to the question of placing the complement after the verb, it needs to be made clear that contrast is found with the pattern SVC, but only of the type οὐ/μὴ . . . ἀλλά, which type is *not* found with the pattern SCV. There are three examples of SVC contrast in 1 Corinthians:

2:5 ἵνα ἡ πίστις ὑμῶν μὴ ᾖ ἐν σοφίᾳ ἀνθρώπων ἀλλ᾽ ἐν δυνάμει θεοῦ
"so that your faith might not rest (= be) on human wisdom but on God's power"

3:7 ὥστε, οὔτε ὁ φυτεύων ἐστίν τι οὔτε ὁ ποτίζων, ἀλλὰ ὁ αὐξάνων θεός.
"So then, the one who plants is not important, nor is the one who waters the plants; it is God who makes the plants grow who is important."

12:14 καὶ γὰρ τὸ σῶμα οὐκ ἔστιν ἓν μέλος, ἀλλὰ πολλά.
"For the body does not consist of (= is not) just one part, but of many parts."

There is also one contrastive example in which the verb is in the form of a participle:

9:21 μὴ ὢν ἄνομος θεοῦ, ἀλλ᾽ ἔννομος Χριστοῦ
"not being without any law of God, but being under the law of Christ"

The fact that οὐ/μὴ . . . ἀλλὰ contrasts place the negated complement after the verb is undoubtedly significant. There are also eight
examples in 1 Corinthians of the pattern VC in which the complement is negated. It would be easy to simply say that when the complement is negated, it follows the verb. However, while this is
generally true, it is not universally and invariably true. Certain
"counter-examples" need to be considered:

15:58 εἰδότες ὅτι ὁ κόπος ὑμῶν οὐκ ἔστιν κενὸς ἐν κυρίῳ.
"since you know that your hard work is not useless in the Lord"

15:10 καὶ ἡ χάρις αὐτοῦ ἡ εἰς ἐμὲ οὐ κενὴ ἐγενήθη, ἀλλὰ περισσότερον
       αὐτῶν πάντων ἐκοπίασα
"And his grace shown to me was not useless, but I have toiled more
abundantly than all of them."

In the second example, the complement κενή is negated as part of
an οὐ . . . ἀλλά contrast, yet it precedes, not follows, the verb.

7:23 μὴ γίνεσθε δοῦλοι ἀνθρώπων
"Do not be the slaves of human beings."

10:7 μηδὲ εἰδωλολάτραι γίνεσθε
"Do not be idolaters."

How are such contrasting examples to be explained? My own preference is to say that when the complement follows the verb, it can be
described in general terms as "downplayed," the opposite of "highlighted." In the case of contrast, this is already well established—the
negative side of a contrast is almost invariably less significant, in the
context, than the positive side. In the three examples given earlier,
this seems reasonably clear. The negative side of the contrast is being
rejected by the apostle as erroneous, unacceptable, and undesirable.

How about the above examples, then? In 15:10, it seems reasonable
to posit that we have here an emotionally-charged evaluative and personal statement from the apostle, an "I" statement comparing himself
with the other apostles. The factor of emphasis is, therefore, considered to be operative, and so κενή precedes the verb. 15:58, on the
other hand, is a grounds or motivation for the preceding exhortation. The concept κενός is not being contrasted, or emphasized. It is
not, in any obvious sense, a key concept such as focussing requires.
(In fact, it would seem to follow from the predominance of negated
complements following verbs that negated concepts are rarely focussed—but this needs further research and refining.)

The difference between the two γίνεσθε commands in 7:23 and
10:7 can be explained along similar lines, but put a bit differently.

The command in 10:7 is clearly the point that Paul is making along with other negative commands in verses 8, 9, and 10: it is thematic. The command in 7:23, important though it is, is to one side of the main thrust of verses 17–24. It is in verse 24 that Paul returns to the main theme, stated in verse 20. In fact, verse 23 is the final part of a γάρ unit, consisting of verses 22 and 23.

There is a further striking pair of opposite examples in 12:2 and 13:11.

12:2   οἴδατε ὅτι ὅτε ἔθνη ἦτε
"You know that, when you were pagans"

13:11   ὅτε ἤμην νήπιος . . . ὅτε (δὲ) γέγονα ἀνήρ
"When I was a child . . . but when I became an adult"

In both cases, the copula clauses are ὅτε clauses, both consist only of complement and verb, yet they are in the reverse order relative to each other. Why is one CV, the other VC? Doubtless various answers could be given, and quite possibly more than one factor is operative. My own answer is to observe that 13:11 is an illustration. The main point is given in verse 10: "When that which is complete comes, that which is only partial is removed." Paul then illustrates this main point from childhood and adulthood in verse 11, and in other ways in verse 12. However, even verse 10 is a subsidiary point to the opening clause in verse 8, "love never comes to an end." This main point is then picked up again in verse 13. Hence, verses 9–12 are, in some sense, illustrative and subsidiary to the main theme. To adapt narrative terminology, "they are off the theme-line." If this is so, it implies, by way of contrast, that 12:2, in some sense, is "on the theme-line." In fact, 12:2, 3 appear to be stating some vital initial information concerning "spiritual" experiences before Paul talks in detail about spiritual gifts. (It is also possible that there is an implicit contrast in 12:2 with their present status as believers; this would also require the complement before the verb.)

What is being suggested, then, is that the placing of the complement after the verb signaled to the Koine Greek reader that that information was "off the theme-line." I am well aware that this is generic terminology, a skeleton which needs fleshing out, and I am aware of immediate questions in my own mind. An appreciable number of (S)CV examples were in γάρ units or εἰ clauses or ὅτι clauses. Can such units be considered thematic? Until there is a well-defined and tested theory of theme-line in non-narrative materials, the question will have to be left hanging. Some further examples of (S)VC are given below:

7:7   θέλω δὲ πάντας ἀνθρώπους εἶναι ὡς καὶ ἐμαυτόν
"I would like everyone to be like myself."

14:10   τοσαῦτα, εἰ τύχοι γένη φωνῶν εἰσιν/ἐστιν ἐν κόσμῳ
"Doubtless, there are all sorts of languages in the world."

15:9   ἐγὼ γάρ εἰμι ὁ ἐλάχιστος τῶν ἀποστόλων
"for I am the least of the apostles"

16:22   ἤτω ἀνάθεμα
"Let him be cursed."

12:15   ὅτι οὐκ εἰμὶ χείρ, οὐκ εἰμὶ ἐκ τοῦ σώματος
"Because I am not a hand, I am not a part of the body."

15:17   ἔτι ἐστὲ ἐν ταῖς ἁμαρτίαις ὑμῶν
"You are still in your sins."

15:9 and 16:22 are obviously difficult, as they certainly give the impression of being evaluative, and hence, emphatic. Such examples show that the analysis needs improving, until such examples can be accounted for satisfactorily.

Finally, there are four instances of the relative clause and one article-and-participle clause, all with the pattern SVC, S being the relative pronoun in the one case, the article in the other.

1:30   ὃς ἐγενήθη σοφία ἡμῖν ἀπὸ θεοῦ
"who was caused to be wisdom for us by God"

3:11   ὅς ἐστιν Ἰησοῦς Χριστός
"who is Jesus Christ"

4:17   ὅς ἐστιν μου τέκνον/(τέκνον μου) ἀγαπητὸν καὶ πιστὸν κυρίῳ
"who is my beloved and faithful child in the Lord."

15:9   ὃς οὐκ εἰμὶ ἱκανὸς καλεῖσθαι ἀπόστολος
"who am not worthy to be called an apostle"

1:2   τῇ οὔσῃ ἐν Κορίνθῳ
"which is in Corinth"

In principle, it would be expected that such clauses as these could exhibit both SVC and SCV patterns. However, such clauses do seem rather unlikely to exhibit contrast, emphasis, or focus, so if there are SCV examples in the New Testament corpus, it would be expected that they would be rare.

(Note: the quick survey of Romans, mentioned in the Introduction, has yielded two examples of article-and-participle clauses in which the order is SCV. The first is in 8:5, οἱ γὰρ κατὰ σάρκα ὄντες "those who are controlled by the flesh," in which κατὰ σάρκα is the complement, and precedes the verb. Here the context would indicate contrast with οἱ δὲ κατὰ πνεῦμα "those who are controlled by the Spirit."

The second is found in 8:28, τοῖς κατὰ πρόθεσιν κλητοῖς οὖσιν "to those who are called according to [God's] purpose." Since the following two verses are introduced by ὅτι "because," it seems likely that the complement, κατὰ πρόθεσιν κλητοῖς, is in cataphoric focus, providing a key concept for the following ὅτι group.)

Complement-initial Copula Clauses

We now come to patterns which are much less frequent. My count of complement-initial copula clauses is seventeen, less than 10% of the total. Further, all those with the pattern CVS fall into three distinct groupings and account for thirteen of the total seventeen.

The Pattern CVS

There is one example in the data of a relative clause, the relative pronoun being the complement:

3:17 οἵτινές ἐστε ὑμεῖς
"which is what you are"

There are also two examples of what some linguists call **information interrogatives**. (These two examples are obviously parallel with each other, and there are various textual variants. In particular, the question which is placed second in the sequence has the verb omitted in some MSS, present in others. But these textual variants do not materially affect the analysis, nor does the fact that they are actually rhetorical questions.)

3:5a τί(ς) οὖν ἐστιν Ἀπολλώς;
"Who/What then is Apollos?"

3:5b τί(ς) δέ (ἐστιν) Παῦλος;
"Who/What is Paul?"

The third group is the biggest of the three. Here, **the subject is in the form of a clause** and is placed at the end; the complement precedes the verb. Since the form of the subject clause varies somewhat, all eight examples are given.

4:3 ἐμοὶ δὲ εἰς ἐλάχιστόν ἐστιν ἵνα ὑφ' ὑμῶν ἀνακριθῶ
"It doesn't matter to me at all that I should be critically assessed by you."

6:7   ἤδη μὲν [οὖν] ὅλως ἥττημα ὑμῖν ἐστιν ὅτι κρίματα ἔχετε μεθ᾽
ἑαυτῶν
"In fact, however, you have already suffered a (serious) defeat in that
you are having lawsuits with each other."

7:8   καλὸν αὐτοῖς (ἐστιν) ἐὰν μείνωσιν ὡς κἀγώ
"It is good for them if they remain in the same state that I am in."

7:9   κρεῖττον γάρ ἐστιν γαμῆσαι ἢ πυροῦσθαι
"For it is better to marry than to be aflame with desire."

(The subject here is γαμῆσαι "to marry"; ἢ πυροῦσθαι completes the
comparison and is the peripheral part of the complement, the head
being κρεῖττον.)

9:16   οὐαὶ γάρ/δὲ μοί ἐστιν ἐὰν μὴ εὐαγγελίσωμαι
"Woe to me if I don't spread the good news!"

11:13   πρέπον ἐστὶν γυναῖκα ἀκατακάλυπιον τῷ θεῷ προσεύχεσθαι;
"Is it fitting for a woman to pray to God with her head uncovered?"

14:35   αἰσχρὸν γάρ ἐστιν γυναικὶ λαλεῖν ἐν ἐκκλησίᾳ.
"It is disgraceful for a woman to talk in the public meetings of
the church."

16:4   ἐὰν δὲ ἄξιον ᾖ τοῦ κἀμὲ πορεύεσθαι
"if it is appropriate for me to go also"

It would be tempting (and simple) to say that these are fixed orders so that there is no choice involved, and, therefore, no further
factors need be discussed than those already mentioned of relative
clause, information interrogative, and clausal subject. There are two
further examples, not in this pattern, but related to it, which cast
doubts on such a simplistic approach.

9:18   τίς οὖν μού/μοί ἐστιν ὁ μισθός;
"In that case, what reward is there for me?"

16:12   καὶ πάντως οὐκ ἦν θέλημα ἵνα νῦν ἔλθῃ
"And it wasn't at all his will to go now."

The first example is clearly a case of an information interrogative,
but the periphery of the complement, μού, is placed before the verb
while the head follows the verb, giving the pattern CSV rather than
CVS. In the second example, there is a clausal subject (cf. the ἵνα
ἔλθῃ πρὸς ὑμᾶς of the preceding clause; the subject repeats this information in abbreviated form). The new information is the οὐκ ἦν θέλημα and is the complement in this case, and being negated, follows
the verb, giving the pattern VCS.

Further, when the clausal subject examples are looked at more closely, many of them are evaluative and/or emotional examples in which the complement typically precedes the verb in (S)CV patterns. It seems reasonable to assume, therefore, that although either the complement (in relative clauses and information interrogatives) or the subject (in clausal subject clauses) is fixed in position, the other two constituents have freedom of movement according to the factors already discussed in connection with (S)CV and (S)VC patterns. It may well be the case, therefore, in the clausal subject examples, that the complements precede the verb because they are emphasised or focussed (they are not contrastive, however).

The Pattern CSV

That leaves just four other examples of complement-initial clauses, all with the same pattern CSV. This being so, the complement precedes the verb, and should exhibit the same factors of contrast, emphasis, or focus that (S)CV patterns show. The subject is also the topic, as is always the case in copula clauses, and precedes the verb as in SCV and SVC clauses. So the key question appears to be why the complement—very untypically—precedes the subject.

The four examples are the following:

6:11　καὶ ταῦτά τινες ἦτε
"And that's what some of you were!"

9:1　οὐ τὸ ἔργον μου ὑμεῖς ἐστε ἐν κυρίῳ;
"You are my work in the Lord, aren't you?"

9:2　ἡ γὰρ σφραγίς μου τῆς ἀποστολῆς/(τῆς ἐμῆς ἀποστολῆς)
ὑμεῖς ἐστε ἐν κυρίῳ.
"For you are the seal of my apostleship in the Lord."

10:17　ὅτι εἷς ἄρτος, ἓν σῶμα οἱ πολλοί ἐσμεν
"because there is only one loaf, we—the many—constitute (= are) only one body"

The conditions for complement before the verb are clearly met. 6:11 is emphatic and also contrastive, followed as it is by a sequence of three ἀλλά's. 9:1 and 2 are in the context of Paul defending his apostleship to the Corinthians, so that they are not only emotionally charged statements, but in each the complement is a key concept in his defence. 10:17 is clearly contrastive internally.

Why CSV rather than SCV? Possibly it has something to do with the fact that all four examples are first and second person examples of copula clauses so that the subjects are free pronouns, or, as in 6:11

and 10:17, a descriptive phrase. There are only two examples of this sort with the common pattern SCV:

5:2   Καὶ ὑμεῖς πεφυσιωμένοι ἐστέ
"And yet you are full of yourselves!"

9:27   μή πως, ἄλλοις κήρυξας αὐτὸς ἀδόκιμος γένωμαι.
"lest, after having preached to others, I myself might be rejected"

These have both been analyzed earlier as having emphasized complements. In 9:27, however, αὐτός is in contrast with ἄλλοις, and in 5:2 the context makes it likely that there is emphasis on ὑμεῖς. So, it seems a reasonable hypothesis to say, in first and second person clauses, in which there is also a "free" subject, the complement, if contrasted, emphasized, or focussed, precedes that free subject, unless the subject itself is also contrasted, emphasized, or focussed. Put in other terms, a highlighted complement, in these non-third person clauses, precedes the subject, unless that subject is itself highlighted, in which case the order is SCV. Obviously more data and research are needed.

Verb-initial Copula Clauses

Existential Clauses

We now come to the smallest group of all, VSC and VCS patterns; there are just nine examples in all. However, before these are commented on, it needs to be pointed out there are eight V-initial clauses which are not being considered here. Some of the grammar books distinguish between the "existential" use of the verb "to be," and its "copulative" use, and this is a distinction which is accepted here.[3] Existential clauses are distinguished from copula clauses by having only two constituents, the verb and the subject, existence being predicated of the subject or being denied.

The examples are as follows:

---

[3] "Existentials" as a distinct meaning of einai or as a distinctive subgroup of copula clauses, is vigorously rejected by McGaughy (1972:119–25). In this he follows the arguments of Charles M. Kahn in an article "The Greek Verb 'To Be' and the Concept of Being" (1966) and is, he claims, supported by John Lyons and Halliday (p. 104). He takes the view that "existential" uses of "to be" as well as its "possessive" use, are all to be traced to a "locative" sense or use of the verb. I am not persuaded, as I think that there is confusion in what is said between form, context, and meaning, but I would not deny that the "existential" use has closer links semantically with the "locative" use than with other uses of the verb. For the purposes of this paper, existentials are distinguished by consisting of subject and verb only.

8:5a   καὶ γὰρ εἴπερ εἰσὶν λεγόμενοι θεοὶ
"For even if there are so-called 'gods' "

8:5b   ὥσπερ εἰσὶν θεοὶ πολλοὶ καὶ κύριοι πολλοὶ
"as there are undoubtedly many gods and many lords"

14:28   ἐὰν δὲ μὴ ᾖ διερμηνευτής
"if there happens to be no interpreter present"

15:44a,b   (εἴ) ἐστιν σῶμα ψυχικόν, καί ἐστιν/ἐστὶν καὶ σῶμα πνευματικόν
"(Since) there is a physical body, so there is also a spiritual body."

15:54   τότε γενήσεται ὁ λόγος ὁ γεγραμμένος
"then the (following) written message will take place (= come
    into existence)"

The seventh example appears to be a case of an existential in
which the subject is clausal in form:

11:20   οὐκ ἔστιν κυριακὸν δεῖπνον φαγεῖν
"It is not the Lord's supper you are eating" (literally "to eat
    the Lord's supper does not exist").

There are, however, another nine clauses which can be analysed as
existentials, but in which the subject *precedes* the verb, rather than
follows it, as in the above examples. The reasons for the subject being before the verb are as follows:

(a) The subject is an information interrogative; in this case, it appears to be used idiomatically:

214:15 and 26   τί οὖν ἐστιν;
"So what is to be done/concluded then?"

(b) Article and participle clauses (the article, i.e., the subject, has
to be first):

1:28   τὰ μὴ ὄντα
"the things which do not exist" (= the things which are of no importance)

15:37   τὸ σῶμα τὸ γενησόμενον
"the body which will be" (= will come into existence)

(c) Contrast, i.e., the subject is in contrast with another (following) concept:

12:4   διαιρέσεις δὲ χαρισμάτων εἰσίν, τὸ δὲ αὐτὸ πνεῦμα
"There are many varieties of 'grace-gifts,' but it is the same Spirit
    (who gives them)."

12:5 and 12:6 are essentially the same as 12:4 and closely parallel it.

(d) The subject is focussed (15:12 is cataphoric; 16:2 is both cataphoric and anaphoric):

15:12   πῶς λέγουσιν ἐν ὑμῖν τινες ὅτι ἀνάστασις νεκρῶν οὐκ ἔστιν;
"how can some of you say that there is no resurrection?"

16:2   ἵνα μὴ ὅταν ἔλθω, τότε λογεῖαι/λογίαι γίνωνται
"so that, when I come, there won't be collections at that time"

Before leaving the existentials, it is interesting to note that negation appears to have no effect on the order. Negative existentials are found with both patterns, VS and SV. This is obviously different from the copula clause (and supports the view that existentials are a distinct grouping, with their own patternings).

The Pattern VSC

There are nine examples of verb-initial clauses, five with the pattern VSC and four with the pattern VCS. These verb-initial patterns raise one essentially new question and another older question. The new question is: Why is the subject found *following* the verb? In what way do these examples differ from the many where the subject precedes the verb? The older problem is as to what accounts for the relative ordering of the subject and the complement.

It would be very satisfying if there were one solution to the first, major question, rather than half-a-dozen solutions. Two factors do stand out in this group of V-initial copula clauses: one is the fact that seven of the nine are negative; the other is that four of the nine are purposes, and that three of these four purposes are found in the VSC group. This latter figure is obviously significant when it is compared with the same figure of three for the (S)CV patterns, which are ten times as many as the VSC. A further three purpose clauses are found in the (S)VC patterns.

The most attractive overall solution to the motivation for these patterns is to propose the theory that when both subject and complement follow the verb then *the whole clause* is being negated, rather than the complement only, as in many of the cases when the complement follows the verb. Radney (1982) postulated that if the negative particle immediately precedes the verb, then the whole clause is negated. This obviously cannot be applied unmodified to copula clauses, since in most of the examples of (S)VC, the negative particle immediately precedes the verb, but only the complement is negated. It does not seem unreasonable to say that, *for copula clauses*, when the whole clause is negated, then both subject and complement follow the verb, and, it seems reasonable to posit, *in that order*. In other words, the pattern neg-VSC signalled to the Greek reader that the proposition represented by S,C and their relationship was being denied.

The three examples of VSC which would be explained by this approach are:

10:6   εἰς τὸ μὴ εἶναι ἡμᾶς ἐπιθυμητὰς κακῶν
"so that we should not be those who desire all sorts of evil"

(A quick survey of copula clauses in Romans revealed no less than nine examples of εἰς τὸ εἶναι clauses, all but one with the order VSC; the ninth was VCS. In such clauses, can we consider the position of the verb fixed?)

11:8   οὐ γάρ ἐστιν ἀνὴρ ἐκ γυναικός, ἀλλὰ γυνὴ ἐξ ἀνδρὸς
"For man does not originate from woman, but woman from man."

(This example is an obvious οὐ . . . ἀλλά contrast, so the pattern SVC would be expected. The present hypothesis is saying that the order VSC is denying the claim, or assumption, that "man originated from woman" and is replacing it with the opposite statement.)

12:25   ἵνα μὴ ᾖ σχίσμα ἐν τῷ σώματι
"so that there won't be any division in the body"

(Compare the three affirmative statements about divisions discussed in the SCV section. In 12:25, the stated purpose is to avoid the situation of divisions in the body.)

That leaves two affirmative VSC patterns to account for. These are the following:

12:19   εἰ δὲ ἦν τὰ πάντα ἓν μέλος, ποῦ τὸ σῶμα;
"Now if all the parts of the body were just one part, where would the body be?"

15:28   ἵνα ᾖ ὁ θεὸς [τὰ] πάντα ἐν πᾶσιν.
"so that God may be everything to everyone"

The first example is the only example in 1 Corinthians of a copula clause which is a contrary-to-fact condition, but since it inherently denies the main thesis of chapter 12, that the body consists of many parts, it functions effectively as a negated statement, though not formally negated. (It would be an interesting piece of research to verify, modify, or reject this suggestion.)

The second example is much more puzzling. The second half of 15:27 (beginning with ὅταν δὲ εἴπῃ . . .) appears to be introducing a "don't get me wrong" unit (see Werner 1984) which ends with the copula clause of 15:28 cited above. Hence, it can be argued that the whole unit is off the theme-line, a correction of a possible misunderstanding. This explanation would account for the complement following the verb, but not (obviously) for the subject also following the verb. However, it could also be posited that the whole proposition "God is all in all" is the purpose, so that the positive pattern VSC would be interpreted in a similar manner to the negative pattern VSC.

The Pattern VCS

This is the most puzzling of all the patterns, and is the complete reverse of the dominant pattern SCV.

Of the four VCS examples, one has already been discussed in connection with the CVS patterns:

16:12 καὶ πάντως οὐκ ἦν θέλημα ἵνα νῦν ἔλθῃ
"and it wasn't at all his will to go now"

This is subject-final because the subject is clausal in form; the complement follows the verb because it is negated.

The other three are all negative. As already stated, this is taken to signal that the whole proposition is being denied. Why the order complement-subject? The answer to this question is no simpler than for the corresponding pattern CSV, but suggestions are made for each example:

1:10 καὶ μὴ ᾖ ἐν ὑμῖν σχίσματα
"and that there be no divisions among you"

In this case, σχίσματα is the theme of verses 10–17, so the subject may well be placed final to signal its thematic significance. (Contrast 12:25, discussed under the VSC patterns, where the subject, σχίσμα, is not thematic.)

9:16 ἐὰν γὰρ εὐαγγελίζωμαι, οὐκ ἔστιν μοι καύχημα . . .
"For if I spread the gospel, I have no grounds for boasting."

The concept of "boasting" may well be a key concept in verses 15–18, though expressed in different ways. In verse 15 his καύχημα is given as the main reason why he makes known the gospel free of charge. This would be a similar explanation to that given for 1:10, just above, viz., that S is placed final because it is thematic.

14:33 οὐ γάρ ἐστιν ἀκαταστασίας ὁ θεός, ἀλλ᾽ εἰρήνης
"For God is not a God of disorder, but of harmony/peace."

Here there is an οὐ . . . ἀλλά contrast relating to the complement, which may account for the complement preceding the subject in this case.

Unresolved Issues

It may be useful to conclude this paper by restating some of the more major questions that have not been answered, and which it is hoped that others will be able to elucidate.

1. The main unresolved question, to my mind, concerns the factors that motivate or control the placing of the subject phrase before or after the verb in a copula clause, and, in particular, whether the answer to this question lies in the realm of a theory of the "theme-line." That is to say, subjects placed before the verb would be on the theme-line, whereas subjects that followed the verb would be off the theme-line. Is this really the case? And just what is a "theme-line"?

2. While the factors affecting the position of the complement seem reasonably well explained, "emphasis" needs more careful definition, and "focus," I suspect, needs relating to such higher-level matters as theme-line or theme-development, schematic structure, genre type, etc.

3. What is it about negation and purpose that produce an unusually high number of verb-initial clauses?

4. Under what conditions does an author choose to use a verbless copula clause, rather than one with a verb?

References

Callow, Kathleen 1974. *Discourse Considerations in Translating the Word of God.* Grand Rapids: Zondervan.

Kahn, Charles M. 1966. "The Greek Verb 'To be' and the Concept of Being." *Foundations of Language* 2.245–65.

Levinsohn, S. H. 1991. *Discourse Features of New Testament Greek: A Coursebook.* Prepublication draft.

McGaughy, Lane C. 1972. *A Descriptive Analysis of Einai.* Society of Biblical Literature Dissertation Series 6.

Radney, R. J. 1982. *Some Factors that Influence Fronting in Koine Clauses.* M.A. Thesis, University of Texas at Arlington.

Werner, John R. 1984. "Don't Get Me Wrong: A New Testament Discourse Feature." *Notes on Translation* 102. Dallas: Summer Institute of Linguistics. Pp. 29–35.

5

Discourse Analysis, Synoptic Criticism, and Markan Grammar: Some Methodological Considerations

David Alan Black

The idea that Matthew and Luke have in numerous places "corrected" Markan grammar is presupposed in most contemporary discussions of the Synoptic Problem. Ironically, several recent studies have shown that peculiarities in Markan grammar do not necessarily prove Mark to be chronologically prior to Matthew and Luke (see Farmer 1964; Sanders 1969; Orchard 1987). These studies have also shown that the argument from grammar cannot *logically* deduce the priority of Mark, although many scholars continue to use it as if it could (e.g., Stein 1988; McKnight 1991). The purpose of this essay is to reexamine some of the presuppositions upon which the argument from grammar rests, and to see if discourse analysis can shed any light on the questions of Markan priority and the Synoptic Problem.

First, it is necessary to ask what constitutes a grammatical "error." Once this question is posed, it becomes evident that the assertion that Matthew and Luke have "corrected" Markan grammar is an obvious oversimplification. Professor Scot McKnight's recent discussion of one such "correction" may serve to illustrate the point. In rehearsing the arguments for the Two Document Hypothesis, McKnight writes (1991:149):

> At Mark 14:3 we find an unusual concurrence of two genitive absolutes in the same sentence; Matthew avoided this grammatical irregularity by rephrasing the first genitive absolute and turning the second into a finite verb (26:6). It is more likely that Matthew "corrected" Mark than that Mark took a perfectly normal expression and made it irregular.

This statement raises, of course, a host of questions, both linguistic and methodological. For example, what constitutes a "perfectly normal expression." Just how "unusual" is the concurrence of two genitive absolutes in a single sentence? Is this kind of construction typical or atypical of Mark? Exactly how does one determine whether a particular grammatical construction is "irregular"? Interestingly, it seems that adherents of Markan priority rarely, if ever, ask such questions, though in fairness to Professor McKnight it should be emphasized that he was listing commonly used arguments and was not attempting to discuss each example in detail. On the other hand, scholars who raise questions about alleged Markan "errors" or who challenge conclusions drawn from them about sequence tend to be ignored in modern discussions of the Synoptic Problem. For example, William Farmer, while not denying the presence of grammatical peculiarities in Mark, claimed that because "some writers improve the grammar and style of their sources, while others spoil it, such considerations provide no objective basis by which one document may be adjudged primary or secondary to another" (Farmer 1964:230). Farmer then concluded: "There is no provable correlation between style and chronology in matters involving the question of literary dependence between documents of the same general period and class of literature" (Ibid.).

It is remarkable that these contrary observations about Markan grammar so frequently have been overlooked. Farmer (1964:120–28) has shown that the linguistic data may be perceived in quite different ways and may be used to support quite different conclusions. His point is that alleged instances of "errors" in Mark cannot be invoked to support the Markan hypothesis unless one is willing to stretch the evidence beyond any reasonable norm of proof. In short, Farmer believes that the argument from Markan grammar needs no refutation beyond the demonstration that an alternative reading of the evidence is possible. The present writer, without endorsing any particular solution to the Synoptic Problem, came to the same conclusion in an earlier study of alleged Markan "errors" (Black 1988b).

In estimating the probability of Matthew or Luke purposely correcting Markan grammar, it may be useful to ask what bearing discourse analysis may have on the question. Discourse analysis is a method of determining the way in which words, phrases, clauses, sentences, paragraphs, and whole compositions are joined to achieve an author's purpose (see Louw 1973; Black 1988a:138–39). A useful starting point in our discussion is the observation that discourse structure is fundamentally based on larger units of discourse (macrostructures) rather than on individual lexemes (microstructures). Because it is often assumed that a text is merely a collocation of lexical items, words tend to be studied as isolated units. For example, numerous Markan priorists (e.g., Martin 1975:141; Stein 1988:53) have tried to show that Mark's middle voice verb ἐφυλαξάμην (Mark 10:20) is an "incorrect" grammatical form, and that Matthew and Luke have "corrected" it to the active verb ἐφύλαξα (Matt. 19:20; Luke 18:21). However, we cannot study only the voice of ἐφυλαξάμην. The meanings of words and grammatical forms in the New Testament are determined by the environment in which they are located. This suggests that we should always try to provide a realistic linguistic and historical context when examining any word in New Testament Greek. When this is done, one immediately recognizes from Septuagintal usage that Mark's form was a consistent and grammatically "acceptable" variation of the pattern represented in Matthew and Luke (see the discussion in Black 1988b:95–96).

In this connection, it may be appropriate to remark that the instruction given to students in grammar courses sometimes unwittingly contributes to their becoming poor readers of the Gospels. The student, for example, who learns the grammatical "rule" that a transitive verb must have an object in the accusative case might have considerable difficulty with Mark's ἴδε ὁ τόπος (Mark 16:6). For example, advocates of Markan priority sometimes argue that Matthew's accusative noun τόπον is a correction of Mark's nominative noun (cf. Stein 1988:53–54). There is, however, nothing "incorrect" about Mark's construction. John, for example, uses it frequently, as in John 1:29: ἴδε ὁ ἀμνὸς τοῦ θεοῦ. Illogical? Those who would impose an arbitrary system of logic on language would say, Yes. Those who have studied the fluid patterns of language say that whatever logic resides in language can only be inferred from what has actually happened and not from what should have happened.

To return for a moment to our earlier example, what are we to do when we read that the occurrence of two genitive absolutes in the same sentence comprises a grammatical irregularity so unusual that Matthew felt compelled to "correct" it into a "perfectly normal expression"? Is this argument logical? Yes, say those who would impose mathematical concepts on language. No, say those who recognize that two genitive absolutes were likely to be understandable to any competent user of the language (note the absence in Mark 14:3 of any textual variants that attempt to "clarify" the grammar, and that similar "unusual" constructions are found at Mark 6:21–22 and 8:1). Another way of putting this is that language is the product of *people*; it is therefore as much governed by psychological factors as by logical ones.

Thus, from the perspective of Greek discourse analysis, no *linguistic* basis can be found for assuming that Markan grammar is inferior to that of Matthew or Luke. The term "linguistic" is emphasized because there is no doubt that certain grammatical forms have what might be called "social superiority" in that they are valued from a social (or literary) point of view more than others. Nevertheless, the distinction between a linguistic basis of superiority and a social one is basic. It is one thing to say that the occurrence of two genitive absolutes in a single sentence is rare or unusual or even stylistically awkward, but it is quite another thing to say that such a construction is inherently less correct than the combination of a genitive absolute and a finite verb.

The cumulative effect of focusing in this way on usage and correctness is to call into question many of the assumptions that have long been cherished by Markan priorists regarding the linguistic data. It should not be surprising that these assumptions were attacked vigorously by scholars who held that the correctness or incorrectness of Markan grammar was not to be found in the linguistic form itself. This is not to deny the existence of right and wrong in language from a social or literary point of view. It is rather to refute the basis of the grounds on which grammatical superiority (or inferiority) is claimed to rest. In fact, one of the most important contributions of linguistics to biblical studies is that it has initiated a dialogue on the definition of "correctness" in New Testament Greek (Black 1991:380–82).

Thus it was to be expected that adherents of the Two Gospel Hypothesis would make strenuous assaults on Streeter's famous linguistic argument. Inquiries into the style of Mark led many scholars to conclude that Mark's idiolect was exactly what one might have expected of Peter's agent (ἑρμηνευτής). Some adherents of the Two Gospel Hypothesis, among them Dungan, came to the conclusion that Markan grammar supported neither the priority nor the posteriority of Mark. Other scholars, notably Orchard and Riley, concluded that Mark's grammar was evidence of Mark's lateness. In any case, it soon became clear that Streeter's linguistic argument was in serious trouble. Farmer, as we have mentioned, saw in Mark's Gospel a vivid, aural presentation. More recently Riley has used the expression "colloquial style" to denote the diction of Mark. "Mark," notes Riley, "wrote in a colloquial style, without great literary nicety. He was telling the stories again in the way that came naturally to him. The result was the lively manner of the speaker, rather than the thought-out arrangement of the professional writer" (Orchard 1987:47). A similar position was advanced by Orchard (1987:238): "The language in which Mark was written was certainly Greek, but is not that of a practiced writer. . . . "

What are these scholars—and others like them—saying? First of all, that the study of Markan grammar is part of a larger study of the

ways in which people actually *use* their language. Here "usage" is
equivalent to what we have called discourse structure. Second, these
writers insist that the rules of grammar have no inherent value except as statements of fact. *Whatever is in use in a language is for that
reason "grammatical."* Finally, these scholars have attempted to demonstrate that language, as a form of human behavior, involves important sociological implications. It is necessary, therefore, to observe
the way in which language is used to accomplish an author's purpose
in writing. In the specialized language of discourse analysis, this is
called the *communicative event.* Every discourse is tied to a specific historical and cultural context; one must take into account certain
extra-linguistic factors when attempting to understand the meaning
of any text. Thus, in order to understand Mark's grammar, it is necessary to understand something about his purpose in writing, something about the intended recipients of his message, and something
about the topic of his discourse. We come back, then, to our original
question: What did Mark set out to accomplish? To pose this question is not to demean rigorous grammatical study in Synoptic criticism, nor is it to deny the existence of grammatical peculiarities in
Mark. Rather, it is to assert that it is not enough to know the
"data"—not when data are merely stated without being tested.
Hence from a discourse point of view Streeter's linguistic argument
can be falsified, both because it ignores the *purposive* nature of language and because it reflects a wholly inadequate understanding of
the communicative event.

Markan grammar, then, can be studied by psychological as well as
philological methods. This is even true at the level of single words. A
study of New Testament vocabulary shows that words overlap in
meaning and share common properties. The choice of one word
over another depends on the angle from which the writer views the
action or object being described (Black 1988a:125–28). To take a
very simple example, the noun κράβαττος stands at the point of intersection with such terms as κλίνη and κλινίδιον. Just which term will
be used when describing a "bed" will differ from one writer to another, from one social group to another, and possibly even from one
linguistic situation to another. In this light, the view (see Stein
1988:53; cf. Martin 1975:141) that Mark's κράβαττον (Mark 2:4) was
"corrected" by Matthew and Luke into the more acceptable κλίνης/
κλινιδίῳ (Matt 9:2; Luke 5:19) is misleadingly incomplete and over-
simplified. It is worth noting that κράβαττος is used twice in Acts
(5:15; 9:33). As these examples suggest, one sometimes has to look
beyond a single associative field to find the complete explanation of
a lexical unit.

It is clear that the study of Markan grammar is a borderline discipline that confronts the student of the Synoptic Gospels with a double challenge. Not only does it intersect linguistics and discourse analysis, but it is also intimately connected with the idea of *choice*: the possibility of choosing between two or more alternatives (see Nida 1983; Silva 1983:159–60). These alternatives sometimes mean the same thing but do not express it in the same way. A simple example will serve to elucidate the intricate mechanism of choice. It is well known that in both English and Greek the vast majority of sentences are based on grammatical concord: singular verbs take singular subjects, and plural verbs take plural subjects. In both languages there exists, however, the luxury of discarding the rule of concord and constructing a sentence *ad sensum*. Naturally, the places where this is permissible will depend on grammatical factors: it will be used only in constructions that cause no ambiguity. For example, in Mark 4:41 we find a single verb ("obeys") with a compound subject ("the wind and the sea"). One adherent of Markan priority has called this an "example of incorrect grammar," noting that both Matthew and Luke use a plural verb (Stein 1988:53). When seen as a stylistic variation, however, Mark's syntax is no more incorrect than that of Matthew or Luke. A. T. Robertson (1934:405), for example, cites this as an example of the Pindaric construction (σχῆμα Πινδαρικόν), in which two or more third person nouns are used with a singular verb. Elsewhere the present writer has suggested the possibility that Mark's verb agrees with the nearest (and apparently most important) subject (Black 1988b:98). In any case, Mark's usage can be fully appreciated only in the light of contextual considerations and within the overall framework of Hellenistic Greek. This brief example gives an idea, however incomplete, of the subtle and varied effects that a writer can derive from even such a simple grammatical device as using a singular verb with a compound subject.

Three further points ought to be borne in mind in any evaluation of choice. To begin with, the choices that a writer can make are limited by the number of alternatives available in a given situation. In the syntactical system of a language, the number of alternatives tends to be strictly limited. In the lexical system there is a greater degree of flexibility. There is, however, one area where the possibilities of choice are infinitely wider: the realm of figurative expressions (simile and metaphor). A good example of this is Mark's choice of ἐκβάλλει in his narration of Jesus' temptation (Mark 1:12). Not only does Mark use the dramatic historical present, but he also employs a vivid term normally associated with exorcism (11 of 17 occurrences in Mark). Ironically, it has been argued (Stein 1988:53) that Mark's ἐκβάλλει represents a "cruder and more confusing term" than Matthew's ἀνήχθη (4:1) or Luke's ἤγετο (4:1). This argument is unsound both in its premise and its conclusion, for here there can be little doubt that Mark's creative imagination has asserted itself in the realm of figurative language.

In the second place, to say that style is choice is not to claim that it is always *conscious* choice. Indeed, if a person had to make all lexical, syntactical, and stylistic choices consciously, it would take forever to say anything at all. In the Gospels, as in all literature, choice can be intuitive or conscious; yet the result as far as the reader is concerned will be much the same.

Third, it should be emphasized that choice is not limited to forms of expression, for writers obviously choose content, too. Choices in both of these components are in turn the basis for lexical, syntactical, and stylistic choices. For example, it is clearly useful to say that κράβαττος is synonymous with κλίνη/κλινίδιον. Yet these terms are not exactly equivalent. Thus discourse analysis allows for synonymy and at the same time accounts for the fact that synonymous surface forms are not exactly the same.

Enough has been said to show that the concept of choice provides a useful approach to Markan grammar by throwing light on the expressive resources of a language and on the way an author can exploit these resources. It should, however, be added that stylistic analysis depends on two factors, one subjective, the other objective. It depends in the first place on the attitude of the critic—whether she or he is fully aware of the difficulties involved in the study of style and of the ways in which they can be handled. The other factor is that the critic has sufficient information about the linguistic background at the time when the text was written. In this sense, Hellenistic Greek texts such as the Gospel of Mark are well-suited to stylistic analysis. If we take a deviant form and treat its deviance simply as a lack of internal coherence, we are left with no way of explaining how the text is comprehensible to us. If, however, we try to establish a "grammar of discourse" for a deviant form, we can show how it is internally consistent and exactly what is deviant about it and, therefore, how we understand it.

In summary, then, the study of style as choice helps us to focus on the internal cohesion of a text and to recognize that what may be perfectly normal in one text may be unusual in another. To speak of style as choice also helps us to focus on the contextual basis for choice, including such factors as audience, topic, degree of formality, and genre. As we discussed earlier, the more one understands the entire discourse and the communicative event, the more one appreciates the variety of possible choices and combinations of choices available to an author.

We have also attempted to show that the notion of "correct" Greek has no basis in the language itself, though such a notion well serves the purpose of those who (often dangerously) wish to establish a standard for comparison. There is no intrinsically "best" Greek, although one can with full justification speak of the more appropriate or effective variety of language for some particular type of communication. The question becomes one of sociolinguistics, and not of linguistics per se.

This essay was intended to illustrate how discourse analysis can be used to make explicit the internal workings of a text. Current interest in discourse analysis among biblical scholars is due mainly to the fact that this approach gives a new perspective on a central concern of literary theory, namely the relations between author, reader, and text (see, e.g., Dockery 1988). Of course, many problems with respect to Markan grammar remain unsolved. It has not been the purpose of this essay to survey all these problems or to summarize their proposed solutions. For example, the writer is aware of the importance of the question of how far in investigating Mark one is studying the linguistic usage of the evangelist or the usage of the tradition before him. Nor has it been possible here to examine the Markan Gospel with a view to discovering what kind of a person the author was or what were his purposes in writing. It does seem clear, however, that one's awareness of the communicative event and of the role of choice in language plays an important role in how one goes about doing Synoptic criticism. As long as scholars direct attention to isolated structures of a text, they will encourage the view of the text as an autonomous object. Discourse analysis corrects this view by requiring that a text be viewed not only as an object of grammatical analysis but as an act of communication between a writer and a reader. This concern to relate surface forms with particular communicative goals is a central aspect of all linguistic research. We have also seen how language users adjust their speech habits according to the degree of formality required, the subject being spoken about, the genre, and the medium. All such shifts contribute greatly to the speech act itself. Yet it is these kinds of variations that require further discussion if we are to get beyond the current impasse in Synoptic research.

In an important sense, then, the study of Markan grammar is at a crossroads, and the direction it will take may determine its future for a long time to come.

References

Black, David Alan. 1988a. *Linguistics for Students of New Testament Greek.* Grand Rapids: Baker.

_____. 1988b. "Some Dissenting Notes on R. Stein's *The Synoptic Problem* and Markan 'errors.'" *Filologia Neotestamentaria* 1. 95–101.

_____. 1991. "The Study of New Testament Greek in the Light of Ancient and Modern Linguistics." In *New Testament Criticism and Interpretation*, ed. by D. A. Black and D. S. Dockery. Grand Rapids: Zondervan. 379–406.

Dockery, David S. 1988. "Author? Reader? Text? Toward a Hermeneutical Synthesis." *Theological Educator.* 7–16.

Dungan, David L. 1970. "Mark—the Abridgement of Matthew and Luke." In *Jesus and Man's Hope*, vol. 1. Pittsburgh: Pittsburgh Theological Seminary. 51–97.

Farmer, William R. 1964. *The Synoptic Problem: A Critical Analysis.* New York: Macmillan.

Louw, J. P. 1973. "Discourse Analysis and the Greek New Testament." *The Bible Translator* 24. 101–18.

Martin, Ralph P. 1975. *New Testament Foundations*, vol. 1. Grand Rapids: Eerdmans.

McKnight, Scot. 1991. "Source Criticism." In *New Testament Criticism and Interpretation*, ed. by D. A. Black and D. S. Dockery. Grand Rapids: Zondervan. 137–72.

Nida, Eugene A. et al. 1983. *Style and Discourse. With Special Reference to the Text of the Greek New Testament.* Cape Town: South African Bible Society.

Orchard, Bernard and Harold Riley. 1987. *The Order of the Synoptics. Why Three Synoptic Gospels?* Macon: Mercer University Press.

Pryke, E. J. 1978. *Redactional Style in the Markan Gospel.* Cambridge: CUP.

Robertson, A. T. 1934. *A Grammar of the Greek New Testament in the Light of Historical Research.* Nashville: Broadman.

Silva, Moises. 1983. *Biblical Words and their Meaning. An Introduction to Lexical Semantics.* Grand Rapids: Zondervan.

Part II

*Applications
to
Specific
Texts*

6

A Tale of Two Debtors: On the Interaction of Text, Cotext, and Context in a New Testament Dramatic Narrative (Luke 7:36–50)

Ernst R. Wendland

The Nature of Dramatic Narrative

There are basically two types of narrative account: dramatic and non-dramatic. In the case of the latter, the narrator simply recounts a sequence of actions as they occurred (or in reordered form) with no special attempt to distinguish one event or situation from another. Dramatic narrative, on the other hand, is decidedly different. Here the narrator emphasizes, to a greater or lesser degree, a certain conflict which both motivates the events that he or she is telling or writing and directs them to some sort of resolution. This general progression from conflict to resolution may involve different types of crisis situations, whether major or minor, from the perspective of the participants involved as well as the storyteller, e.g., task/test–success, lack–satisfaction, goal–attainment, battle–victory, and so forth (the resolution may also reflect the opposite outcome, such as failure, defeat, rejection, frustration, etc.). Good narrators thus try to develop tension or suspense when telling their tale, especially when the account happens to be fictitious. They will carefully construct the events so that they build to a climax, after which the story is quickly concluded. Other typical narrative features may also be included, depending on the situation, purpose, and skill of the storyteller—for example, a fuller characterization of the major participants, a multiple plot line, the flashback or foreshadowing of events, a shifting point of view, an intensification of the emotive "atmosphere," and the inclusion of additional background information to provide "local color."

All of these features and more may be detected in the various Gospel narratives of the New Testament, though no literary device is allowed to overshadow the particular evangelist's theme or to detract attention from his focal participant, Jesus the Christ. On the contrary, everything is carefully structured to keep the spotlight firmly fixed on the crucial words, deeds, and implications of His ministry of mercy to save a lost humanity. Why did the Son of God have to become man, live and work as a poor itinerant teacher in a colonized society, suffer, and die only to rise again and return to His heavenly home—what was, and is, the significance of it all? That, essentially, is the overall message of the four Gospel writers, but each makes use of somewhat different narrative materials and methods in order to convey distinctive themes and subthemes to a particular early Christian constituency.

The purpose of this essay is to examine a specific Gospel pericope in some detail in order to reveal how a careful linguistic study can help interpret these artistic narratives that are seemingly far removed from us in language, style, and setting (historical, geographical, cultural, religious). The account chosen for consideration is familiar, namely, the story of a notorious woman's anointing of Jesus at the house of Simon the Pharisee (Luke 7:36–50). It was selected not only because of its dramatic nature, i.e., it involves a powerful conflict of personalities, values, and ideals, but also because the central content, conveyed through various means, epitomizes one of the major emphases of the Gospel of Luke. Furthermore, the story illustrates the dynamic interaction of text, cotext, and context, to communicate simultaneously on several planes of cognitive and emotive significance. A recognition, therefore, of the multidimensional nature of this narrative (and many others like it) will hopefully increase our understanding and appreciation of its timeless, universal message; facilitate our ability to apply it, first of all to ourselves; and finally—should the opportunity arise—enable us to communicate it meaningfully to fellow "sinners" of a diverse sociocultural background.

The Import of a Parabolic Inclusion

The dramatic narrative recorded in Luke 7:36–50 is one of the many Gospel accounts which is distinguished by the incorporation of a parable within the discourse of Christ. It is not possible here to undertake detailed discussion of this important New Testament genre, which has received increased attention from conservative Bible scholars in recent years (e.g., Blomberg 1990; Kistemaker 1980; Stein 1981; Wenham 1989), but a few summary remarks are in order due to the vital role which the brief parable of the Two Debtors (vv. 40–42) plays both structurally and thematically in this pericope as a whole. We notice, first of all, its placement at the center of the story; it forms the crucial hinge that bridges the first part of the drama (conflict) with the second (resolution), thus serving to organize the entire narrative with respect to form, content, and functional intent. The significance of this position will be considered later in a structural analysis of this text.

In order to properly understand the purpose of parables, one must correctly discern something of their unique nature and function as manifested in the discourses of Christ. In essence, a "parable" (παραβολή) is simply a verbal analogy in which a comparison is made between two events or situations which either correspond or contrast in certain critical respects, but not in others. In literary terms, a parable functions as an extended simile—or better, a metaphor— whereby imagery selected from the realm of concrete, everyday experience in first-century Palestine, especially rural Galilee (Stein 1981:36–38), is used as an illustration (or "vehicle") to convey a deeper level of meaning (the "tenor"). The latter normally concerns some religious truth about the Kingdom of God as initiated and established by Jesus Christ. The ancestor of the New Testament parable was the Hebrew *mashal* (usually translated by παραβολή in the LXX), a term used to refer to all types of figurative as well as didactic speech in the Old Testament, but especially to proverbs, riddles, enigmas, and other wise sayings (cf. Brown 1976:Vol. II, 744–45; Stein 1981:16–17). Thus a parable could be long or short, simple or complex in construction, plain or elaborate in development, and more or less figurative in nature.

The biblical parables uttered by Christ and composed specifically in realistic, *narrative* form (as defined above) are undoubtedly the best known to most listeners/readers. These metaphors expanded into theological folktales are also classified as "*allegories*" by some scholars (e.g., Blomberg 1990:36; Ryken 1987:65), whereas others prefer to maintain the distinction (e.g., Caird 1980:162; Cotterell and Turner 1989:311). The difference would seem to be a matter of relative degree in relation to both cognitive content and emotive effect: the parable does not contain as many independent denotative elements or symbols requiring independent interpretation. Furthermore, it acts more as a progressively intensified whole with respect to both form and meaning (Williams 1988:90), moving to convey a "sense of shock, disclosure, revelation, or reorientation" (Thiselton 1985:85–86) at its conclusion, thus conforming to the typical folk principle of "end stress" (Ryken 1984:142). There is obviously a continuum of referential possibilities involved here, that is, "a kind of sliding scale, ranging from the most explicitly allegorical . . . at one extreme, to the most elusive, anti-explicit . . . at the other" (Frye 1957:91; cf. the "allegorical circle," Blomberg 1990:38–39, 51).

More important than its precise designation or formal categorization, however, is the major discourse *function* of a given literary genre and, as suggested above, this is what gives the parable its distinctive preeminence, at least in the teachings of Christ. According to one scholarly estimate, parabolic speech is manifested in roughly one-third of our Lord's didactic discourse as recorded in the Scriptures (Brown 1976:743; cf. Wenham 1989:12). Here it operates as a prominent example of low-keyed rhetoric; that is, its primary purpose in most instances was to *persuade* listeners to change their thinking on some important theological or ethical issue, usually one that was well established in current religious convention. This motivation is not often apparent on the uncomplicated, seemingly secular, narrative surface. Only upon reaching the underlying, or indirect, level of interpretation can its dramatic impact be felt and the appropriate reaction generated. Furthermore, the "illocutionary force" of a given parable as an intensive and concentrated speech event did not normally end merely with an appeal to alter one's opinion. Each little story, when properly construed, typically conveys another prominent implication, and that is to elicit a particular *behavioral response* in its specific sociocultural and religious setting.

The popular notion that Christ's parables were designed mainly to *teach* needs to be modified. Certainly, instruction was a prominent element, but that was only the first step. Just as God's "kingdom" is more accurately thought of as a dynamic concept, involving the heavenly Father's benevolent rule in the lives of believers through His Son, the Savior, to counteract the designs of Satan and the forces of evil, so also a parable is speech in *action*, the verbal realization of the Kingdom of God. It is provocative and confrontational as well as informational, for it summons all hearers to make a decision, either for or against the divine dominion. Christ wanted to jolt people into viewing the status quo of socioreligious reality in a new light. Moreover, He called for a complete reversal of traditional norms and expectations along with the total repudiation of any kind of activity which somehow put self in place of God. In short, He demanded genuine *repentance*—a sincere sorrow for sin, faith in His power to grant forgiveness, and a life dedicated to the service of God and humankind. We see this threefold Kingdom-imperative clearly illustrated in the text of Luke 7:36–50.

It is important, moreover, to recognize the considerable diversity that often distinguishes one parable from another, either in form, content, theme, style, or objective (cf. Westermann 1990:183–93), and to investigate the reason for such disparity. Some narratives are more artistically developed than others—or more illustrative than imperative, more positive or optimistic than negative in attitude, more confirmatory of the audience than critical (or even satiric in tone, Ryken 1987:64), or more covertly than explicitly conveyed. It all depends on the particular *context* in which each is found with respect to the larger discourse organization of the text itself, the situational setting described (time, place, occasion, atmosphere), and especially the nature of the audience on the scene. These are the various distinct but related factors that we wish to explore in the present study of Luke 7:36–50 to see how an explication of the interaction of text, cotext, and context can help one both to perceive as well as to personally experience the powerful message which this gospel passage, like many others, seeks to communicate to "all who have ears to hear" (Luke 8:8).

The fact that a majority of listeners, at least at Christ's time, did "not understand" (Luke 8:10b) was not due to the density, opacity, or figurative nature of the story itself. Like most instances of popular oral literature, Christ's narrative parables generally feature a transparent plot consisting of a single line of action carried out by a minimum of clearly contrasting archetypal personages in a setting characterized by familiar scenes and motifs (Ryken 1984:143). Rather, hermeneutical problems arise (then and now) because of a basic unwillingness on the part of receptors to put forth the mental exertion necessary to reach an understanding of the story's deeper sense and significance in its original context (8:9)—or worse, because of an obstinate refusal to take the crucial next step, that is, to make a personal commitment to apply its message to one's own situation and put its implicit imperatives into practice (Mark 12:12).

The TEXT:
Interwoven Layers of Syntagmatic and Paradigmatic Structure

A careful, linguistically informed reading of any biblical text generally pays abundant dividends to anyone willing to invest the effort—provided, of course, that the individual is also led by the Spirit of Christ (Luke 8:10a). Diligence and care are necessary in order to recognize and interrelate the several structural layers of form and meaning that lie in different degrees of proximity to the surface of the passage. An awareness of these major features of discourse organization (i.e., segmentation, connectivity, prominence, and patterning; cf. Wendland 1985:164–67) helps one not only to appreciate more fully the literary and artistic value of the text, but more importantly, to appropriate its communicative significance in broader, yet at the same time, more personal terms.

The most obvious tectonic component perhaps is the simple *plot* of the dramatic narrative recorded here (which I assume to be an essentially accurate, albeit selective and structured, report of events that actually transpired on a particular occasion during the ministry of Christ). We might summarize its basic syntagmatic, or sequential, development as follows:

(a) *Setting* (v. 36)—Jesus is having dinner as an invited guest at the home of Simon the Pharisee.

(b) *Trigger* (vv. 37–38)—An infamous woman, a "sinner," bursts in upon this stately scene and performs a series of expressive acts in worshipful honor of Christ.

(c) *Conflict* (v. 39)—Simon silently criticizes the woman's behavior as well as Jesus' apparent acceptance of it.

(d) *Comment* (vv. 40–43)—Jesus turns to the offended Pharisee and tells him the Tale of the Two Debtors.

(e) *Confrontation* (vv. 44–46)—Jesus contrasts the woman's loving acts of devotion with Simon's failure to accord Him the expected acts of hospitality.

(f) *Climax* (v. 47)—Jesus applies His parable: the greater "debtor" (the woman) is forgiven; the lesser one (Simon), we infer, is not.

(g) *Resolution* (vv. 48–50)—There are two contrasting reactions to the events: outrage and resentment burn in the hearts of the noble guests present, while the woman, having been "forgiven," hence "saved," goes her way "in peace."

This fully conforms to the classic structure expected for dramatic narrative. The events move from one "steady state" to another, the latter being quite different however as a result of what has taken place. The first part of the drama is characterized by action as the stage is set and the essential conflict is initiated. There is an apparent pause in the rising tension when Jesus inserts His simple parable. In the conversation that ensures, things quickly heat up again as Christ applies His text to the two "debtors" who are spotlighted on the scene. There is a progressive build-up of emotions as He deliberately spells out the glaring dissimilarity in behavior which everyone present witnessed. The climactic pronouncement of forgiveness, and by implication the withholding of remission, while not unexpected, nevertheless carried a powerful impact due to the forceful way in which it was stated. The denouement is swift and to the point. Here we have dramatized the two antithetical reactions which typify people's response to the ministry of Christ in general and, more specifically, to the summons to spiritual decision enunciated by His parables: a bitter, even hostile, rejection by the majority contrasts with grateful acceptance by a faithful few.

There are a number of linguistic and literary markers that distinguish this sequence of plot segments. The more important of these features are listed below in their order of occurrence:

(a) major shift in the setting (time/place) and cast of characters; initial verbal form followed by the conjunction δέ (the signal of "something distinctive" in Acts [and presumably Luke as well] according to Levinsohn 1987:87, 90);

(b) new participant after initial καὶ ἰδού; connected action sequence;

(c) shift in subject/primary agent following an initial verbal + δέ; stretch of uninterrupted direct speech (thought) to close the unit;

(d) shift in speaker; a brief, closely connected quote-response couplet is found both at the beginning and the ending of the segment, with the parable sandwiched in between;

(e) shift in focus to the third major participant; series of three contrastive utterances paralleling one another in form and content;

(f) prominent transitional to introduce a conclusion, i.e., οὗ χάριν; the central character (Christ) refers in turn to each of the two other major participants, highlighting the principal theme of the narrative in a highly rhetorical utterance characteristic of "peak";

(g) initial verbal followed by δέ; after a reiteration of the preceding climactic conclusion, there is a shift in perspective, and back again (verbal + δέ) to round out the pericope (the latter utterance could also be considered to be a distinct "closure"); Καὶ ἐγένετο and a major shift in setting signals, the start of a new discourse pericope at 8:1.

Complementing the *linear* structure of the unfolding narrative plot is a corresponding *concentric* pattern of organization which highlights the tense interaction among the three central characters of this drama. A structural introversion is thus formed to confirm the shocking inversion that takes place both on the level of narrative content and also in relation to the principal theological theme being communicated at the same time. The chiasm in question is outlined below with only the major correspondences being noted. Other liter-ary-structural features giving unit and cohesion to the various seg-ments posited will be pointed out later in a more detailed commentary on this passage.

A.   *Introduction*: the principal characters (a Pharisee, Jesus, a "sinful" woman) (vv. 36–37a)
 B.   *Action*: the woman demonstrates her love for Jesus (vv. 37b–39)
  C.   *Response*: Simon makes a wrong judgment about the woman (and Jesus Christ too) (v. 39)
   D.   *Comment*: parable of two debtors, illustrating grace, forgiveness, and gratitude (vv. 40–42)
  C′   *Response*: Simon makes a correct judgment about the woman (and by implication, Christ as well) (v. 43)
 B′   *Action*: Christ compares the woman's outpouring of love with Simon's complete lack of it (vv. 44–47)
A′   *Conclusion*:   the principal characters in retrospect (the Pharisees, Jesus, a "forgiven" woman) (vv. 48–50)

We observe that the introversion coincides almost completely with the linear plot development. There is a bit of structural ambiguity on the inner borders of the two [A] segments, i.e., verse 37a when the "sinner"-woman is introduced and again at verse 48 when Jesus for-mally announces her absolution. The obvious correspondence be-tween the two segments in both topic and position suggests that the slight fuzziness of larger form here may well be deliberate since it serves to draw attention to the great reversal that has taken place in the woman's spiritual standing and in the dramatic situation of the narrative as a whole.

The parable of the Two Debtors is situated in the *structural center* of the introversion [D]. This is not the "climax" of the construction, as some literary analysts might claim (e.g., Bailey 1976:50), but it does provide the hermeneutical key that unlocks both the meaning and the significance of the entire narrative. The placement of the para-ble also serves to foreground its twofold integrated theme on the na-ture of divine forgiveness as an act of grace which should elicit an appropriate human response. The pressing *need* for this subject to be considered in the socioreligious setting of that day is brought out by the [B] and [C] segments of the story, and the spiritual principle elucidated in the parable by Christ is subsequently applied to that very context via the [C′] and [B′] elements. The central notion of debts and debtors is developed somewhat further theologically in the concluding portion of the account [A′] as the crucial event of "forgiveness" is examined in relation to the two contrasting character/religious groups: the supercilious, self-righteous elite as opposed to lowly, penitent "sinners."

In his thorough study of the parables of Christ, Blomberg concludes that their interpretation depends on a recognition of "what a small handful of characters, actions or symbols stand for and fitting the rest of the story in with them" (1990:55). He goes on to apply this to the narrative parables of the New Testament, basing his approach primarily upon the correlation of a major thematic element with each principal character. This results in a classification of the entire corpus into "three-point" (simple or complex), "two-point," and "one-point" parables, with the tripartite category being the most prevalent. The three main participants of this latter group, sometimes called "monarchic" parables, normally feature a central authority figure, such as a king, father, or judge, who must act in relation to a pair of subordinates. These two typically manifest contrasting attributes and behavior, positive or negative with respect to the norm or message of the story (1990:171; cf. Funk 1982:29–54).

Christ's tale of two debtors clearly fits this pattern. The dramatic triad involves a "moneylender" (δανιστής) and two men who were in debt to him (χρεοφειλέται)—one for the equivalent of two months' work and the other for ten times as much. The two debtors do not contrast completely, for they are not positive-negative types and both have their debts completely cancelled (χαρίζομαι). The difference lies rather in their contrasting responses to the creditor's generosity: the greater debtor would be expected to show more gratitude (Blomberg 1990:184). The following thematic "triangle" thus emerges, with one relevant point being highlighted by the actions of each of the major characters:

Creditor: God (Christ) graciously forgives all people their sins, whether many or few, large or small.

Major Debtor: A person who recognizes the greatness of her debt of sin will demonstrate this in a life of love and devotion to the Lord.

Minor Debtor: Someone who does not fully acknowledge his sinfulness before God will not be prepared to evince any special gratitude.

It is important for an appreciation of Luke's tension-building narrative technique to observe his creation of a retrogressive pattern of realizing (or withholding) the principal actions which embody the story's threefold theme as it relates to the fundamental question: Who is the greater debtor/sinner? The full "significance" of the woman's overt acts of devotion (i.e., an integrated series of "signifiers"), namely, that these are a manifestation of forgiveness already received, becomes apparent in the second half of the account, when Jesus confronts Simon over the forgiveness of sins and absolves her. In this bluntly censorious speech, we also have a *flashback* to the beginning of the discourse where there was a "significant absence" of expected activity. In other words, there is the socially inexcusable lack of a corresponding set of significant actions whereby Simon would have demonstrated a fitting measure of respect for Jesus as an eminent "teacher" (v. 40), and perhaps also a "prophet" (v. 39).

In Christ's critical words of verses 44–46, therefore, we have a backward-looking fusion of contrasting concepts pertaining to the dramatic setting of the narrative. This is coupled in verse 47 with an explicit merging of the parable text and its context as Jesus spells out the import of the tale's message in relation to the real-life situation that motivated it. In short, He reveals Himself as the divine Creditor, Simon the Pharisee as the minor debtor (at least in his own eyes), and the shameless woman (once in immoral living, now in heartfelt thanksgiving) as the major debtor. There is a further thematic implication here: in disclosing the remission of the woman's sins, Jesus suggested that a major role-reversal occurred. In God's eyes, Simon stood in spiritual bondage as the great "debtor" while the woman could leave the scene debt-free "in peace."

The denouement then brings to the fore a subsidiary theme, one suggested earlier in this pericope and which later increases in importance as Luke develops his Gospel: Who is Jesus of Nazareth? The issue is raised first by Simon in depreciation as he disparages Christ in his heart: "If this man were a prophet . . . " (v. 39). The importance of the question—as well as a correct reply—is underlined later when the offended dinner guests ask themselves, "Who is this who even forgives sins?" (v. 49). Both queries are uttered silently in this setting. The parallelism found in both the narrative plot as well as the syntax (viz., ἐν αὐτῷ λέγων and λέγειν ἐν αὐτοῖς) would argue in favor of construing the latter as referring to an internal rather than an audible disputation (contra most English versions). In any case, here we have another excellent example of the narrator's art as Luke carefully recalls the seed of controversy planted earlier (5:21), a conflict which will subsequently generate both a supportive and also a hostile reaction (the former especially in ch. 9 [Peter's confession and the transfiguration], the latter in ch. 23 [Christ's trial]).

Returning to the major theme of this account, we find it concentrated, and appropriately so, at the climax of the narrative:

> Therefore, I tell you, her many **sins** have been **forgiven**—for she **loved** much. But he who has been **forgiven** little **loves** little" (7:47, NIV).

This notion is reiterated for good measure in the next verse at the onset of the drama's resolution:

> Then Jesus said to her, "Your **sins** are **forgiven**" (7:48).

So the thematic sequence goes something like this:

SIN → [penitence (v. 38) + faith (v. 50)] → **FORGIVENESS** → **LOVE**

We might note here that that verb "love" (ἀγαπάω) in this setting may be a way of expressing the concept of "thank-fulness" for which there is no precise equivalent in Semitic languages (Jeremias 1972:127). These focal activities and those related to them (synonyms [+], opposites [−], specific instances, etc.) form three cognitive networks which constitute the thematic/ideational backbone of the story (i.e., the conceptual counterpart of the sequential narrative event-line). This vertical, or *paradigmatic,* structure may be outlined as follows [implicit elements are indicated in brackets]:

v.	SIN	LOVE	FORGIVENESS
	⋮	⋮	⋮
37	a woman . . . a **sinner**		
38	⋮	weeping . . . tears . . . wet . . . wiped . . . kissed . . . anointed
	⋮	(+ **love**)	⋮
39	⋮	⋮	who and what sort of woman (− **forgiveness**)
	she is a **sinner**		⋮
41	two **debtors** . . . **creditor**		⋮
	one **owed** 500 denarii, the other [**owed**] 50		
42	having nothing to **repay** with		
	⋮	⋮	both he freely **forgave**
	⋮	who of them will **love** him more?	
43	⋮	⋮	the one to whom he freely **forgave**
	more [**debt**]	⋮	⋮
	⋮	[will **love** him more]	
44	⋮	no water for feet (− **love**)	
	⋮	wet feet with tears and wiped with hair (+ **love**)	
45	⋮	no kiss (− **love**)	
	⋮	continued kissing of feet (+ **love**)	
46	⋮	no oil for head (− **love**)	
	⋮	expensive ointment for feet (+ **love**)	

```
47  her many sins              ┊
    ┊              ┊            have been forgiven
    ┊              indeed she loved much
    but to whom [few sins]     ┊
    ┊              ┊            are forgiven
    ┊              he loves little
48  your sins      ┊           ┊
    ┊              ┊            have been forgiven
49  ┊              ┊            who even forgives
    sins?          ┊           ┊
50  ┊              ┊            your faith has saved you (i.e., "saved" as a
                               consequence/outcome of being forgiven)

    ┊              ┊           ┊
```

As the diagram illustrates, this condensed soteriological theme, which exhibits several of the principal interrelationships associated with the concepts of sin, forgiveness, and love operates as a continuous triple threat intertwined throughout the narrative. It is expressed in one form or another (i.e., a transformation), whether explicitly or implicitly, in virtually every utterance of the discourse, in direct as well as indirect speech. The parable text, which crystallizes the message in figurative form, helps to reinforce its application in the situational setting at Simon's house. Thus the three major characters of the drama also evince its thematic nucleus through their varied interactions from conflict to resolution. These variants may be signified in abstract conceptual terms as follows:

Jesus: [– SIN, + LOVE, + FORGIVENESS]
Woman: [+ SIN, + FORGIVENESS, + LOVE]
Simon: [+ SIN, – FORGIVENESS, – LOVE]

To explain: Jesus, of course, is sinless; His love, or grace, moves Him to forgive the penitent woman's "debt" of sin. The sinful woman abundantly demonstrates her love (or thankfulness) for the forgiveness that she received freely through faith in Christ. The position of Simon (and the other dinner guests) is a little ambiguous because it depends on one's perspective: in his own eyes, and probably in the opinion of everyone else on the scene, his status before God was that of [– SIN]. Therefore, he thought that he really needed no forgiveness—and hence no Savior (Messiah) either. Accordingly, he felt under no obligation to accord any special honor ("love") to someone who claimed to be the Christ of God. Indeed, his insulting treatment of Jesus, as well as his silently expressed opinion (v. 39), showed the opposite opinion: he would endeavor publicly to put this false "prophet" in his rightful place! In this attitude he was supported by the entire company of his self-righteous comrades (v. 49)—all except for the "sinner" whom they could not forgive!

In this connection, we might draw attention to another instance of the subtle interweaving of the structure and theme of Luke. The special prominence of women in Luke and Acts, compared to the other Gospels is obvious. Women figure prominently throughout this carefully selected and ordered account (Luke 1:1–4), for they constituted a prominent segment of the socio-economically disadvantaged "poor" to whom Christ gave special attention in His revolutionary ministry of the Kingdom (e.g., 4:18, 7:22; cf. Wenham 1989:96). It has also been observed that Luke frequently conjoins his stories or parables involving women with those featuring men, either in similar situations or having a corresponding function. D'Angelo gives a helpful listing of these "Lukan pairs" (1990:444–45), but she overlooks the possibility of character contrast as well, specifically with respect to the narrative of Luke 7:36–50, where the sinful woman and Simon the Pharisee exemplify opposing poles of the thematic core concerning Christ's teaching about the forgiveness of sins.

It was noted above that the parables of Christ are not only informational (cognitive) in nature. They, along with the narratives in which they are embedded, also perform a number of important *affective* (conative) functions in discourse, and these may be emotive and/ or imperative in operation, that is, utterances intended to modify (to change, motivate, or reinforce) the feelings and attitudes as well as the behavior of receptors (cf. Wendland 1985:22–31). This particular aspect of verbal interaction was aimed specifically at the religious dimension of His hearer's worldview, especially as this concerned the newly inaugurated "Kingdom of God." Its prominence in the Gospels is confirmed by the sheer amount of highly poetic and rhetorical language whereby the various admonitions, exhortations, promises, warnings, and other directives of the Lord are communicated, whether by overt injunction or more subtle implication (cf. Tannehill 1975:ch. I.1).

One informal method whereby the extent of this interpersonal influence can be estimated and evaluated in dramatic texts involves the notion of *illocutionary force* as presented in speech act theory (Wendland 1985:94–98, 175–79). Thus, it is possible to trace the sequence of simple and complex communication intentions, or illocutions, that are conveyed both explicitly and implicitly by the specific utterances (locutions) of a text. Some of these, in particular those recorded as expressions of direct speech, are difficult to identify with certainty due to the loss of certain vital contextual factors such as facial expressions, gestures, audience reactions, and paralinguistic features like intonation, volume, tempo, stress, and so forth. Does Simon, for example, invite Jesus to "tell him something" (v. 40) with enthusiasm, in expectation of an important piece of instruction, or reluctantly out of obligation, since he feared from the Teacher's formal introduction that some sort of critical remark was on the way? In the speech setting, of course, the latter seems to be more likely. Similarly, did Simon's colleagues question Christ's act of absolution in genuine amazement, admiration, anxiety, or antagonism (v. 49)? It is probable that theirs was an angry, reproachful response to the event, as is suggested by a similar incident recorded in the cotext of this passage (5:21). It is not easy to tell, however, from the actual linguistic form of their query, although the marked usage of οὗτος and καί would in this instance argue for a more pejorative inference.

The complete text could be analyzed in this same fashion, resulting in yet another linear construct, the illocutionary structure, which also contributes to its unique form, character, and communicative import. Space prevents us from carrying out such an exercise at this time, but several additional remarks pertaining to the interactional dynamics of this discourse will be noted in the more detailed sequential commentary below. However, we wish to point out what may be posited as the principal illocution of this discourse, or "speech event," as a whole. This may be stated in terms of the thematic nucleus identified earlier, which it complements. Accordingly, in this narrative, there is manifested a compelling threefold appeal to each and every listener/reader to: (a) honestly repent of one's sinfulness; (b) trust in (the) Christ for full and free forgiveness; and (c) produce abundant fruits of faith, namely, through concrete deeds of love.

We will conclude this portion of our analysis with a few observations of more general hermeneutical relevance. We have seen how both the syntagmatic (linear and concentric) as well as the paradigmatic structures of this text function in concert to realize and to reinforce the primary message of the narrative as a whole. This is indeed "concentrated" communication, that is in more technical terms, discourse with a high level of "redundancy" (i.e., in the specialized sense of information theory; cf. Nida 1964:125–29). There is recursion on every hand operating simultaneously on several (at least) textual levels: similar, contrastive, synonymous, exact, repetition of form and content, figurative and literal terms, overt surface of the text and tacitly (implicitly) as well. This is typical of many Gospel accounts, especially those which incorporate the discourses of Christ.

Such textual plurisignification is not open-ended, as many current relativistic critics have assumed (cf. Blomberg 1990:152–56; Cotterell and Turner 1989:55). Rather, it is closely controlled by the original author (or compiler-editor) who by means of the linguistic signs and literary features of discourse (assuming now a written composition), in conjunction with established modes and conventions of interpretation, conveyed to intended receptors a definite and definable meaning, consisting of both denotative and connotative elements (cf. Black 1988:131). This means that the central message of a given biblical text, such as that found in Luke 7:36–50, including its illocutionary implication(s), should turn out to be largely the same—or at least essentially equivalent—for any reader (or hearer), whether "real," "implied," "narrative," "ideal," or any of the others conjured up by modern literary theorists (cf. Combrink 1988:191; Longman 1987:38).

Thus the discourse itself operates both structurally and conceptually to limit the number of valid possible "interpretations" of this (or any other) pericope. Therefore, instead of "deconstruction" (à la Derrida and many "reader-response" critics, cf. Culler 1981:14–15; Detweiler 1978:188–89), we have in effect an ongoing *reconstruction* of sense and significance whereby the text, if understood correctly in its original linguistic and sociocultural (including religious) setting, reconstitutes itself for each generation of new readers, in whatever contextual environment they may happen to be. However, receptors must read and interpret the discourse as originally designated and designed in order to be able to respond appropriately to its built-in signifiers of meaning—cognitive, emotive, and imperative. If this is not done, then other divergent or even completely erroneous "readings" might well arise, e.g., ones overly "contextualized" in favor of the contemporary situation. We cannot pursue the theoretical implications of this critical hermeneutical issue here (cf. Cotterell and Turner 1989:ch. 2). The pervasive effect of context, that is, the specific setting of interpretation, will be illustrated in a closer reading of the narrative below.

The COTEXT:
Convergent Lines of Formal and Semantic Influence

The cotext of a given text, or oral/written speech event, is any discourse that is somehow associated with it in linguistic or literary terms. We might distinguish between two types of cotext; the *intra*textual, which refers to any passage that is related to another *within* the demarcated text itself; and *inter*textual, which then applies to any other relevant text. Intertextual influence may, in turn, be categorized into "internal" and "external" varieties, the former referring to works by the same author and the latter to the texts produced by other writers or speakers. Thus, when considering a specific portion of a larger verbal composition, as was done in the preceding discourse analysis, the cotext obviously refers to the various sentences, paragraphs, chapters, and sections surrounding it (Cotterell and Turner 1989:16).

Relationship, of course, is a matter of degrees. As far as linguistic texts are concerned, we may specify this notion in terms of *proximity* with respect to both form, including spatial position, and content. The more closely one pericope is related to another, the more semantic influence, or "resonance," the former exerts upon the latter—and vice-versa. The lexicographical principle that the precise sense of a given lexical item is determined by the other words with which it occurs, i.e., its cotext (Nida and Wendland 1985:28–29), may therefore be extended to the meanings of larger segments of discourse. The overall meaning and import of a passage such as Luke 7:36–50, for example, is modified, indeed amplified, by the chapters which have already preceded it in the Gospel and, assuming a multiple reading of the text, also by those which follow, as will become apparent in the discussion below.

The relationship of the short parable recorded in 7:41–42, 43 to the verses that come before and after it is somewhat more complicated. The surrounding sections consisting of verses 36–40 and 44–50 do comprise the cotext of the parable. These two segments also act as its context (in the more restricted sense of the present study) since they refer to the extralinguistic setting in which the tale was told. There is, in fact, a dynamic interplay between these three components of the discourse—the text, cotext, and context—as has already been suggested and will be illustrated further later. It is this vital interaction which initiates, guides, and gives substance to the hermeneutical process (interpretation and exposition/application) right up to the present day.

In comparison with the composition-internal influence noted above, *external* intertextual applicability is certainly not as great, nor is it as apparent (cf. Wendland 1990:308). However, it is important to recognize the fact that to a greater or lesser extent "any text is an intertext . . . a set of relations with other texts" (Steyn 1990:229, 232). Furthermore, "interpretation is always intertextual; a single text cannot interpret itself" (Aichele 1990:95). Accordingly, a definable *continuum of relevance* with regard to interpretation may be also established with respect to intertextuality on the basis of linguistic, structural, thematic, and situational proximity (the last feature pertaining to time, place, audience, environment). Different works by the same author, e.g., Acts in relation to Luke, would naturally be the most significant as far as such a partial delineation of meaning is concerned, for example, with respect to the Lukan compositional style of balancing one series of persons and events with another that corresponds in some significant way (cf. Talbert 1974:40, 62–63). Similar texts, with respect to form (e.g., the parable genre, Talbert 1988:53) or content (e.g., theological topic), by different writers and compilers are also of considerable importance in this regard, depending on how much correspondence there actually is in comparable settings (Steyn 1990:243). As it turns out, the other synoptic pericopes usually cross-referenced to Luke 7:36–50, that is, Matthew 18:23–34, 26:6–13, and Mark 14:3–9, do reveal some prominent disparities, but they are valuable nevertheless for comparative purposes.

Other gospel passages that reflect the Lukan theme of [sin → forgiveness → loving response] are pertinent to any theological study—first of all, those actually attributed to Christ and, to a lesser degree, analogous texts from the Epistles (e.g., Jas. 2:5; cf. Matt. 5:3). The Old Testament cannot be ignored either, not only for background information on Jewish social customs (e.g., rites of welcoming guests, cf. Gen. 18:4, 19:2; Judg. 19:21; Ps. 23:5; Eccl. 9:8) and religious thought (e.g., regarding "the prophet," cf. Deut. 18:15), but just as significantly in this case, for an important parallel in the technique of parable telling, i.e., Nathan's tale of the poor man's lamb, which he used to allow King David to condemn himself in the Bathsheba-Uriah affair (2 Sam. 12:1–7). The Septuagintal tradition is particularly important in relation to Luke's Gospel, as Steyn has shown (e.g., in the account of the resurrection at Nain, Luke 7:11–17 [1990:240–41]). On the outer fringes of the orbit of cotext, then, would be passages from contemporary literature, both religious and secular, that would shed light either on certain motifs and events of the narrative at large or on specific words, phrases, and grammatical constructions used within it, such as the relationship between "remitting a debt" (Luke 7:42) and the "forgiveness of sins" (7:47) (cf. Brown 1976:Vol. II, 697ff).

Indeed, much more could be said about the varied cross-textual influence which is manifested on the Gospel of Luke. We must limit our attention, however, to a consideration of several important intertextual lines of narrative development which converge on the pericope at hand, thus revealing the care, as well as the artistry, with which the author composed not only this discourse (its larger rhetorical-poetic structure has already been observed), but also his work as a unified aesthetic and theological whole. There appears to be a larger pattern in the mind of Luke which is intended to reveal a corresponding pattern in the ministry of Jesus (Wilcock 1979:88). The following comments therefore are merely suggestive of the many cohesive strands of topical significance, similar as well as contrastive, which permeate the text of this Gospel to form interrelated structural patterns and thematic networks of varying size, scope, and complexity (for some possibilities, see Gooding 1987:passim).

We will briefly survey what may be posited as the two major themes of Luke's Gospel, each of which may be introduced by a question that demands an unequivocal response on the part of the hearer. The pair are integrally related, for the one pertains to the person of Jesus Christ: *Who* is He (5:21)?—the other concerns His work: *What* was His message (4:36)? Luke's point is, first of all, to demonstrate that Jesus of Nazareth is the Son of God and promised Messiah. He also shows that Jesus came to establish the Kingdom of God by bringing salvation to the penitent "poor" through a preaching of the gospel of the forgiveness of sins through faith. As has been demonstrated, both themes find clear expression in the pericope of 7:36–50, but we are now interested in how they are realized in the discourse prior to this point and also immediately afterwards. Our aim is to indicate, at least in a superficial way, the skillful manner in which our text is anticipated in literary terms and built up to so that it functions as a minor peak in the framework of the entire composition.

In a most striking way, the verses immediately preceding our text announce the central theme in terms of its three primary character groups. Christ Himself quotes fickle popular opinion, especially that of the religious leadership, which was critical of Him because of the company He was keeping: "Here is . . . a friend of tax collectors and '*sinners*' " (Luke 7:34). The pericope closes with a cryptic saying that has elicited a host of interpretations by commentators. In the present textual setting, however, this proverbial statement could well apply both to what Jesus had just said and also to the story that Luke was about to narrate. That is to say, true wisdom in God's eyes is manifested by those such as the "tax collectors and sinners" who believe the good news which was proclaimed by Jesus and His forerunner John the Baptist (cf. Reiling and Swellengrebel 1971:315). This is then followed appropriately by the account illustrating Jesus' association with those regarded as religious outcasts by the self-centered, spiritual "upper-class," which focuses on an unlikely example of "wisdom" in the person of the repentant woman (perhaps not incidentally, a feminine noun like σοφία) and her antithesis, Simon the Pharisee.

The ideological controversy over "sinners" between Jesus and the local religious authorities is a matter of central concern in Luke's

Gospel (cf. Neale 1991). Clear evidence for this interest is provided by a direct comment on the subject by the author which interrupts the preceding pericope, i.e., 7:24–35. Thus in verses 29–30 Luke draws explicit attention to the contrasting responses to Jesus' words on the part of most common people—"even the tax collectors"— and "the Pharisees and experts in the law." This aside also serves to prepare the way for the section beginning at verse 36 which, as we have seen, dramatically brings together individual representatives of the two parties in the religious conflict and confronts them both with Christ's gospel proclamation, offering the free remission of sins through believing in Him.

It is compositionally significant that a similar scenario appears earlier in Luke in the account of Jesus' healing a paralytic (5:17–26). Here we see the same emphasis on a dynamic faith that displays itself in action and forgiveness for the "poor" (v. 20). There is, in addition, a highlighting of the bitterly hostile, though as yet unspoken, reaction by the clergy (v. 21). This story also brings to the fore the associated theme regarding Jesus' divine identity (v. 24), but it is not quite as critical of the faith and religious life (or deadness!) of the Pharisees and their colleagues. That aspect of Luke's message begins to take shape in the next episode, the story of Levi's conversion, in which Christ clarifies the spiritually therapeutic nature of His call to repentance and the typical responses by the two divergent groups of "patients" (7:29–32). We might also note a subtle touch of contrastive characterization in the account of Jesus' enrolling His first disciples at the beginning of chapter 5. Here we have a completely different sort of "Simon," a common Galilean fisherman who humbly confesses his sinfulness before the Lord (5:8).

There are many other lines of thematic importance which function together to forge a well-marked conceptual path leading up to the climactic text of Luke 7:36–50, but it is not possible to discuss them all here (in addition to the passages of ch. 5, for example, on the Messiah: 1:32–33, 35; 2:11, 26; 4:34, 41; on His message: 1:68–69, 77; 2:31–32; 3:3, 6; 4:18–19, 43). However, it is worth observing in passing that the general theme of "salvation" is treated from various perspectives in the narrative section covering chapters 7–8 (Gooding 1979:124). We witness, for example, the miraculous healing of serious illnesses and resurrections from death in two pairs of stories which begin and end this unit (7:1–17; 8:40–56) along with Christ's own comment on the significance of these events (7:18–33). He also manifests His divine power over nature and demonic supernatural forces (8:22–39). Personal salvation is effected through the power of God's Word (8:1–15), a message intended for all people (8:16–18),

not any privileged group or class (7:24–28), not even His own family
(8:19–21). The growing opposition to this gospel of the Kingdom is
introduced to reveal the contrary reaction to Christ's work (7:29–
35). The text of 7:36–50 thus stands in the midst of this cluster of diverse but related episodes as a dramatic example of the nature, purpose, and consequences of His ministry.

We will conclude this study of the influence of cotext upon text by
briefly considering a few important passages that lie beyond the
Luke 7 pericope, just to exemplify the expert manner in which these
complementary threads of theological significance are drawn out in
different ways in the discourse. Christ's special concern for sinners,
and troubled women in particular, is further illustrated by Luke in
the summary report that follows our text (i.e., 8:1–3). This was a
unique aspect of "the good news of the Kingdom" (8:1; cf. 9:1–2),
the dynamics of which had just been demonstrated in the text and
cotext of the Tale of Two Debtors (cf. 7:22; 4:18, 43). This is followed
by the allegorical parable of the seed and its interpretation (8:4–15),
which includes at its core Christ's explanation of the nature and purpose of parables (vv. 9–10, discussed above). There are some interesting parallels to the pericope of 7:36–50 in the account of Jesus'
healing a woman subject to bleeding (8:40–48; cf. Gooding
1987:131), especially in His final words of benediction, which correspond exactly (i.e., 7:50 and 8:48). The thematic element involving
Christ's true identity reaches a twin peak in the confession of Peter
(9:20) and the heavenly Father's affirmation (9:35), passages which
are prefigured by the paradoxical fact that, while the demons
seemed to know exactly who He was (8:28), those who should have
understood did not—the theologians (7:49), royalty (9:9), witnesses
to His mighty miracles (8:37), even His own disciples (8:25)!

The parallel motif unfolding the unusual character of Christ's
kingdom is also progressively developed, both in relation to the Savior Himself (9:22, 44, 58) as well as His followers (8:15, 18, 21; 9:23–
27, 48–50, 59–62). One outstanding example of this is recorded in
the parable of the Good Samaritan (10:25–37), which highlights a
theme similar to that of the Two Debtors, but which is centered on
the loving concern that should characterize the relationship between
fellow "debtors" in real life. Who is a good "neighbor" in God's eyes
(vv. 29, 36)? Clearly, the person who has already forgiven those who
have "sinned" against him (cf. Jewish–Samaritan antagonism) and
then demonstrates this attitude in deeds of love (for additional parallels with Luke 7, see Wallis 1979:8). This compositional pattern,
which explores many different facets of what it means to accept, or
reject, the Kingdom of God, is persistently extended to encompass

the remainder of the discourse. It reaches another climax in the passion account, where the question of who Jesus is receives special attention (e.g., 22:67, 69–70; 23:2–3, 35, 37, 39). Luke ends his "careful investigation" of "the things which have been fulfilled among us" (1:3, 1) with a concluding statement in the words of our Lord Himself in which He summarizes the essence of His ministry and message:

> The Christ will suffer and rise from the dead on the third day, and *repentance and forgiveness of sins* will be preached in his name to all nations . . . " (24:46–47).

Truly, this is a theme which resonates throughout the Gospel from beginning to end, with one text being artistically reflected off of another (cotext) both to enrich and to reinforce the point on each occurrence (cf. Wendland 1990:312–14)

The CONTEXT:
Diverse Levels of Situational Relevance

Due to ambiguous usage in the literature, it is necessary to define the term "context." In the present framework of analysis, this concept has two wider dimensions, one pertaining to the particular setting of text *composition*, the other to that of interpretation. With specific reference to stories in writing, the compositional context also has two aspects: the *narrative* context denotes the total *non*linguistic environment that surrounds a given discourse (Cotterell and Turner 1989:16). It includes all pertinent features of the original historical, natural (geographical/biological), and cultural (social/economic/political/religious, etc.) milieu that underlie the various events being reported in the text. This is to be distinguished from the *authorial* context, that is, the actual circumstances and setting within which the writer produced the work under consideration. However, in the case of ancient documents such as those found in the Scriptures, it is not always possible to delineate the latter with certainty. For the purposes of this study, therefore, we will focus our attention on the narrative background, both specified and implied by the text.

In addition to the compositional context just described, one must also take into consideration both the original and the current setting of *interpretation*. Since little if anything is known about the initial interpretive context, we will concentrate on the contemporary scene. This has an objective and a subjective component. The former, *concrete* context has its basis in the real world of receptors today, but from the perspective of communication, the latter is much more important. This subjective *conceptual* context, or "cognitive environment" (Gutt 1991:25), is a psychological construct comprised of the sum of a person's presuppositions and assumptions about the world of reality, the supernatural as well as the natural (should such a distinction even be made). The conceptual context of a community of socio-ethnically related individuals is sometimes called their "world view," a convenient abstraction useful in analyzing the hermeneutical process across diverse cultures (cf. Wendland 1987). In addition to this established component of a person's cognitive environment, there is another that is more transient since it arises in a particular situation of verbal communication (oral or written). This refers to the assumptions which the participants, source and receptor(s), arrive at based both on the physical and sociological surrounding which they happen to be in and also on what has already been written/spoken in the discourse at hand.

The so-called presupposition pool, composed of all assumptions, both established and situational, that are shared by participants, is an important part of any communication event (Cotterell and Turner 1989:90). It is obvious that the initially intended reader/hearer(s) of a given message did not require as much explicit background information for correct interpretation as a secondary audience would because they were presumably familiar with the underlying context, compositional as well as interpretive. An author/speaker normally takes this into consideration when producing a text and often leaves such known, or commonly-held, material implicit so that he does not bore his audience or confuse them with unnecessary details. He also knows that he will be able to convey a certain portion of his message by implication rather than overt utterance because of the various assumptions that he shares with them.

The notion of *proximity* introduced earlier applies here as well. Thus, the further removed a particular receptor group is from the primary setting of communication, the more danger there is that they will either fail to recognize what has been implied in the text or misconstrue what has actually been said due to interference from the more familiar assumptions relating to their own current physical, historical, sociocultural, or linguistic environment, i.e., their alien conceptual context. In other words, as the presupposition pool common to an author of long ago and a contemporary readership is depleted and becomes less clearly defined, so also the capacity of the original text to communicate by means of implicature is greatly reduced.

An additional difficulty enters the picture in that the notion of initial "audience" (or "readership") itself is ambiguous, and it is not always so easy to determine exactly who this actually was, especially in the case of an ancient literary document. With respect to any narrative passage, then, are we talking about the person(s) to whom some character in the story is speaking, the audience implied by the assumed narrator of the account, or the one actually intended by the real author, whether primary (mentioned by name, e.g., Theophilus) or secondary (i.e., some other receptor group that may be envisioned, e.g., Greek-speaking, Gentile believers in the case of Luke)? An accurate specification (to the extent that this is possible) of the intended audience/readers is important, however, for it helps one to determine the point and purpose of any given passage and perhaps even the composition as a whole. Indeed, without such knowledge, a reliable interpretation may in certain instances be impossible (cf. Aichele 1990:97–98).

We cannot pursue this line of inquiry here, but will orient the discussion below primarily with respect to the contextual situation which seems to be implied by the Lukan text itself. This would include a number of tentative conclusions concerning the response of the original constituency to the dynamics of the text in terms of their presumed conceptual context, or cognitive environment. That is to say, when composing a literary work for a specific group of receptors, an author will give at least some indication of the particular setting and circumstances of communication by means of the selection, arrangement, and proportioning of his material (content). What information does he include, leave out, or modify in comparison with the other Gospels, for example, and how does he rhetorically structure and "shape" what is there, for instance, through repetition, descriptive detail, direct speech, intensifiers, figurative language, inserted commentary, and other literary devices (cf. Gooding 1987:15–16). Although we can only assume how the principally intended audience reacted to these different narrative techniques (Combrink 1988:193), it is possible to come close enough through careful procedures of discourse analysis to justify a study of the context and its influence on the interpretation of a given pericope.

A knowledge of the contextual background of a particular Gospel story is necessary, first of all, for a correct understanding of the *normal* features of daily Palestinian life in the time of Christ—meal customs and conventional hospitality, for examples (cf. Gower 1987:241–50). This is especially important where one of His parables is concerned in order for one to recognize any sociocultural *incongruities* that may be present in the account. This refers to details that are unusual, atypical, surprising, uncustomary, exaggerated, and even unnatural or paradoxical in the narrative setting as it has been described. The significance of such abnormalities lies in the fact that they act as signals which point to another dimension of reality which impinges upon that of ordinary human experience (Via 1967:66). These markers of a second level of meaning in the parable, namely, its crucial metaphorical or allegorical frame of reference, may also give some important clues to its theological interpretation (cf. Bailey 1976:passim). In the Tale of Two Debtors, for example, it would be unheard of for a Jewish moneylender to simply write off large debts of this nature out of pure altruism. Such striking incompatibility with a human way of thinking and behaving thus strongly suggests a divine character who stands behind the surface representation of this personage.

Thus far we have spoken primarily of the *original* setting of communication, but there is another context that is equally important to the interpretation of a given biblical passage, though more in a negative way, and that is the *contemporary* situation. All receptors approach the Scriptures with a built-in conceptual context or preunderstanding (Longman 1987:40), that is, a complex referential grid and associated networks of assumptions which have been constituted and shaped by their own world-view, language, culture, environment, and personal experiences in the historical period in which they are living (cf. Wendland 1987:ch. 1). When people today, therefore, confront the biblical text, they are always under pressure to read it as a *current* document and in the light of their *local* horizon of interpretation (cf. Thiselton 1980:10–23), thus altering the author-intended meaning of the original message in various ways which are contextualized in the direction of the receptor culture. The degree of conceptual skewing that takes place depends upon a variety of interrelated factors pertaining to both the audience concerned, e.g., age, experience, education, level of biblical knowledge, and verbal (literary) competence, as well as the amount and nature of divergence between the original and the receptor contextual settings.

The following sequentially arranged comments on the pericope of Luke 7:36–50 are merely suggestive of some of the things that a more contextually oriented analysis ought to investigate. The point is to highlight the importance of the *mutual* interaction of text and context in biblical discourse and the affect which this has upon the process of interpretation. We will take particular note of several of the special hermeneutical problems that arise for receptors living in a traditional (non-urbanized) Central African (i.e., Chewa and Tonga) cultural setting, which includes their natural environment, world-view, and way of life. This is not intended to be a complete commentary, and thus only a limited number of representative issues have been introduced in summary form for consideration. (All Scripture quotations are from the NIV unless indicated otherwise.)

Verse 36

The fact that Jesus accepted Simon's meal invitation is a significant fact to begin with, a matter which is emphasized by the unusual order of the opening words. He was a "friend," not only of "tax collectors and sinners" (7:34), but also of Pharisees! It was not so long ago in Luke's discourse (the cotext) that these same Pharisees and other religious leaders complained, "Why do you (Jesus and His disciples) eat and drink with tax collectors and 'sinners'?" (5:30). In His typical proverbial reply, Jesus indicated that such self-righteous individuals were actually the spiritually *un*invited guests at Levi's banquet. He was present to minister to repentant "sinners" (5:31–32).

In Luke chapter 7 the situation is reversed, but the theological issue is the same, an implication which becomes more clearly apparent as the discourse proceeds. The force of Luke's subtle irony is increased when one realizes the importance of table fellowship in Near Eastern (and many other societies, including those in Central Africa) culture. Eating together is a sign of interpersonal harmony and mutual acceptance. It can even mark the reconciliation of estranged parties or the restoration of someone to a certain community (as in Levi's case). In biblical literature, the setting of a feast may convey an additional symbolical allusion to the concord that will characterize the heavenly banquet of the eschatological Kingdom of God (Luke 13:29; 14:15; 22:29; cf. Ps. 23:5–6; Isa. 25:6). At Simon's house, however, things were different, for his dinner party was marred by a great deal of animosity on the part of the majority present.

A seemingly minor cultural detail found at the end of this verse is important because it indicates how Jesus and the woman were later situated. Jesus, it is said, "reclined" (κατεκλίθη) at the meal (cf. Gower 1987:246–47). In many other societies, however, to lie down at a meal, if rendered literally, would either be seriously misunderstood (i.e., the guests were lying down upon or beside the table because they were sick!) and/or it would constitute culturally unacceptable behavior. Thus a meaningful translation normally has to state the setting in a generic way (e.g., Chewa): "he rested at the place for eating." To say "he sat down to eat" (Living Bible) as a cultural equivalent would be inappropriate in this instance since it would imply that Jesus' feet were placed underneath the table (or His chair) and hence in a very awkward position for the woman to carry out her ministrations (v. 38).

Verses 37–38

"And look! a woman who was in the city—a sinner!" In this way the literal text grammatically reflects the shock and amazement that was experienced in the context when the ignominious woman suddenly appeared on the scene. Her low character was well known throughout the city, a point which is again highlighted by the unusual word order in Greek. The startling thing was not that a strange woman approached the place where men were eating (as would be the case in a Bantu setting), for at that time uninvited guests were not prohibited from coming in just to observe what was going on at such a banquet. Rather, it was her reputation that was objectionable because the Pharisees tried to isolate themselves from unclean food and people as well. All their meals demanded the strictest ritual purity, and this implicit concern heightens the narrative tension immediately—but only for those familiar with the socioreligious customs involved.

The scene now is carefully structured by a sequence of six culturally significant actions whereby the woman demonstrates the depths of her own personal sorrow and repentance along with the highest reverence and gratitude to her Lord. The particular sequence in which these events are reported must be observed in order to make the necessary logical connections between them and also to recognize their closely coordinated nature (cf. Bailey 1976:6):

    a— she brings a flask of perfume
        b— she stands behind Jesus at His feet weeping
            c— she "rains" (lit.) tears down upon His feet
            c'—she wipes His feet dry with her hair
        b'—she repeatedly kisses His feet
    a'—she anoints His feet with the perfume

This structure of inverted parallelism is complemented by the verbal composition of the different propositions. Three participles (bringing, standing, weeping) refer to activities which, under the circumstances, might be expected. These lead up to the turning point (i.e., [c], she began to rain tears) and then the three main actions, which are expressed as finite verbs (wiped, kissed, anointed). The latter are definitely unexpected, a spur of the moment reaction, either to the personal feelings that overwhelmed her or perhaps to the Pharisee's blatant neglect of proper social etiquette toward Jesus.

It may well be that the most expressive—and for the Pharisees, offensive—event is the one at the center (c'). For a woman of that day to unbind and let down her hair in public before strangers was considered most disgraceful and indecent. Indeed, had she been properly married, she could have been divorced for such an open display of intimacy. In any case, we notice that virtually all of the woman's actions are focused upon Jesus' feet. The feet were considered by the Jews to be among the most unclean and dishonorable parts of the body, just the opposite of the head. Because of the nature of the land, climate, and common dress (i.e., sandals), a person's feet were usually dusty and dirty. Thus the woman demonstrated her complete unworthiness by restricting her attention to Jesus' feet. This is also indicated by her silence; according to the text, the woman did not utter a single word to Jesus during this entire episode. Her actions spoke much louder than words.

This is perhaps the most dramatic display of humility and penitence as well as gratitude, reverence, and devotion directed toward Christ that we have recorded in the Scriptures. The various gestures packed into these two verses are so filled with unspoken meaning that it is almost impossible for any commentary, let alone translation, to do them justice. Not only are the woman's actions culturally conditioned, but even in the social context in which they occurred, they were grossly misinterpreted by everyone on the scene—everyone but the One who saw, and later revealed, their true motivation. Needless to say, in another cultural environment, a Central African context, for example, nearly all of these actions, with the possible exception of the weeping, would sound curious at best (e.g., for a woman to let down her hair), meaningless to most (e.g., anointing someone's feet with perfume), and would undoubtedly involve behavior which in the local setting would be regarded as socially and sexually taboo (e.g., for a woman to kiss another man's body, let alone his feet).

Verse 39

Simon's soliloquy seems to reveal his true motive for inviting Jesus to dinner: he wanted to personally see whether there was any basis to the rumor that Jesus was a prophet, or possibly someone even greater (cf. Luke 7:16–17, 19). The manner in which he expresses himself, that is, in a contrary-to-fact conditional construction, clearly indicates that he had already come to a negative conclusion. The forefronted οὗτος is emphatic and pejorative, i.e., "this [fellow]." Simon's critical judgment naturally extends to the woman, the redundancy of his expression here highlighting his contempt not only for her, but by implication also for Jesus as well: "who is touching him and what kind of woman she is—that she is a sinner." It is hard to find equivalents in other cultures for the harshly antagonistic social and religious connotations associated with the general term ἁμαρτωλός. The best solution in Chitonga, for example, is to employ the more specific word "adulteress" to convey some correspondence in negative emotive impact.

Simon's faulty conclusions were based upon two erroneous assumptions, either of which would, in his opinion, disqualify Jesus as a genuine prophet: (a) He did not know the true character of the woman, in which case He lacked the power of moral discernment that a prophet was supposed to possess; or (b) if He really did know what kind of person she was and still allowed such an unclean person to honor Him, then He definitely lacked the holiness demanded of a prophet of God. Of these two presuppositions generally held in devout Jewish circles (Marshall 1978:309), the first would correspond to traditional Chewa and Tonga beliefs about prophets, but the second would not. In the latter case, the fault would be entirely a woman's for presuming to get so close as to touch a man in public. Prohibitions concerning ritual defilement through physical contact are common, but these primarily involve certain sexually related taboos and not individuals with religious deficiencies, who were grouped together with those having physical deformities or who were suffering from various bodily emissions, as in the Jewish setting (cf. Lev. 15). The challenge facing translators in this verse is to reproduce in their language the strong feelings of sanctimonious indignation and revulsion implicit in the Pharisee's unspoken condemnation of Jesus and the repentant "sinner."

Verse 40

At this juncture, seemingly in ironic response to Simon's first false assumption (v. 39), Jesus answers the Pharisee's critical thoughts. These are the first recorded words of Christ, in fact, the first overt direct discourse of the entire story. Everything up to this point has consisted of wordless actions and soundless (internal) speech. The tension has thus been building up, and now the issue comes to a head in the Lord's reply. He does not ask for permission to speak, as a more literal translation might imply. Rather, with this formal introduction He is indicating to Simon the fact that He has something very important to say—something which Simon might not like to hear.

Simon's response is non-committal; he shows no surprise, but neither is he very encouraging, in Chitonga: "So what is it, O Teacher?" There is an initial suggestion that he recognized Jesus' authority in his use of the honorific term "Teacher," which in Luke is equivalent to "Rabbi." Then again, coming from Simon, this vocative could also be sarcastic, for his real opinion of Christ had already been made clear in word and deed.

Verses 41–42a

Christ's simple parable begins abruptly, without an indication of speaker, which does not work in either Chewa or Tonga. The beginning of the tale must also be appropriately marked in these languages, e.g., Chewa: "There were [some time ago] two people who . . . " (as the indefinite "certain" [τίς] frequently does in the original). The mention of "two debtors" is emphatic in Greek by virtue of its clause-initial position. The parable closes with a corresponding front-shifted reference to them "both," a rhetorical structuring device termed *inclusio*. The parable as a whole is also symmetrically arranged as follows (in literal translation):

A   Two debtors there were
  B   to a certain creditor [i.e., he lent money to them]:
    C   and one owed 500 denarii,
    C'   and the other 50.
  B'   Not having anything to repay [i.e., to the creditor]
A'   both (of them) he freely forgave.

The major contrast of the parable is found in the center (C/C'), while its climax occurs unexpectedly at the very end (A'). The discourse construction artistically mirrors the sudden thematic reversal which is the point of the tale.

The interaction between text and context here is readily apparent; it is only in terms of the latter that the significance of the former is manifested. The parable's three principal characters patently correspond with the three persons of the setting who were in the narrative spotlight. It is important to note that, while the two debtors differed greatly in the respective amounts which they owed, with regard to their essential indebtedness and inability to repay, the were exactly the same. They both needed grace (cause) and the remission of their debt (effect), a concept that was very closely related to the forgiveness of sins in Jewish religious thought (cf. Luke 11:4; Matt. 6:12; "in Aramaic the word *chobha* means both debt and sin," Bailey 1976:13). The provision of this crucial need, with respect to both of its dimensions, is effectively summarized at the very end of the parable in the verb ἐχαρίσατο "cancel a debt/graciously forgive" (cf. Louw and Nida 1987 [vol. I]:583, 503). The similarity between this thematic peak of the story and God's relationship to sinners in general as well as to the two specific "sinners" in the foreground of events should have been obvious to all those present on the scene—to anyone, that is, who was not blinded by his own religious prejudices.

Verses 42b–43

Jesus' question at the end of verse 42 serves to mark the transition from text to context (in terms of the parable). The Greek particle οὖν indicates that the query requires the addressee to make an inference based upon what has just been said. Thus Simon is called upon to make a judgment, one whereby he would indirectly implicate himself and contradict the false conclusions he arrived at in verse 39. He seems to be reluctant to come out with the answer which he knows is expected (contra Cotterell and Turner 1989:273). That is to say, gratitude (love) tends to be proportionate to the amount of grace (remission) recognized and received. Undoubtedly Simon was beginning to see the direction of Christ's argument and to anticipate its ultimate application to the present situation. In any case, he hedges in his reply with a guarded "I suppose" (ὑπολαμβάνω). The conclusion is inescapable, and Jesus holds him to it with the emphatic pronouncement: "*Rightly* (ὀρθῶς) have you judged!" The stage is now set for Jesus to fuse text and context in bringing the verdict that Simon had correctly verbalized to bear upon the central characters of that suspenseful scene.

There is a communication problem that arises here in a Central African setting with respect to Christ's climactic question (in literal translation), "Which of them will love him more?" For many listeners the answer is clear: it is the gracious creditor! Obviously, he demonstrated the greatest love *to God* in this whole affair. The significance of tense distinctions and precise pronominal reference is not always attended to with care. Besides, the differences in individual actions, especially in a situation of overt conflict, are often played down in a communal society. Therefore, *both* debtors would be expected to "love" the creditor more or less the same since each had been forgiven a debt which he could not repay. Thus the whole point of the parable is likely to become blurred or even lost entirely unless some semantic restructuring is able to help restore the original focus, e.g., Tonga: "Now which of those (two) persons will greatly love the person who unloosed them (from the debt)?"

Verses 44–46

The conversation continues, but now Christ does all the talking, and a sharply critical speech it is at that. His censure of Simon's lack of hospitality, here emphatically revealed for the first time, strikes home with even greater force because it contradicts culturally acceptable norms. There, in the presence of all the invited dignitaries, the second shocking event of the day occurs: a guest calls public attention to the inferior, unworthy treatment which He had received from the host. Only someone who comes from a face-to-face society, where the shame factor is an important element in all interaction, can fully appreciate the magnitude of what Christ does here. In these communities (as are many still in Africa today), a guest is always expected to voice great appreciation for any bit of hospitality offered. The host, for his part, must downplay whatever service he has rendered as being inadequate for such an honored guest.

In this case, as the parable makes clear, the unthinkable has happened: the upstanding Pharisee has been measured up against the town harlot with respect to common courtesy and has been found wanting by a great deal. Surely, this must have caused everyone in that hall to gasp in amazement and to give their undivided attention to what was coming next. That was precisely what Jesus wanted to happen. His purpose was not to humiliate Simon out of spite, but simply to break down that shell of self-righteousness which was blocking a recognition of his sin.*

"And having turned to *the woman*, to *Simon* he (Jesus) said . . . " The syntax juxtaposes the two primary antagonists and the individuals who will be featured in the sequence of comparative statements which follows. By His very posture Jesus stresses her worth as a person, and He encourages Simon to do the same: "Do you see this woman?" The question is rhetorical—and theological. Of course Simon saw her; that was the very problem from his point of view. Blinded by sanctimonious pride, he did not "see" the significance of either her actions or her new relationship with the Christ. With this pointed question, Jesus also implies that His parable applies both to the woman and also to Simon. The Pharisee was thereby encouraged to see himself as one of the two debtors in the story, in fact, the very one whom he had negatively evaluated by implication. This is brought out in the subsequent clause by an emphasis in the word order of the original, which we might render in English like this: "*Yours* was the house that I entered . . . " The social obligation here is only too obvious to most Africans: to accept a guest into one's home (compound) is to assume full responsibility for taking care of his every need. Any dereliction in this regard reflects badly upon the host.

There is a break in the syntax at this point, i.e., the absence of a conjunction (asyndeton), which signals the onset of the focal comparison. Three key aspects of the woman's prior behavior, in the order reported earlier (vv. 37–38), are now contrasted with three expressions of Near Eastern hospitality which Simon had failed, no doubt deliberately, to accord Jesus. The form of the discourse here reveals a highly balanced pattern of development, one reminiscent of Hebrew poetic parallelism. In the New Testament, such structured speech, normally in direct discourse, is frequently used to highlight content of an especially significant nature:

> "Water for me on the **feet** you (Simon) did not give,
>> *but this* (woman) [αὕτη δὲ] with (her) tears wet my **feet**
>>> and with (her) hair wiped (them) off;
>
> a kiss to me you did not give,
>> *but this* (woman) from the time I entered
>>> has not stopped covering my **feet** with kisses;
>
> with oil my head you did not anoint,
>> *but this* (woman) with perfume anointed my **feet**."

Repetition of form and content, word order, ellipsis, emphatic pronouns—these are some of the linguistic features which are used here to cause these utterances and the contrasts that they convey to stand out more forcefully. Simon's disrespectful omissions, which had been kept implicit earlier, are now dramatically exposed. Such artistically composed discourse (text) serves to reinforce the higher theological message which these social conventions (context) were intended to prefigure as part of the total communication event. The problem of cross-cultural inequivalence remains, however. It may even be exacerbated as a result of this detailed reiterative reference to unfamiliar customs and their unspoken implications.

Verse 47

Jesus does not dwell upon the social import of Simon's behavior, just as He mentions nothing about the woman's past. He has a weightier message to bring, one that concerns the present spiritual condition which motivated their respective actions towards Him. "Therefore (οὗ χάριν) I tell you . . . "—this solemn introduction foregrounds the climactic conclusion. This, too, is stated in the form of a contrasting pair of parallel expressions which enunciate what turns out to be the third shocking event of the day (after the woman's actions and Jesus' public rebuke of Simon), namely, a mere human being (or so they thought) imputing to another the forgiveness of sins:

> " . . . they have been forgiven her many sins,
>> *that is why* she loved a lot;
> but he who is forgiven little,
>> loves (only) a little."

Many versions, both ancient and modern, mistranslate the first couplet. Among the worst is this rendering from the New American Bible:

"I tell you, that is why her many sins are forgiven—because of her great love."

According to this version, the woman's works become the basis of her subsequent forgiveness, which appears then to occur at this point in the narrative. Such an interpretation is faulty. It contradicts (a) the tense of the verb ἀφέωνται, a perfect passive form which focuses upon the present effect of a past action; (b) the point of the parable, which clearly moves from cause to effect; and (c) the second half of this compound parallel construction, where Christ again puts reason before result. In this instance then, the ambiguous conjunction ὅτι appears to have a consequential or evidential force, i.e., "that is why," rather than the usual causative sense (Bailey calls this a "consecutive use," 1976:18). One of the clearest of the newer versions is the *Good News Bible*, which translates the utterance in this way (but see also the *Jerusalem Bible* and the *New English Bible*): " . . . the great love she has proves that her many sins have been forgiven."

Thus, the measure of love demonstrates the measure of forgiveness, instead of determining it. This interpretation of the text also sheds some light upon the situational context referred to in verses 37–38. Evidently the woman had come to repentance and faith in Jesus sometime *before* she appeared on the scene at Simon's house. When she learned where He was going to be therefore (v. 37a), she decided to go and show her gratitude no matter what the consequences.

Turning then to the opposite case, Jesus softens the blow by making a general (present tense) rather than a specific reference to Simon. The statement is also ironic in that "forgiven little" implies "sins little," which is certainly not what Christ meant. The problem for Simon was one of perception: he did not realize what a great sinner he was, and so he had no sympathy for a woman whom the entire community had branded as one. The generic form of Christ's principle here also forced Simon to make the personal application for himself, a task which preceding events (the dramatic context) should have made evident, if not easy, for him. Indeed, the tables had been turned as far as he was concerned. If he would honestly assess the matter, he would find himself now in the position of the greater "sinner," for his lack of love toward Christ showed that he had not accepted the forgiveness that was freely available to him too. What is more, he would have to conclude that the "prophet" whom he had so rashly misjudged was One who not only had the power to read hearts and lives, but also to heal them.

The problems which this passage presents for many receptors of Central Africa are twofold, both textual and contextual. In the first place, the generalized expression of Christ's second statement on forgiveness makes it sound almost like a universal proverb. Thus listeners (and readers) tend to focus on the extraneous issue of which type of people need to be forgiven "only a little bit!" Hence the implicit indictment of Simon and the powerful irony of the situation are often missed. Second, there is a larger question which pertains to the relevance of the theological component of "forgiveness." From a traditional perspective, only the person (or family) that has been wronged can grant remission to the offender(s). Thus God is really not involved at all, for "sin" is primarily a social issue and hence of vital concern to the departed members of the clan, the ancestral spirits. The difficulty of perception is increased in this case due to the use of the passive of divine avoidance in the original. Consequently, in most translations the "forgiver" and also recipient of "love" is not mentioned at all. People's reaction therefore to Christ's pronouncement of absolution (v. 47) sometimes approximates that of the Pharisees (v. 48), though it is quite different in both attitude (i.e., genuine surprise) and motivation (i.e., a naive misunderstanding due to conceptual interference arising from the traditional belief system).

Verses 48–50

Jesus begins this concluding section by directly addressing the woman for the first time. Previously He spoke to her only indirectly through the Pharisee; now He speaks indirectly to Simon—and all those with a pharisaic mentality—through her. He thereby manifests a masterful communications strategy which encouraged everyone present (as well as those following the story in a subsequent setting) to actively participate in the apprehension and appropriation of His message. Overtly then, Jesus reaffirms the absolution which He has just declared to be hers and thus gives this courageous woman the special assurance that her sins, all of them, "stand (have been) forgiven." The specific function of this repeated declaration of forgiveness needs to be clarified in many translations so that it does not sound as if a second act of remission is being referred to.

With this same speech act, Jesus implicitly asserts His deity by exercising the divine prerogative of absolving sins. This unspoken message was all too clear to the other Pharisees and religious leaders in the crowd. They rejected this implication, as suggested by the cotext (Luke 7:29–30), but they did not presume, at least at this stage, to contradict Jesus openly. Their rhetorical question, "Who is this . . . ?"—

often needs to be restructured, e.g., as an intensive expression of skepticism, so that it is not misunderstood to be a genuine interrogative. Another pair of presuppositions is operative here, one textual, the other contextual, and these are the occasion for the guests' hostile reaction. In rabbinic theology, even the Messiah could not forgive sins; this right belonged to God alone (Luke 5:21). The Christological significance of the parable becomes further apparent here: Who else could the gracious creditor be than the person who was pronouncing forgiveness in their hearing? In the parabolic tradition of that time, this central power figure was conventionally identified with God (Blomberg 1990:64). Who did Jesus of Nazareth think He was by ascribing to Himself such authority? According to their thinking, therefore, He was guilty of blasphemy (cf. Mark 2:7). Thus a skeptical and rationalistic cognitive environment, misinformed by contextually based theological assumptions, made it difficult, if not impossible, for many religious leaders to evaluate the person and work of Jesus Christ. Sad to say, all too often the same thing happens today.

Jesus does not respond to the guests' doubts directly, as He had done earlier in Simon's case. He simply allows them to consider what they are seeing and hearing so that they can come to their own conclusions, but He leaves no doubt as to the direction which He wants their thinking to take. Thus Jesus continues His divine pronouncement to the woman: "Your faith has saved you." This sort of utterance often occurs at the end of some healing story, where faith in Christ leads to a physical as well as a spiritual restoration (e.g., Luke 5:20; 8:48; 18:42). The perfect tense here corresponds to that of the forgiveness previously declared, for the two concepts go together: those who have been forgiven before God are in the state of salvation, or spiritual deliverance from Satan and oneness with God. These logical links, however, are not always evident to new or poorly instructed Christians. For them the meaning of a concentrated theological proposition like "your faith has saved you" is not at all apparent, even in this context—faith in whom? and saved how? The relevant spiritual roles and relationships need to be clarified, e.g., "God has saved you because you believe in me."

The woman's new, transformed condition is confirmed by the final utterance (and lesson) of this texts: "Be going (a present tense softens the edge of the imperative) in peace!" This customary Jewish word of farewell (i.e., "may peace from the God of Israel be yours," cf. 1 Sam. 1:17; 2 Sam. 15:9; 1 Kings 22:17; Acts 16:36; Jas. 2:16) assumes a greater significance in contexts such as this where forgiveness and salvation have been bestowed. Here it refers to the subjective state of blessing that results from the two preceding objective facts. Due to the absence of an adequate contextual background, however, this expression often conveys little of its religious import in another language. The common farewell in Chewa and Tonga ("may you travel well") does not have the necessary theological impact, while a literal substitution of "in peace" for "well" is meaningless, even if the result is accepted as an instance of ecclesiastical jargon. A fuller explication may be helpful, e.g., "you may go now and may God bless you"; but only a better understanding of the biblical context and cotext can enable one to comprehend something of the spiritual richness of this divine farewell.

The underlying message of this portion of Scripture is, like many other Gospel texts, a two-edged sword, one converting the penitent and one convicting the proud (cf. Heb. 4:12). As Bailey observes: "In a confrontation with Jesus the options are faith or offense—there is no middle ground" (1976:21). It is an excellent example of a passage which derives much of its theological significance, artistic qualities, and emotive impact from the sociocultural setting in which it arose and the traditional literary patterns wherewith it was shaped. As we have attempted to show in this study, the adoption of an analytical perspective which carefully distinguishes among, yet also closely integrates, the three factors of text, cotext, and context (i.e., discourse structure, narrative dynamics, textual setting, literary background, and Near Eastern culture) provides an essential tool that enables one to more fully plumb the depths of meaning hidden beneath the surface of these magnificent parable pericopes.

The challenge facing translators and other Christian communicators today is how to convey this message, in all of its power and diversity, to a current constituency which lacks much of this original background and is instead strongly influenced in their interpretation by a cognitive context informed by their own culturally specific worldview and life-style. Certainly one will not be able to fill in *all* of the semantic gaps and pragmatic imperatives for contemporary readers and hearers. One should, however, adopt some sort of strategy to convey, whether textually in the translation itself or cotextually by means of explanatory notes, the contextual implications necessary to make possible an accurate transmission of the closest functional equivalent of the essence of the original message in a stylistic form which is acceptable to and understood by the majority.

Conclusion:
On the Hermeneutical Relevance of Text, Cotext, and Context

A new, somewhat reductionistic approach to the sociolinguistic, or pragmatic, interpretation of verbal discourse has recently been proposed by Sperber and Wilson (1986) and applied to the exegesis and translation of biblical texts by Gutt (1991), among others. Advocates of this so-called *relevance theory* advance the claim that all of the various "felicity conditions," "co-operative maxims," and so forth that have been formulated for the explication of utterances by Austin, Searle, Grice, etc. (for a useful survey, see Levinsohn 1983:passim) may be neatly subsumed under the all-embracing "principle of relevance." This rather opaque and, indeed, debatable postulate is stated as follows (Sperber and Wilson 1986:158): "Every act of ostensive communication communicates the presumption of its own optimal relevance." The twofold "presumption of optimal relevance," in turn, is this (Ibid.:158):

> (a) The set of assumptions [I] which the communicator intends to make manifest to the addressee is relevant enough to make it worth the addressee's while to process the ostensive stimulus.
> (b) The ostensive stimulus is the most relevant one the communicator could have used to communicate [I].

RT proposes that communication is entirely an inferential process which depends only on this principle of relevance for success. The latter, in turn, has two corollaries: there must be "adequate contextual effects" in the situation at hand, but this is to be attained with "minimal processing cost" (Gutt 1991:30; cf. Sperber and Wilson 1986:125). The realization of contextual effects involves some definite modification of a receptor's state of mind, i.e., there must be either: an addition of new cognitive assumptions (inferred from propositional content and contextual presuppositions), a reinforcement of certain assumptions already held, or the elimination of erroneous or unprofitable ones (Gutt 1991:27).

This is a highly subjective process, for each receptor not only experiences but also evaluates these contextual effects according to the standard of his or her personal *cognitive environment* or assumptions about the world at the time of a given speech event (Gutt 1991:25). However, the description and assessment of what is taking place conceptually is usually done by some outside observer or analyst. Furthermore, this is apparently carried out with reference to cognition alone, at least initially, as if this could be isolated in every instance from the emotive and volitional components of the human psyche.

There is another, more serious problem with the relevance theory as it is currently formulated. The preceding study has indicated that the parables of Jesus (and similar literary genres) would seem to contradict certain aspects of the two major premises of the relevance theory, particularly the need for the lowest possible processing effort in the estimation of communicative relevance. There are many Gospel passages, for example, which speak of the great difficulty involved in understanding at least some of Jesus' parables. This was true not only for cultural "insiders," but even for those who were the closest to Christ theologically, namely, His own disciples (e.g., Mark 4:11–12). Now why was (and is) this the case? Does this mean that His parables were not relevant for the majority who heard them initially—and throughout the ages ever since?

As we have seen, the difficulty involved here did not seem to be so much a matter of high-level theological language or of great literary sophistication. Rather, the issue has to do with the hermeneutic and spiritual implications of the parabolic form of communication. These stories were obviously told with a double (at least!) meaning in mind. People simply expected such semantic density from *mashal*-type discourse. Thus, it required some mental exertion on their part to get to the bottom of the message, that is, to the religious truth that Jesus was trying to convey via the story surface. Here was a case of sound pedagogy in practice: the extra intellectual energy expended during interpretation would reinforce the learning process. It was not "intended to yield all of its meanings at once" (Ryken 1984:150), but would rather stimulate thought and discussion, thus making a greater impression on the mind. With regard to casual listeners, on the other hand, "Jesus used parables in order to prevent premature understanding unaccompanied by inner change" (Thiselton 1985:112).

The problem was that in order to arrive at a correct interpretation of a given parable—the Tale of Two Debtors, for example—the listener had first to adopt Christ's own central core of cognitive assumptions regarding the Kingdom of God, e.g., that the divine Creditor had, in fact, freely forgiven people their debts of sin both great and small. Such a notion was revolutionary in that it flatly contradicted the beliefs of many of His listeners, especially the work-righteousness oriented religious elite. Thus, the communication would fail at this initial stage of comprehension because the contextual implications of Jesus' message were entirely negative from their point of view. Did He not realize that this was likely to happen—did He deliberately choose to communicate in a way that was "inconsistent with the principle of relevance" (Gutt 1991:92) as far as His receptors were concerned? Or is some other mode of communication involved here, almost the antithesis of the "principle of relevance," as it were, in that the twin barriers of initially *antithetical* contextual effects and considerable processing effort first had to be overcome?

Second, even in cases where an adequate grasp of the deeper level of meaning-content had been gained, there was another psychological hurdle to cross, namely, its *volitional* imperative or invitation to action. Here is where another large group of hearers balked, refusing to make the consequential ethical/religious decision with which Jesus was confronting them. Surely there was considerable mental strain involved here, for the inner conflict had to be resolved, one way or the other (Luke 8:18; 10:36–37). Is it possible at this point to limit the notion of contextual effects only to certain modifications in the cognitive sphere? Surely there were also crucial *behavioral* implications as well, having to do with one's own personal life-style, which would have to be radically transformed in keeping with the demands of discipleship, and also the social ramifications of a decision for Christ, which could well result in one's ostracism from family, friends, and even the community at large.

Thus the task of understanding and applying Jesus' parables and other sayings normally required a great deal of processing because consequential communication was taking place on three different psychological levels at once: the intellectual, emotive, and imperative. Furthermore, the message being conveyed often demanded alteration or complete change in traditionally established cognitive assumptions as well as customary patterns of behavior. In a sense Jesus deliberately "flouted," to use Grice's term (Levinsohn 1983:104), the usual principles of relevant message transmission in order to better achieve His theologically unique and rigorous goals of communication. Much of His discourse was almost "performative" (Ibid.:229ff) since, as people put forth the effort to understand His words, believed them, and made a commitment to carry out His commands, His larger purpose was achieved. Such individuals actually became members of the Kingdom of God through hearing and doing the Word. The Holy Spirit guarantees that this same interactive process of conversion continues unabated today throughout the world.

As diverse communication boundaries are crossed, even greater consideration must be given to interrelated variables of processing effort and contextual effects as these are evaluated with respect to a given receptor-group situation. The former is to a large extent governed by the factor of *accessibility*, or relative distance from the original speech event, both conceptually and in terms of the actual linguistic, historical, cultural, and environmental features of the real world. The matter of contextual effect(s), on the other hand, is very much dependent on the *compatibility*, that is, the degree of correspondence with or divergence from the indigenous worldview and way of life, especially in relation to religious behavior. We might posit in any given communicative situation a number of pertinent facilitators or inhibitors of accessibility and/or compatibility in the minds of receptors which would together determine the relative difficulty involved in interpretation and ultimately also the overall acceptability of the message. This sort of cross-cultural comparative evaluation would naturally have to pay serious attention to the interaction of text, context, and cotext with respect to both the source and the receptor settings, as was illustrated in our earlier study of the Lukan pericope.

The goal of such study would be to convey the *essence* of the original message, as determined by sound exegetical procedures (including a complete discourse analysis), in a functionally equivalent way via a text in the receptor language (cf. Wendland forthcoming). The specific nature and application of functional equivalence in this process would in turn be guided by the principles of relevance as discussed and modified above. Accordingly, the translation would be appropriately shaped with respect to text (e.g., an idiomatic/natural vs. a more literal rendering), cotext (e.g., in stating certain critical implicit information explicitly in the text), and context (e.g., the use of supplementary notes, illustrations, maps, tables, a glossary, etc.). This would have to be done in view of both the expectations and desires as well as the needs (intellectual and spiritual) of the receptor constituency. The latter requirement is an important safeguard to the integrity and vitality of the biblical message in the face of possible opposition raised by receptors on the grounds of culture (e.g., to sanction familiar pre-Christian customs) or ecclesiastical tradition (e.g., to preserve favorite doctrines).

It is not possible to develop these ideas further here (cf. Gutt 1991:ch. 7; Wendland 1987:ch. 8). But the implications for exegesis should be clear enough in light of our examination of the Two-Debtors pericope. Verbal communication is a complicated interactional process involving senders and receivers engaged in the exchange of messages, whether vital or trivial depending on one's perspective and purpose. These may be oral or written (or mixed), and are manifested either with or without non-verbal, paralinguistic correlates, under the dual influence of prior language events as well as the current circumstantial setting. All of these dimensions need to be analyzed separately and in conjunction with one another according to the principles of relevance and (selective) functional equivalence in order to determine the interpretation (sense + significance) of the particular text being communicated.

The factors of reduced proximity and an altered perspective complicate things immensely. Thus, some of the most difficult problems of hermeneutics are encountered on the current-application side of the discipline: How do we increase both the accessibility and the acceptability of communication aimed at the more distant receptors of Scripture? This involves an ongoing process of modified and modulated transmission which, as was illustrated earlier, requires comprehensive analysis of both text and cotext in the contextual setting of the original message as well as that of the contemporary cross-cultural community of forgiven sinners in Christ. Surely all those who recognize themselves as belonging to the latter group ought to be willing to put forth the effort needed to sow the seed effectively so that they who have ears to hear, *can* hear (Luke 8:8)!

References

Aichele, George, Jr. 1990. "The Fantastic in the Parabolic Language of Jesus." *Neotestamentica* 24:1. Pp. 93–105.

Bailey, Kenneth E. 1976. *Poet & Peasant* [and] *Through Peasant Eyes: A Literary-Cultural Approach to the Parables in Luke* (combined edition). Grand Rapids: Eerdmans.

Black, David Alan. 1988. *Linguistics for Students of New Testament Greek.* Grand Rapids: Baker.

Blomberg, Craig L. 1990. *Interpreting the Parables.* Downers Grove, IL: InterVarsity.

Brown, Colin. 1976. *Dictionary of New Testament Theology.* Vol. 1–3. Grand Rapids: Zondervan.

Caird, G. B. 1980. *The Language and Imagery of the Bible.* Philadelphia: Westminster.

Combrink, H. J. B. 1988. "Readings, Readers and Authors: An Orientation." *Neotestamentica* 22. Pp. 189–204.

Cotterell, Peter and Max Turner. 1989. *Linguistics and Biblical Interpretation.* Downers Grove, IL: InterVarsity.

Culler, Jonathan. 1981. *The Pursuit of Signs: Semiotics, Literature, Deconstruction.* Ithaca, NY: Cornell University Press.

D'Angelo, Mary Rose. 1990. "Women in Luke-Acts: A Redactional View." *Journal of Biblical Literature* 109:3. Pp. 441–61.

Detweiler, Robert. 1978. *Story, Sign, and Self: Phenomenology and Structuralism as Literary-Critical Methods.* Philadelphia: Fortress.

Frye, Northrup. 1957. *Anatomy of Criticism.* Princeton: Princeton University Press.

Funk, Robert W. 1982. *Parables and Presence.* Philadelphia: Fortress.

Gooding, David. 1987. *According to Luke.* Grand Rapids: Eerdmans.

Gower, Ralph. 1987. *Manners and Customs of Bible Times.* Chicago: Moody.

Gutt, Ernst-August. 1991. *Translation and Relevance: Cognition and Context.* Oxford: Blackwell.

Jeremias, Joachim. 1972. *The Parables of Jesus.* Philadelphia: Westminster.

Kistemaker, Simon. 1980. *The Parables of Jesus.* Grand Rapids: Baker.

Levinsohn, Stephen H. 1987. *Textual Connections in Acts.* Atlanta: Scholars Press.

Longman, Tremper, III. 1987. *Literary Approaches to Biblical Interpretation.* Grand Rapids: Zondervan.

Marshall, I. H. 1978. *The Gospel of Luke.* Grand Rapids: Eerdmans.

Neale, David A. 1991. *"None but the sinners": Religious categories in the Gospel of Luke* (JSNT Supplement Series, 58). Sheffield: Sheffield Academic Press.

Nida, Eugene A. 1964. *Toward a Science of Translating.* Leiden: E. J. Brill.

_____, and Ernst Wendland. 1985. "Lexicography and Bible Translating." In *Lexicography and translation,* ed. by J. P. Louw. Cape Town: Bible Society of South Africa. Pp. 1–52.

Reiling, J. and J. L. Swellengrebel. 1971. *A Translator's Handbook on the Gospel of Luke.* Leiden: E. J. Brill.

Ryken, Leland. 1984. *How to Read the Bible as Literature.* Grand Rapids: Zondervan.

_____. 1987. *Words of Life: A Literary Introduction to the New Testament.* Grand Rapids: Baker.

Sperber, Dan and Deirdre Wilson. 1986. *Relevance: Communication and Cognition.* Oxford: Blackwell.

Stein, Robert. 1981. *An Introduction to the Parables of Jesus.* Philadelphia: Westminster.

Steyn, G. J. 1990. "Intertextual Similarities Between Septuagint Pretexts and Luke's Gospel." *Neotestamentica* 24:2. Pp. 229–46.

Tannehill, Robert C. 1975. *The Sword of His Mouth.* Philadelphia: Fortress.

Talbert, Charles H. 1988. "Once Again: Gospel Genre." *Semeia* 43:53–73.

_____. 1974. *Literary Patterns: Theological Themes, and Genre of Luke-Acts.* Missoula, MT: Scholars Press.

Thiselton, Anthony C. 1985. "Reader-Response Hermeneutics, Action Models, and the Parables of Jesus." In *The Responsibility of Hermeneutics,* ed. by R. Lundin, A. Thiselton, and C. Walhout. Grand Rapids: Eerdmans. Pp. 79–113.

_____. 1980. *The Two Horizons: New Testament Hermeneutics and Philosophical Description.* Grand Rapids: Eerdmans.

Via, Dan O. 1967. *The Parables.* Philadelphia: Fortress Press.

Wallis, Ethel. 1979. "Theological exposition embedded in Luke's narration." *Notes on Translation* 75. Pp. 6–9.

Wendland, Ernst R. 1990. "What is Truth? Semantic Density and the Language of the Johannine Epistles (with special reference to 2 John)." *Neotestamentica* 24:2. Pp. 301–33.

_____. 1987. *The Cultural Factor in Bible Translation.* New York: United Bible Societies.

_____. 1985. *Language, Society, and Bible Translation.* Cape Town: Bible Society of South Africa.

_____. Forthcoming. *The practical assessment of functional equivalence in interlingual communication: An initial evaluation of the applicability of "relevance theory" to Bible Translation* (MSS).

Wenham, David. 1989. *The Parables of Jesus: Pictures of Revolution.* London: Hodder & Stoughton.

Westermann, Claus. 1990. *The Parables of Jesus in the Light of the Old Testament.* Minneapolis: Fortress.

Wilcock, Michael. 1979. *The Message of Luke.* Downers Grove, IL: InterVarsity Press.

Williams, James G. 1988. "Parable and Chreia: From Q to Narrative Gospel." *Semeia* 43.83–114.

7

Οὖν, Δέ, Καί, and Asyndeton in John's Gospel

Randall Buth

In the Gospel of John, the connectors between sentences (i.e., non-subordinating conjunctions) have attracted previous scholarly attention during this century.[1] The problems encountered with John are two-fold. The first problem is to determine exactly how John uses his conjunctions, and the second is to compare and explain any differences with other Gospel writers and Greek narrative in general.

This paper will contribute to the discussion by providing a feature matrix that adequately describes the main narrative connectors οὖν, δέ, καί, and asyndeton (Null, Ø). Some explanation as to why John deviates from other Gospel writers and Greek narrative will also be proposed.

Background

An important area in the study of texts is the system of connectors that is used. In all genres and periods Greek distinguishes between sentences[2] that begin with καί and those that begin with δέ.[3] The result of

---

[1] Discussions within major studies on John's style include Abbott (1906) (this already makes some use of the papyri) and Colwell (1931) (this is mainly concerned with the question of Semitic sources and illustrating Johannine style in contemporary Greek sources). More recent studies specifically related to Johannine connectors include Waltz (1976), Poythress (1984) (a thorough study though rather "etic"), M. Reimer (1985) (suggestive but needing work in distinguishing functions of other connectors), and Stephen H. Levinsohn (1991) (suggestive and recognizing peculiarities of John). Turner (1963:329) says succinctly, "Fascinating problems arise for the meticulous student. Why does οὖν occur so often in the fourth Gospel and what does it signify?"

[2] "Sentence" is difficult to define. See Poythress 1984:313–317. He calls a sentence a "maximal" clause, which is a clause that includes all the embedded and subordinated clauses attached to it. However, there are still ambiguous situations where two clauses

144

studying these connectors in the Gospels has led to a recognition that John deals with them differently. This can be illustrated in Table 1.

Table 1: Main Narrative Connectors (Levinsohn 1991:33)

	Acts	Luke	Mark	Matt	John
unmarked connector	καί	καί	καί	καί	∅
development connector	δέ	δέ	δέ	δέ	δέ,οὖν
other	τέ,τότε	—	—	∅,τότε	καί

Καί is certainly the unmarked connector in the Synoptic Gospels and Acts. Δέ is used by the same authors to mark significant changes in the presentation of the text. However, in John οὖν frequently occurs in contexts where a δέ would be expected according to the synoptic patterns. In addition to that, asyndeton is very frequent and seems to take over as the unmarked device for linking sentences.

As mentioned above, the problem is to explain the phenomena in John as well as to explain how and why John got into that situation. While I think that we can arrive at a helpful and simple solution, I will admit that the connectors in John are a "can of worms" that may not be completely satisfying, even if we get it right.

---

joined together could be thought of as two maximal clauses, yet semantically they seem to be one compound maximal clause. Would Mark 2:11 be one, two, or three sentences? ἔγειρε ἆρον τὸν κράβαττόν σου καὶ ὕπαγε εἰς τὸν οἶκόν σου "arise, pick up your cot, and return to your house." The following verse breaks down the three imperatives into two main verbs with a participle: καὶ ἠγέρθη καὶ εὐθὺς ἄρας τὸν κράβαττον ἐξῆλθεν ἔμ-προσθεν πάντων, "and he arose and immediately, having picked up his cot, he went away from all of them." The simplest approach is to say that in cases of ambiguity the clauses will be defined as maximal and as sentences. Mark 2:11 would be three sentences while 2:12 would be two. That means that a few "got up and wents" or "answered and saids" in the Gospels will be treated as two sentences. Such a definition does justice to the surface structure since a writer has a choice of using subordination or two coordinated sentences. Compare ὁ δὲ ἀποκριθεὶς εἶπεν (Matt. 4:4) versus Ἀπεκρίθησαν καὶ εἶπαν αὐτῷ (John 8:39) and ἀπεκρίθη Ἰησοῦς καὶ εἶπεν αὐτῷ (John 14:23). (A curious feature of John is that he never uses the participles ἀποκριθεὶς, ἀποκριθέντες; he always has an explicit subject in the singular and he frequently uses asyndeton.)

[3] For a discussion on καί and δέ see Levinsohn (1987, 1991) and Buth (1981). A popular treatment summarizes much of the import of this for the Gospels in Buth (1991). Basically, καί is the unmarked connective. Δέ can be said to mark a change in the text. It is what Stephen Levinsohn calls a "development" marker, with the priviso that it can also mark an "un-development" of background material.

Before discussing each of the devices οὖν, δέ, καί, and asyndeton, we will look at some suggestions and contributions made by a scholar before discourse grammar and text linguistics were academic disciplines.

Edwin A. Abbott and οὖν

John has long been recognized to be different, so different that one scholar, Edwin Abbott, wrote a separate Greek grammar for John. When we look at some of his treatment of John's connectors we will see that certain semantic relationships can be signaled by more than one connector. This can be doubly helpful. Such analyses show what kind of collocations and situations are permissible for the various connectors, and they also lead toward the recognition that there are pragmatic factors involved. When an author chooses one connector over another he or she is signaling more than the simple semantic relation between the sentences.

In his *Johannine Grammar*, Edwin Abbott discusses several functions of οὖν. Abbott (1906: 472–474) recognizes a "resumptive" usage, something that may be called a "return to main-line" today.[4] "A parenthesis is frequently followed by a resumptive οὖν." His examples include 2:16–18 (where it does not follow a parenthetical δέ), 3:23–25, 4:8–9 (following γάρ), 6:3–5, 9:4–6, 11:12–14, 11:57–12:1, 18:1–3, and 18:5–6. I accept Abbott's basic analysis, and we will need to account for it in any description of Johannine connectors.[5]

Abbott (1906) also discusses a "thematic οὖν," which is sometimes marked with δέ [sic].

> In many cases opinion may be divided as to whether a δέ clause is, or is not, parenthetical: but it is certain that οὖν (far more frequently than δέ) *introduces* the more weightly words and deeds of Christ, and that an οὖν clause is often *preceded* by a parenthetical, explanatory, or subordinate statement (p. 474). . . . the use of "therefore" often helps the reader to receive the impression that what Christ said or did was not an accident but a consequence, an effect proceeding from a cause, and that cause from a cause still higher, reaching to the First Cause of all (p. 480).

Again, Abbott has recognized something important that is basically correct even though he has extended his grammatical definition into

---

[4] Cf. F. Blass, A. Debrunner, and R. W. Funk 1961:sec. 451(1).

[5] A caveat: Abbott has been criticized for theologizing his definitions. At John 6:3–5 he suggests that οὖν may not be simply resumptive after a parenthetical digression. Instead, he claims that δέ (6:4) is "probably not parenthetical . . . the mention of the passover may have a mystical meaning connected with what follows."

the realm of theology. Οὖν in John does seem to pragmatically mark some sentences as more significant. Notice, also, that he equates δέ with the function of introducing "weighty words and deeds." An analysis is insufficient if it does not also distinguish the difference between οὖν and δέ with the "weighty" deeds.

Abbott made two more general observations that need to be remembered whenever dealing with John. Genre distinctions can affect the functions and frequencies of connectors. The difference between narrative and expository discourse is quite pronounced: "John . . . uses οὖν very frequently in his gospel, about 195 times in all, but in Christ's words very rarely, only 8 times . . . (p. 164)."

Because this paper deals mainly with narrative, the lack of οὖν in non-narrative portions is not treated at length. If someone were tempted to speculate that the difference between the narrative sections and the words of Jesus was caused by John's using a source for Jesus' words while using his own style in the narrative sections, then they may be surprised to find that the Epistle of 1 John is completely lacking οὖν. The problem of the differences between narrative and speech in the Gospel is one of genre, not sources.

Another observation of Abbott's that bears repeating is that John is not normal Koine. John writes a simple Koine, but it cannot be called "normal." "The discussion of the Johannine οὖν in narrative cannot be quite satisfactory because it is not at present capable of illustration from contemporary or earlier writers (p. 479)."

Preliminary Analysis[6]: Οὖν

When we look at examples of οὖν in John we find backing for many of Abbott's observations with a few other collocations that are worth noting.

1. Resumptive. Οὖν is resumptive after background material, but only when thematic development and a close connection[7] is implied:

---

[6] The examples and categories under each connector have been called preliminary because a more comprehensive analysis will be synthesized from these sections later in the paper.

[7] Poythress (1984:330) would agree that close connection is a primary function of οὖν: "The presence of *oun* can assure the reader. Of course, *oun* does *not* assure him that what follows is directly related to what *immediately* precedes, but it assures him that it is directly related to *something* preceding, whether immediate or further back. In such a way it might be seen as appropriate at the close of a parenthesis. It says, as it were, 'Now we take up again on the *same* narrative, not an independent one.' "

John 6:3–5

3 ἀνῆλθεν δὲ εἰς τὸ ὄρος Ἰησοῦς,
DE Jesus went up to the mountain,

καὶ ἐκεῖ ἐκάθητο μετὰ τῶν μαθητῶν αὐτοῦ.
KAI there he sat with his disciples.

4 ἦν δὲ ἐγγὺς τὸ πάσχα, ἡ ἑορτὴ τῶν Ἰουδαίων.
DE the Passover was near, the feast of the Jews.

5 ἐπάρας οὖν τοὺς ὀφθαλμοὺς ὁ Ἰησοῦς
καὶ θεασάμενος ὅτι πολὺς ὄχλος ἔρχεται πρὸς αὐτὸν
λέγει πρὸς Φίλιππον . . .
OUN Jesus, lifting his eyes
    and seeing a large crowd coming to him,
    says to Philip . . .

The material in verse 4 is not an event in the Gospel but is explanatory information spliced into the sequence of events of the story. The events of the story jump from verses 3 to 5. That is the sense in which οὖν is called resumptive. The events of verses 3 and 5 are closely related in time but they are not logically related or part of a cause-effect relationship.

2. Οὖν is used with sentences that have a logical, close connection.

John 1:39

λέγει αὐτοῖς, Ἔρχεσθε καὶ ὄψεσθε
∅ he says to them, "Come and see"

ἦλθαν οὖν καὶ εἶδαν ποῦ μένει
OUN they came and saw where he stays

The imperatives are the direct stimulus of the events in the second half of the verse.

John 11:46–47

46 τινὲς δὲ ἐξ αὐτῶν ἀπῆλθον πρὸς τοὺς Φαρισαίους
καὶ εἶπαν αὐτοῖς ἃ ἐποίησεν Ἰησοῦς.
DE some of them went to the Pharisees
    and told them the things that Jesus did.

47 συνήγαγον οὖν οἱ ἀρχιερεῖς καὶ οἱ Φαρισαῖοι συνέδριον . . .
OUN the chief priests and Pharisees gathered a Sanhedrin council . . .

The events of verse 46 are the stimulus for the events in verse 47.

3. Οὖν can be used at the beginning of new units and event groupings (cf. Levinsohn 1991:39).

John 4:28-34

[28] ἀφῆκεν οὖν τὴν ὑδρίαν αὐτῆς ἡ γυνὴ
OUN the woman left her water jar

καὶ ἀπῆλθεν εἰς τὴν πόλιν
KAI she went to the city

καὶ λέγει τοῖς ἀνθρώποις, Δεῦτε . . .
KAI she says to the men, "Come . . .

[30] ἐξῆλθον ἐκ τῆς πόλεως
∅ they went out of the city

καὶ ἤρχοντο πρὸς αὐτόν.
KAI they were coming to him.

[31] Ἐν τῷ μεταξὺ ἠρώτων αὐτὸν οἱ μαθηταὶ λέγοντες, Ῥαββί, φάγε.
∅ Meanwhile the disciples were asking him, "Rabbi, eat!"

[32] ὁ δὲ εἶπεν αὐτοῖς, Ἐγὼ βρῶσιν ἔχω φαγεῖν ἣν ὑμεῖς οὐκ οἴδατε.
DE he said to them, "I have bread to eat that you don't know."

[33] ἔλεγον οὖν οἱ μαθηταὶ πρὸς ἀλλήλους, Μή τις ἤνεγκεν αὐτῷ φαγεῖν;
OUN the disciples were saying to each other, "Has no one brought him something to eat?"

[34] λέγει αὐτοῖς ὁ Ἰησοῦς, Ἐμὸν βρῶμά ἐστιν . . .
∅ Jesus says to them, "My bread is . . . "

Verses 28–30 form a series of events that can be viewed as a unit, and οὖν begins the sequence. At verse 33 the conversation changes to a new point of discussion. In effect it becomes a new series of interactions.

4. Background Οὖν(?!). This is suggested somewhat facetiously, because the other examples of οὖν suggest that οὖν is actually signaling that the sentence is NOT "background." Be that as it may, non-events, by definition, are usually "background." So if someone were to define "background" with strictly semantic definitions without allowance for pragmatic choices, then we could include "background" as one of the collocations/"functions" of οὖν.

John 11:54

Ὁ οὖν Ἰησοῦς οὐκέτι παρρησίᾳ περιεπάτει ἐν τοῖς Ἰουδαίοις,
OUN Jesus was no longer traveling openly in Judea

ἀλλὰ ἀπῆλθεν ἐκεῖθεν εἰς τὴν χώραν ἐγγὺς τῆς ἐρήμου, εἰς Ἐφραὶμ λεγομένην πόλιν,
ALLA he departed from there to the area near the wilderness, to a city called Ephraim,

κἀκεῖ ἔμεινεν μετὰ τῶν μαθητῶν
KAI there he stayed with the disciples

The sentence with οὖν describes what Jesus did not do, so it is a non-event and would normally qualify as "background" material. A better analysis would be to say that John has pragmatically marked some material as though it were part of the main story line.

5. Switch Subject, New Agent. Poythress (1984:328) suggests that οὖν is "the unmarked way of continuing the narrative whenever there is a shift to a new agent." There are two reasons for not including this among the functions of οὖν. First, all of the other connecting devices can be used with a change of agent. Second, οὖν can be used with the same agent, as illustrated in the following example.

John 4:40

> ὡς οὖν ἦλθον πρὸς αὐτὸν οἱ Σαμαρῖται ἠρώτων
> OUN when the Samaritans came to him they were asking . . .
> (The subject of the previous sentence is πολλοὶ . . . τῶν Σαμαριτῶν "many of the Samaritans.") Compare John 4:4,45.[8]

Rather than imply that οὖν is *marking* the change of agent, it is better to find out what οὖν does mark and then list an ad hoc notation that the factors that have generated οὖν usually occur with changes of agent and subject. It is a useful piece of information to know that a very high frequency of sentences with οὖν have a different subject from the previous sentence. The same is true for δέ.

Preliminary Analysis: Δέ

1. Background. Δέ is regularly used in background descriptions and with interruptive, authorial comments. (Apparently, asyndeton is used for such comments when the author considers them more incidental.)

John 6:71

> ἔλεγεν δὲ τὸν Ἰούδαν Σίμωνος Ἰσκαριώτου,
>   οὗτος γὰρ ἔμελλεν παραδιδόναι αὐτόν
> DE he was speaking about Judah son of Simon from Kariot
>   for that one was going to betray him

---

[8] Poythress (1984:328) would argue that in these cases οὖν is being chosen for some other reason than a change of agent. However, he ends up with a system of exceptions of exceptions (p. 329).

2. Switch Subject. Δέ is used idiomatically with the pronoun/article ὁ "the,he" and οἱ "the,they" (without an explicit subject nominal) to refer to a different subject than the previous sentence. To my knowledge ὁ δέ cannot be used with the same participant, in John or in Greek in general, but infrequently δέ by itself can be used with the same participant (e.g., John 6:6,71;12:6).

John 2:8

καὶ λέγει αὐτοῖς, Ἀντλήσατε νῦν καὶ φέρετε . . .
KAI he says to them, Now draw water and bring it . . .

οἱ δὲ ἤνεγκαν.
DE they brought.

3. Contrast. In many examples of δέ the reader may discern some contrast with the preceding context.[9] A problem with such an analysis is that not only δέ but also ἀλλά, asyndeton, and καί can be argued to mark contrast if the criterion for the analysis is that some contrast is perceived by the reader. It is necessary to specify what is different among these connectors. Contrast is an "etic" collocation for δέ.

John 11:45–46

[45] Πολλοὶ οὖν ἐκ τῶν Ἰουδαίων οἱ ἐλθόντες πρὸς τὴν Μαριὰμ καὶ θεασάμενοι ἃ ἐποίησεν ἐπίστευσαν εἰς αὐτόν
OUN Many of the Jews who came to Mary and saw what he did believed in him,

[46] τινὲς δὲ ἐξ αὐτῶν ἀπῆλθον πρὸς τοὺς Φαρισαίους καὶ εἶπαν αὐτοῖς ἃ ἐποίησεν Ἰησοῦς.
DE some of them went to the Pharisees
    and told them the things that Jesus did.

In the above example the action of the two groups of people is opposite and contrastive. Yet in his narrative John is more concerned with building up points of the story than with simply contrasting the two kinds of action. Verse 46 is certainly a fitting candidate for being marked as a significant change (cf. point 5 below under δέ). Between οὖν and δέ one would expect δέ to be more commonly used in contrastive situations since the close connection implied in οὖν would need to be avoided.

---

[9] Poythress (1984:322) claims that in the expository material of John δέ can "consistently be translated 'but.'" It is better to try to account for δέ in harmony with its other functions, if possible.

4. New unit—event complex. As with οὖν, δέ is also used to mark off groups of sentences.

John 11:54–55

54 Ὁ οὖν Ἰησοῦς οὐκέτι παρρησίᾳ περιεπάτει ἐν τοῖς Ἰουδαίοις,
OUN Jesus was no longer traveling openly in Judea

ἀλλὰ ἀπῆλθεν ἐκεῖθεν εἰς τὴν χώραν ἐγγὺς τῆς ἐρήμου, εἰς Ἐφραὶμ λεγομένην πόλιν
ALLA he departed from there to the area near the wilderness, to city called Ephraim

κἀκεῖ ἔμεινεν μετὰ τῶν μαθητῶν
KAI there he stayed with the disciples

55 Ἦν δὲ ἐγγὺς τὸ πάσχα τῶν Ἰουδαίων
DE the Jewish Passover was approaching

καὶ ἀνέβησαν πολλοὶ εἰς Ἱεροσόλυμα ἐκ τῆς χώρας πρὸ τοῦ πάσχα ἵνα ἁγνίσωσιν ἑαυτούς.
KAI many went up to Jerusalem from the countryside before the Passover to purify themselves.

The string of events from verses 54 through 55 is divided into two groups by the δέ at the beginning of verse 55 (cf. John 2:9).

5. On-line and a significant change; in Levinsohn's terms, a "development." In fact, this should cover all of the above examples of δέ that are not part of the background. The term "significant change" is not completely testable because one cannot state where such a δέ must be used. The author is the one who makes that choice. Such an analysis is useful, though, because it allows one to decode the message and interpret the author's choice. It is also flexible enough to fit real language data where definitions of δέ based on logical relationships and specific situations invariably break down (cf. John 12:3,14,44).

Preliminary Analysis: Καί

1. Καί marks a close connection and some continuity.[10] Usually this implies that the same subject continues (e.g., in John 12 there are same subjects with καί in verses 3,13,13,21,22,22,30,36,44, and partially in 12:2).

---

[10] Poythress (1984:331) speaks about "close narrative continuation" where the same subject is not being continued. His analysis implicitly recognizes that καί and οὖν have continuity in common (Ibid.). "It appears difficult if not impossible to give hard and fast rules in such cases to specify at exactly what point *kai* will cease to be used and *oun* used instead." In the present paper it will be suggested that οὖν and καί differ in the feature of significant change, which is an authorial choice in the same way that marking or not marking continuity is an authorial choice.

2. Καί can join sentences together into a block or an event complex.[11]

John 1:19–21

[19] Καὶ αὕτη ἐστὶν ἡ μαρτυρία τοῦ Ἰωάννου ὅτε . . .
KAI this is the testimony of John when . . .

[20] καὶ ὡμολόγησεν
KAI he confessed

καὶ οὐκ ἠρνήσατο
KAI he did not deny

καὶ ὡμολόγησεν ὅτι Ἐγὼ οὐκ εἰμὶ ὁ Χριστός.
KAI he confessed that "I am not the Christ."

[21] καὶ ἠρώτησαν αὐτόν, Τί οὖν; Σύ Ἡλίας εἶ;
KAI they asked him, "So then? Are you Elijah?"

καὶ λέγει, Οὐκ εἰμί.
KAI he says, "I am not."

Ὁ προφήτης εἶ σύ;
∅ "Are you the prophet?"

καὶ ἀπεκρίθη, Οὔ.
KAI he answered, "No."

3. Background. I would not suggest that καί *marks* background, but καί can be used with material that could be called "parenthetic" and/or "background." This will help to reinforce the difference between etically listing the situations in which a connector is attested and emically explaining why the connector was chosen.

John 2:9

ὡς δέ ἐγεύσατο ὁ ἀρχιτρίκλινος τὸ ὕδωρ οἶνον γεγενημένον
DE when the host tasted the water which had turned to wine

καὶ οὐκ ᾔδει πόθεν ἐστίν
KAI he did not know where it was from

οἱ δὲ διάκονοι ᾔδεισαν οἱ ἠντληκότες τὸ ὕδωρ
DE the servants who drew the water knew

φωνεῖ τὸν νυμφίον ὁ ἀρχιτρίκλινος
the host calls the groom . . .

---

[11] Both Levinsohn (1991:36) and Poythress (1984:331) recognize this associative feature of καί. It is the reciprocal complement of οὖν and δέ in the function of delimiting a block of text.

John does not allow the parenthetic material above to break apart the sentence. The καί structurally joins the parenthetic material to the "when" clause so that the whole unit becomes preparatory for the main clause. Without the καί John would have needed to make three sentences and to structurally slow down the pace of his presentation (the second δέ is joining clauses within the parenthesis).

Preliminary Analysis: Asyndeton [∅] in John

A characteristic of John's narrative is the frequent use of asyndeton to begin sentences. Asyndeton occurs fairly frequently in the Epistles of the New Testament when two sentences are juxtaposed in a "Head-Head" semantic relationship[12] or when producing a list. The frequent use of asyndeton in narrative is what should catch our attention, especially in comparison with the Synoptics.

1. Unmarked. The most direct and accurate analysis of asyndeton is that asyndeton is "unmarked" in John. That means that vis-a-vis οὖν, δέ, and καί, asyndeton marks nothing. It neither marks whatever the others are marking nor does it necessarily mark the opposite of them. Asyndeton is the noncommittal connecting device.

John 12:22 (Some Greeks have come to Jesus' group)

ἔρχεται ὁ Φίλιππος καὶ λέγει τῷ Ἀνδρέᾳ
Philip comes and speaks to Andrew

ἔρχεται Ἀνδρέας καὶ Φίλιππος καὶ λέγουσιν τῷ Ἰησοῦ
Andrew and Philip come and speak to Jesus.

These are not new units and not thematic developments. We can argue that they are not *marked* as closely connected since καί is marking that within both of the above sentences.

2. Parenthetical comments.

John 6:59

Ταῦτα εἶπεν ἐν συναγωγῇ διδάσκων ἐν Καφαρναούμ
∅ These things he spoke in a synagogue while teaching in Capernaum.

John 2:17

ἐμνήσθησαν οἱ μαθηταὶ αὐτοῦ ὅτι γεγραμμένον ἐστίν . . .
∅ His disciples remembered that it was written . . .

---

[12] See Beekman, Callow, and Kopesec (1981) for explanations and illustrations of the term "Head-Head."

John 1:39

ὥρα ἦν ὡς δεκάτη.
It was about the tenth hour.

There is a tendency for the asyndetic parenthetical comment to co-occur with aorist main verbs (but note ἦν "was" in 1:39), while the δέ background descriptions tend towards imperfect verbs. Further study is needed to confirm the extent of this correlation.

3. With topicalized time settings that function as quasi-connectors[13]: μετὰ ταῦτα "after these things" and τῇ ἐπαύριον "the next day."

John 12:12

Τῇ ἐπαύριον ὁ ὄχλος πολὺς . . . ακούσαντες . . . ἔλαβον . . .
The next day the great crowd . . . having heard . . . took . . .

This begins a new narrative unit and has a paragraph indentation in the Nestle-Aland 26th edition.

4. Resumptive. Asyndeton can be used after background comments when the narrative resumes (cf. the comments under οὖν and δέ above).

John 2:6–7

⁶ ἦσαν δὲ ἐκεῖ λίθιναι ὑδρίαι ἓξ . . .
De there were six water jars . . .

⁷ λέγει αὐτοῖς ὁ Ἰησοῦς . . .
∅ Jesus says to them . . .

5. List. Multiple sentences can be juxtaposed as an unmarked list of sentences.

John 9:9

ἄλλοι ἔλεγον ὅτι οὗτός ἐστιν.
Others were saying that it was the man.

ἄλλοι ἔλεγον Οὐχί, ἀλλὰ ὅμοιος αὐτῷ ἐστιν.
Others were saying, "No, he resembles him."

ἐκεῖνος ἔλεγεν ὅτι ἐγώ εἰμι.
That man was saying, "It's me."

---

[13] With asyndeton these temporal phrases look like expanded conjunctions. However, they can also occur with other connectors, e.g., John 7:1 καὶ μετὰ ταῦτα and John 19:38 μετὰ δὲ ταῦτα.

6. Contrast(?). There are many contexts where two sentences juxtaposed with asyndeton have an inherent contrast. However, it is important to remember that asyndeton does not *mark* contrast.

John 4:22

ὑμεῖς προσκυνεῖτε ὃ οὐκ οἴδατε
Ø you worship what you do not know

ἡμεῖς προσκυνοῦμεν ὃ οἴδαμεν . . .
Ø we worship what we know . . .

The question of contrast becomes very significant when we consider a verse like John 1:17 in Greek and in the Living Bible:

John 1:17

ὅτι ὁ νόμος διὰ Μωϋσέως ἐδόθη
ἡ χάρις καὶ ἡ ἀλήθεια διὰ Ἰησοῦ Χριστοῦ ἐγένετο.
for the Law was given through Moses
grace and truth have come through Jesus Christ.

John 1:17 (Living Bible)

For Moses gave us only the Law with its rigid demands and merciless justice, while Jesus Christ brought us loving forgiveness as well.

Translation does not get much worse. Instead of recognizing an unmarked syntactic relationship,[14] the translator has added theological contrasts that appear to know no bounds. Verse 17 is given in the context of explaining "a blessing on top of a blessing" (verse 16), not a blessing for a curse!

An Emic Analysis

The connectors οὖν, δέ, καί, and asyndeton are marking something, but they cannot all be marking the same thing, e.g., background, switch subject, new unit, resumption, etc. Those are collocations where the author is adding or marking something else. At the same time, certain affinities have been noted between some pairs of connectives. Both οὖν and καί seem to be on one side of a continuum marking close connection, both οὖν and δέ share aspects of marking significant change, while both δέ and asyndeton share aspects with interruptive, backgrounded, and contrasting material.

---

[14] Leon Morris (1971:111) made a pertinent grammatical observation even though he ended up interpreting the verse contrastively: "We should have expected the contrasting μέν and δέ. But John simply puts the two statements side by side."

My proposal is that we view these four connectors as reflecting a four-celled matrix composed of two parameters: "close connection" and "significant change" (see Table 2). Both of those parameters are basically pragmatic in nature. They reflect values assigned by the author and are therefore not predictable in the sense that an analysis can say when one or another connector *must* be used. In addition, "significant change" means a change in the development of the text that the author considered worthwhile to mark. That includes a change from main-line events to background material, something common for δέ. It does not mean that all δέ or οὖν sentences contain dramatic points of the story. They are merely signals that the reader should expect "something different." These are pragmatic, structural devices for presenting the continuous flow of sentences and for aiding the reader in processing the information.

Table 2: The parameters signalled by οὖν, δέ, καί, and asyndeton

		+close connection		–close connection
+significant change	οὖν	*closely related* *signif. material* (logical resumptive new unit change subject non-event)	δέ	*significant change* (background new unit on-line contrast change subject)
–significant change	καί	*coordinated* *sameness* (same subject continuity with change subj. parenthesis new unit)	∅	*unmarked* (parenthesis resumptive contrast time phrase list new unit change subject)

This grid is what we need to interpret John's text. It is simple and practical for exegetes and easy to remember. It is a system. It has a real chance of being psychologically real.[15] The categories within the

---

[15] On the necessity of psychological adequacy and pragmatic adequacy in linguistic theory, see Dik 1989:4–17.

parentheses are not intended as part of the system but show where the systemic categories can occur and how they are able to overlap.

This is not to deny that some etic work remains to be done. Listing every sentence in John under etic contexts within the emic categories is especially important for comparative, philological work and for persons interested in questions like the linguistic influences on the Gospel of John. In addition, it is the frequent use of particular etic contexts that eventually allows a language to develop and change. At first, a particular context may become idiomatically frequent, then fixed, and finally the system may change to accommodate it. Several devices were in such potential flux with John or in Greek in general: οὖν as a standard narrative connector, μετὰ ταῦτα as an independent connector, ὁ δέ as a switch subject, asyndeton with the word "answer" and as a standard narrative device, καί beginning a new unit (paragraph level) or for parenthesis or author's comment.

Comparisons with Koine Greek

Several questions arise from a study on John's connectors. How can an analysis be acceptable if it does not occur in other known Greek literature?[16] Granting a unique ideolect in John, how did he develop it? What caused him to develop such a style?

There are several factors that may have contributed to John's style. We need to explain from where his common narrative use of οὖν and asyndeton comes. Earlier Greek grammarians (e.g., Robertson [1934]; Moulton [1908]) pointed to colloquial Greek as a source for asyndeton. Evidence for this comes from the increased use of asyndeton in the non-literary papyri published during the past one hundred years. However, most of the non-literary papyri are short letters or various business documents. These represent a different genre from the long narrative of John. There are two other influences "near at hand" that must also be considered. In biblical Aramaic asyndeton became frequent in narrative. Some of the contexts correspond to common examples of John. For example, many speech margins in the Gospel (i.e. "he said," "he answered") use asyndeton. In the same way "answered and said" is regularly with asyndeton in Daniel. The other local influence is Mishnaic Hebrew. Rabbinic discourses are regularly strung together without "and," the connector which is otherwise so frequent in the more literary Hebrew of the

---

[16] It is not enough for Colwell (1931:10) to compare asyndeton in John's narrative with Epictetus' exposition and diatribe. During the first half of this century many scholars were content to show that something in the Gospels also exists in the papyri or in Greek literature. The relative frequencies are often different for comparable genre.

Dead Sea Scrolls and the Old Testament. So it appears that a colloquial substratum in Hebrew, and probably Aramaic and Greek, could
all have influenced John in the direction of a "normal" narrative
function for asyndeton.[17]

There is also a precedent for the feature behind οὖν. In literary
Aramaic, exemplified in books like the Genesis Apocryphon from the
Dead Seas Scrolls as well as Imperial Aramaic, two degrees of a narrative connector occur. There is a simple relator אדין "then" and a
"more-closely connected" relator באדין "so then, (lit.) in-then."[18] Admittedly, the common equivalent between Aramaic אדין and Greek
was not οὖν, but τότε. However, without other clear stylistic models
for John's use of οὖν, it is not too much to suppose that John would
independently develop an otherwise unexploited, common, non-
narrative Greek connector in the direction of an Aramaic connector.

A parallel phenomena to John's use of οὖν may be found in the
Septuagint. Nigel Turner (1963:337) has pointed out that, while
LXX Genesis 1–25 only has three examples of οὖν, there are twenty-
seven examples in Genesis 26–50. LXX Exodus has twenty-six examples of οὖν in chapters 1–24 while only three examples in 25–
40.[19] These frequencies of οὖν in the Septuagint do not match John
but they do suggest a possible source or parallel influence on his
own style. Apparently, one or more of the Septuagint translators was
moving in John's direction.

An appendix to this paper comments on a papyrus example that uses
οὖν for marking the major propositions. It is not intended to explain
John's background since it is so short and is a non-narrative text. However, it does illustrate the usefulness of paying attention to connectors
in interpreting a text (οὖν marks the points of significant change).[20]

Appendix to Johannine Connectors
Letter—100 AD [Fayum 114] (*Select Papyri*, vol 1:300)

1   Λούκιος Βελλῆνος Γέμελλος
2   Σαβίνωι τῶι οἰείῶι
3   χαίρειν.
4   εὖ οὖν πυήσας

[17] Nigel Turner (1963:340–341) thinks that Aramaic influence was probable for the
frequent use of asyndeton with verbs of speaking.
[18] Cf. Buth 1990.
[19] However, Exodus 25–40 has long procedural sections on building projects, so
there is a genre difference to consider.
[20] Already in 1906 Abbott referred to this papyrus as a potential illustration for
John's use of οὖν.

5   κομισάμενος μου τὴν ἐπιστολὴν
6   πέμσις μυ Πίνδαρον εἰς τὴν πόλιν
7   τὸν πεδιοφύλακα τῆς Διονυσιάδος,
8   ἐπὶ ἐρώτησέ με Ἑρμῶναξ
9   εἵνα αὐτὸν λάβῃ εἰς Κερκεσοῦχα
10   καταμαθῖν τὸν ἐλαιῶνα αὐτοῦ,
11   ἐπὶ πυκνός ἐστιν
12   καὶ θέλι ἐξ αὐτῶν ἐκκόψαι φυτά,
13   εἵνα ἐνπίρος κοπῇ τὰ μέλλοντα ἐκκόπτεσθαι·
14   καὶ τὴν εἰκθυὶν πέμσις τῆι κδ΄ εἶ κε΄ εἰς τὰ γενέσια Γεμέλλης.
15   μὴ ο(ὖ)ν ληρήσῃς τὸν ἐκτιναγμόν σου.
16   ἔρρωσο.
17   δ΄ Αὐτοκράτορος Καίσαρος Νερούα Τραϊαν(οῦ) Σεβαστοῦ
        Γερμανικοῦ Χύακ ιη΄

Summary of letter:

   3 main commands:
     1. Send Pindar, 4–13
     2. Send fish, 14
     3. Don't quibble, 15

Conjunctions:
   οὖν for main sentences #1 and #3
   καί for main sentence #2

Word order:
   Fronting with "pro"verbs "do," "have" et al.
   Normal VO order after participle clause
   Normal VO for main line at 6, 15
   But OV at 14 as marked Topic after lengthy sentence
   Fronted Focus at 13: with experience

Thematic statement[21]
   "Send Pindar
     because Ermonax wants experienced help.
   Also send the fish.
   And don't give foolish excuses."

---

[21] See Beekman, Callow, and Kopesec (1981) for a background to a theory of "thematic statements."

References

Abbott, Edwin A. 1906. *Johannine Grammar.* London: Adam and Charles Black.

Beekman, John, John Callow, and Michael Kopesec. 1981. *The Semantic Structure of Written Communication.* 5th ed., draft. Dallas: Summer Institute of Linguistics.

Blass, F., A. Debrunner, and R. W. Funk. 1961. *A Greek Grammar of the New Testament and Other Early Christian Literature.* Chicago: University of Chicago Press.

Buth, Randall. 1981. "Semitic 'kai' and Greek 'de'." *Selected Technical Articles Related to Translation* 3.12–19.

_____. 1990. "EDAYIN/TOTE—Anatomy of a Semitism in Jewish Greek." *Maarav* 5–6.33–48.

_____. 1991. "'And' or 'but', so what?" *Jerusalem Perspective* (March–April) vol. 4, no. 2.13–15.

Colwell, Ernest C. 1931. *The Greek of the Fourth Gospel.* Chicago.

Dik, Simon C. 1989. *The Theory of Functional Grammar.* Part 1: *The Structure of the Clause.* (Functional grammar series 9). Dordrecht: Foris Publications.

Hunt, A. S. and C. C. Edgar. *Select papyri.* vol. 1: *Non-literary papyri, private affairs.* (Loeb classical library 226). London: Heineman and Cambridge, Mass.: Harvard University Press.

Levinsohn, Stephen H. 1987. *Textual Connections in Acts.* Scholars Press.

_____. 1991. *Discourse Features of New Testament Greek: A Coursebook.* Dallas: Summer Institute of Linguistics, April 1991 draft copy.

Morris, Leon. 1971. *The Gospel According to John.* (The New International Commentary). Grand Rapids: Eerdmans.

Moulton, James Hope. 1908. *A Grammar of New Testament Greek,* vol. 1: *Prolegomena.* Edinburgh: T & T Clark.

Poythress, Vern S. 1984. "The use of the intersentence conjunctions DE, OUN, KAI, and asyndeton in the gospel of John." *Novum Testamentum* 20.312–340.

Reimer, M. 1985. "The functions of *oun* in the Gospel of John." *Selected Technical Articles Related to Translation* 13.28–36.

Robertson, A. T. 1934. *A Grammar of the Greek New Testament.* Nashville: Broadman.

Turner, Nigel. 1963–1976. *A Grammar of New Testament Greek,* vol. 3: *Syntax* (1963), vol. 4: *Style* (1976). Edinburgh: T & T Clark.

Waltz, Nathan. 1976. "Discourse patterns in John 11." *Notes on Translation* 59.2–8.

8

The Imperativals of Romans 12

Neva F. Miller

Introduction

There are times when all of us need comfortable walking shoes, for a walking time that is long, for a path that is off the beaten track and rough underfoot, for a new and untried destination. After I spent a year on a sabbatical leave in Israel and Biblical lands, I occasionally took small groups back for what I called "spiritual pilgrimages." Preparatory instructions to group members always included such advice as this: "We will be going to some wonderful and meaningful places. But often the pathways to reach them are rough, so be sure to take along some comfortable walking shoes!"

Biblical exegesis on the detailed and exacting level required for translation is somewhat like that—going on spiritual pilgrimages into wonderful and meaningful places in the Bible, but often the mental pathways are rough and challenging. So when we are going down into the depths of exegesis, looking intently into God's message for humankind, and trying with integrity to come up with what the author intended to say to his people in his day amid the problems and challenges of his world situation, our task becomes easier amid the complicated exegetical factors if we have some familiar and tested "standbys" among the helps we use. Often the best helps are not commentaries, rather they are the result of considerations we come to in our effort to solve an exegetical problem. For example, there is Bruce Hollenbach's article, "Two Constraints on Subordination in New Testament Greek." The ordering constraint states that if two or more constructions are subordinate to the same construction, they are typically ordered from least specific to most specific. Finite constructions are the most specific, with participial constructions, infinitive constructions, and nominal constructions following down the line of specificity in that order (Hollenbach 1985:2). Roger Van Otterloo's study on the functions of ἰδού and ἴδε "behold" in the Greek New Testament is one I consult again and again. Van Otterloo's paper presents three basic meanings for these Greek particles: (1) Pay attention, here comes the main character; (2) Pay attention, because even if you doubt it, what I am about to say is true; (3) Pay attention, for what I am about to say will require a response from you (Van Otterloo 1988:34). Likewise, the insights gained through examining the imperativals of Romans 12 have been constantly helpful. The different kinds of imperativals enable the author to give firm ethical teachings with unusual refinement and sensitivity.

We shall look first at the complicated verb system of Romans 12, which constitutes a challenge and a potential problem for the interpreter and the translator. We shall then think about grammatical considerations, attempting to account for the use of participles, adjectives, and infinitives as imperatival forms. We shall also seek to account for the change from plural to singular imperatives in the final propositions of the passage. In the third place, we shall look at some pragmatic considerations to be derived from the communication situation. Finally, we shall examine the semantic implications, asking why the author chose the particular imperatival forms he used, and why he put them into the sequence in which they are found.

A Display of the Verb System of Romans 12

Verse	Connecter	Finite Verbs Verbals and Subordinate clauses
1	οὖν Therefore	παρακαλῶ ὑμᾶς, ἀδελφοί, παραστῆσαι τὰ σώματα ὑμῶν I urge you, brothers, to present your bodies,
2	καὶ and	μὴ συσχηματίζεσθε τῷ αἰῶνι τούτῳ, do not model yourselves after the world's behavior patterns,
	ἀλλὰ but	μεταμορφοῦσθε . . . be transformed by a whole new attitude of mind
		εἰς τὸ ὑμᾶς δοκιμάζειν so that you may prove what is God's will.
3	γὰρ For	λέγω . . . μὴ ὑπερφρονεῖν I say to everyone of you not to think of yourself more highly

Verse	Connecter	Finite Verbs	Verbals and Subordinate clauses
			παρ' ὃ δεῖ φρονεῖν than you ought to;
	ἀλλὰ rather,	(λέγω) φρονεῖν think of yourself	
			εἰς τὸ σωφρονεῖν, with sober judgment,
			ὡς ὁ θεὸς ἐμέρισεν ἑκάστῳ μέτρον πίστεως. each according to the measure of faith God has given him.
4	γὰρ For		καθάπερ πολλὰ μέλη ἔχομεν, just as we have many members in one body,
	δὲ but		τὰ μέλη πάντα οὐ τὴν αὐτὴν ἔχει πρᾶξιν, all those members do not have the same function,
5	οὕτως so also	οἱ πολλοὶ ἓν σῶμά ἐσμεν ἐν Χριστῷ we the many are one body in Christ,	
	δὲ but in fact,	τὸ καθ' εἷς ἀλλήλων μέλη (ἐσμέν). individually, we are members of one another.	
6	δὲ Now then,	_____	ἔχοντες χαρίσματα . . . διάφορα having gifts differing
			κατὰ τὴν χάριν τὴν δοθεῖσαν ἡμῖν, according to the grace given to us,
	εἴτε if	_____	_____ προφητείαν _____ κατὰ τὴν ἀναλογίαν τῆς πίστεως, prophecy, (let us use our gift) in proportion to our faith;
7	εἴτε or if	_____	διακονίαν _____ ἐν τῇ διακονίᾳ, service, (let us use our gift) in serving others;
	εἴτε or if	_____	ὁ διδάσκων _____ ἐν τῇ διδασκαλίᾳ, (anyone of us) is the one teaching, (he should use his gift) in teaching
8	εἴτε or if	_____	ὁ παρακαλῶν _____ ἐν τῇ παρακλήσει, (anyone of us is) the one exhorting, (he should use his gift) in exhorting others;

Verse	Connecter	Finite Verbs	Verbals and Subordinate clauses
	(or if		ὁ μεταδιδοὺς _____ ἐν ἁπλότητι, anyone of us is) the one contributing, (he should contribute) generously (to the needs of others);
	(or if		ὁ προϊστάμενος _____ ἐν σπουδῇ, anyone of us is) the one exercising authority, (he should exercise authority) diligently;
	(or if		ὁ ἐλεῶν _____ ἐν ἱλαρότητι. anyone of us is) the one helping others in distress, (he should help them) cheerfully.
9		ἡ ἀγάπη _____ ἀνυπόκριτος.	(Let) love (be) genuine;
			ἀποστυγοῦντες τὸ πονηρόν, hating the evil,
			κολλώμενοι τῷ ἀγαθῷ, holding firmly to the good,
10			τῇ φιλαδελφίᾳ εἰς ἀλλήλους φιλόστοργοι, with brotherly love toward one another (being) warmly affectionate
			τῇ τιμῇ ἀλλήλους προηγούμενοι, in respect (for each other) taking delight,
11			τῇ σπουδῇ μὴ ὀκνηροί, in zeal untiring;
			τῷ πνεύματι ζέοντες, in spiritual fervor never lacking,
			τῷ κυρίῳ δουλεύοντες, to the Lord doing service;
12			τῇ ἐλπίδι χαίροντες, in hope rejoicing,
			τῇ θλίψει ὑπομένοντες, in trouble holding steady,
			τῇ προσευχῇ προσκαρτεροῦντες, in prayer persisting;

Verse	Connecter	Finite Verbs	Verbals and Subordinate clauses
13	____	____	ταῖς χρείαις τῶν ἁγίων κοινωνοῦντες, to the needs of God's people contributing,
	____	____	τὴν φιλοξενίαν διώκοντες. as for hospitality, practicing it zealously.
14	____	εὐλογεῖτε τοὺς διώκοντας [ὑμᾶς], Bless the ones who are persecuting you;	
		εὐλογεῖτε bless	
	καὶ and	μὴ καταρᾶσθε. do not curse.	
15	____	____ (You ought)	χαίρειν μετὰ χαιρόντων, to rejoice with rejoicing people,
	____	____ (you ought)	κλαίειν μετὰ κλαιόντων. to weep with weeping people;
16	____	____	τὸ αὐτὸ εἰς ἀλλήλους φρονοῦντες, with one another living harmoniously,
	____	____	μὴ τὰ ὑψηλὰ φρονοῦντες not acting haughtily
	ἀλλὰ but	____	τοῖς ταπεινοῖς συναπαγόμενοι. with lowly people associating.
		μη γίνεσθε φρόνιμοι παρ' ἑαυτοῖς. Do not be conceited.	
17	____	____	μηδενὶ κακὸν ἀντὶ κακοῦ ἀποδιδόντες, To not one person evil for evil repaying,
	____	____	προνοούμενοι καλὰ ἐνώπιον πάντων ἀνθρώπων· taking thought for what is right in the sight of all people
18			εἰ δυνατόν, if possible,
	____	____	μετὰ πάντων ἀνθρώπων εἰρηνεύοντες· living at peace with all people,
	____	____	μὴ ἑαυτοὺς ἐκδικοῦντες, not trying to get revenge, dear friends;
	ἀλλὰ but instead,	δότε τόπον τῇ ὀργῇ, leave that for God to take care of with His wrath;	

Verse	Connecter	Finite Verbs	Verbals and Subordinate clauses
	γὰρ for	γέγραπται, it is written,	
		Ἐμοί (ἐστιν) ἐκδίκησις, To Me belongs vengeance,	
		ἐγὼ ἀνταποδώσω, I will repay,	
		λέγει κύριος. says the Lord.	
20	ἀλλὰ Rather,		ἐὰν πεινᾷ ὁ ἐχθρός σου, if your enemy is hungry,
		ψώμιζε αὐτόν· feed him.	
			ἐὰν διψᾷ, if he is thirsty,
		πότιζε αὐτόν· give him a drink;	
	γὰρ for		τοῦτο ποιῶν if you do that,
		ἄνθρακας πυρὸς σωρεύσεις ἐπὶ τὴν κεφαλὴν αὐτοῦ. coals of fire you will be heaping on this head.	
21		μὴ νικῶ ὑπὸ τοῦ κακοῦ, Don't be overcome by evil,	
	ἀλλὰ but	νίκα ἐν τῷ ἀγαθῷ τὸ κακόν. overcome evil with good.	

The Problem

Romans 12 is a hortatory passage with verbs and verbals turned into exhortations and imperatives in all English versions but which reveals a much more complicated system in the Greek text. Orienters plus infinitives and imperatives appear to be used in a normal way in the opening propositions (vv. 1–5). Beginning with verse 6 there appears a series of participles intermingled with adjectives, infinitives, and imperatives, all acting as imperatives and ordinarily translated as injunctions. A final complication appears in the change from plural to singular imperatives in the final propositions of the passage.

In the attached display, finite verbs are to the left with other verbal forms indented. The modifiers are rearranged to show the rhythmic patterns in the propositional clusters which might serve to assist memorization as well as show more clearly the variations in verbal patterns. Lines are inserted where no normal grammatical connections are expressed, to show subordination or relationship to the rest of the propositions. Examination of the display will reveal the problem of finding meaning in the complication of the verbal system, beginning in verse 6 and continuing through verse 21. Outstanding are the three series of the participles, with the first closed by the key verse, "Love ought to be genuine" (v. 9a), the second series intermingled with adjectives and ended by a brief series of infinitives and imperatives, the third, briefer still, ended by a series of imperatives. The change from plural to singular imperative apparently comes from a quotation from the Old Testament, with the singular being retained in the closing two propositions of the chapter.

Grammatical Considerations Toward a Solution

The verbal system of Romans 12 includes two performative verbs, seventeen imperatival participles, three adjectives with imperatival function, two imperatival infinitives, and eleven imperatives. After Paul has completed the doctrinal portion of his letter (chs. 1–11), he begins the practical portion (chs. 12–16) with a strong performative verb παρακαλῶ ὑμᾶς "I urge you." In this way he signals his purpose for the latter part of his letter: to teach the believers in Rome how to apply the gospel message to their own behavior. A second performative adds prominence to the specific ethical points he intends to cover in chapter 12: λέγω παντὶ τῷ ὄντι ἐν ὑμῖν "I say to everyone among you." Most of the imperativals which follow serve to encode injunctions having to do with the influence of the Spirit in service and behavior. In verses 7 and 8 there is a series of five attributive participles which give direction concerning the exercise of spiritual gifts. They are to be translated as exhortations. Following the thematic injunction in verse 9: "Let love be genuine," there is a long series of imperativals and imperatives relating to the transformed behavior which is to be manifested in the daily life of the believers as the fruit of the Spirit. We will consider the grammatical aspects of these various forms of imperativals.

Imperatival Participle

It is apparent that imperatival participles are most frequently employed, with imperative verbs next in frequency. Paul uses the imperatival participle prominently in the practical sections of his letters to both the Romans and the Ephesians (Eph. 4:1ff. and 5:19–21). Peter makes use of it in his first letter when he gives ethical instructions to household servants (2:18), to husbands (3:7), and to wives (3:1–6).

In such usage, the participle functions independently in the communication situation. It is used descriptively, pointing out how those being referred to should act in a given situation. The participle encodes event propositions. Blass, Debrunner, and Funk (1961:245–246) in their Greek grammar conclude that this use is related to a type of anacoluthon where a construction is begun with a finite verb and continued by means of coordinated participles, sometimes in a long series. In the imperatival use, the initial finite verb is omitted as injunctions are encoded in a long series. Robertson (1925:945, 1133) goes further by positing the absolute use of the participle as an imperative. He observes that although the participle itself is neither imperative or indicative, examples can be found in both the papyri and the New Testament where the participle is used to carry on the verbal functions of either the indicative or the imperative. Asyndeton in such cases makes it impossible to connect the participle with any verb in the context. Moulton (1908:180ff., 22ff.) claims that any discussion of the independent use of the participle as a verb is removed from the realm of controversy by the proof from the papyri. It is found more frequently as an indicative, but clear examples of its use as an imperative have been found, including its use in decrees.

Dana and Mantey (1927:229) regard the imperatival participle as a peculiarity of Koine Greek, found in the New Testament and papyri. Even though it occurs in the papyri in other situations that can be explained on the basis of Hebrew usage, there is a strong likelihood that both Paul and Peter are drawn by their own orientation toward using a typical Hebraism when they are listing injunctions about the Halacha, the daily walk.

Lange (1971:390–394) and Barrett (1975:237–243), in their commentaries on Romans, concur in seeing an imperatival use of the participle here. Barrett calls it evident and undisputed; the participles must be understood as imperatives.

Imperatival Use of Adjectives

Grammatically, the substitution of adjectives for verbals in the exhortations of Romans 12:9–21 is not difficult to understand or account for. Three descriptive adjectives are not joined grammatically to their context, ἀνυπόκριτος (v. 9), φιλόστοργοι (v. 10), and μὴ ὀκνηροί (v. 11). However, an injunction later in the series (v. 16) contains an adjective as the predicate nominative with the imperative of γίνομαι: μὴ γίνεσθε φρόνιμοι παρ᾽ ἑαυτοῖς. This proposition undoubtedly helps to account for the grammatical connection in the previous three adjectives on the basis of ellipsis.

Dana and Mantey (1927:229) confirm the above analysis: "Adjectives are also (in addition to participles) used in what appears to be an imperatival construction, but doubtless in these cases the imperative of the verb *to be* is to be understood."

The independent use of the adjective as an imperatival is rarely found. The context must furnish the sense. Meyer (1983:475) comments that in this hortatory section of Romans 12, because they occur in the midst of other grammatical types of recognized imperatives, the participles and the predicate adjectives are to be translated by the imperative of the corresponding verb as a natural mode of expression.

Three adjectives are used with imperatival function. The verb is ellipsed, and the adjectives occur in the predicate position. Paul places them in context in such a way that they do more than the attributive adjective which provides an incidental description of the substantive. In the predicate position they provide the main point (Robertson 1923:656). The predicate position describes what *attitudes* those being referred to will exhibit in a given situation. We may understand the three independent adjective imperativals as follows:

"When you show someone that you love them, really mean it." (v. 9)

"Be warmly affectionate toward one another with brotherly love." (v. 10)

"Be untiring in your zeal." (v. 11)

Imperatival Infinitive

While admittedly rare, the imperatival use of the infinitive is well established, and its use is noted in standard grammars. For example, Goetchius points out: "Rarely in the New Testament, the infinitive may be used independently as an imperative (i.e., expressing a command or request)" (Goetchius 1930:324).

Blass, Debrunner, and Funk (1961:196, 197) comment that the imperatival infinitive is extremely old, being mostly found in Homeric Greek. It has become less frequent in Attic Greek. In Paul's writings it is limited to a very few passages: Romans 12:15, Philippians 3:16, 2 Thessalonians 3:14. If a governing verb were to be supplied, it would be something like δεῖ "it is necessary" or χρή "one ought." Imperatival infinitives in the papyri occur primarily in official orders and the like.

Moulton (1908:179) points out that the imperatival use of the infinitive was common in laws and maxims, and it recurs in the papyri. Robertson (1923:1092) adds that the Attic inscriptions frequently have the absolute infinitive as imperative.

Imperative Verb

The finite form of the imperative is characteristically used to give a direct and positive command. As Dana and Mantey (1927:174, 175) have pointed out, it is the genius of the imperative to express the appeal from will to will. Where ordinary communication is characterized by an appeal from intellect to intellect, in the imperative mode one will addresses the will of another. The imperative expresses intention, not possibility, probability, or fact. When we turn to considering semantic implications, we shall see that in certain injunctions Paul employs the imperative when he wants to make a more forceful appeal to the will of people, urging them to decide to act in certain ways.

The change to second person singular of the imperative in the final propositions of the passage appears first in the Old Testament quotation from Proverbs 25:21–22. It continues beyond the end of the quotation to the last appeal, which undoubtedly serves as a climax of thought about what genuine love can accomplish: "Don't be overcome by evil; but overcome evil with good." Beekman and Callow (1974:109) suggest that the final propositions in Romans 12 have been changed to the singular for rhetorical effect. However, there is also the possibility that the final two injunctions have been attracted into the singular under the influence of the singulars in the Old Testament injunctions.

Pragmatic Considerations Toward a Solution

Before turning to semantic implications in Paul's choices in the verbal system of Romans 12, we will look briefly at two pragmatic factors in the communication situation, factors which may prove helpful in understanding why he uses the particular forms of ethical teachings which he does.

The Time and Place of the Writing of the Letter

It is generally determined, by correlation with the Acts narrative, that Paul wrote the letter to the Romans during a comparatively quiet three month stay in Corinth (see Acts 20:2, 3). The most probable time reckoning is in the early months of A.D. 58. At that time his third missionary journey was drawing to a close.

One cannot help but be impressed, in this respect, with the similarity of the subject matter and the handling of it in chapters 12 and 13 of 1 Corinthians as compared with the second and third paragraphs of Romans 12. The problems arising from overemphasis on certain gifts of the Spirit and the lack of regulation in the exercise of them, along with the need to control the use of the gifts with redemptive love, are echoed in Romans 12. It is as if the apostle wrote with the Corinthians' experience fresh in his mind. He may have no specific situation to speak to in Rome as he did in Corinth, but he lays down directions and injunctions based on his experience. Sanday and Headlam (1895:359, 360) are undoubtedly correct in pointing out that just as in the doctrinal portion of the letter he writes with fresh memory of past experience, discussing and laying down in a broad spirit positions which had been gained in the course of those controversies, so in the practical portion Paul lays down broad and statesmanlike positions which are the result of past experience and which deal with circumstances likely to arise in any community.

The Occasion and Purpose of the Letter

A further pragmatic factor bearing upon the interpretations of Paul's injunctions to the Roman church is that out of all his writings preserved in the Scriptures, only the letter to the church at Rome is addressed to someone other than his own converts, fellow workers, or members of churches he had been instrumental in founding. The church at Rome may indeed have been formed through the influence of his converts who migrated to the heart of the empire from the East, but even so, he addresses the church in different tones. He longs to visit it on his way to new labors in the West (15:23, 24). He hopes to be of some spiritual benefit to its members (1:11). He is solemnly aware of the possible danger awaiting him in his upcoming trip to Jerusalem (15:25–32). First he will write ahead to the group in Rome, sharing with them his best in doctrinal and ethical teachings. He will do it in ordered fashion. The injunctions of Romans 12 seem calmly written, though they are intensely written for daily life situations. They are set forth in measured cadences, suitable for easy memorizing. He passes on to them the best of the Old Testament code of behavior and merges it with elements from the apostolic traditions. In this way he provides a sort of moral catechism for the New Testament church, and in this way he presents principles and codes which transcend time and place to become permanent and universal.

Semantic Considerations Toward a Solution

Paul begins the practical portion of his letter by urging a deep surrender to God which will lead on toward transformed living. His exhortations and injunctions which follow will bear upon realizing this consecration in life. We are not aiming for a commentary on the content of those injunctions, but we are rather asking why Paul chose to cast them into the forms he used, and why he put them into the particular sequence we find in Romans 12. Do the verbals of the passage represent a system at all? What can he convey with imperatival participles and infinitives and with the imperatival use of adjectives which he cannot or will not convey with straight imperatives of command or prohibition? What relation do the verb forms have to the content? to the communication situation?

We cannot hope to have come up with all the answers to those questions, but we will present some suggestions and considerations which may serve to point the way for further observations and possible research. We will look first at some semantic implications in the verbal forms, and then turn to semantic implications in the sequence.

Semantic Implications in the Verbal Forms

The imperative use of the participle. The first unusual use of verbals which meets us in the passage is the imperatival use of the participle. In the propositional cluster dealing with the exercise of the gifts (vv. 6–8) the participles function differently from those in the ethical passage (vv. 9–21). A new sentence begins with ἔχοντες δὲ χαρίσματα, where the participle has no antecedent but is in its meaning joined with the ἐσμεν of the previous verse to form a kind of apposition: "We have many members. . . . We have differing gifts." The attributive participles, without verbs, which follow ἔχοντες in a patterned sequence, must function in a double way. Each points to a possessor of a particular gift and implies, along with its adverbial phrase, the third person imperative verb needed to complete the exhortation: "If he is one who teaches, let him teach with his teaching gift; if he is called to give to others, let him give generously," etc. It would seem that this patterning suits the apostle's purpose to *convey directions* without giving direct commands. The participles communicate more politely and are addressed to the reason rather than to the will.

As for the long series of seventeen imperatival participles, even though they are interrupted occasionally by other verbals or adjectives, the choice to use them seems mainly due to Rabbinic usage, where participles are employed to express, not direct commands, but rules and codes. It is quite probable that both Peter and Paul are encoding Hebrew participial injunctions into the Greek. If this is a correct linguistic explanation, then we may see a picture of early Christian living finding its ethical code from the heritage of Judaism and the Old Testament rather than from Gentile systems of thought and behavior. We have some of the Christian counterpart of the Halacha of Judaism, patterned in such a rhythmic way as to provide for easy memorization and recitation.

A further consideration is that the participial injunctions appeal to the reason and the emotions more than to the will. They are intended to teach the one who genuinely loves others how to *act* in given situations. For instance, in the presence of evil, he will abhor it; in troubles, he will hold steady; in praying, he will continue steadfast; he will share the necessities of life with needy believers; he will be very attentive to the demands and opportunities of hospitality. In all these imperatival participles there is an encoding of the principle of love in action.

A third consideration to account for the use of imperatival participles is found in the communication situation. As pointed out above, Paul does not intend to "throw his apostolic weight around" with the Romans. Rather, he is seeking to share with them in fellowship for mutual benefit. One may suggest, therefore, that he deliberately chooses a softer form of command, a more polite appeal to reason and affections, when he talks about applying the principle of love in ordinary daily life situations.

The imperatival use of adjectives.   A second uncommon use of verbals in this passage is the imperatival use of adjectives. As pointed out earlier, the three adjectives without grammatical connection can undoubtedly be completed by an ellipsed γίνεσθε, since it is actually found with the fourth adjective in the hortatory series. We go on to ask, then, what Paul is hoping to communicate with these adjectives which he could not do as well with participles or some other imperatival form?

First, we note that adjectives encode a state proposition, while participles and infinitives encode event propositions. Here Paul uses adjectives which identify characteristics the person who genuinely loves will exhibit. These characteristics will be manifested in the behavior not so much by acts as by *attitudes*. Thus, the genuinely loving person is to be warmly affectionate towards others with brotherly love (v. 10), he is to be untiring in his zeal (v. 11), and he is not to be conceited (v. 16).

Second, we may note a psychological factor, that adjectives appeal primarily to the emotions rather than to the intellect or will. They hold up an ideal to reach for, a vision of what one would like to become. Thus, when Paul seeks to exhort his hearers to take certain attitudes and strive for certain ideal characteristics, he finds the adjective the best suited to his purpose.

The imperatival infinitive.   A third verbal form found in this hortatory passage is the imperatival infinitive. If participles encode actions to be followed in given situations, and adjectives encode attitudes which are acceptable, what does the imperatival infinitive communicate which would not better be communicated by other imperatival forms?

The sense of the imperatival infinitive is best brought out by accepting for a moment the suggestion of Blass, Debrunner, and Funk which says that if a governing verb were to be supplied, it would be something like δεῖ or χρή. One use of the impersonal verb δεῖ is to denote the compulsion of duty, "one ought" or "one should." An inner necessity grows out of a given situation. The conscience is being deliberately activated. What is proper or fitting shades over into what is necessary. Χρή likewise denotes "it is necessary" or "one ought." Both are completed by infinitives. The exhortations in Romans 12:15 would then become like this: "You ought to rejoice with those who are rejoicing. You ought to weep with those who are weeping."

If the suggestion to supply δεῖ or χρή is valid, then we can conclude that the author chooses the imperatival infinitive to encode *moral duty*. By activating the conscience he has come close to an outright command, but he still stops short of it. He supplies a delicate urgency instead. The given situation does not allow a direct command, but pressure is still being put on the will to make a deliberate choice. This would seem to be the case when love is enjoined to prove itself genuine by becoming involved in the joys and sorrows of others (v. 15).

The imperative mode. The fourth and last verb form used in the exhortations of Romans 12 is the imperative mode itself. Here there is a direct appeal to the decision of the will. The communicator speaks with authority and the hearer is presented with a *choice*. The assumption is made that in a given situation both speaker and hearers have moved beyond the need for more arguments and emotional appeals. A choice must now be made. It could be expected that in ethical codes the command would be reserved for those situations where it is difficult, if not impossible, to carry out a needed course of action from appeal to reason or emotions alone. The will must be brought to bear more powerfully upon the situation. A deliberate choice must be made. Higher forms of motivation must come into play to help a person make a difficult choice.

It is exactly in such difficult kinds of situations that Paul uses imperatives in Romans 12. Some of love's highest service will be to motivate the Christian to pronounce a blessing instead of a curse on those who are persecuting him, to help him refuse to try to get revenge upon an enemy who has wronged him.

It is also those very injunctions which are highlighted and brought into sharper focus by repetition and by reinforcement with Old Testament quotations: "Bless those who are persecuting you, bless them and do not curse them" (v. 14). Leave vengeance to God to take care of, for it is written, "Vengeance belongs to me, says the Lord, I will repay. But if your *enemy* hungers, feed him; if he is thirsty, give him a drink." "Don't be overcome by evil, but overcome evil with good" (vv. 19–21).

The use of imperatives to encode choices which must be made in a deliberate way is further reinforced by the fact that such injunctions are either the words of Jesus Himself as He spoke them in the Sermon on the Mount (compare Matt. 5:44; Luke 6:28) or are the words of the Lord drawn from the Old Testament (see Deut. 32:35; Prov. 25:21, 22). The highest authority of all is behind these commands. Again we see Paul's delicate handling of his present hearers. He does not impose his own apostolic authority, but he points them to the highest authority of all in these difficult issues.

Semantic Implications in the Sequence of the Hortatory Injunctions

The most challenging aspect of the problem of the verbal system in Romans 12 is to try to discover whether the injunctions encoded by the four imperatival forms are placed in such a sequence that they constitute a system at all. What, if any, is the thought process of the passage? Does it reach a climax? What would be its effect on the hearer who is receiving his moral and ethical instructions first as participles mingled with adjectives, then as infinitives, imperatives, more participles, more imperatives, somewhat in that order? At this point in our study we can only suggest some answers and hopefully point the way toward further needed observation and investigation. As a kind of moral catechism for believers, the evidences of thought movement within the passage appear to be as follows:

- There is movement from basic spiritual experience to transformation of behavior. The believer's presentation of his body to the Lord as a living sacrifice is to lead on to a life lived according to God's good will.
- Instructions concerning the exercise of spiritual gifts in the service of the church are followed by exhortations to show the fruits of love to the community, bringing benefit to others. Ecclesiastical conduct is to be correlated with social duties.
- The setting forth of principles is followed by the spelling out of codes based on these principles. The principle of unity in the body, the church, is encoded first. The principle of loving redemptively is then set forth in a code covering much of the daily life.
- There is movement, of course, from the general to the specific, as one would expect in hortatory passages. Gifts are to be exercised in proportion to one's faith. Specific gifts are then highlighted. Likewise, hating what is evil and holding fast to what is good is to be manifested in many specific ways.
- In general, there is progress from exhortations which appeal to the reason to those which appeal to the emotions and finally to those which direct decision in the will. The first two, however, are intermingled more than the third kind, which tends to cluster to-

ward the close of the passage. Along with this may be noted a general movement from outward expression to inward motivation.

- If, as Barrett points out (1975:241), Paul draws his code from both Rabbinic sources and apostolic traditions, then there is a movement from the Old Testament teachings to the New Testament distinctives.
- Finally the passage appears to move toward a climax of thought. Love becomes more and more energetic and aggressive until it moves right into the camp of the enemy and succeeds in winning out against him. There is a hint that love can even effect a transformation of an individual and turn him from an enemy into a friend. The mercy of God becomes triumphant over rebellion and disobedience of people. The victory comes as believers love with God's love, genuinely and redemptively.

Summary

We have seen some evidences that the verbal forms of Romans 12 constitute a system and that there is definite thought movement from the lesser to the greater and to the greatest achievement of love.

There is also evidence that each form of the imperatival has its own distinctive function in encoding behavior. The form has been chosen not only according to the communication situation, but also according to what the author wishes to accomplish in his hearer in that situation.

It has been demonstrated that hortatory codes are more likely to be encoded in rhythmic patterns, to provide for easier memorization and recall.

Further observation and investigation needs to be carried out to determine the validity of positing psychological factors in interpreting Scripture. The findings concerning imperativals need to be applied to other passages of Scripture. The source of hortatory codes in the New Testament can be further checked. Further examples of change of number from singular to plural or vice versa in verbs following Old Testament quotations could be sought.

Conclusion

With an increased understanding of the verbal system of Romans 12, the student and translator should be able in a clear and concise way to express the propositions with the sensitive differences Paul intended as he dealt with the delicate issues of the believers' service and behavior.

The following meaning-based paraphrase is intended as a guide for translators, with each kind of imperatival expressed in a different way.

"You should" is used for participles and adjectives, "you ought" is used for infinitives, "you must" or "do this or that" is used for imperatives.

A Meaning-based Paraphrase of Romans 12

1   So then, my friends, (in view of all that God has done to rescue people from wrongdoing, I will tell you in what ways you should live to please God:)

I urge you to give yourselves as a gift to God, to belong completely to Him as long as you remain alive here on earth. God is really pleased with that kind of gift from you, and that is really the proper way for you to worship Him.

2   In addition to that, do not follow any longer the ways of the people around you who do not know God.

Instead, by your thinking completely new and different thoughts about how God wants you to live, (you must) become completely new and different in your ways. In that way you will be able to find out what God has decided you should do. (And keep this in mind:) what He decides is always good, and He is always pleased when you do what He says, and what He tells you to do is exactly the right thing for you to do.

3   You see, God has acted kindly toward me, giving me a task to do for Him.
That is why I am talking to everyone in your group (telling you how to act in your ways).

(First, as you work for the Lord,)
you ought not to think that you are more important than you are.

Instead, you ought to think sensibly about yourself
in agreement with the way God enables you to strongly trust Him to help you.

4   I will tell you what I mean to say by that:
(As you know,) each of us has one body with many different parts,
and yet each part has its own work to do in a different way.

5   So like that,
even though we (believers) are many distinct persons,
yet by being together with Christ
we are just like one body.

Furthermore, we are all joined together to help one another
just like the different parts of a body help all the others.

6   So then, God has given to each one of us different abilities to do some kind of work for Him.
    (That is why it is proper for us to use the special abilities we have) in the way God kindly helps us to do our task for Him.

    (For example:)
    when God gives to someone the ability to tell God's message to people, then whenever God gives him a message to tell them in His name,
    then he should faithfully do it,
    believing that God has given him the task of doing that.

7   When God gives to someone else the ability to help (other believers),
    then that person should help them in a trustworthy way.

    When God gives to someone else the ability to teach (other believers),
    then that person should teach (others) with God's help.

8   When God gives to someone else the ability to urge (other believers) to carefully follow God's ways.
    then that person should do that, trusting God to help him.

    When God gives to someone else the ability to share his possessions (with others who need help),
    then he should do that generously.

    When God gives to someone else the ability to take the lead (over other believers),
    then he should try really hard to guide them well.

    When God gives to someone else the ability to help people who are experiencing heaviness,
    then he should gladly help them.

9   (That is the way I want you to do your work for God. And here is the way I want you to behave toward other people:)

    When you show people that you love them,
    you should really be sincere about it.

    (For example:)
    You should firmly turn your backs on whatever is wrong.

    You should strongly join your thoughts to whatever is right.

10 (Because you belong to God,)
    you should think about one another affectionately
    like brothers in one family group do.

You should go out of your way to treat each other with respect.

11   You should not be lazy (about following God's ways) but you should go on doing your best.

You should always be ready and eager (to please Him),
(and) you should serve the Lord in whatever ways He asks you to.

12   When you think about (the surpassingly good things the Lord is going to do for you in) the future,
you should really be happy, thinking about that.

When you meet up with hardships,
you should endure them without complaining.

When you speak to God about something,
you should never give up thinking that He will do what you ask Him to.

13   When God's people do not have enough food to eat or clothes to wear,
you should give some of what belongs to you to help them.

When another (believer) is visiting your area and needs food and a safe place to stay in for the night,
you should make it a point to go and ask him to come and stay with you.

14   When people cause you to suffer,
ask God to make something good happen to them.
(I will say that again:) ask God to make something good happen to them.
Don't (try to pay them back by) asking God to make something bad happen to them.

15   When something happens to make others feel happy,
then you ought to show them that you are happy too.

When something happens to make others feel really sad and cry,
then you ought to show them that you are sad with them by crying too.

16   When you are telling one another your opinions about things,
you should do your best to come to an agreement.

You should not think that you are more important than others.
    Instead, if there are some people whom others look down on,
you should make friends with them.

Do not be thinking about yourselves that you are really smart.

17   When someone does something bad to you,
      you should not try to pay him back by doing something bad to him.

      You should decide ahead of time that you are going to live in
         honest ways,
         so that no one can accuse you and say that you have done
         something wrong.

18   You should not begin using angry words with anyone, but you
      should do all you can to live peaceably with all the people
      around you.

19   My dear friends,
         when someone treats you unfairly,
      you should not try to get even with him by yourselves.
      No, let the Lord decide what He will do to punish him.

      (I tell you not to try to get even) because that is what God caused
         to be written down in His book long ago. Here is what it says:
         "If someone deserves to be punished,
      I myself will punish him.
         If someone has done evil,
      I myself will cause evil to happen to him."
      That is what the Lord says.

20   However, (He also tells us in His Book to do this:)
         "Whenever your enemy is hungry,
      give him food to eat.
         Whenever he is thirsty,
      give him water to drink.
         By acting toward him in that way,
      you will be helping him to change his thoughts so that the Lord
         can make him new and different."
      (That is what the Lord tells you to do.)

21   So don't try to win out over someone
         by doing something hurtful to him.
      No, win out over him
         by doing something helpful for him.

References

Aland, Kurt, Matthew Black, Carlo M. Martini, Bruce M. Metzger,
and Allen Wigren, eds. 1975. *The Greek New Testament.* 3d ed. London: United Bible Societies.

Arndt, William F. and Wilbur Gingrich. 1957. *A Greek-English Lexicon of the New Testament and Other Early Christian Literature.* Chicago: University of Chicago Press.

Barrett, C. K. 1957. *A Commentary on the Epistle to the Romans.* Harper's New Testament Commentaries. New York: Harper and Row.

Beekman, John and John Callow. 1974. *Translating the Word of God.* Grand Rapids: Zondervan Publishing House.

Blass, F., A. Debrunner, and R. W. Funk. 1961. *A Greek Grammar of the New Testament and Other Early Christian Literature.* Chicago: University of Chicago Press.

Dana, H. E. and Julius R. Mantey. 1927. *A Manual Grammar of the Greek New Testament.* Toronto: Macmillan.

Goetchius, Eugene Van Ness. 1930. *The Language of the New Testament.* Boston: Ginn and Company.

Hollenbach, Bruce E. "Two Constraints on Subordination in New Testament Greek." *Selected Technical Articles Related to Translation* No. 14:1–16. Dallas: Summer Institute of Linguistics.

Louw, Johannes P. and Eugene A. Nida. 1988. *Greek-English Lexicon of the New Testament Based on Semantic Domains.* Vols. 1 and 2. New York: United Bible Societies.

Meyer, H. A. W. [1883] 1983. ed. *Critical and Exegetical Handbook to the Epistle to the Romans.* Peabody, Mass: Hendrickson.

Moulton, J. H. 1908. Prolegomena. *A Grammar of New Testament Greek.* 3d ed. vol. 1. Edinburgh: T & T Clark.

Robertson, A. T. [1914] 1923. *A Grammar of the Greek New Testament in the Light of Historical Research.* 4 ed. New York: Hodder and Stoughton.

Sanday, William and Arthur C. Headlam. 1905. *A Critical and Exegetical Commentary on the Epistle to the Romans.* The International Critical Commentary. Edinburgh: T & T Clark.

Van Otterloo, Roger. "Towards an Understanding of 'Lo' and 'Behold,' Functions of ἰδού and ἴδε in the Greek New Testament." *Occasional Papers in Translation and Textlinguistics.* OPTAT 2 (1):34–64.

9

The Disappearing Δέ in 1 Corinthians

Kathleen Callow

Introduction

The purpose of this paper is to use techniques of discourse analysis, such as may be applied to any language, to shed light on how the particle δέ is used in 1 Corinthians, and particularly on the significance of its occurrence and nonoccurrence in specific contexts. The author makes no claim to be familiar with the vast literature available on this epistle: the aim is to bring a new discipline to bear on old problems.[1]

In the absence of a total semantic/pragmatic analysis of the book, this paper cannot claim to be exhaustive. Every occurrence of δέ in 1 Corinthians has been considered, however, and also numerous places where it does not occur. The author is satisfied that what is presented here does account satisfactorily for a large proportion of the evidence, and hopes that it will provide stimulus for further and more detailed study, in this and other New Testament writings.

Essential Theory

Three main theoretical presuppositions undergird this paper.

---

[1] Between 1979 and 1982, several articles about the use of δέ in discourse appeared in publications of the Summer Institute of Linguistics, specifically in *Notes on Translation* (NOT) I-79 (limited edition) and in issues of *Selected Articles Related to Translation* (START). See, for example, the article by Stephen Levinsohn, "Four Narrative Connectives in the Book of Acts" in which he states that δέ is a "developmental particle" signalling "progression *from* some element *to* some corresponding element" (NOT I-79, p. 1). The debate is helpfully reviewed in Scott Youngman's unpublished dissertation, *The Stratificational Analysis of a Hortatory Text: 1 Cor 8.1–11.* (M.A. Thesis for University of Texas at Arlington, August 1987.) The present writer has worked for the last decade with the conclusions of this debate, and here both accepts and develops them.

First, it is assumed that a particle such as δέ may occur in texts with several different meanings or functions, and that such multiple function causes no ambiguity to a native speaker of the language. This can only be the case if other linguistic signals co-occur with the δέ, differing with the different functions of δέ, and in effect providing the hearer or reader with a package of signals on each occasion, the δέ being one component in the package. A major purpose of this paper is to explore such signals.

Second, it is assumed that if the other components of the package are present, and yet δέ does not occur, this nonoccurrence is significant. It is not absent because those components were sufficient without it, or because Paul forgot to use it, or because it really does not matter whether it is there or not. Paul had the choice of using a δέ-package, and many times elected to use it; where he elected not to do so that choice was significant. This can, of course, be stated equally well from the point of view of the reader: being accustomed to being presented with δέ along with certain other signals, its absence from that environment would be significant. In other words, if we do not find δέ where we expect it, this is because Paul did not mean δέ at that point. This should enable us to discover more exactly what δέ does and does not mean, and to explore what factors caused Paul to use other constructions and signals instead.

Third, our assumption that multiple function is possible does not preclude the existence of some shared factor of meaning at a very generalized level, common to all functions. Since such a shared factor, if it exists, is of necessity realized only through the spectrum of specific examples, we will here study the multiple functions first, reaching conclusions about a generalized, shared factor or factors at the end of the paper.

These three theoretical presuppositions provide a ready-made threefold structure for our investigations. We will first consider the multiple functions of δέ, then consider its significant absences, and finally, its generalized substratum of meaning.

The Multiple Functions of Δέ

Even a superficial reading of Corinthians reveals that δέ occurs at a variety of different discourse levels. It may occur with high-level significance, initiating a new topic which will form a major discourse-block, such as in 7:25, περὶ δέ τῶν παρθένων "Now concerning the unmarried." It may occur with low-level significance, being relevant only to the clause or sentence in which it is located, as in 14:14: τὸ πνεῦμά μου προσεύχεται, ὁ δὲ νοῦς μου ἄκαρπός ἐστιν "my spirit prays but my mind is unfruitful."

It therefore appears that the span or domain of a δέ in any instance is a considerable clue to its function. We will for convenience consider first long-span uses, then short-span uses, and finally will use our findings to analyze intermediate-span functions.

When δέ occurs in the first clause of a long span, the main accompanying signal is a major change of topic from the preceding material. In the earlier part of chapter 7 Paul was talking about married people, and then about circumcision and about slaves: περὶ δὲ τῶν παρθένων (7:25) marks a clear switch, signaling to the reader to tune in now on a different set of people. There is no further long-span δέ until 8:1, περὶ δὲ τῶν εἰδωλοθύτων, when a new topic, food offered to idols, is introduced.

These examples indicate, of course, that in addition to the change of topic under consideration, the very formula περὶ δέ plus genitive is itself an accompanying signal of the long-span function of δέ. This formula is, however, optional. A number of long-span uses are accompanied instead by a reference to Paul's own attitude or purpose, as in 11:2 ἐπαινῶ δὲ ὑμᾶς "I praise you," and 15:1 γνωρίζω δὲ ὑμῖν "I remind you." See also 1:10; 4:6; 11:17.

A further long-span use of δέ is to terminate the discussion of a topic, as in 9:23 where πάντα/τοῦτο πάντα/τοῦτο δὲ ποιῶ[2] has a retrospective span which began at verse 12. See also 12:11 (span 4–11), 12:31 (span 1–31), and 13:13 (span 1–13). In all these instances the accompanying signal is a generic term with back-reference to the specifics preceding it—τοῦτο (9:23); πάντα . . . ταῦτα (12:11); τὰ χαρίσματα (12:31); πίστις, ἐλπίς, ἀγάπη, τὰ τρία ταῦτα (13:13). Such a concluding generic statement also provides a clue that what follows will constitute a new topic-unit at some level.

When we turn to short-span uses of δέ, most of the occurrences signal either contrast or an aside. For examples of contrast, consider 13:12, where ἄρτι "now" contrasts with τότε in the δέ clause, and δι᾽ ἐσόπτρου "in a mirror" with πρόσωπον πρὸς πρόσωπον "face to face," and 15:6b, where οἱ πλείονες/πλείους μένουσιν "the majority remain" contrasts with τινὲς . . . ἐκοιμήθησαν "some fell asleep" in the δέ clause. The contrastive lexical signals here are obvious.

When used as a marker of an aside, δέ is accompanied by a different package of signals. The aside may function to mark an exception or restriction (1:16; 3:15c), an explanation (10:4; 14:2), or to prevent a possible misunderstanding on the part of the reader (10:29; 15:10c). In each of these cases, some lexical item already mentioned is taken up again in the δέ clause, and something new is added, which is not

---

[2] Variant readings are noted throughout this paper to aid the reader, but do not affect the analysis.

then further referred to. Thus in 1:16 ἐβάπτισα picks up ἐβαπτίσθητε at the end of 15, while τὸν Στεφανᾶ οἶκον is not mentioned again. Similarly, in 10:4 πέτρας is taken up as ἡ . . . πέτρα; the new information is Χριστός, which receives no further mention. The repeated information is not always lexically identical: in 15:10c the ἐγώ in the δέ clause is taking up the first person ending in the preceding ἐκοπίασα; in 3:15c σωθήσεται is taken up in the δέ clause by οὕτως, here acting as a verb-substitute, the clause being otherwise verbless.

Another short-span use of δέ is in listing (15:39), sometimes with cumulative, climactic effect (3:23; 12:8–11). Again the lexical clues (items from same lexical domain, often partial clause repetition) are obvious.

We now turn to occurrences of δέ which operate with an intermediate span. They do not introduce a new topic, like long-span δέ, but they often introduce a new aspect of an existing topic, and this new subtopic does not terminate with the δέ clause. See, for example, 4:18, where Paul, still talking about his relationship with his converts, takes up the new subtopic of his postponed visit. Similarly in 7:32 where, in the context of the inadvisability of marriage in view of the times, Paul introduces the related subtopic of being ἀμερίμνους "without worries," which he develops up to the end of verse 3. In both these instances, some of the referential material (e.g. person reference) maintains the existing topic, while some introduces new ideas in a compatible area. In addition 7:32 starts with θέλω δέ, a phrase reminiscent of long-span introducers.

Once a topic or subtopic is introduced, it is common for major successive points to be marked with δέ, while supporting material is marked with γάρ, ὁμοίως, participles, etc. Sometimes the successive points are simply additive, as in 10:7–10 where a series of negative exhortations (γίνεσθε . . . πορνεύωμεν . . . ἐκπειράζωμεν . . . γογγύζετε) are each introduced by μηδέ. Sometimes the progression is strictly logical, as in 15:12–17, where each new point is marked by δέ. The conclusion reached by one deductive step becomes the protasis of the next, marked with δέ, and building up a chain of reasoning. Note verse 16, however, which repeats the argument of verse 13: this is now known information and is not being used to present a point, but to support the argument of verse 15; in this case the introductory particle is γάρ.

Sometimes the progression of thought takes a slight side-step: Paul moves from fact to evaluation (10:6) or from evaluation to exhortation (10:7) using δέ each time. Sometimes, while still talking of one situation as his main topic, Paul introduces envisaged possibilities, as in 14:28, 30: he has been speaking of the church meeting, but he steps a little tangentially to envisage a possible situation where no interpreter is present introducing this aside by ἐὰν δέ (v. 28). Verse 29 uses a δέ to return us to the mainline with instructions about prophets, and verse 30 envisages a different alternative situation, again signaled by ἐὰν δέ, in which the prophet who is speaking is instructed to give way to another.

Often intermediate-span units use δέ in a way which matches the short-span ones we have already considered. Thus in 4:19 Paul uses a contrast with δέ (. . . I didn't come [v. 18]; I δέ will come quickly) as a point of departure for some comments about his proposed visit. At this intermediate level contrasts tend to be less tight, the argument progresses not so much by opposites as by a sort of counterbalancing relationship. Thus in 10:13 the faithfulness of God is presented with δέ in a counterbalancing relationship to the trials referred to in verse 12, and it is this faithfulness which is developed in the remaining clauses of verse 13. Likewise it is possible to have an intermediate-span aside, to prevent possible misunderstanding (9:15b, a disclaimer; he is not pleading for support) or to provide an explanation (15:27b, the forefronted πάντα of verse 27a has one exception, which is then spelt out). In counterbalancing examples it is common to have lexical similarities on both sides of the pivotal δέ (4:18 ἐρχομένου . . . ἐφυσιώθησάν, 4:19 ἐλεύσομαι . . . πεφυσιωμένων; 10:13a πειρασμὸς ὑμᾶς, 10:13b ὑμᾶς πειρασθῆναι . . . πειρασμῷ). The same balancing of lexical items is found in asides: 15:27a πάντα . . . ὑπέταξεν, 15:27b πάντα ὑποτέτακται . . . ὑποτάξαντος . . . πάντα. In 9:15b the balancing referents after the δέ are generic, ταῦτα and οὕτως. In addition, asides frequently have an introductory formula signalling their removal from the mainline: 9:15b οὐκ ἔγραψα; 15:27b ὅταν δὲ εἴπῃ.

As presented here, it is obvious that δέ has a wide variety of functions. Moreover, it may occur with several different functions in successive verses. To illustrate how this works out in practice, let us consider all occurrences of δέ in 7:1–9 (realising seven different functions occurrences in all eight)

7: 1	Περὶ δὲ ὧν ἐγράψατέ (μοι) . . .	Long-span topic introducer
2	Διὰ δὲ τὰς πορνείας . . .	Counterbalance, subtopic introducer
3	Τῇ γυναικὶ ὁ ἀνὴρ . . . ὁμοίως δὲ καί	Short-span counterbalance
4	Ἡ γυνή . . . ὁμοίως δὲ καὶ ὁ ἀνὴρ	Short-span counterbalance
6	Τοῦτο δὲ λέγω κατὰ συγγνώμην . . .	Transfer from commands to evaluation
7	ὁ/ὃς μὲν οὕτως, ὁ/ὃς δὲ οὕτως.	Short-span contrast
8	Λέγω δὲ τοῖς ἀγάμοις . . .	Authorial subtopic introducer; return to commands
9	Εἰ δὲ οὐκ ἐγκρατεύονται . . .	Alternative situation within topic

The point being made is that because of the packaged nature of the signals, Paul's readers would have had no difficulty in distinguishing exactly how δέ was developing the argument with each occurrence.

Significant Absence of Δέ

Our second theoretical assumption was that the nonoccurrence of δέ is significant, that where Paul did not use it, he did not mean it, and he did mean something else. Obviously to pursue this thesis in detail would require an in-depth study of every conjunction in the epistle, and of asyndeton—a task which we have no intention of tackling. Rather, we want to consider a rather surprising phenomenon, that there are several fairly long passages (eight to ten verses or more) in which δέ does not occur at all. If evenly distributed throughout the epistle, δέ would occur approximately every other verse, so long stretches with no occurrence merit investigation. There are also several other passages in which the only occurrences of δέ are short-span contrastive ones: intermediate-span δέ is conspicuously absent, yet no one would claim that Paul was not developing his argument. Why does he choose to develop it without δέ?

The obvious answer to this question would presumably be that Paul was developing a different kind of argument, and hence different signals would be required. On examination, however, this proves not to be the case. If we review the functions of δέ listed in the last section, we find that almost all of them can be paralleled in passages without δέ, or with only short-span contrastive δέ. In the following discussion, examples previously quoted will be cited by reference in parentheses, to facilitate comparison.

Contrast: 15:42b–44   A sustained contrast of σπείρεται "it is sown" with ἐγείρεται "it is raised," linked with the contrasting pairs φθορᾷ . . . ἀφθαρσίᾳ "perishable . . . imperishability," ἀτιμίᾳ . . . δόξῃ "dishonor . . . glory," ἀσθενείᾳ . . . δυνάμει "weakness . . . power." See also verses 47–49 (13:12; 15:6b).

Logical argument: 6:2–4   Here the logical argument follows the same pattern as previously noted, with the conclusion already reached forming the protasis of the next deductive step. Particularly noteworthy is 15:32c, d, where the protasis εἰ νεκροὶ οὐκ ἐγείρονται "if dead (people) are not raised" echoes εἰ δὲ ἀνάστασις νεκρῶν οὐκ ἔστιν "if there is not resurrection of dead (people)" in verse 13. (15:12–17)

Transition from fact to evaluation: 5:1, 2a   The fact is that of πορνεία, the evaluation—a negative one—and you are still puffed up!

Envisaging possibilities: 7:18, 21   Paul addresses different groups within the church, but instead of using conditional clauses (e.g., if any of you were slaves when you were called) he uses questions throughout, as in 21 δοῦλος ἐκλήθης "Were you a slave (when) called?" (14:28, 30)

Generic summing up: 7:20   The different groups are summed up in ἕκαστος and their different states at conversion in τῇ κλήσει ᾗ ἐκλήθη "the calling in which he was called." See also verse 24. (9:23; 12:11)

Expression of Paul's own attitude: 11:22e, ἐπαινέσω ὑμᾶς . . . οὐκ ἐπαινῶ "will I praise you? . . . I do not praise you!" (11:2, 17)

Just as significant as the examples of individual functions listed above is the evidence from studying longer passages without δέ such as 6:1–11, 15–20, and 10:14–20, where it is clear that Paul is distinguishing mainline from less prominent material but is using rhetorical questions instead of δέ. In chapter 6 his main points are expressed by οὐκ οἴδατε plus a question (as in 9, 15, 16) while in chapter 10 the same function is performed by a rhetorical question with οὐχί.

It seems clear, therefore, that functions which are regularly signaled using a δέ-package can also be signalled in different ways, and that Paul had a genuine choice available to him. We need now to investigate the motivating factors which determined his choice. What causes the disappearance of δέ?

Factors Motivating Δέ and Not-δέ

The longest passages without any occurrence of δέ are 1:1–9; 6:1–11; 9:1–14; 15:42–49. In addition there are other passages of similar length which contain short-span contrastive δέ but no others. These are 1:18–29 and 5:1–13; shorter passages are 3:1–7; 4:8–13; 7:17–21; 9:19–22; 10:14–20; 15:29–34.

Excluding 1:1–9, which is introductory, the remaining passages fall into two major categories, of which the larger consists of those expressing strong emotion. Usually this emotion was a negative one, such as indignation, and was directed at Paul's addressees. Thus in 3:1–7 he expostulates concerning their divisions, in 5:1–13 concerning their failure to deal with πορνεία, in 6:1–11 concerning their suing fellow-believers in secular courts, and in 10:14–20 concerning the idolatry involved in participating in heathen ceremonies. (The latter example provides an interesting contrast. When Paul discusses food sacrificed to idols in chapter 8 it is in connection with Christian liberty, and he discusses the issue quite dispassionately, with normal use of δέ. In chapter 10 he makes it clear that while eating εἰδωλόθυτα in a private house is acceptable, eating it in connection with heathen ceremonies is emphatically not.) In two other passages Paul expresses strong emotion concerning himself and his ministry (9:1–14; 15:29–34).

In all these passages there is frequent use of rhetorical questions (as τί . . . κινδυνεύομεν πᾶσαν ὥραν? 15:30). All the passages also contain evaluations of some sort (as οὐ καλὸν τὸ καύχημα ὑμῶν 5:6). Most contain metaphors, e.g., those concerning soldiers, cultivators of vineyards, and shepherds in 9:7. We will consider the significance of this later.

The other passages, while obviously expressing emotion, are less indignant than ironical (4:8–13, concerning their being puffed up) or scornful (1:18–29, concerning human wisdom, and expressed almost in paradoxes). These show the same characteristics as discussed above.

The other group of passages is completely different, in that no strong emotion is being expressed. Two of the passages (3:18–23 and 7:17–21) are hortatory: we could say that the addressees are themselves the topic, especially in the case of the latter passage. The other two passages (9:19–22 and 15:42–49) are in no way addressee-oriented, the former expounding Paul's pattern of serving all men, and the second comparing believers with seeds in their contrasting death and resultant life. No explanation of emotion or relation to the addressee will suffice here, a closer look at these passages is necessary.

In 9:19 Paul affirms in generic terms one of the apostolic principles on which he bases his whole evangelistic approach: ἐλεύθερος . . . ὢν ἐκ πάντων, πᾶσιν ἐμαυτὸν ἐδούλωσα ἵνα τοὺς πλείονας κερδήσω. For the next three verses he expounds this in a series of illustrative examples, followed in each instance with a repetition of the purpose, ἵνα . . . κερδήσω. The successive examples are τοῖς Ἰουδαίοις (v. 20), τοῖς ὑπὸ νόμον (v. 20), τοῖς ἀνόμοις (v. 21), and τοῖς ἀσθενέσιν (v. 22). In verse 22c he summarizes all this in τοῖς πᾶσιν . . . ἵνα . . . σώσω. In this entire passage there is no occurrence of δέ. (In the next verse, in which Paul explains his motivation for this behaviour [πάντα/τοῦτο . . . ποιῶ, a backward-looking generic clause] δέ reappears. We will consider the significance of this in a moment.)

When we turn to 15:42–49 we find something similar. The entire passage is a prolonged illustration of the nature of the spiritual body, or rather, it consists of two illustrations, that of the sown seed, and that of the first and last Adam, both bearing on the contrast between our present body (τὸ ψυχικόν) and our future one (τὸ πνευματικόν). The entire passage is strongly marked by asyndeton and from verse 45b to verse 48b (the "Adam" metaphor) it is also verbless.

The absence of δέ cannot be attributed in these cases simply to the use of figurative language: in 9:25 we have a metaphor (πᾶς . . . ὁ ἀγωνιζόμενος) which is introduced with δέ. The explanation seems rather to be that in these instances the comparisons, contrasts, or illustrations are prolonged: Paul is not moving on steadily from point to point, but is hovering, as it were, over the one point which he is developing more like an artist than like a lawyer. (I make no apologies for lapsing into figurative language myself here: discourse analysis cannot be handled purely by rules, there are some things which the human mind grasps best by metaphor. The constraint is that linguistic evidence must be available in the surface structure forms to back all claims, but the claims may be expressed in whatever way language and circumstance permit.) When we look more closely at these passages we see this claim borne out by the frequent repetition of ideas and the frequent use of parallelism. In 9:19–22 the structural pattern of repetition is inescapable: the formula X(dative) ὡς X(nominative) ἵνα X(accusative) κερδήσω, where X stands for a group of people, covers four illustrations and with a little variation the generic summary. Paul is painting his canvas with bold strokes and a great sense of symmetry.

Similarly in 15:42–49, the pattern σπείρεται ἐν Y, ἐγείρεται ἐν not-Y, where Y is a negatively evaluated abstract noun, likewise covers four examples. The contrast between the first and second Adam is likewise built up by repetition. Unlike Paul's style in more logically-reasoned passages, sentences are short, subordination is infrequent, connectives are also infrequent, and lexical repetition within a short compass is a very prominent feature.

We conclude, therefore, that when Paul is developing an argument by a succession of points, linearly, the use of δέ is appropriate and frequent. When Paul is developing a single point, holistically, δέ is inappropriate, and the progression of thought is marked instead by repetition and the other factors we have noted.

This can be confirmed by looking at a very different passage, this time strictly factual and not at all figurative. In 15:1–8 δέ occurs three times, but the first of these is a long-span introducer, and the other two are short-span uses (v. 6c, contrast; v. 8a, last item in list). There is no intermediate-span δέ; the main development of Paul's thought, as he piles up the evidence for Christ's resurrection, is carried first by *Prepositional Phrase + καί + 2pl. verb* (3 times, vv. 1, 2a), then by ὅτι + *3p verb (Χριστός the subject)* (4 times, vv. 3b–5a), and finally by ὤφθη + *dative* (4 times, vv. 5a–8).

Why should Paul use his "artist" approach in such a judicial matter as the listing of evidence? I suggest that there are several very valid reasons. First, he is not making a succession of points, even though he is referring to a succession of events: rather he is making one point—the abundance of evidence for the central fact of Christ's resurrection. Second, the point that he is making is not new to his readers, he says γνωρίζω . . . ὑμῖν, "I remind you." It is very easy to lose one's audience by presenting them with a series of facts which they already know, and Paul does not make the mistake of attempting to do so: he is not here *presenting* facts but *recalling* them to his readers, and he does so by presenting the issue globally rather than linearly, by the use of grammatical parallelism and lexical repetition. The point that the risen Christ was repeatedly seen is hammered home, not as a new fact, but as a very significant one: this fact is meant to engage not only the mind but the heart. Third, important though this is, Paul has not yet reached his main polemical point, which he does in verse 12a, and which he makes with δέ: since Christ is proclaimed (and now demonstrated) to be risen, it is utterly inconsistent for some to hold that there is no resurrection. The audience will have been waiting for some such point to be made: in his holistic prolegomena he has been setting the scene, as a description would do in narrative; the audience is now expectant, waiting for the action to start.

We may say, therefore, that δέ characteristically occurs where there is linear development of thought, and that it marks new development in the progression of the message. It does not occur when the message is emotional, or when there is a poetic or rhetorically motivated dwelling on one point. Two matters remain to be discussed. First, does this cover all the evidence? Second, can we find any rationale lying behind this usage?

Of the passages listed at the beginning of this section (thirteen in all), eleven are accounted for satisfactorily by the explanation already presented. The two not yet adequately explained are 3:18–22 and 7:17–21, which were already mentioned as being hortatory and non-emotional. It is possible that the passage in chapter 3 is coloured by previous discussion of σοφία, with its underlying argument-by-paradox. No such explanation is available for 7:17–21, where Paul is giving instructions to different subgroups among the Corinthians. However, this is a very "you-directed" passage, and this factor is not unrelated to those already discussed. It remains to be seen whether an underlying rationale can coherently relate these various strands.

Why should linear development be marked with δέ, and global, figurative, or emotional development be marked by its absence? Let us think a little further about what is happening in the minds of speaker and hearer when δέ is used. The speaker uses δέ as a signal, saying, "This is the next step." It may be a little step or a big one, it may be a step forwards, or sideways, or even backward-looking, but it is always the next step, and with it the speaker or writer is progressing one thought at a time along a purposeful line of development. Resorting to metaphor again, we can say that δέ knits thoughts together into a chain, very reasonably and rationally, one thought at a time.

Emotional communications, however, do not develop a reasoned chain or progress a thought at a time: they leap from point to point by some emotive association; sometimes the speaker almost explodes with the effort to express so much at one time. To do so he often resorts to poetical forms and figurative language: he is not appealing now to the reason but to the heart.

It is necessary in studying discourses to distinguish between mind and heart, reason and emotion. The mind is concerned with facts, the heart with attitudes and evaluations; facts are third-person things, attitudes and emotions are I-and-you related. The characteristic uses of δέ are at the factual, third-person end of this scale, its absence is most clearly noted at the I-and-you end. If there is a fuzzy area in the middle, represented by two cases out of thirteen, this is not in discourse terms surprising. It will suffice as an explanation until a better appears.

Meantime, the evidence of 1 Corinthians—we claim no more—is that δέ is a particle of calm, reasonable progression, a step at a time. The absence of δέ is occasioned by the dominance of any factor operating not linearly, but emotionally and holistically.

10

Patterns of Thematic Development in 1 Corinthians 5:1–13

Kathleen Callow

Introduction

The aim of discourse analysis is obviously, in the long term, the analysis of discourses, i.e., whole passages. To do this, we often have to start by analysing low-level surface-structure signals which have discourse significance, such as connectives, word order, and verb mood. Such analysis is essential in order to have good, objective evidence for their function on any particular occasion of use, but it is not our only aim: our future purpose is to see how a whole passage fits together to express the intended meaning of the writer and what contribution each constituent element makes to the whole.

At the present stage of research into New Testament Greek, neither type of study is complete. We do not have a full analysis available of the low-level signals, nor can we yet analyse a whole passage comprehensively and satisfactorily. Yet the two types of study must be pursued in parallel, each providing evidence to illuminate the other. The analysis presented here of 1 Corinthians 5:1–13 uses a variety of low-level signals as evidence in establishing the overall thrust of the unit as a whole. It is hoped that such a high-level analysis will fulfill at least two purposes: (1) To show the current state of higher-level analysis as I see it and to develop our thinking further, and (2) To provide a clear picture of higher-level factors in the light of which further study of low-level signals can be pursued.

Method of Analysis

It is assumed that a communicator always communicates *about something* and *for some purpose*: his message is referentially and purposively coherent. These two parameters are taken as defining meaning units at all levels of discourse. Thus the passage under consideration will be seen to exhibit both referential and purposive unity. The passage can, in its turn, be divided into smaller units each having the same characteristics, i.e., coherence with respect to reference and purpose. It is beyond the scope of this paper to defend these subdivisions in detail; the reader must accept them as based on objective criteria.[1] They are established in this paper in order to study the contribution made by each such unit to fulfilling the purpose of the whole passage.

When we assess the purpose of a passage, or the contribution of a sub-unit, we find that some of the content is more significant than the rest: those parts which relate most closely to the purpose of the unit are the prominent parts, and these constitute its theme. (Prominence is signaled in a variety of ways which will be commented on at the appropriate points). Our method will be to identify the global theme (i.e., of the whole passage), and also to distinguish between prominent and supporting material in each sub-unit. This will provide the evidence on the basis of which we will seek to evaluate the contribution made by each sub-unit to the thematic development of the passage as a whole. We thus establish a sort of thematic pattern: this may be expected to exhibit similarities to the thematic patterns of other hortatory passages, which is a subject that merits further study.

To facilitate reference to the Greek text, verses are divided roughly into clauses, each clause being identified by a lower-case letter, thus 2b, 7c, etc. Relative clauses and embedded clauses are included as part of the matrix clause. A major purpose of this paper is to identify different kinds of thematic pattern characteristic of volitional, expressive, and factual messages.

Topic

Any communicative unit is about something. The topic of this passage (which we call the global topic, to distinguish it from lower-level topics) is the immoral man.

The man is first mentioned indirectly, in verse 1a, by the use of πορνεία "immorality." Obviously a person or persons must be committing this immorality; verse 1c makes it immediately clear that the topic is not immorality in general (or, πορνεία as a sin, in the abstract) but one particular person who was acting immorally. The same person is

---

[1] Types of evidence are detailed in Kathleen Callow and John Callow, article to appear in *Discourse Description*, eds. Sandra Thompson and William Mann, Pragmatics and Beyond NS, Benjamins.

mentioned overtly in verses 2c, 4, 5a, 5b, and 13b, and metaphorically referred to (as "old yeast" which had to be removed) in verses 6b, 7a, and 8. He is also subsumed under a more general command in verses 11b and 11c. It is clear, therefore, that this person is Paul's topic.

It is worth noting the ways in which Paul refers to this man. Apart from the neutral τινα in verse 1c (a far from neutral context!) and το πνεῦμα in verse 5b, all the references are unequivocally negative. Twice (vv. 5a, 11c) Paul calls him "such a fellow" (τὸν τοιοῦτον, τῷ τοιούτῳ); twice he identifies him by the wrong which he has committed (τὸ ἔργον τοῦτο πράξας/ποιήσας (v. 2c), τὸν οὕτως τοῦτο κατεργασάμενον (v. 3b, 4)); speaking metaphorically he twice uses the term "old yeast" (τὴν παλαιὰν ζύμην (v. 7a), ἐν ζύμῃ παλαιᾷ (v. 8)), and once, more bluntly still, he uses the figure "yeast of sin and evil" (ἐν ζύμῃ κακίας καὶ πονηρίας (v. 8)). Finally, Paul demands his expulsion as τὸν πονηρὸν (v. 13b)—an inherently negative evaluation.

We have said that this is a volitional passage: Paul is aiming at getting the Corinthians to do something. All willed action is based on some evaluation, and it is therefore common in volitional messages that at least some of the supporting material is evaluative, presenting certain situations and actions as good, others as bad. Here we see that, quite aside from any supporting arguments, Paul presents the person he is talking about as bad, simply by his lexical choices. There is no neutrality here, nor any trace of softness or wavering towards an erring brother—he is πονηρόν. Paul presents his topic packaged up, as it were, with its own condemnation. The fact that he can do this without any supporting arguments probably implies that he knew that his readers would accept that verdict as a true one.

Constituent Units and Theme

The passage subdivides into four constituent units.

Unit 1 (vv. 1 and 2) introduces the topic of πορνεία but moves on immediately to a negative evaluation, not of the sin or the sinner, but of the Corinthians themselves: they have been smug and self-satisfied, rather than mourning as they should have. Paul then immediately tells them what they *should* do—remove the offender from their fellowship. In other words, this initial unit moves from fact (v. 1) to evaluation (v. 2a, 2b) to command (v. 2c), in line with what we are calling the "purposive chain." This is posited in order to encapsulate in theory what happens so frequently in our thought processes, and hence in our communications. Human beings seldom rest content with plain facts, but by an almost self-propelling mental process go on to evaluate those facts, and from there to either propose or perform the appropriate activity. The term *purposive chain* is used as a sort of verbal shorthand to refer to this pattern of mental progression. Unless the text provides evidence to the contrary, material at the factual end of the purposive chain is considered to be less prominent than material at the activity end; there is a graded increase in prominence as we move away from fact towards volition and action.

I am taking the ἵνα clause in verse 2c as imperatival, following Turner (Moulton 1963:95), who says that it is "usually taken as final, but only imperat . . . will make good sense. . . . " See also Zerwick (1963:142) and Zerwick and Grosvenor (1981). (One would expect that a ἵνα imperative would have some different discourse significance from a normal imperative, but there are so few undisputed biblical examples that this would be hard to establish, and examples from Hellenistic sources also seem to be rare. For clear New Testament examples, see Mark 5:23, Ephesians 5:33, 2 Corinthians 8:7.) It is taken as imperative in the RSV, NEB, and (English) Jerusalem Bible. However, even if it is interpreted as the purpose or result of ἐπενθήσατε, it is clear that Paul thinks that this is what they should have done, and now should do. On any interpretation it is clearly volitional, and hence (being at the prominent end of the purposive chain), the most naturally prominent element in the unit.

In fact, each major unit in the passage ends with a repetition of this command in one form or another. In unit 2 (vv. 3–5) Paul puts his own authority behind the judicial sentence παραδοῦναι τὸν τοιοῦτον τῷ Σατανᾷ (v. 5a). In unit 3 (vv. 6–8) the command occurs twice in the form of metaphors, or rather, as elements in the sustained metaphor of yeast and the Passover. As soon as the figure is introduced in verse 6, Paul immediately moves to the command in verse 7, "Get rid of the old yeast." And this is taken up again at the end of the unit ("Let us celebrate the feast, *not with the old yeast.*" [v. 8]). This time, however, Paul expands the command into a positive exhortation (still partially metaphorical) to sincerity and truth—which he obviously felt were lacking in the Corinthians' handling of the situation.

The final, longer unit (vv. 9–13) contains three semantic paragraphs: the first (vv. 9–10) corrects their misunderstanding of a previous command; the second (v. 11) says exactly what he now commands, in the form of a general principle which includes, but goes beyond, the issue of πορνεία. These two semantic paragraphs form a closely knit unit, to which the third (vv. 12, 13) is somewhat more loosely appended. They are considered to form one larger unit on the grounds of referential and purposive continuity: τοὺς ἔξω (v. 12a) refers back to verse 10a, and τοὺς ἔσω (v. 12b) to verse 11b, while purposively the commands to μηδὲ συνεσθίειν (v. 11c) and ἐξάρατε/ἐξαρεῖτε are, in practical terms, equivalents. The introduction of the idea of judging could, however, be taken as contrary evidence, in favour of a stronger boundary between verses 11c and 12a. On either analysis, both the second Semitic paragraph and the third end with a strong command to discontinue fellowship with the erring brother.

We thus see that what is effectively the same command is presented no less than six times in these thirteen verses. Since, in general, volitionals outrank evaluatives and factuals in natural prominence, these commands each constitute the prominent element in their unit or sub-unit. This is borne out by the fact that it is to this command that most of the supporting material relates: it is supported by reasons in verses 3, 6b, and 12b, and by purposes in verses 5b and 7b. It is presented literally (vv. 2c, 13b), metaphorically (vv. 5a, 7a, 8), and in a larger context (v. 11). It is quite possible in hortatory material for the commanded action to be mentioned only once, and for supporting material to provide reasons, consequences, and so on, without any further repetition of the exhortation. Its multiple occurrence in this passage indicates that it is not only thematic, but urgently and vigorously so.

It is worth noting that in every case except one the imperative or its surface-structure equivalent (e.g., παραδοῦναι, v. 5a) occurs initial in its clause: one function of the initial position seems to be the carrying of material most closely related to the theme of the unit.[2] This is borne out by verse 11 where the focus of attention is not on the act of refusing to associate with sinners, but on which sinners Paul was talking about: in this instance only, the person to be shunned/ejected (ἀδελφὸς ὀνομαζόμενος, taken up as τῷ τοιούτῳ) takes precedence over the command (μηδὲ συνεσθίειν).

Simultaneous Thematic Strand

The theme as outlined in the preceding section is carried by what we may call naturally prominent material: it is signaled by imperatives or their grammatical equivalents, and these function as head elements to which supporting material relates. There is, however, an-

---

[2] This is not the view taken by Levinsohn (1991), who considers initial verb as a default word order, used when no other word in the clause is being fronted for prominence. However, this observation is based primarily on narrative material. My own rather different observation here could be due to difference in genre, or to the fact that we are in this passage dealing with imperatives and their semantic equivalents, which may well invest word-order factors with different thematic significance.

other kind of prominence which we may call special prominence: this is signaled by special devices such as exclamations or rhetorical questions and is used by a writer to express or arouse emotion. The passage before us is particularly rich in examples of special prominence: Paul makes no attempt to hide his strong feelings about the matter.

Of particular interest to us here is the fact that these expressions of emotion, which are found in almost every unit, *always occur in connection with the attitude of the Corinthians themselves.* They thus constitute what may be considered a separate thematic stand, intertwining with the structural theme of ejection and expressing an attitude which does not fall far short of exasperation. The fact that this special prominence is referentially homogeneous (carrying some second person marker in all but one case) and that it occurs throughout the passage gives strong grounds for calling it thematic. Its emotional impact makes the label *secondary theme* somewhat inappropriate. We prefer to call it a *thematic strand* and will discuss it in detail at the appropriate points.

Thematic Pattern

The thematic pattern of a passage is the way its thematic material is fitted together, the way the author develops his thought in prosecuting his communicative intention. One of the purposes of this paper is to explore the possible categories which may be used to define such thematic development. A theme is not a static thing; there is progress and development throughout a passage. We want, if possible, to pinpoint certain categories which will provide criteria for describing different kinds of thematic patterning.

Paul's obvious purpose here is to get the Corinthians to expel the immoral man: the way in which he prosecutes that purpose provides the developmental/thematic pattern for the whole. Since we may assume that Paul chose his arguments carefully, addressing them to real needs or weak points, we can learn quite a bit about the Corinthian church by studying how he directs his arguments.

Volitional messages exhibit very different patterns according to what the writer perceives to be the main obstacle to carrying out the command. Sometimes the addresses need convincing that the situation to be changed is bad, or that the situation to be brought about is good. Such arguments, which we may categorise as those of *evaluative persuasion,* may take the form of "X is good (in itself)" or "X is consistent with your present values" or "X produces good consequences." Alternatively, the argument can take the form that "not-X" is the opposite of these. With one possible exception to be discussed below,

Paul does not use arguments of this category. Rather, he uses arguments from a different range of possibilities, those of *motivation to action*. Such arguments may take the form of an appeal to the self-interest of the addressees, or of an appeal to authority, or of a rebuke for inactivity: values are not the problem; the appeal is addressed to whatever is blocking the performing of the commanded activity. Obviously, in Paul's view, the problem was not that they were evaluating the situation wrongly, but that they were not responding to it with the appropriate action.

We will now discuss the thematic contribution of each unit in turn.

Unit 1 (vv. 1, 2)

There are two possible interpretations of this unit. It is either a unit of evaluative persuasion ("you must realise that πορνεία is wrong") or a unit of motivation to action (rebuke for inactivity). Rebuke there certainly is here (v. 2a, b), but it is because they had done nothing or because their evaluation of the situation was wrong? The issue turns on the interpretation of πεφυσιωμένοι "puffed up" in verse 2a. Were the Corinthians πεφυσιωμένοι *because* of the πορνεία, or was Paul saying that their already being πεφυσιωμένοι was utterly inappropriate in the circumstances?

NIV seems to take the former view ("A man has his father's wife. And you are proud! Shouldn't you rather have been filled with grief . . . ?") Phillips, Jerusalem (English), and NEB take the latter view, NEB particularly clearly with "And you can still be proud of yourselves!"

Only one possible reason is ever put forward for their possibly being proud of the πορνεία, and that is that they thought it exhibited their Christian liberty to an unusual degree, but the evidence of the rest of the passage is against this. First, Paul does not take up either the issue of liberty (which is not mentioned), or of the evil of immorality (which is assumed but not argued, as we have seen). If liberty had been the issue here, it seems inconceivable that Paul would not have tackled it head on. Further evidence is found in unit 3, where καύχημα "boasting" (v. 6a) is surely just an expression of their being πεφυσιωμένοι. This vocal high opinion of themselves was οὐ καλόν, not because they were proud of the wrong things, but because they were ignorant of the effect on themselves of sin tolerated in their midst.

In fact there is positive evidence for the alternative interpretation, that the Corinthians were already puffed up. In the early part of the letter Paul twice warns them against boasting (1:31; 3:21), and in the immediately preceding verses he refers to those who were puffed up (ἐφυσιώθησάν τινες [4:18]; τῶν πεφυσιωμένων [4:19]), specifically because he himself had not visited them when expected. The best interpretation of verse 2a, therefore, seems to be that Paul was expostulating with them because their smug and self-satisfied attitude had continued unabated and was so inappropriate in the circumstances. The use of καί in verse 2a also tends to confirm this interpretation: if πεφυσιωμένοι had been new information, relating directly rather than indirectly to verse 1, the appropriate conjunction would have been δέ: καί claims no specific connection between the two verses.

The special prominence in verse 2a (exclamation) and 2b (rhetorical question conveying rebuke) thus highlights both the complacent attitude of the Corinthians and their failure to respond appropriately to the πορνεία situation. These, combined with the implied command in verse 2c, provide evidence for a thematic contribution of *motivation by rebuke*, the rebuke being both for inappropriate attitudes, and for failure to act.

It is also possible that the use of καί rather than δέ in verse 2a makes it more likely that they were already puffed up: no specific connection is claimed between verses 1 and 2a.

We therefore conclude that the thematic contribution of this unit is that of motivation by rebuke for inactivity.

One additional factor in this unit is worthy of note. On any interpretation, the rebuke is expressed particularly strongly, as an exclamation in verse 2a and a rhetorical question in 2b. Special prominence (prominence signaled by special devices) is found later in the passage also, at points which we will note, *but always in connection with the attitude of the Corinthians themselves*. It is as if the main thematic development of the passage is signaled by natural prominence (repeated commands), but that there is a simultaneous thematic stand surfacing at intervals, in which Paul addresses the attitudes of the addressees, using devices signaling special prominence.

Unit 2 (vv. 3–5)

In verse 3, Paul puts all the weight of his own authority behind a formal expulsion. Why does he need to do this? Perhaps there were no leaders among the Corinthians with acknowledged authority— Paul clearly indicates that the act of expulsion was one of the whole church fellowship (συναχθέντων ὑμῶν, v. 4b). Possibly there were leaders who saw no need to act, being as smug and self-satisfied as the rest of the congregation. Perhaps the leaders felt inadequate, in Paul's absence, to tackle such an issue: this interpretation would be supported by verse 2b, where the point highlighted by the contrast in Paul's presence or absence (not his body versus his spirit, which are also contrasted, but are not clause initial).

For some or all of these reasons, Paul obviously saw the lack of a locally exercised authority as one of the main reasons for their failure to act, and he himself provides that authority. The thematic function of unit 2 is therefore that of motivation by exercise of authority.

This interpretation conflicts with the NIV note on verse 3a, which takes ἐγώ here as contrasting with ὑμεῖς in verse 2—but in that case I would have expected δέ, not μὲν γάρ. κέκρικα does not really contrast with πεφυσιωμένοι, so a contrast here is not convincing. Certainly the initial ἐγώ requires explanation, however. The occurrence of γάρ indicates that ἐγὼ . . . κέκρικα is supporting the command for expulsion, but μέν seems to relate ἐγώ forward, not backward. In the light of this, and of the thematic role of the unit, we take ἐγώ as certainly prominent—but Paul comes on stage here not to contrast his attitude with theirs, but as an authority figure, no less authoritative because of his absence.

Nothing has been said here about the thematic stand signaled by special prominence—for the good reason that, in this unit only, none appears. Sentence length and style are also both noticeably different from unit 1. The whole of unit 2 consists of one long, flowing sentence with much subordination: by comparison with unit 1, it has a formal, almost judicial atmosphere. It would not be appropriate that the passing of a most solemn sentence (παραδοῦναι . . . τῷ Σατανᾷ) should be expressed emotionally.

Unit 3 (vv. 6–8)

In this unit Paul urges the expulsion (ἐκκαθάρατε, v. 7a) in the light of the effect of evil on their fellowship as a whole, and of their own status as ἄζυμοι—a purified community. Their failure to be aware of this is given special prominence in verse 6a (a negative evaluation of the addressees is always prominent!) and verse 6b (rhetorical question).

The unit has a double thematic function, of warning and assurance—a warning of danger to themselves if they fail to act, and an assurance of benefit (appropriate to their status as a purified people) if they do. These, of course, are like two sides of one coin, or the stick and the carrot which both in different ways induce a donkey to action. Together they constitute an *appeal to the (spiritual) self-interest* of the Corinthians, and falls once more in the area of motivation to action.

Unit 4 (vv. 9–13)

This final unit sheds further light on the reasons for the Corinthians' failure to deal with the offender. They had misunderstood previous strong instructions not to have fellowship with any such people, thinking that Paul meant they should not associate with anyone at all who sinned in such ways. Now, logically, this warning, even if misunderstood, should clearly have covered the present instance. Obviously they had failed to carry out these instructions as they understood them—hence Paul's use of ὠφείλετε ἄρα, and also the forefronting of ἐκ τοῦ κόσμου, "you would have had to come out of the world altogether!" It seems that they had dismissed the whole issue from their minds as totally impracticable.

The question is, what function does this correction have? Is it simply support for the final command in verse 13b? Then the thrust would be, "You misunderstood before, but since you now know what to do, go ahead and do it." This might then have the thematic function of facilitation, that is, clearing the way for the command to be carried out by removal of some obstacle, but this facilitating function is strictly completed by the end of verse 11. We must therefore consider it as the thematic contribution of the first two semantic paragraphs only (vv. 9–11): with verse 12a the whole unit takes a slightly unexpected turn.

It would have seemed quite a natural train of thought to progress straight from verse 11c to verse 13b, giving us something like, "I was talking about sinners who claim to be Christians—don't even eat with such people! Expel the wicked man from among you!" Instead Paul introduces another factor into the situation, that of passing judgment. At first glance this seems to be simply an argument supporting his correction of their mistake: the γάρ in verse 12a signals that sentence as a reason and would indicate that verses 12a–13a had a supporting role. The thread of the argument would then be, "Of course I wasn't talking about sinners who aren't Christians—what business is it of mine to judge *them?* No, leave that to God."

This analysis, however, fails to take account of several factors. First, 12a and 12b are both cast as rhetorical questions, and as such are quite strongly prominent. Second, they are linked closely with each other in a chiastic structure, again a mark of prominence. Third, the chiastic structure develops a new train of thought; it does not simply support previous material.

Let us look at this more closely. The chiasmus involves the two elements in each question which immediately precede κρίνειν/κρίνετε.

| 12a | Τί γάρ | μοι | τοὺς ἔξω | κρίνειν? |
| 12b | Οὐχὶ | τοὺς ἔσω | ὑμεῖς | κρίνετε? |

We have here a third example of special prominence focused on the Corinthians and their attitudes. Paul's strong assertion in verse 12a that it is not his business to judge non-Christians is not primarily supporting previous material but leading in to what follows: it undoubtedly is the Corinthians business to judge members of their own fellowship.

Moreover, the responsibility of Christians to exercise judgment within their own community is taken up as a strong theme in the following verses, as is also the contrast between "outsiders" and "insiders." So the content itself is prominent, as well as the grammatical form and the chiasmus.

For these reasons it is necessary to consider verses 12a–13a, not as a unit supporting verses 9–11, but as prominent in its own right, the head of the whole unit verses 9–13a. The thematic role of the whole unit is to support the structural head (v. 13b), presenting yet another kind of motivation, that of responsibility. This confirms the picture that has been steadily emerging, of the Corinthian church as so self-satisfied that the thought of exercising any kind of internal discipline never even crossed their minds. Paul's punch line here is that dealing with the situation is their responsibility; they must actually get down to doing something about it.

If this interpretation is to stand, we must give consideration to two surface-structure features which might point in other directions. The first is the occurrence of γάρ in verse 12a, which would seem to subordinate verses 12 and 13 to what preceded them. The second is the sudden introduction of ὁ θεός in verse 13b—the judging of unbelievers is to be left to Him. This could be seen as downplaying the exhortation to the Corinthians in verse 12b concerning their responsibility to exercise judgment within the church. We will consider these two issues in turn.

The correct analysis of γάρ requires the recognition that special prominence may, and frequently does, overrule natural prominence. In terms of natural prominence, a reason signaled by γάρ is less prominent than the assertion it is supporting. If there had been no special prominence here, verses 12 and 13 would have been taken as supporting the facilitating function of verses 9–11 and would have been allocated no thematic function of their own. The degree of special prominence here is such that Paul seems to be making a separate point, and making it strongly, and our analysis should reflect this. In other words, we must recognize that the normal prominence patterns associated with γάρ have been overridden at this point by the emotional intensity with which Paul presents the argument of verse 12. Thus, while γάρ retains its logical flavor (thus providing a smooth transition between v. 12a and what precedes), it surrenders its normal prominence function.

We now turn to Paul's assertion in verse 13a that God will judge unbelievers: the fronted element is *unbelievers*—there is not need for the Corinthians to judge them; God will do that. The question facing us is not that of its meaning, which is clear, but of its significance within the discourse. The answer hinges on the function of δέ.

Among the recognized functions of δέ, two are relevant here. It may mark progress along the main line of discourse development, or it may mark an aside, a departure from that main line. Obviously the first interpretation would give verse 13a thematic prominence, the second would downgrade that prominence. Mercifully we are not left to decide the issue at the flip of a coin: there are clear discourse signals which indicate its interpretation here as marking an aside.

First, comparison with other verses in 1 Corinthians shows that verse 13a exhibits a pattern commonly found in asides: something which has just been mentioned is repeated at the beginning of the clause with δέ. Then something new is said about it, which is not mentioned again thereafter. Parallel examples are given here, with the reference followed in turn by the repeated information (in both forms) and the new.

1:16	(ἐβάπτισα)	ἐβάπτισα δέ	τὸν Στεφανᾶ οἶκον
7:11	(χωρισθῆναι)	ἐὰν δὲ . . . χωρισθῇ	ἄγαμος . . . καταλλαγήτω
10:4	(πέτρας)	ἡ πέτρα δὲ	ὁ Χριστός
5:13α	(τοὺς ἔξω)	τοὺς δὲ ἔξω	ὁ θεὸς . . .

Obviously, verse 13a fits readily into this pattern: a native speaker would have been aware of such signals and would have interpreted δέ accordingly.

In addition, signals are missing which would have indicated an interpretation as mainline progression. The only other occurrences of δέ in this passage (vv. 3a and 11a) are clearly contrastive. The mainline in this passage is not carried by δέ at all, and evidence from the rest of the epistle indicates that this is normal in emotional sections of the letter. The reader or hearer would not have been expecting δέ as a mainline signal.

We thus interpret verse 13a as an aside, leaving verse 12 to carry the emotive thematic strand, and verse 13b as the main structural theme of the passage.

Summary

We may summarize the thematic pattern of this passage as follows, using X for the commanded act of expulsion:

1–2	You should do X!	Rebuke
3–5	Do X with my authority!	Authoritative Support
6–8	Doing X will benefit you	Appeal to (Spiritual)
	Not doing X will harm you	Self-interest
9–11	Misunderstanding corrected	Facilitation

| 12–13a | The responsibility is yours | Assertion of Responsibility |
| 13b | Do X | Thematic Head |

We have attempted to show in this paper that a wide variety of discourse signals contribute to our awareness of the author's purpose and attitudes. In particular, we have tried to make clear the importance of prominence, both natural and special, in determining that purpose and as evidence in the case of doubtful interpretations (as with γάρ and δέ). It is important to realize that where signals such as connectives have multiple functions, there was *no ambiguity for the native speaker,* and appeal to the full range of evidence will normally solve the issue.

The thematic patterns discovered here all relate to the area of motivation, except the function of facilitation which belongs in the area of removing obstacles. When someone is trying to get addressees to perform an action, he may either evaluate the action, remove obstacles, or provide motivation. Since this passage so strongly emphasizes motivation we may assume that this was needed. We will need to look to other passages to provide patterns in the areas of evaluation and facilitation.

References

Levinsohn, Stephen H. 1991. *Discourse Features of New Testament Greek: A Coursebook.* Dallas: Summer Institute of Linguistics, draft copy.

Moulton, James Hope. 1963. *A Grammar of New Testament Greek.* Vol. 3. Syntax. Edinburgh: T & T Clark.

Zerwick. 1963. *Biblical Greek.* Rome: Biblical Institute Press.

_____, and Grosvenor. 1981. *An Analysis of the Greek New Testament.* Rome: Biblical Institute Press.

11

Dimensions of Discourse Structure: A Multidimensional Analysis of the Components and Transitions of Paul's Epistle to the Galatians

H. Van Dyke Parunak

Introduction

A text is like a machine. We presume that it does something, that it works. Machines work when they carry us along a road, or mix our pancakes, or print our papers. Texts work when they generate in our minds a vision of a world that was present in the mind of the writer. If indeed a text or a machine does work (and there are both texts and machines that do not), it does so by virtue of the interactions of its parts.

From this perspective, the task of discourse analyst is very much like that of a mechanic exploring an unfamiliar mechanism. Our first task is to identify the parts of the text and understand why each one is where it is and how it interacts with those around it.

Many scholars have developed systems for analyzing the relations among the entities of a text. Some of these systems differ widely from one another. These differences can be accounted for by noticing that the various methods look at different things about a text. Thus, in principle, they ought to be complementary to one another, and an analyst who understands the relations among them ought to be able to gain a fuller understanding of a text than one who follows only a single methodology, just as a mechanic who understands the fuel, electrical, and air subsystems of an internal combustion engine is in a better position to understand the entire engine than someone who is only an electrician. Unfortunately, published studies of structure in texts tend to follow one or another system almost exclusively.

This paper reviews three approaches to literary structure, shows how they complement one another, and then exercises all three concurrently in analyzing the Book of Galatians, with special emphasis on the function of Galatians 2:15–21. In the balance of the paper, Section 2 describes three different approaches to studying the structure of literary texts and explains why they should be viewed as complementary to one another. Section 3 prepares the laboratory in which we will explore the concurrent use of these three approaches by reviewing the anomalies in the position of 2:15–21 and anticipating the structural conclusions. Sections 4 through 6 illustrate the multidimensional approach by using the three approaches concurrently to derive the macrostructure of Galatians. Section 7 brings the results of this analysis to bear on 2:15–21.

Three Kinds of Structure

This section develops a simple metamodel for structural models and shows how it embraces three structural models that have been applied to the understanding of biblical texts.

A Unified Theory of Discourse Structure

In constructing a framework for discussing discourse structure, two dichotomies are useful. The first is between a text and the (mental) world that it generates in its audience. The second is between entities and the relations among them. The intersection of these two dichotomies provides a useful framework for comparing different structural methodologies.

Texts and Worlds.   One of the first sentences acquired by a person learning another language is, "What does X mean?" where X is some construct in the language being learned. This experience bears witness to one of the most important characteristics of linguistic entities: they point to other entities. Classically, these entities are psychological constructs called *concepts* or *significations*, and they often designate objective things, events, processes, or states in the external world. Thus the medieval schoolmen taught *vox significat [rem] mediantibus conceptibus*, "The word signifies [the thing] by means of mediating concepts." This conceptualist view is an oversimplification from several perspectives (Lyons 1977), but the notion that two kinds of entities in the world outside of the mind (texts and the realia of daily life) are mapped to one another by means of some kind of *deep structure* in the mind is widely accepted.

In some ways these mental structures are shared by a person's perceptual and articulatory systems, so that, for example, the mental structure generated when I see a cow grazing in the field enables me to generate a stream of phonemes or graphemes that describes this state of affairs. While these mental structures mediate between word and thing, they can exist without the corresponding thing (e.g., "unicorn," "the present king of France").

Such mental structures seem to be hierarchical, with some levels deeper than others (Longacre 1976:233–310). At levels near the surface, the components of the structure map fairly directly into entities (words, clauses, episodes) in the text. At deeper levels, the structure broadens out to include other connections that are not explicit in the text but that would occur to people who hear the text. This conclusion emerges from the last thirty years of research on natural language understanding in the Artificial Intelligence community. Efforts to understand a text on the basis of a restricted representation encompassing only the entities and relations named explicitly in the text have repeatedly failed (Winograd and Flores 1987). Text understanding seems to require access to an extremely large body of common-sense knowledge that at first glance lies far beyond the domain of any single text (Guha and Lenat 1990). "All things are connected" (Seatlh 1955).

For example, the text *The cow is grazing in the field* inevitably leads to a mental image that includes a great deal besides a cow and a grassy field. Some details are entailed by the text, though not stated explicitly: there is grass in the field; the cow is outside; there is a barn nearby; there are hoof prints in the field. Other details depend on one's experience, but are certainly present. The cow may be brown, white, or spotted; the field may be flat or rolling; perhaps there are some trees and a pond; the sun is shining, or the sky is overcast. That is, experiencing a text leads us to construct a whole (mental) world. This world is consistent with the text, but usually includes many default concepts that the text does not specify. We may in fact say that a text generates a set of possible worlds that are consistent with it. Similarly, from a speaker's perspective, any of those possible worlds could generate the text. When we translate or paraphrase a text, we seek to produce another text that will generate the same set of possible worlds. The fact that a given text is associated with a set of possible worlds rather than a single world is a refinement that does not bear on the rest of my argument, so I will simplify and speak of *the* world associated with a text.

Entities and Relations.   The mechanistic metaphor of a text developed in the introduction invites us to view a text as a set of entities and to explore the relations among those entities. Because a text is so closely bound to its world, we can gain insight into a text by considering entities in the text itselfs (morphemes, clauses, paragraphs), and also by considering entities in the mental world associated with the text (times, people, places, things). Similarly, some of the relations that we can describe are visible purely at the level of the text, while others require us to enter into the text's world, descending at least part-way into the mental structures underlying the text. We can summarize the options graphically, bearing in mind that the "World" really represents a series of hierarchical levels.

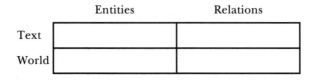

The insight that permits us to unite various structural systems is that the entities and relations with which they deal are drawn from different portions of this diagram. In the balance of this section, we explore this insight by briefly reviewing three well-known structural models.

Symmetric Structure

In the mid-eighteenth century, Bishop Lowth observed certain patterns of symmetry in the arrangements of words in Hebrew verse (Lowth 1753). Ancient text is essentially aural (Parunak 1983) and thus one-dimensional, so the only patterns of symmetry that are available are mirror symmetry (leading to chiastic patterns, such as ABC-CBA or ABCBA) and translation symmetry (leading to alternation, such as ABC-ABC). Lowth's insights were expanded to larger sections of discourse by Jebb (1820), Boys (1824), Forbes (1854), and lately, stimulated by Lund (1942), many others. For references, see Parunak (1978, 1981b, 1982, 1983). It is now widely recognized that ancient literature commonly uses symmetric patterns of repetition, sometimes in a rather baroque fashion. The linguistic functions of these patterns have been compared (Parunak 1981b) to the use of modern typographic devices such as white space, different font sizes, and placement of blocks of material, and include delineation of discourse units, various kinds of prominence (Callow 1974:52), and summary.

The entities with which this approach is concerned are sometimes in the text (repetition of specific words or even graphemes), and sometimes in the higher levels of the text's world (for example, the common referent of a pronoun in one place and a proper name elsewhere). The distinctive feature of symmetric structure is that the relations among these entities are described purely at the surface level, in terms of symmetries in the sequencing of the elements. In terms of our metamodel, symmetric structure looks like this:

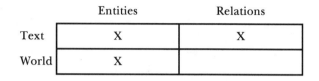

	Entities	Relations
Text	X	X
World	X	

The symmetries observed in these studies can be continuous, as in chiasm, alternation, and inclusio (a rudimentary chiasm in which corresponding elements mark the extremes of a block of material). The textual aspects of what biblical scholars call *form criticism* can be considered a species of symmetric structure if we allow the notion of *discontinuous* symmetry. That is, a literary form (say, a letter form) is recognizable as a structural unit because the same series of elements (salutation, body, closing) recurs in the same order in different (therefore discontinuous) texts. Particular in continuous symmetry, a series of elements that is repeated (for example, ABC in the chiasm ABC-CBA or the alternation ABC-ABC) is called a *panel*.

A useful tool in discovering and studying symmetric structure is the linguistic density plot (Parunak 1979, 1981a, 1984), for example, Plot 1. Such a plot depicts the distribution of occurrences of a linguistic phenomenon (in this case, first person singular verbs and pronouns) throughout a text (here, Galatians). Each dot on the plot represents an occurrence of the phenomenon under study. The horizontal location of a point shows its location in the book. The X-axis is linear in words, and the vertical bars show where successive chapters begin. The vertical position of a point shows how close it is to the points on either side. If a phenomenon is repeated at three successive words, the central occurrence is plotted at the top of the chart. Less densely spaced occurrences appear lower. Thus peaks on the chart represent areas in which the phenomenon is concentrated, and valleys represent areas where it is less common. The dashed line across the plot shows where all the dots would be plotted if occurrences were evenly distributed throughout the book.

Such a plot permits us to see at a glance how a given phenomenon is distributed. For example, Plot 1 immediately calls our attention to five concentrations of first person singular verbs and pronouns: a broad group that begins in the middle of chapter 1 and tapers off through chapter 2; a very narrow but concentrated group at the end of chapter 2; and less impressive groups in the middle of chapter 4,

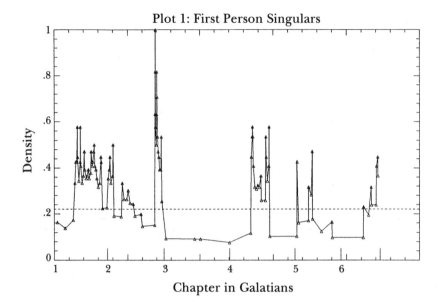

Plot 1: First Person Singulars

the first half of chapter 5, and toward the end of chapter 6. Such distributions are clearly important data in understanding the surface structure of a text, and our analysis of Galatians will take into account this and other distributions.

Studies of continuous symmetry in Galatians are available in Bligh (1966), Jeremias (1958), and Ellis (1982). Studies that compare the sequence of elements in Galatians with other texts (discontinuous symmetry) include Betz (1979), who analyzes Galatians as an apologetic letter, and Hall (1987), who prefers the pattern of a deliberative speech.

Semantic Structure

Another approach to the structure of biblical texts takes its inspiration from the structuralist work of scholars like C. Levi-Straus, V. J. Propp, and A. J. Greimas. Its proponents in biblical studies include Patte (1976), Polzin (1977), and E. Güttgemanns (Petersen 1976). Both the elements and the relations of interest to this community reside rather deeply in the world of the text, not in the text itself. In terms of our metamodel,

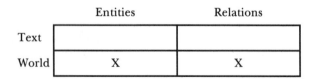

	Entities	Relations
Text		
World	X	X

Because it is the text's world that provides the semantics for the text, and because this approach focuses so strongly on the text's world, I designate it the study of *semantic structure*. This use of the term should be distinguished from that of Beekman (*et al.* 1981), which is concerned more with what I call *syntactic structure*.

For example, Greimas (1966:172–191) observes that many texts follow an *actantial schema* in which a sender seeks to convey an object to a receiver. The protagonist of this transfer is the subject, aided or opposed by various helpers and opponents. Graphically,

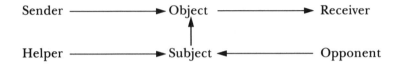

Such a structure is more abstract than the plot of a narrative. It identifies the *actants* (characters and prominent props) and defines the classes of interaction among them, but does not articulate the relative prominence of the respective actants, or the sequence and development of their interactions. In fact, one can imagine a single actantial schema that gives rise to several very different narratives. Such a schema really defines the world of the text more than it does the text itself.

I am not aware of previous studies of Galatians from the perspective of semantic structure. For examples at the level of whole Bible books, see Polzin (1977:54–125) on Job, or Collins (1987) on Psalms. In fact, Galatians does follow Greimas' actantial schema. God seeks to convey salvation to the Galatians, supported by the subject, the gospel. Paul is the helper of this gospel, but there are also opponents, the false teachers, who seek to corrupt it and so blunt its effectiveness as a vehicle of salvation:

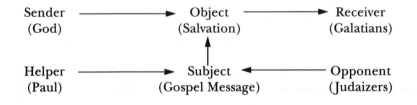

Syntactic Structure

For most people, the terms *discourse analysis* and *text linguistics* denote the analysis of how clauses (which are defined to be minimal paragraphs) join into larger paragraphs, these paragraphs in turn form still larger ones, and so on hierarchically until the entire text has been accounted for as a single paragraph. This approach has been extensively developed and demonstrated by members of the Summer Institute of Linguistics as a mechanism for interpreting existing texts (Longacre 1976, 1980, 1989; Grimes 1975; Beekman and Callow 1974; Beekman et al. 1981), and recently adopted in the computer science community in an effort to enable computers to generate coherent text (Mann and Thompson 1987). The entities manipulated by this approach are either textual elements such as explicit paragraphs (including clauses), or entities in the text's world that can be mapped rather closely to textual paragraphs (for example, a proposition that is realized in the text as a rhetorical question). The relations among paragraphs are logical, and thus belong to the text's world.

For example, the sequence paragraph consists of a series of sub-paragraphs that follow one another in time and is ubiquitous in narrative (Longacre 1980, 1989). The notion of the passage of time *in the text's world* (as opposed to the time taken in reciting the text) is central to the definition and recognition of this paragraph type. The same textual markers that accompany a sequence paragraph can be used in other paragraph types as well. For example, *waw* consecutive, commonly regarded as a hallmark of Hebrew sequential paragraphs, can also mark logical sequence without temporal implications (Gen. 45:6–7), epexegesis (2 Sam. 14:5), or a pluperfect rather than sequential temporal situation (1 Kings 13:12) (Waltke and O'Connor 1990:ch. 33). The analysis as a sequential paragraph thus appeals to relations in the text's world. I describe this approach as *syntactic* because syntax in general deals with meaning-based relations among surface-level elements. In terms of our metamodel,

	Entities	Relations
Text	X	
World	X	X

Rogers (1989) offers a thorough syntactic analysis of Galatians which, because it follows Beekman (1981), is called a *semantic* structure analysis, not to be confused with what I term *semantic structure.* One aspect of syntactic structure in Galatians, the functional role of phase order, is surveyed in Levinsohn (1989). In my syntactic comments, I will use the terminology of Longacre (1980).

Summary on Structure

This brief survey of structural approaches illustrates how they differ in their approach to the interacting dichotomies of ⟨text, world⟩ and ⟨entity, relation⟩. None of them covers the entire field. Furthermore, no two of them together take into account all of the pairwise relations among the cells in the metamodel. For instance, though symmetric and semantic structure together occupy all four cells of the model, only the syntactic approach addresses the critical question of how relations in the text's world are encoded in the text itself.

Because of these differences, the three methods yield qualitatively different insights. Semantic structure, the most remote of the three from the text itself, highlights relations and developments that are possible within the text's world, including some that may not be exploited by the text. Syntactic structure shows not only what relations are possible, but also just how the text develops them. Symmetric structure is most useful for identifying the hierarchical ranking of high-level structural divisions and identifying differences of prominence between successive sections of text.

Syntactic and symmetric structure are particularly synergistic. Because syntactic features are identified between contiguous units of text, they often show that a discourse division falls at a particular location in the text, but are less clear about the rank of that division relative to others. Figuratively, they yield a model of text like a string of pearls, isolating individual pearls clearly but leaving some question about how those pearls group into larger substrings and those substrings into still larger ones. Symmetric relations can span units that are not contiguous, and thus can show (to return to the figure) that the third through the eighth pearls belong together and form a distinct unit with respect to those before and after. For example, though I prepared this analysis of Galatians before I learned of Rogers (1989), we use similar syntactic data, and the locations of the divisions that I identify correspond in the main with hers, at least to her subpart constituent level. However, I draw on insights into the symmetric structure of the text that she does not, and as a result I propose a very different hierarchical organization of these divisions from hers.

The Ambiguity of 2:15–21

This section turns from theory to application. I describe some anomalies in Galatians 2:15–21 that make its function an interesting quarry in our hunt. Then, to provide some context for later sections,

I sketch out the overall structure of Galatians that they will justify, and finally I anticipate how this structure elucidates the role of the problematic paragraph.

Questions about 2:15–21

The raw data of 2:15–21 that bear on its function in the book seem to be straightforward.

1. The section is followed in 3:1 by a vocative to the readers, without any logical connective. Rogers (1984) and Larson (1991) argue that vocatives are not necessarily boundary markers, but in fact, with one exception, vocatives elsewhere in Galatians mark a significant paragraph break (1:11; 3:15; 4:12, 19; 5:11; 6:1, 18). The exception is 4:31, which is integrated with its preceding context by the strong inferential particle *ara* "therefore."

2. The preceding context relates a conversation between Paul and Peter. Paul's direct discourse to Peter begins in 2:14, in the second person singular. Until we reach the vocative of 3:1 (accompanied with second person plurals), there is no reason to think that the direct discourse is over. The verbs and pronouns do shift to first person plural in 2:15–17, but this shift is easily understood as Paul's effort to place himself in Peter's position as a Jew facing the question of Gentiles, rather than polarizing the discussion. In 2:18–21, the verbs and pronouns shift to first person singular, but very plausibly in order to present Peter with Paul's personal experience.

3. The subject matter of 2:15–21 is strongly anticipatory of chapters 3–6 and has little if anything to do with the broad theme of the first two chapters, which seems to be Paul's independence of human teachers.

These data lead us in two different directions. On the one hand, the first two items encourage us to see the paragraph as the continuation of Paul's remarks to Peter, an analysis that is endorsed by Brown (ND:88), Lightfoot (ND:113–114), and Hendriksen (1968). On the other hand, the third item is so strong that Betz (1979:114–115), Bruce (1982:136), and Burton (1921:117), with varying degrees of certitude, view the actual quotation of Paul's words as ending in 2:14, and take 2:15–21 as an introduction to the latter half of the book. Brown (ND:88) has an extensive summary of older commentaries that are likewise divided.

How far does the discourse with Peter extend—only to 2:14, or through 2:21, or somewhere in between? Syntactically, is the paragraph deeply embedded in the text of a quote paragraph that is itself part of the last build up of an extended sequence paragraph, or is it a very high-level summary that is amplified in the latter half of the book? If it is so deeply embedded, why do its themes fit the second half so well? If it is intended as an introductory summary to the second half, why are the textual marks of division much stronger at its end than at its beginning?

Previewing the Structure of Galatians

In our effort to understand 2:15–21, the bulk of this paper will develop the overall structure of Galatians. This development will be easier to follow if I anticipate its results. The structure of Galatians is broadly chiastic. The outer layer consists of the epistolary hardware, the formal salutation (1:1–5) and closing greeting (6:11,18), required by the Greek letter form. The next layer (1:6–10; 6:12–17) sets forth the circumstances that lead to the letter. These two paragraphs realize the same underlying semantic structure, contrasting the true gospel with counterfeits.

Setting aside 2:15–21 for the moment, 1:11–6:10 consists of four paragraphs arranged chiastically. The first two (1:11; 1:12) are extremely short, only one verse each, and summarize the material developed in the latter two (1:13–2:14; 3:1–6:10). The outer two paragraphs of this structure argue for the substance of the message that Paul preaches, while the inner two insist on the independence of the messenger, Paul, from human influence.

We can diagram these correspondences:

Epistolary hardware	1:1–5	6:11,18
Existential setting	1:6–10	6:12–17
Substance of the Message	1:11	3:1–6:10
Independence of the Messenger	1:12	1:13–2:14

Linearizing this structure, we can summarize Galatians thus: "Paul, finding the Galatians confronted with a choice between the true gospel and various counterfeits [Existential Setting], writes to them [Epistolary Hardware] to defend the content of his message [Substance] and its divine origin [Independence]."

The bulk of the epistle is devoted to the two topics at the center of the chiasm, the substance of the message and the independence of the messenger. Arguably, these are the epistle's main points, the two things that Paul most wants his readers to carry away. Significantly, the paragraph that has attracted our attention (2:15–21) lies just at the transition between the expositions of these two major themes. In this position, it has a claim to being the most significant transition in the entire book.

LINGUISTICS AND NEW TESTAMENT INTERPRETATION

2:15–21 as a Transition

The transitional nature of 2:15–21 sheds considerable light on its syntactic ambivalence. Characteristically, transitions in biblical literature are ambivalent in their connections with the units that they integrate (Parunak 1982). They engage the reader in the new material before the old has been fully left behind. It is completely in keeping with this pattern that Paul's words to Peter at the end of one major section should anticipate the burden of the next section. Such a scheme, while awkward to describe syntactically, is extremely effective pragmatically. Our subsequent analysis of the paragraph will show in more detail just how it moves readers from Paul's first major point to his second, and so maintains the integrity of the argument.

To confirm our hypothesis about the overall structure of the epistle and the function of 2:15–21, the following sections expound the structure of the various components of the book. In doing so, they draw on all three of the varieties of structural analysis that I have reviewed, demonstrating how these techniques can reinforce and supplement one another.

Epistolary Hardware, 1:1–5; 6:11,18

A literary form (such as an epistle) is marked by the occurrence of a series of sections in a specific order in the text. This ordering is a surface-level phenomenon and is thus an example of (discontinuous) symmetric structure.

Galatians has the same components as other letters in the Pauline corpus: a tripartite salutation (sender, addressee, and word of greeting), either a doxology or a prayer beginning with thanksgiving (only Ephesians has both), a body, and a closing. The doxology is unremarkable, as is the close, except that 6:11, which seems to be part of it, is uncharacteristically separated from the final benediction (6:18) by a substantive paragraph. The salutation, though, deserves special comment.

Paul's salutations range from 93 words (Rom.) to 19 (1 Thess.). Galatians has the second longest (66), followed closely by Titus (65). The addressee section of Galatians is as short as any (4 words, matched only by 2 Tim.), so the extra length is devoted to the description of the sender (26) and the greeting (36).

The only sender sections longer than Galatians are Romans (72 words) and Titus (47). Both Romans and Titus devote this space to expounding the content of the gospel. When we consider the basic thrust of these epistles, this emphasis is in order. Romans is a systematic exposition of the gospel, and Titus (like Galatians) deals with the problem of false teachers.

The salutation of Galatians also contains a summary of the gospel, but in the greeting section, not the description of the sender. In fact, the greeting section of Galatians (1:3–4) is three times as long as any other Pauline greeting. No other greeting section, not even in Romans or Titus, goes beyond the highly stylized "Grace unto you, and peace, from God our Father, and from the Lord Jesus Christ," and some abbreviate even that. In Galatians alone, Paul not only proclaims grace and peace, but describes its genesis in the work of the Lord Jesus, "who gave himself for our sins, that he might deliver us from this present evil world, according to the will of God, even our Father."

The expanded sender section of the Galatians salutation describes, not the gospel, but the apostle Paul. The sender sections of the various epistles contain a number of stylized epithets for Paul ("servant," "apostle," "called one") or a list of his associates. Of these, Galatians mentions only "apostle." Commonly, his apostleship is traced to "the will of God," Galatians expands this concept considerably: he is "an apostle, not of men, neither by man, but by Jesus Christ, and God the Father, who raised him from the dead."

The two prominent themes in the salutation are two of the six main actants highlighted by the actantial analysis proposed earlier: Paul the *helper* (to whose credentials the expanded sender section is devoted), and the gospel message *subject* (summarized in the expanded greetings section). Thus semantic analysis enables us to articulate the various concepts that are in view, and (at least in the salutation) symmetric analysis permits us to determine the relative emphasis to identify those that are thematically prominent.

Existential Setting, 1:6–10; 6:12–17

Once we peel off the epistolary hardware, the body of the letter begins and ends with a description of the existential circumstances that led Paul to write it. The overall structure that I have suggested for Galatians ties these two paragraphs closely together as corresponding members of a chiasm. This correspondence can be seen both semantically and symmetrically, and a syntactic view provides a further integrating insight.

Semantic Perspective

Every verse in these paragraphs realizes some combination of four semantic oppositions. Though these oppositions appear elsewhere in the book, nowhere else is the complete system displayed in as short a span as in these paragraphs. These four oppositions, with verses illustrating them, are:

- the true gospel vs. the false gospel, 1:8,9;
- Paul vs. other teachers, 6:13,14;
- the physical vs. the spiritual plane, 1:10 (pleasing men vs. God);
- the possibility of incurring favor vs. disfavor: 6:12,13 (the false teachers avoid persecution and seek to boast in the Galatians); 6:14,17 (Paul's glory and persecution).

Aristotle's logical square (On Interpretation 10) is a useful tool for visualizing two binary oppositions. For example, if we combine the opposition "true vs. false gospel" with "Paul vs. other teachers," we obtain the figure below, where only the vertices occupied by **X** are occupied in the world of Galatians.

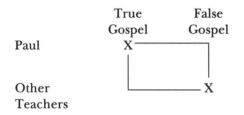

Just as two oppositions define a square, three oppositions define a cube, with eight vertices that can be occupied. Three vertices are occupied in the cube formed by combining "Paul vs. others," "physical vs. spiritual," and "favor vs. disfavor": "Paul, physical, disfavor" (6:17, Paul is persecuted physically), "Paul, spiritual, favor" (1:10, Paul seeks to please God), and "others, physical, favor" (6:12,13, the Judaizers are avoiding persecution). (Bringing 1:8,9 into the picture makes it a fair bet that we should also mark "others, spiritual, disfavor" as occupied as well, but this can only be shown by considering the contrast between the true and false gospels as well.) Physical analogs fail us with four or more oppositions, but mathematically we can define hypercubes of any dimensionality, and our four oppositions yield a four-dimensional hypercube, with a total of sixteen vertices, of which only four are occupied (since the "Paul vs. other" opposition is completely correlated with the "true gospel vs. false gospel" opposition).

Every verse in these two paragraphs comments on some aspect of this four-way opposition:

- 1:6, The Galatians must choose between the true and the false gospel.
- 1:7, Other teachers promote the false gospel.
- 1:8,9, The false gospel differs from the true, and yields spiritual disfavor.
- 1:10, Paul chooses spiritual rather than physical favor.

- 6:12, Others promote a false gospel to avoid physical disfavor.
- 6:13, Others promote a false gospel to obtain physical favor.
- 6:14, Paul rejects physical favor.
- 6:15,16, The true gospel leads to spiritual favor.
- 6:17, Paul has experienced physical disfavor.

Semantically, these two paragraphs thus define a world in which Paul, teaching the true gospel, expects God's blessing but suffers physical persecution, while other teachers, promoting a bogus gospel, avoid persecution but incur God's wrath. Between these two alternatives the Galatians are hesitating. The rest of the epistle exploits this semantic framework, but is not necessary to establish it. If we had nothing more than the 11 verses in 1:6–10 and 6:12–17, we could define both the hypercube and its occupied vertices. Furthermore, with the exception of three paragraphs at structurally critical junctures in 3:1–6:10, no other portion of the epistle exhibits the density of reference to these oppositions that we observe in 1:6–10 and 6:12–17.

Symmetric Perspective

In addition to the semantic evidence relating these two paragraphs, symmetric considerations (both continuous and discontinuous) show that they are closely related.

The possibility of discontinuous symmetry invites us to ask whether other Pauline letters include statements of the letter's existential setting, and if so, where these statements occur in the overall letter.

Paul's letters frequently include descriptions of the occasion for writing:

Romans 1:8–15; 15:14–33	Preparation for a personal visit to Rome
1 Corinthians 1:10,11	News about dissensions in the church
Philippians 4:10–20	Receipt of a material gift from the church
Titus 1:4,5	Instructions for helping the church in Crete
Philemon 21–22	Preparation for a personal visit

Romans shows that the setting can be discussed both at the beginning and at the end. The epistolary hardware of Romans includes 1:1–7 and chapter 16. The second and penultimate paragraphs describe Paul's frequent desire to see the Romans (1:13; 15:23), his proposed trip to Rome (1:10, 15; 16:23, 29), and his fruit among other gentiles (1:13; 16:28). Arguably, Philippians is another example of this construction. The last paragraph before the closing, 4:10–20, thanks the Philippians for their material gift to Paul, described with the verb κοινωνέω "to share" (4:15) or a compound of this verb (4:14), while the opening paragraph acknowledges their κοινωνία "fellowship" in the gospel (1:5). The epistle is widely held to be in response to this gift, and if the opening paragraph does indeed allude to it, then Philippians, like Romans and Galatians, is bracketed by paragraphs describing its existential circumstances. Thus discontinuous symmetry suggests that it is not uncommon for an epistle to begin or end (or both) with references to its circumstances, reinforcing our analysis of such a construction in Galatians.

From the standpoint of continuous symmetry, the material in Galatians 1:6–10 and 6:12–17 is ordered similarly. Each paragraph begins with discussion of the false teachers and their impact on the Galatians (1:6–7; 6:12–13), and ends with Paul's claim to seek spiritual favor, even at the expense of physical disfavor (1:10; 6:14–17). The symmetric perspective thus confirms the close correspondence between the paragraphs suggested by their semantic content.

Syntactic Perspective

In discussing the similar ordering of material in the setting paragraphs, I passed over the function of 1:8–9, in which Paul anathematizes anyone who preaches any other gospel. These verses have no clear parallel in the second setting paragraph and do not fall into either of the sections that do correspond between the two paragraphs. Yet their repetition of the same sentence shows that they are clearly in focus. This focal position may actually explain why they are not repeated at the end of the book: a broken symmetry is a common prominence mechanism (Parunak 1981b), and one that we will later observe in two other contexts in Galatians.

A syntactic analysis clarifies the function of these two verses. They present the hearer with a choice between the true gospel and any other, and curse those who pursue alternatives, implying a blessing on those who accept the true gospel. These two verses present this choice as abstract. The verses on either side offer specific instances: the other teachers who are offering a false gospel, and Paul who offers the true one. Thus the entire paragraph is a chiastic exemplification paragraph, with 1:8–9 as the text and 1:6–7, 10 as two examples. Chiastic paragraphs, with one tagmeme flanked by replications of another, are common in biblical literature (Andersen 1974:119–140).

Message and Messenger, 1:11–6:10

Jeremias (1958) suggests that Galatians 1:11–12 sets forth a twofold theme that the main body of the book expounds: the gospel is not κατὰ ἄνθρωπον (1:11) "according to man," but rather "according to the Scripture" (3:1–6:10); and Paul did not receive it παρὰ ἀνθρώ-πον (1:12) "from man," but directly from the Lord (1:13–2:21). Though Jeremias does not mention it, his thesis is supported by the emphasis we have already seen in the salutation on the credentials of the messenger (corresponding to 1:12 and 1:13–2:21) and the content of the message (corresponding to 1:11 and 3:1–6:10).

I will further develop his thesis in two steps. First, I show that the device of introductory chiastic summary is common in biblical literature. Second, I establish the internal structural integrity and subject matter of 1:13–2:14 and 3:1–6:10, respectively, leaving aside for the moment the question of 2:15–21. If these are integral blocks of material; if the themes to which they address themselves are the very themes summarized in 1:11–12; and if chiastic summary is elsewhere attested as an introductory device, then we may reasonably conclude that the same device is being applied here as well.

The Device of Introductory Chiastic Summary

Paul commonly introduces large blocks of material with one or two verses that summarize his main themes, often in inverse order. In this section I illustrate this device with two examples, without any claim to being exhaustive.

First Corinthians 15:35. First Corinthians 15 has three major parts: 1–11, 12–34, and 35–58. The first section is marked as a unit by its own internal symmetries. The second and third form an alternation, with three correspondences between them. They both begin by citing an error concerning the resurrection, in the form of a question posed by a hypothetical hearer (vv. 12, 35). Then they give an answer to the error (vv. 13–32, 36–57) and close with an exhortation to the Corinthians (vv. 33–34, 58).

Purely surface characteristics prompt us to divide the second answer (vv. 36–57) into two parts. Verses 50–57 use the first and second person throughout, while verses 36–49 use the third person (with the exception of a second person singular in verse 36, addressing the answer to the supposed questioner of verse 35, and a first person plural in verse 49, which serves as a transition into the second part). Semantically, this division makes sense. Verses 36–49 deal with the nature of the resurrection body, comparing it with grain and the heavenly bodies, while verses 50–57 deal with the mechanism by which the natural body is transformed into the resurrection body at the return of Christ.

Jeremias (1958) observes that these two divisions correspond in inverse order to the two questions of 35. The first question, "How are the dead raised?", is answered in verses 50–57, while the second, "With what body do they come?", corresponds to verses 36–49.

Ephesians 1:18–19. At the beginning of Ephesians, Paul prays that his readers might receive divine help in understanding three subjects: the hope of God's calling, the riches of the glory of God's inheritance in the saints, and the greatness of God's power toward believers (1:18–19). The rest of the epistle discusses these three subjects, in inverse order.

The third subject is the power that God can display in the believer, a theme expounded in 1:20–2:10. There we learn first that Christ's resurrection and ascension manifest the power of God (1:20–23), then that the believer is made alive, raised up, and seated in heavenly places, all with (συν-) Christ.

The second subject is God's inheritance in, or consisting of, the saints. In the Old Testament, God's inheritance is Israel (Ps. 78:71; Isa. 19:25). Now, Paul emphasizes, Jew and Gentile merge in a new body, the church, which is discussed in detail in 2:11–3:20.

Corresponding to the "hope of his calling" in 1:18 is the "hope of your calling" in 4:4. The two phrases have the same reference, the subjective genitive of the first being replaced by an objective genitive in the second. We might paraphrase both phrase as, "the hope to which God has called you." The context in 4:4 associates this hope with the one body in which believers function, while the calling in 4:1 is closely tied with the conduct expected of a new creature in Christ. The following verses (4:11–16) show how the conduct of believers in the church leads to Christlikeness, the hope to which believers are called, and the practical injunctions in chapters 4–6 serve as guides to this end.

Thus Ephesians 1:18–19 summarizes three points that are developed and expounded, in inverse order, throughout the rest of the book.

The examples of 1 Corinthians 15:35–57 and the Book of Ephesians show that it would not be surprising to find introductory chiastic summary elsewhere in Paul's writings. To conclude that the device governs Galatians 1:11–6:10, we must now show that the summary (1:11–12) is followed by blocks of material that correspond with the elements of the summary and that have their own structural integrity.

The Structural Integrity of 1:13–2:14

Symmetric and syntactic analyses of 1:13–2:14 reinforce one another and confirm the integrity of the block, which is semantically consistent with 1:12.

Syntactically, the section is a sequence paragraph with a setting (1:13–14) and five build ups (1:15–17; 1:18–20; 1:21–24; 2:1–10; and

2:11–14 [or further, depending on the disposition of 2:15–21]), each beginning with a temporal particle. The table below summarizes several observations about these build ups.

Reference	Particle	Location	Length (Words)
1:15–17	ὅτε	Arabia	54
1:18–20	ἔπειτα	Jerusalem	39
1:21–24	ἔπειτα	Syria, Cilicia	44
2:1–10	ἔπειτα	Jerusalem	177
2:11–14 (-21)	ὅτε	Antioch	79 (219)

The divisions among the build ups are confirmed symmetrically by an alternation between action out of Jerusalem and in Jerusalem. The completeness of the sequence is suggested by the chiastic use of ὅτε for the first and last of the build ups, reserving ἔπειτα for those in the center. The final build up is the climax of the entire sequence: the increased length of the last two build ups relative to the first three (and in particular of the last, if it includes 2:15–21) reflects the increased attention to detail and crowding of action common in the vicinity of the peak of a narrative (Longacre 1989:34), and the last build up is the only one including reported speech, another index of climax (Longacre 1980:9).

The broad peak of first person verbs and pronouns visible on Plot 1 coincides with this section and further reflects its internal coherence. (The extremely strong peak at the end of chapter 2 is 2:18–21, part of the ambiguous section.) The section is marked not only by a high concentration of first person narrative, but also by an almost complete lack of second person plural verbs and pronouns, as seen in Plot 2. The only occurrences are the rhetorical interjections in 1:13,20; 2:5. It is not inevitable that first singular and second plural forms should be in complementary distribution, for both Plots 1 and 2 have peaks in the same general regions in the middle of chapters 4 and 5. Rather, the complementary distribution is characteristic of Paul's narrative genre and a further mark of the internal integrity of 1:13–2:14 and its distinction from its environment on either side.

The integrity of 1:13–2:14 seems clearly established. How does it correspond with 1:12? The γάρ "for" in 1:13 suggests that verse 13 (at least) furnishes a reason for the statement in verse 12 that Paul

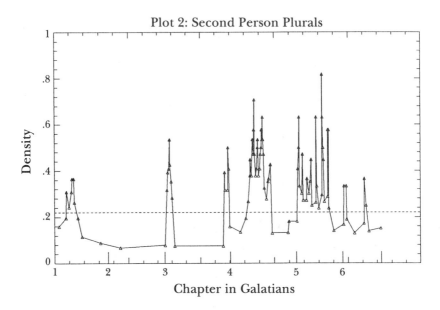

Plot 2: Second Person Plurals

received his gospel by direct revelation rather than through human tradition. This role is not filled adequately by 1:13–14, which do not discuss either means of learning the gospel, but only why one might not expect Paul to be sympathetic to it at all. Those verses simply establish the setting for the sequence of events that extends through chapter 2. As many commentators have noted, each episode in that sequence shares the common semantic thread of establishing Paul's independence of those who were in Christ before him. Thus it is all of 1:13–2:14 that forms the reason for 1:12, and Jeremias' suggestion that 1:12 anticipates the balance of chapters 1 and 2 seems well confirmed.

The Structural Integrity of 3:1–6:10

The proposed correspondent to 1:11 is both longer and more complex than that to 1:12. To exhibit its integrity, I shall first offer some general observations about the entire section, then discuss each of its parts, and finally display its relation with 1:11.

Overview. The distribution of person markers in this section suggests that from a symmetric perspective it is an alternation of three panels.

Plots 1 and 2 show that 3:1–6:10 is punctuated by two peaks of first person singular constructions, in 4:11–21 and 5:2–12, that coincide with concentrations of second person plural constructions. The genre here is not first person narrative, but a highly personal entreaty between Paul and the Galatians. Semantically, these sections resume the set of oppositions that characterize the existential setting sections at the beginning and end of the epistle. The Galatians are hesitating between the true gospel and a false one (4:9; 5:4). They are abandoning their love for Paul (4:14,15) in favor of someone else (4:17; 5:7,10,12) and in the process risk spiritual disfavor (4:17; 5:2), though faithfulness to the truth will bring physical disfavor (5:11). Even the "I-you" tone of entreaty reflects the setting paragraphs, each of which begins with a "you" section describing the Galatians' tenuous position, and ends with an "I" section reminding them of Paul's faithfulness to the gospel, even under persecution.

Both the personal entreaty and the oppositions of the setting paragraphs are absent elsewhere in 3:1–6:10, except for 3:1–5. Though the latter paragraph has only one first person reference, it does have a concentration of second person plurals and repeats themes from the setting paragraphs: the contrast between true and false gospels (3:1,2), the physical disfavor and spiritual favor associated with the truth (3:4,5), and the false teachers who have promulgated the error (3:1). Thus we tentatively associate this section with 4:11–21 and 5:2–12. (The second person plural peak in 3:26–29 is different, since it shows neither concurrent first person singulars nor the oppositions of the setting paragraphs.)

Since first person singular constructions (referring to Paul) and second person plural constructions (referring to the Galatians) seem to be such strong structural indices, it is interesting to consider the distribution of first person plurals and second person singulars in Plots 3 and 4.

Plot 3 shows twenty-four first person plural constructions in 3:1–6:10. Of these, only two fall in the entreaty sections that open each panel, and then only in the final entreaty section (5:5). In the entreaty sections Paul distinguishes himself from his readers with an "I-you" contrast, but then in each case takes his place at his readers' sides with "we." Twice he makes this move clearly and without exception. The third time the polarization of the entreaty is softened with "we," perhaps in an effort to emphasize harmony over confrontation as his argument concludes.

Plot 4 shows the second person singular constructions. Most of those (12 of 15) occur in 3:1–6:10, and of these 12, 9 are embedded in quotations from the Old Testament, which occur only in 3:1–6:10 and are only in the non-entreaty sections.

Thus the distribution of all four classes of person markers, together with the semantic oppositions observed in the setting paragraphs, suggests that the macrostructure of 3:1–6:10 is an alternation of three panels, AB-AB-AB. Each panel begins with a personal *entreaty* in which Paul confronts the Galatians ("I-you") with the concerns of the existential

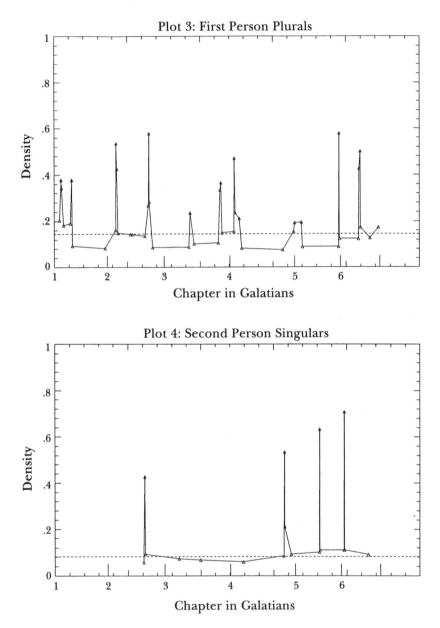

Plot 3: First Person Plurals

Chapter in Galatians

Plot 4: Second Person Singulars

Chapter in Galatians

setting paragraphs, and continues with a less confrontational ("we") *didactic* section that leans heavily on expositions of Old Testament texts.

Each didactic section develops a significant contrast between two concepts. The contrast is different in each panel: works vs. faith in 3:1–4:7, bondage vs. freedom in 4:8–5:1, and flesh vs. spirit in 5:2–

6:10. The concentration of these themes in these particular sections of the book is clear from density plots that cannot be presented here for reasons of space. In each case the contrast helps articulate the difference between the true and false gospels. Each section cites the Old Testament, and in fact these sections are the only places in the epistle where the Old Testament is cited.

Turn from Works to Faith, 3:1–4:7. Though 3:1–5 lacks the coincidence of first and second person constructions that mark the openings of the other two panels, its nature as personal entreaty is seen in the concentration of rhetorical questions and Paul's evident desire to correct his readers' folly (vv. 1,3).

The governing contrast in this section is between faith in God's promise and the works of the law, reflected in the concentration here of νόμος "law," πίστις "faith," πιστεύω "to believe," ἐπαγγελία "promise," and ἐπαγγέλλομαι "to promise." (Terms for "law" and "faith" in fact become dense just at the end of chapter 2, explaining why some expositors see 2:15–21 as an introduction to what follows rather than a continuation of 2:11–14.) The opening entreaty associates the false gospel that is tempting the Galatians with the works of the law, an association that becomes explicit in the closing setting paragraph (6:12,13). The false teachers are preaching adherence to the law as the means of salvation. In this section, Paul sets this approach in contrast with salvation by faith in the promise of God and shows that only the latter is in keeping with the teaching of Scripture.

Though all three didactic sections cite the Old Testament, this section draws on the widest variety of texts. The catena of citations in 3:6–14 references no fewer than six different texts, while 3:16 cites a phrase from yet another. Furthermore, the historical argument in 3:15–22 relies implicitly on the pentateuchal history.

Turn from Bondage to Freedom, 4:8–5:1. The general location of the personal appeal that begins the second panel of 3:1–6:10 is not precisely marked, a circumstance that does not compromise our analysis but rather reflects the ambiguity that we have already associated with transitional material. Strong parallels between 4:8–9a with earlier material tempt us to include these verses in the first panel, but the shift from second person singular in 4:7 to plural at 4:8 suggests that we have entered the entreaty section of the second panel. Syntactically, it is easiest to divide the material between 4:7 and 4:8, so I prefer to see the primary break there and recognize the parallels between the opening clauses and the previous paragraph as a linked keyword transition (Parunak 1982).

The dominant contrast in this panel is no longer between works and faith, but between bondage and freedom, as is evident in the concentration of nominal cognates of δουλόω and παιδίσκω "to serve," ἐλευθερία "freedom," ἐλευθερόω "to free," and ἐλευθερός "free" (adjective). The first panel described the means by which people access salvation; this one describes the state in which they find themselves as a result of exercising those means.

As does the first panel, the second both cites and alludes to the Old Testament. Paul cites Isaiah 54:1 in 4:27 and Genesis 21:10 in 4:30, and the entire didactic section is an allegorical exposition based on Genesis 16 and 21.

Turn from Flesh to Spirit, 5:2–6:10. The appeal in the third panel extends from 5:2 through 5:12, where the vocative in the next verse suggests a break. The contrast in the didactic section is now between flesh and Spirit, a theme that was adumbrated in the appeal of the first panel and the allegory of the second, but that is clearly concentrated here. The first panel shows that faith, not works, is the means by which people access God's promise of salvation. The second shows that the result of this salvation is a state of freedom, not bondage. Now Paul describes the resource by which believers are to live in this state of freedom: not the efforts of the flesh, but the power of the Holy Spirit.

The emphasis on the Old Testament is weakest in this panel, but not absent. In 5:14, Paul cites Leviticus 19:18 to show that love, the head of the fruit of the Spirit (5:22), is required by the law, and in fact asserts that this single requirement sums up all that the law demands.

The Correspondence between 1:11 and 3:1–6:10. We can thus establish in 3:1–6:10 an alternation between personal entreaties and didactic expositions. The similarities among the entreaties (dense allusions to the oppositions of the setting paragraphs; second person plural and usually first person singular constructions) and among the didactic sections (extensive Old Testament allusions and citations; semantic focus on contrasts characterizing the difference between the true gospel and the false one) establish the integrity of this construction, which does not begin earlier than 3:1 or extend beyond 6:10. The emphasis on the Old Testament is particularly impressive, since nowhere else in the epistle does Paul cite it. Thus we can legitimately describe this section as characterizing Paul's gospel and defending that characterization from the Scripture. Jeremias' intuition is correct: 3:1–6:10 shows that the true gospel, the one advocated by Paul is, "according to the Scripture," not κατὰ ἄνθρωπον "according to man," and thus corresponds to 1:11.

Because of the physical separation between 1:11 and 3:1, we have no particle to guide us in assessing the relation between the summary and the amplification. The relation between 1:12 and 1:13–2:14 is that of reason, a relation that certainly makes sense here as well. The Galatians should believe that Paul's gospel is not from man (1:12) because his history shows that he could not have received it through human tradition (1:13–2:14). They should believe that it is not according to man (1:11) because in the essential points at which it deviates from the false gospel, it is based on the Old Testament (3:1–6:10).

Syntactically, 1:11–6:10 is a single paragraph that merges the functions of amplification and reason, and does so within a chiastic framework. The schema for a reason paragraph is ⟨Text, Reason⟩; that for an amplification paragraph is ⟨Text, Amplification⟩. Here, we have ⟨Text-1, Text-2, AmplifiedReason-2, AmplifiedReason-1⟩. It is hardly parsimonious to christen this a new elemental paragraph type and register it alongside simpler structures. Scores of examples could be cited of similar hybrid structures that embed different rhetorical relations. Rather, basic clause-level syntactic relations and symmetric patterns can actively combine to form nonce hybrids like the body of Galatians.

The Transition, 2:15–21

We are nearing the end of our journey. Using the same tools that have proven so successful in the rest of Galatians, I will now explore the inner structure 2:15–21 in more detail, showing how symmetric, semantic, and syntactic structures interact with one another, and then will discuss the role of this paragraph in the rest of the book.

Symmetric and Syntactic Interplay

The structure of 2:15–21 is driven by the close interaction of symmetric and syntactic devices. The highest structural distinction is at the surface level. Based on this distinction, I discuss each of the two paragraphs that emerge, then analyze their joint syntax.

The role of Grammatical Person. At the surface level, pronouns and verbs shift from first person plural in 2:15–17 to first person singular in 2:18–21. These constructions in 2:15–21 are in turn set off from those before 2:15 (which are second person singular) and after 2:21 (second person plural). The absence of first person singulars in 3:1–5 is probably intended to heighten the break with 2:15–21. Had Paul used them in the first entreaty section, the articulation of 2:15–21 as a whole, and of its two main parts, would have been less crisp.

While the shift from "thou" (Peter) to "we" between 2:14 and 2:15 is deliberate, it hardly justifies a major division. Each panel in 3:1–6:10 shows a shift from confrontational entreaty (always marked with "you" [Galatians] and sometimes with "I" [Paul]) to collegial exposition (marked with "we"). The shift between 2:14 and 2:15 can be understood in just the same way, as indicating a shift from confrontational entreaty to brotherly encouragement. We shall see other indications that Paul is drawing a parallel between Peter's failing and the temptation faced by the Galatians.

The "We" Paragraph. The analysis of the first person plural section (2:15–17) is complicated by the ambiguity of 2:17, on which the exegetical commentaries offer copious discussion. A coherent structural picture emerges if we understand the verse as advocating the personal piety of believers, reading it as a contrafactual indicative rather than an interrogative: "If, while we seek justification by Christ, we also [along with the gentiles of 2:15] are found to be sinners, then Christ would be the minister of sin. God forbid!" This interpretation represents a deviation from Paul's usual usage in which μὴ γένοιτο "God forbid!" typically follows an interrogative (though some occurrences are ambiguous, and at least 6:14 is different). It has the advantage of understanding ἄρα "then [Christ would be . . .]" as the common Pauline inferential particle rather than as the interrogative particle, which Paul never uses. It is also appropriate in view of the clearly impious behavior of Peter that, whatever the formal connection of 2:15–21, his behavior can hardly avoid being in the reader's mind at this point (Moule 1968:196).

On this reading, 2:15–17 sets two complementary principles side by side. The **faith principle** is that salvation is by faith and not by works (vv. 15–16). The **piety principle** is that the lives of those who have been saved must be characterized by good works and not by sin (v. 17). This pair of principles is a common semantic structure in Paul (e.g., Eph. 2:8–9, 10; Titus 3:4–7, 8). To some of Paul's hearers, the association seemed paradoxical, leading to the charge that he advocated antinomianism (Rom. 6:1), but he consistently links the two together, insisting that only a salvation that issues from divine rather than human initiative can yield a life that conforms to divine standards.

The "I" Paragraph. The faith and piety principles reappear in the outer verse (2:18, 21) of the first person singular section, which correspond with one another symmetrically as conditional paragraphs (in the case of v. 21, embedded in the reason slot of a reason paragraph). Corresponding with the specifying move from "we" to "I," we now encounter specific examples of violations of the two principles contrasted in 2:15–17. Paul argues that to go back to the law, as Peter endorsed by his actions in Antioch and as the Galatians are considering doing, violates both the doctrine of salvation by faith apart from works and the requirement that believers should live righteous lives.

The first condition, 2:18, resumes the piety principle of 2:17. Putting himself in Peter's place, Paul argues that to build up what one has destroyed, to behave in accordance with justification by the law after forsaking that approach, would be a transgression, which (according to 2:17) should be unthinkable for a believer. Similarly, the second conditional paragraph, 2:21, resumes the faith principle of 2:15–16. To act in accordance with justification by law nullifies the grace of God, in effect claiming that Christ's death was unnecessary.

Thus the outer verses of the "I" section echo the contrast between the two halves of the "we" section. The verses in between, 2:19–20, go beyond what is explicit in the "we" section, explaining the mechanism by which a person avoids claiming credit for salvation and yet remains responsible for daily piety. These verses repeatedly contrast the believer's death and life in Christ: the agency of the believer that is at the same time the agency of Christ. This contrast explicates the supposed paradox of 2:15–17 (and 2:18,21) between salvation by faith and a working life. The very identification with Christ that permits me to be saved through His merit rather than my own also embues me with His life, a life that must manifest itself in my daily practice.

An Integrated Syntactic Summary. Thus understood, 2:19–20 give the reason, not for 2:18 alone, but for 2:18 and 2:21 together, and 2:18–21 thus forms a chiastic reason paragraph. In turn, 2:18–21 at once specifies 2:15–17 (by moving from general principles that govern *us* to a specific case involving *me*) and amplifies it (through the addition of 2:19–20).

This analysis suggests two extensions to the syntactic mechanisms described by Longacre (1980). The first is the notion of a chiastic paragraph, which we have already encountered in 1:6–10. The second suggests that multiple syntactic relations may be combined in a single paragraph, sharing a single slot-filler. In this case, 2:18–21 both specifies and amplifies 2:15–17.

Such complexity is further illustrated in 2:15–16. The overall structure is a comment paragraph, in which verse 15 comments on the subject of verse 16. In turn, 2:16 is symmetrically a chiasm that includes circumstance, purpose, and reason slots in a way that defies parsimonious analysis into separate circumstance, purpose, and reason paragraphs. In previous examples of chiastic paragraphs the symmetry has been in discourse function. Here, it is in catch-words and phrases repeated between corresponding elements.

Complex paragraph:

A   **circumstance:** 2:16 knowing that a person is not justified
B   by deeds of the law
C   but by faith of Jesus Christ,
D   **text:** we also have believed on Christ Jesus,
C   **purpose:** that we might be justified by faith of Christ
D   and not by deeds of the law,
      reason: for by deeds of the law
A   no flesh shall be justified.

Symmetric and Semantic Interplay

The basic framework of 2:15–21 embodies two oppositions, one between "we" and "I," the other between how one is justified and how one lives as a believer. From a symmetric perspective, the paragraph is an amplified chiasm, **AB-bca**, where the difference in case reflects the "we-I" distinction between the two panels; the difference between **A** (or **a**) and **B** (or **b**) reflects the distinction between justification and conduct; and the added element in the second panel is the additional information in 2:19–20.

Thus a chiasm with two panels, each of two corresponding elements, encodes all four possible interactions of two oppositions, as does the logical square. The relations defined on the classical logical square (contraries, subcontraries, contradictions, and implications) depend on the particular nature of the oppositions that generate it (quantification and negation). Our passage uses one of these oppositions (quantification, between "we" and "I") but not the other; we do not see the same set of relations, but the symmetric structure of 2:15–21 shares with logical square analysis the basic idea of examining all possible interactions of two oppositions.

Such a two-by-two analysis is common in biblical literature. Without conducting an exhaustive search, I have noticed the pattern in Jeremiah 25:5–6; 27:16b–17; 30:12–17; 34–38; Matthew 7:6; Romans 10:1–21; 1 Corinthians 13:7; Ephesians 4:11; Colossians 3:8–14; 2 Timothy 4:14–18; and Hebrews 2:9. (The preponderance of instances in Jeremiah is an effect of sampling, not any indication of a preference by Jeremiah for this device.) In addition, alternations extend this device by permitting larger matrices to be examined. Perhaps the fascination of biblical writers for symmetric structures, seemingly so remote from the methods of modern analysis of semantic structures, actually reflects a very modern concern to organize their material so as to make explicit the interplay of multiple oppositions in the world they are trying to describe.

The Transitional Effect of 2:15–21

At the outset I hypothesized that 2:15–21 is a transition between Paul's defense of himself as an independent messenger in 1:13–2:14 and his exposition of the true gospel as according to the Scripture rather than according to man in 3:1–6:10. We are now in a position to confirm this hypothesis by reviewing the overall effect of the shift in grammatical person that structures 2:15–21 and the alignment between the content of this section and those on either side.

The shifts in grammatical person that articulate 2:15–21 parallel the shift from confrontation to encouragement in the three panels of 3:1–6:10. This observation suggests that Peter is in some sense architypical of the Galatians, and that Paul's comments to him are equally relevant to the Galatians in their current situation.

We observed that Paul's conversation with Peter is the climax of the sequence paragraph that demonstrates Paul's independence of human authority. Peter's prominence among the twelve is legendary. If Paul's gospel were derived from Peter or others of the twelve, Paul could hardly have rebuked Peter on the basis of that gospel. The rebuke of 2:14–21 establishes at once Paul's independence of Peter and the content of his gospel. Paul reminds Peter that it is not enough to claim to believe in justification by faith. Such belief carries with it the commitment to live in a certain way. Peter's compromise with judaizing forces in Antioch amounts to transgression (2:18), thus violating the piety principle of 2:17. Furthermore, by casting into question the sufficiency of the death of Christ (2:21), it challenges the faith principle of 2:15–16. The disputed paragraph is entirely consistent with the conversation with Peter.

The same independent authority that permits Paul to challenge the Petrine "thou" in the climax of the first half of the book also enables him to rebuke the Galatian "you" in the second. The twofold emphasis if 2:15–21, on justification by faith and the importance of consistent works, emerges immediately in 3:3. "Having begun in the Spirit, are you now made perfect by the flesh?" This same emphasis is extended in the first and third panels of 3:1–6:10. The first panel, contrasting works and faith as means of justification, develops the principle of 2:15–16, 18, while the third, contrasting the sinful results of life in the flesh with the piety produced by life in the Spirit, develops 2:17, 21. For the Galatians as for Peter, the gospel by which one is saved has implications for how one lives. Peter seems clear on the faith principle but stumbles on the piety principle. The Galatians are confused about the faith principle, and are in danger of missing the piety principle as well.

This analysis leaves the middle panel of 3:1–6:10, the allegory of Abraham's women contrasting freedom with bondage, without a clear antecedent in the transition. Such an asymmetry is no defect. For example, we have seen it already in the amplification of 2:15–17 by 2:18–21 and in the presence of 1:8–9 in 1:6–10 without a correspondent in 6:12–17. The asymmetry between 2:15–21 and 3:1–6:10 would draw the attention of an astute reader to this middle panel, which therefore comes into special focus. Such focus is particularly appropriate polemically, since this panel claims that (contrary to superficial appearance) the adherents of the true gospel, not the judaizers, are the proper heirs of Abraham. Whatever their physical lineage might be, and in spite of their claim to represent the continuity of the Old Testament faith, the false teachers are spiritually illegitimate.

Where does 2:15–21 Fit?

The question with which we began was the place of 2:15–21 in Galatians. Our analysis supports the description of this passage as a transition, a function that contributes to the very ambiguity that generations of commentators have noticed.

There is no reason to exclude the passage from Paul's rebuke to Peter.

- The break at 3:1 (vocative to the Galatians; discontinuation of first person singulars in spite of their presence in other entreaty sections) is much stronger than that at 2:15.
- The content of 2:15–21 fits well in the rebuke to Peter.
- The shift from "thou" (Peter) to "we" (Paul and Peter together) between 2:14 and 2:15 does not mark the end of direct discourse but reflects similar transitions in 3:1–6:10.
- Including 2:15–21 in the rebuke to Peter makes 2:11–21 the longest build up of the sequence paragraph of which it is a part, consistent with its role as climax of the narrative.

At the same time, the two main points developed by the transition (justification by faith and consistent conduct) are amplified in two of the three panels that make up 3:1–6:10. As we would expect of a transition, 2:15–21 moves the user without discontinuity from one major section of the epistle to another.

In fact, retaining 2:15–21 as part of the rebuke to Peter strengthens its role as introduction of the second half of the book, for Peter's error adumbrates that of the Galatians, and Paul rebukes the Galatians mainly by amplifying and expounding what he has already said to Peter.

Conclusions

We can carry useful conclusions from this study at three levels. At the finest level of detail, our analysis has yielded many useful results on the structure of Galatians. Our target has been a better understanding of the transitional nature of 2:15–21, but along the way we have learned much about how the rest of Galatians works, including the introductory chiastic summary of 1:11–12 and the role of grammatical person as a key to the structure not only of 2:15–21 but also of 3:1–6:10.

At a higher level, we have observed a number of interesting linguistic patterns that will be useful in understanding other texts. For example, our analysis suggests that syntactic analysis of paragraph types can usefully be extended beyond static single-function paragraph types such as sequence, reason, and purpose, to complex paragraph like 2:16 that embody multiple syntactic functions concurrently and use symmetric devices to organize them. Another example is the use of a two-by-two chiastic pattern (such as AB-ba or Ab-aB) to capture the kind of structural regularity for which semantic analysis use the logical square.

All of these specific insights are subsidiary to the main burden of the paper. Our primary purpose in analyzing Galatians has been to observe how three structural methods in common use can complement and reinforce one another. Discourse structure is not one-dimensional. Its analysis requires the identification of entities and relationships both in the text itself and in the many cognitive layers in which the text is encoded in the mind of the writer or reader, what I have called the text's world. No single method yet proposed can capture all of the richness of the miracle that is language. An eclectic, multidimensional approach gives us a much fuller appreciation for the text's structure on many levels.

This research has been considerably assisted by the power and flexibility of the GRAMCORD package for search and retrieval in the Greek New Testament, and I am deeply indebted to Paul Miller for making it available to me.

References

Beekman, J. and J. Callow. 1974. *Translating the Word of God.* Grand Rapids: Zondervan.

Beekman, J., J. Callow, and M. Kopesec. 1981. *The Semantic Structure of Written Communication.* Dallas: Summer Institute of Linguistics.

Betz, H. D. 1979. *Galatians.* Philadelphia: Fortress.

Bligh, J. 1966. *Galatians in Greek.* Detroit: University of Detroit.

Boys, T. 1824. *Tactica Sacra.* London: Hamilton.

Brown, J. ND. *An Exposition of the Epistle to the Galatians.* Marshallton, Del.: Sovereign Grace, 1970 (reprint).

Bruce, F. F. 1982. *The Epistle to the Galatians: A Commentary on the Greek Text.* The New International Greek Commentary. Grand Rapids: William B. Eerdmans.

Burton, E. D. 1921. *A Critical and Exegetical Commentary on the Epistle to the Galatians.* Edinburgh: T & T Clark.

Callow, K. 1974. *Discourse Considerations in Translating the Word of God.* Grand Rapids: Zondervan.

Collins, T. 1987. *Decoding the Psalms: A Structural Approach to the Psalter. JSOT* 37.41–60.

Ellis, P. F. 1982. *Seven Pauline Letters.* Collegeville, MN: Liturgical Press.

Forbes, J. 1854. *The Symmetrical Study of Scripture.* Edinburgh: T & T Clark.

Greimas, A. J. 1966. *Semantique structurale.* Paris: Larousse.

Grimes, J. E. 1975. *The Thread of Discourse.* The Hague: Mouton.

Guha, R. V. and D. B. Lenat. 1990. "Cyc: A Mid-Term Report." *AI Magazine* 11:3. 32–59.

Hall, R. G. 1987. "The Rhetorical Outline for Galatians: A Reconsideration." *JBL* 106:2. 277–287.

Hendriksen, W. 1968. *Galatians.* New Testament Commentary. Grand Rapids: Baker.

Jebb, J. 1820. *Sacred Literature.* London: Cadell and Davies.

Jeremias, J. 1958. "Chiasmus in den Paulusbriefen." *ZNTW* 49.145–156.

Larson, I. 1991. "Boundary Features." *Notes on Translation* 5:1.48–54.

Levinsohn, S. H. 1989. "Phrase Order and the Article in Galatians: A Functional Sentence Perspective Approach." *OPTAT* 3:2.44–64.

Lightfoot, J. B. ND. *The Epistle of St. Paul to the Galatians.* Grand Rapids: Zondervan, 1957 (reprint).

Longacre, R. E. 1976. *An Anatomy of Speech Notions.* Lisse: Peter de Ridder.

_____. 1980. "An Apparatus for the Identification of Paragraph Types." *Notes on Translation* 15.5–22.

_____. 1989. *Joseph: A Story of Divine Providence.* Winona Lake: Eisenbrauns.

Lowth, R. 1753. *De sacra poesie Hebraeorum; praelectiones academicae Oxonii habitae.* Oxford: Clarendon.

Lund, N. W. 1942. *Chiasmus in the New Testament.* Chapel Hill: University of North Carolina.

Lyons, J. 1977. *Semantics.* vol. 1. Cambridge: Cambridge University Press.

Mann, W. C. and S. A. Thompson. 1987. *Rhetorical Structure Theory: A Theory of Text Organization.* ISI Reprint Series ISI/RS-87-190. Marina del Rey: Information Sciences Institute. Reprinted from L. Polyani, ed., *The Structure of Discourse.* Norwood, NJ: Ablex, 1987.

Moule, C. F. D. 1968. *An Idiom-Book of New Testament Greek.* Cambridge: Cambridge University Press.

Parunak, H. V. D. 1978. *Structural Studies in Ezekiel.* Ph.D. Dissertation, Dept. of Near Eastern Languages and Civilizations, Harvard University.

_____. 1979. *Linguistic Density Plots in Zechariah.* The Computer Bible. vol. 20. Wooster: Biblical Research Associates.

_____. 1981a. *Prolegomena to Pictorial Concordances.* Computers and the Humanities 15.15–36.

_____. 1981b. "Oral Typesetting: Some Uses of Biblical Structure." Biblica 62:2.153–168.

_____. 1981c. "A Structural Outline of the Epistle of Paul to the Romans." Unpublished memorandum.

_____. 1982. "Transitional Techniques in the Bible." *JBL* 102:4.525–548.

_____. 1983. "Some axioms for literary architecture." *Semitics* 8.1–16.

_____. 1984. "Linguistic Density Plots in Ezekiel." The Computer Bible. vol. 27. Wooster: Biblical Research Associates.

Patte, D. 1976. *What is Structural Exegesis?* Philadelphia: Fortress.

Petersen, N. R. 1976. ed. *Semeia 6: Erhardt Güttgemanns' "Generative Poetics".* Missoula: Scholars Press.

Polzin, R. 1974. "The Framework of the Book of Job." *Interpretation* 28:2. 182–200.

_____. 1977. *Biblical Structuralism.* Missoula: Scholars Press.

Propp, V. 1968. *Morphology of the Folktale.* 2nd ed., Austin: University of Texas (orig. 1928; 1st ET 1958).

Rogers, E. 1984. "Vocatives and Boundaries." *Selected Technical Articles Related to Translation* 11.24–29.

_____. 1989. *Semantic Structure Analysis of Galatians.* Dallas: Summer Institute of Linguistics.

Seatlh, Chief of the Suquamish, 1855. Cited in Wilson and Hayden 1981: 159.

Waltke, B. K. and M. O'Connor. 1990. *An Introduction to Biblical Hebrew Syntax.* Winona Lake: Eisenbrauns.

Wilson, S. C. and K. C. Hayden. 1981. "Where Oil and Wildlife Mix." *National Geographic Magazine* 159:2.145–173.

Winograd, T. and C. F. Flores,. 1987. *Understanding Computers and Cognition.* Reading: Addison-Wesley.

12

The Function of καί in the Greek New Testament and an Application to 2 Peter*

Kermit Titrud

It is my contention that a reexamination of the meaning of καί is needed. The subtleties of its meaning have been ignored too long, often glossed over in grammars, commentaries, and translations. The study of καί is important because it is used in practically every verse of the New Testament; it occurs approximately nine thousand times. Yet, amazingly, exceedingly few comprehensive studies of καί are available.

Traditional Definitions of καί

It has long been recognized that καί means more than "and" or "even," yet most of the beginning grammars and lexicons still define καί as "and," "also," or "even." Even Lampe (1961) glosses καί merely as "*and*; contrasted with δέ." I am convinced that this simplistic understanding has led to a number of false interpretations concerning the intention of the New Testament authors.

On the other hand, the more comprehensive descriptions such as those of BAGD,[1] Turner (1963:334–36), and Blass and Debrunner (1961:para. 227) present an analysis of the meaning of καί that is complex and confusing, partly due to inconsistencies in their taxonomies and categories (see Titrud 1986:ch. 1). Also too often they

---

* The first part of this article was first published in *Notes on Translation*, Vol. 5(1), 1991, under the title, "The Overlooked KAI." The text has been slightly revised and updated, and the principles presented have been further illustrated by application to the text of the Second Epistle of Peter.

[1] BAGD refers to the 1979 edition of Bauer's *Greek-English Lexicon of the New Testament*, translated by Arndt and Gingrich and subsequently revised and augmented by Gingrich and Danker. (See Arndt and Gingrich 1979 in the references list.)

seek to describe the meaning of καί by relating it to the meaning of various English or German constructions. It must, however, be analyzed within its own system in New Testament Greek, not on the basis of an English or German grid.

As a Bible translator for a language group in the Philippines, I became aware in the course of my work that there are a number of unanswered exegetical questions involving καί in the Greek New Testament. Such questions are often glossed over in commentaries and translations, probably because καί is often judged to be "pleonastic" (redundant or of no real value). Such an opinion is the result, I believe, of interpreting a particle in one language according to the system of another language. So I began to wonder if καί is, in fact, pleonastic or "Semitic" as claimed, for it seems to have an important function and a bearing on many disputed passages. (See Titrud 1986:13–26 concerning problems of the New Testament καί being equated with the Hebrew *waw*.)

Clearly καί cannot always be translated "and," "even," or "also." Matthew 21:5 is my favorite example. As a child I always wondered how Jesus rode on an ass *and* on a colt. Did He straddle the two or did He first ride on an ass and then on a colt?

In Acts 5:29 also, it is misleading to translate καί as "and," as is done in RSV and KJV: "Peter and the apostles." One who does not know that Peter was an apostle would assume from this reference that he was not. If a friend told me he had seen Joe and the elders of the church at a restaurant, I would assume that Joe was not an elder himself. TEV and NIV prevent this misinterpretation of Acts 5:29 by translating it "Peter *and* the *other* apostles" (see also Matt. 26:59; Mark 15:1; and John 11:47).

Thus one striking difference between the Greek καί and the English "and" is that "and" implies that the conjoined items are distinct. Καί, on the other hand, may or may not imply a distinction. The context, the presupposition of the writer/speaker, and his understanding of the presuppositions of the recipients of the message will determine whether or not a distinction exists.

An interclausal example of this is in 2 Thessalonians 1:10, "when he comes on that day to be glorified in the saints, and (καί) to be marveled at in all who have believed" (RSV). Practically all the translations render the καί here as "and." However, by such a rendering one not versed in New Testament theology would probably understand the saints as a distinct group from those who have believed. Are the saints the Old Testament believers, or special people like Peter and Paul, as opposed to the average believer? It is more probable that the second clause is parallel to the preceding one (Milligan 1908:92).

"The saints" and "all those who have believed" are one and the same. The first term emphasizes that their salvation is God's work and the second that they actively embraced Christ (Hendriksen 1955:161). In order to prevent a misunderstanding of the intention of the biblical author, a suggested translation (using words and phrases similar to the RSV) is "when he comes on that day to be glorified and marveled at in his saints, that is, in all who have believed" (see also LB).

Many more verses could be cited to demonstrate that καί does not simply mean "and," "even," or "also." Other clear examples are Mark 15:25, Mark 8:3, Luke 13:7, and 1 Corinthians 15:29, to mention only a few. The examples that have been given are a mere sampling to show how translating καί only in this way produces confusion or even wrong meaning.

Redefining καί in the Light of Linguistics

In the light of recent studies in linguistics, we assume that καί was not just written arbitrarily; it has a particular function in the discourse structure of New Testament Greek. Though often it may seem that the relationship between propositions could have been expressed by a more specific form (e.g., δέ, ὅτι, ὅτε, Ø, etc.), there were pragmatic reasons for the use of καί, for the New Testament writers were concerned for "correctness" and not just the "truth" in a propositional semantics sense.

A serious analyst should ask, "Why is καί used here as opposed to another form" and explore the underlying differences. We can assume that the choices an author makes concerning the shape of his text are meaningful choices. Another fair assumption is that the New Testament authors took it for granted (as all authors do) that their readers possessed a certain amount of knowledge relating to the content of the text (e.g., the characteristics of tax collectors and Pharisees, and that people do not generally walk on water). What any author believes his readers already know has a significant impact on the form and content of his message (Jones 1983:2).

On the basis of these pragmatic assumptions, then, we shall now examine the functions of καί, which Greek grammars and lexicons have rightly divided into two basic categories, καί as an adverb and καί as a conjunction.

The Adverbial Function of καί

The adverbial καί seems to call special attention to what follows it, marking it with prominence. By its use, the writer signals the reader that what follows is important (2 Pet. 1:5, "For this *very* reason"), or surprising (Mark 4:41, "*even* the wind and the waves"; John 7:47, "Did he fool you, *too?*" [TEV]), or bewildering (Matt. 10:30, "*even* the hairs of your head"), or extreme (Gal. 5:12, "*even* castrate themselves"), or a combination of these (2 Pet. 2:1, "*even* denying the Master who bought them"). It may also be used to evoke ridicule (Matt. 5:46, "*Even* the tax collectors do that!"), or to confirm or amplify (2 Pet. 3:16a, "As *in fact* he does in all his letters"). It may be used to emphasize that what is being stated is true (2 Pet. 1:14, "as *in fact* our Lord Jesus Christ has made clear to me"; 2 Pet. 2:12, "they will *indeed* perish"). Especially when followed by a pronoun, the effect of the adverbial καί is to emphasize that the following is to be acted upon (Luke 17:10, "so you *also* . . . should say"; see also Matt. 13:29; Luke 21:31; and Mark 13:29). Thus, it appears that the primary function of the adverbial καί is to indicate that the following component(s) should be intensified or emphasized, just as a spotlight focuses our attention on something. Thus, in English, the adverbial καί could be glossed as "even," "also," "indeed," "as well," "likewise," "too," "very," and so on, depending on the context.

In a number of English versions, the translators often seem to regard the presence of καί as irrelevant. This is probably due to the opinion that καί is often "pleonastic" (redundant, not needed). Yet the use or nonuse of a given particle is not arbitrary. There is a pragmatic difference between the use of καί and its nonuse even though it may be slight.

Having analyzed a number of passages where there is an adverbial καί, I suggest that its function is primarily emotive and that this emotive factor should, if possible, be conveyed in the translation. This admittedly often requires ingenuity. For example, what is the force of the adverbial (emotive) καί in ἱνατί καὶ τὴν γῆν καταργεῖ (Luke 13:7)? None of the translations deal with it except Phillips: "Why should it use up *valuable* ground?" Phillips seems to recognize that the καί here is intensifying, making the "ground" important (understandable coming from a landowner).

BAGD (as well as many other analyses) often refers to καί as pleonastic (s.v. καί, II.3, 4, and 7), failing perhaps to recognize the distinction between the adverbial καί and the conjunctive particles. For example, in Matthew 6:10 and Acts 7:51 (cited by BAGD in II.3), the ὡς indicates the semantic relationship between the two clauses, an intersentential function. The καί, on the other hand, marks what is prominent. In Matthew 6:10, καί is marking "on earth" as the focal constituent. In Acts 7:51, "you" is similarly marked as prominent. (When translating into English, this focus effect can often be created by forefronting: the item in focus is placed before the item with which it is compared.)

When an element is intensified, often there is an implication that it is intensified as opposed to some other element or elements. Hence, καί is often translated as "also" or "even" to imply that there is another element or other elements not being singled out. Many argue that 1 Peter 3:19–20 does not mean that Jesus went to preach to these disobedient spirits after His resurrection but rather that, at the time of Noah, He went and preached to them *through the lips of Noah.* One of the arguments for this over against the position of Jesus' personally going to them after His resurrection is, Why would He have gone only to those who disobeyed in the days of Noah? It is important here to have a clear understanding of the function of καί in verse 19. Verse 19 does not say "only," but rather "even": "he went even to the spirits in prison who formerly disobeyed in the days of Noah." The emphasis on these particular spirits does not necessarily exclude Jesus' having gone to other disobedient ones as well. Rather, these are singled out merely as noted examples and by doing so Peter is then able to introduce his baptism theme.

The idea that the adverbial καί primarily modifies the immediately following constituent and not necessarily the whole clause is demonstrated in 1 Peter 2:21. The focus is on the fact that *even Christ Himself suffered,* so they also should endure suffering. The phrase "for you," although a component of the clause, is not what is intensified. The RSV here is misleading. The meaning is not "Christ also suffered for you," which could give the impression that someone else had suffered for them as well, but rather that Christ had, in fact, also suffered, and that when He suffered He suffered unjustly. The translators of the NIV, TEV, and many other translations realized that to translate καί here as "also" would be problematic so they just ignored it. However, in doing so, they failed to express the emotive feature desired by the writer. The impact of the a fortiori argument is not brought out. It could be translated "Christ Himself had likewise suffered when He suffered for you," making explicit in English that what is being intensified does not include the subordinate constituent ὑμῶν.

The Construction καί . . . καί ("both . . . and")

The construction καί . . . καί ("both . . . and") is classified in BAGD and in Liddell and Scott (1968) under connective/copulative; in Denniston (1959) it is listed in a separate category, namely corresponsive. One could argue that this is a failure to recognize that the first καί in the construction is really an adverb intensifying the phrase and the second καί is acting as the connective. For example, in Matthew 10:28, the first καί in the construction καὶ ψυχὴν καὶ σῶμα "both soul and body" is the adverb, stressing the inclusion of each of the two items specified. In English the word "both" encodes this intensification when two items are coordinated; preceding a single item, "even" encodes the intensification. Note that, in English, "even" and "both" do not co-occur (e.g., I saw *even both* John and Jill).[2]

It is also interesting that English encodes degrees of intensity. For example, the difference between "John also swam across the river" and "John even swam across the river," in a context where other things (or another thing) that John did was mentioned or implied, is the degree of intensity. "Even" evokes a higher degree of intensity than "also." The Greeks apparently did not make this fine distinction. Thus, when we translate καί into English, only by examining the context and the Greek world view can we determine whether "also" or the more intense form "even" is appropriate. In many cases, it is quite difficult to determine the degree of intensity the writer wishes to convey (e.g., in 1 Pet. 1:15; 2:18; 3:5, 19, 21; 4:1, 6).

Distinguishing καί as an Adverb from καί as a Coordinating Conjunction

The function of καί as an adverb and its function as a conjunction is distinguished in Greek by the position in which it occurs. As a conjunction linking clauses, καί only occurs as the first word of a clause, never postpositionally (as δέ and τέ do). When καί does occur postpositionally, it is an adverb. Of course, καί as an adverb is not restricted to postposition. As an adverb καί may occur in the clause initially when clauses are conjoined by asyndeton (∅) or postpositional conjunctions (e.g., γάρ). On the other hand, when clauses are conjoined by either coordinating or subordinating conjunctions, καί as an adverb is always postpositional (except when it occurs with a postpositional conjunction, e.g., γάρ). This is proven by the fact that, in Greek, one never finds καί immediately preceding the coordinating conjunctions ἀλλά, ἤ, διό, οὖν, etc., or even δέ for that matter. One may find καί preceding

---

[2] Interestingly, Friberg and Friberg (1981) treat both of the καί's in the καί . . . καί construction as coordinating conjunctions (CC). After I shared the analysis presented here with John Werner (a consultant for Friberg and Friberg), he noted that all instances of καί rendered as "both" in Young's Concordance were indeed analyzed as CC by Friberg and Friberg with but five exceptions, three of which they labeled AB and two AB/CC, even though these five seemed to have no semantic difference from the CC's. As a result of our discussion, John Werner is recommending that Friberg and Friberg tag all the καί ("both") . . . καί ("and") constructions with "(QE) . . . (CC)," wherein QE would represent emphatic particle (John Werner, personal communication).

the subordinating conjunctions such as εἰ, ὅτε, ὡς, etc. (e.g., Mark 10:1); however, in these cases, καί is functioning as the coordinating conjunction. It is relating the previous propositional cluster(s) with the following propositional cluster(s) which in turn are being introduced by a subordinate clause. When καί *follows* subordinating conjunctions, it is not functioning as a link between propositional clusters but rather as an adverb—an intensifier (e.g., Matt. 18:33b).[3]

There are two kinds of conjunctions: subordinating conjunctions and coordinating conjunctions. The conjunctive καί is a coordinating conjunction; it coordinates grammatical units of equal rank in the same way that "and" does in English. When καί is found between an indicative verb and a participle the καί is an adverb and not a conjoiner. For example, in 2 Peter 2:1b, καί is not conjoining similar grammatical units: the participle "denying" is subordinate to the indicative verb "secretly bring in." This is, therefore, the adverbial καί, meaning "denying *even* the Master who bought them." This signals that this denial of Christ was one of their heresies, more than likely the most destructive one. The emotive element may be one of surprise that anyone could do such a thing.

In 2 Corinthians 5:6 virtually all the translations and commentaries have interpreted καί as a conjunction, surfacing in English as "and" or asyndeton (∅). (E.g., "Therefore we are always confident *and* know that as long as we are at home in the body we are away from the Lord," NIV). This rendering of καί, however, does not make much sense. How does "knowing that while we are at home in the body we are away from the Lord" cause us to be of good courage? The opposite would be assumed since "we would rather be away from the body and at home with the Lord" (v. 8). By looking more closely at the grammatical construction in verse 6, we will note that there is a change of tense/aspect from present (θαρροῦντες) to aorist (εἰδότες). Hence grammatically and contextually it makes more sense to interpret the καί in this verse as an adverb, resulting in "knowing" being dependent upon "being confident." A suggested translation could be "Therefore we are always confident *even though* we know that as long as we are at home in the body we are away from the Lord."

The Conjunctive Function of καί

As a coordinating conjunction much like the English "and," καί serves (1) intraclausally as a conjoiner of words and phrases of equal

---

[3] Moule (1959:167) describes εἰ καί as concessive, "even if," whereas καί εἰ may be purely conditional, "and if." Interestingly, the deep structure of the form κἄν may be either καί ἐάν (Luke 13:9) or ἐάν καί (John 11:25).

grammatical rank and (2) interclausally as a conjoiner of clauses of equal grammatical rank. Also, like "and," καί is used as a function word to express the general relation of connection or addition, especially accompaniment, participation, combination, contiguity, continuance, simultaneity, and sequence. However, unlike "and," which generally encodes an addition, and thus a distinction between the concepts or propositions it is conjoining, καί often does not encode a distinction between the items it is conjoining. In English the formula "A and B" generally implies that A does not equal B (e.g., Jack and Jill; the bat and the ball; Mary and the boys; I went to the grocery store and to the drug store; I cooked dinner and took care of the kids). In Greek, on the other hand, the formula "A καί B" often does imply that A equals B, as in apposition and hendiadys.

The English "and" functions to express a close relationship between the constituents or propositions it is conjoining, but, at the same time, it maintains a distinction between those constituents or propositions except in a few cases, such as in repetition ("I cried and cried") or idiomatic expressions ("I'm sick and tired of you"). The Greek καί, on the other hand, functions to express such a close relationship between the conjoined constituents or propositions that they are often perceived as a single entity.

The Appositive-Introducing Function of καί

Like the Old Testament writers, it was common for the New Testament writers to summarize, emphasize, specify, further explain, or clarify what was previously mentioned. New Testament writers frequently marked an appositive by καί, but when καί is translated as "and" in contexts where it introduces apposition, misunderstandings often arise. Unfortunately, it is often translated this way even in translations intended to be idiomatic, for translators as well as commentators often fail to perceive instances where καί is introducing apposition.

Bruce Moore (1972) has done an extensive study of doublets in the New Testament. He defines doublets as "sets of two or more words or constructions (the "terms" of the doublets) which occur together and which are so redundant in context that, for translation purposes, they may be rendered as a single term plus possible modifying concepts such as intensity" (p. 3). Interestingly, well over half of the doublets listed by Moore are conjoined by καί.

I myself prefer the term "appositive" to "doublet," defining an appositive as that which reiterates, amplifies, specifies, or summarizes the preceding. This would cover all of Moore's doublets and, at the same time, broaden the category to include summary statements (e.g. 1 John 3:23–24 which provides a summary conclusion to the section

vv. 10–24). Moore clearly demonstrates that it was common for New Testament writers to use καί in marking apposition. Indeed, it could be argued that καί introduce an appositive even more frequently than Moore realized. For example, Moore notes five instances in 1 John where καί introduces a doublet/appositive (1 John 1:2, 6; 2:4, 27, 28). All of these examples happen to be interclausal. Yet it could be argued (staying on the interclausal level) that καί also introduces an appositive in 1 John 1:2a, 2:18, 3:1, 4, 9, 12, 23, and 4:3, 7, 21.

In 1 John, of the fifty-six instances where καί conjoins clauses, an appositive is being introduced in fifteen—over 25% of them. John's frequent use of καί in this way is not unique, as a perusal of Moore's doublets demonstrates.

Having determined that καί does in fact often introduce appositives, what is the determining factor in deciding whether καί is introducing an appositive or merely conjoining two distinct entities? Linguists are becoming more and more aware of the fact that there is a great deal of redundancy in communication. Even when we may not understand a particular word or phrase (or when, in the case of spoken speech, noise obliterates some elements), we are still able, more often than not, to receive the information because of built-in redundancy (Silva 1983:154–55). In 1953 Martin Joos suggested the rule of maximum redundancy: "The best meaning is the least meaning" (quoted by Silva 1983:153). This means that the correct meaning in individual contexts is usually that which contributes the least new information to the total context. In applying these maxims, we conclude that there is no need to force a distinction between two virtually synonymous or related terms, phrases, or clauses if apposition is a viable option.

The Word/Phrase-Conjoining Function of καί

As has been demonstrated, the conjunctive καί functions to express a close relationship between the elements it conjoins, whether clauses, phrases, or words. The nature of this close relationship may be one of apposition. On the intraclausal level, using the formula A καί B, B may be equivalent or virtually equivalent to A (Luke 2:4; Acts 7:42; Rom. 13:13; 15:19; 1 Cor. 16:16; 1 Tim. 6:9; Rev. 21:5, 26), or B may be specifying A (Matt. 21:5; Phil. 4:6; Rev. 2:19 where ἔργα "works" is the generic term being specified by the following καὶ τὴν ἀγάπην καὶ τὴν πίστιν καὶ τὴν διακονίαν καὶ τὴν ὑπομονήν σου). Exegetes and translators often do not perceive καί as introducing apposition on the intraclausal level, partly due to the presupposition that it means "and" (therefore the conjoined words or phrases must have contrasting meanings) and partly because their definitions were traditionally based on etymological studies, resulting in dangerous hermeneutics. Whether, in any given context, καί is introducing apposition or not, it is nonetheless still expressing a close relationship between the conjoined elements. In this sense it is like "and."

There is an even closer relationship between constituents conjoined by καί when they share the same article.[4] This is often referred to as the Granville Sharp rule which states:

> if two substantives are connected by καί and both have the article, they refer to different persons or things . . . if the first has an article and the second does not, the second refers to the same person or thing as the first . . . Of course the rule could also be applied to a series of three or more (Brooks and Winbery 1979:70).

This rule applies both in New Testament and Hellenistic Greek (Turner 1963:181–82) as well as classical Greek (Smyth 1956, sec. 1143 ff.).[5]

It is not, however, always the case that the two constituents are one and the same being or thing. This is clearly demonstrated in Acts 23:7 by τῶν Φαρισαίων καὶ Σαδδουκαίων "the Pharisees and Sadducees." Here the doctrinal differences between the two groups are presupposed. They are probably closely linked here because they functioned together as representatives of the Sanhedrin. Nor is it true that if two substantives are connected by καί and both have an article, they always refer to different persons or things. This is illustrated in Revelation 2:8, ὁ πρῶτος καὶ ὁ ἔσχατος "the First and the Last," where both substantives refer to Christ.

I suggest, therefore, the following modification to the Granville Sharp rule:

> If two substantives are connected by καί and both have an article, they refer to different persons or things unless the immediate or even broader context strongly suggests that they refer to the same person or thing. In this case, we are to understand that different aspects of that which is being described are being stressed. If the first substantive has an article and the second does not, the second refers to the same person or

---

[4] The repetition of the article with the second item of the coordinate construction is much more frequent than the use of a single article to govern two (or more) substantives—almost four times as frequent. This was determined by Peter Denton (1985:8) in a study made with the use of GRAMCORD, a computer retrieval system.

[5] Interestingly, the Granville Sharp rule is still in effect in Modern Greek. Helen Werner (nee Eleni Boora), wife of John Werner, says that τοὺς συγγενεῖς (relatives) καὶ τοὺς φίλους (friends) μου would be two groups of people whereas τοὺς συγγενεῖς καὶ φίλους μου would be one group (John Werner, personal communication).

thing as the first unless the context suggests otherwise. In this case, we should understand that they are being considered as a unit in some sense. (This could also be applied to a series of three or more.)

The Clause-Conjoining Function of καί

Like "and" in English, καί is a coordinating conjunction that on the interclausal level functions as a conjoiner of clauses of equal grammatical rank. Some might claim that καί is also a subordinating conjunction since it introduces subordinate clauses such as temporal (Matt. 26:45; Mark 15:25), reason-causal (Mark 8:3), and result (Matt. 26:15). However, such instances are extremely rare. It is important to determine whether καί can function as a coordinating conjunction only or as a subordinating conjunction as well. I maintain that the conjunctive καί is always a paratactic (coordinating) signal in the discourse structure of Koine Greek, even though there may be cases where logically one proposition is subordinate to the other. When this skewing between discourse and logical structure occurs, it is the result of the author's strategy—it is deliberate and significant (see also Larson 1984, ch. 21 for discussions of "skewing"). By syntactically elevating what is logically subordinate, the author is placing more prominence (emphasis) on the clause than it would have had if introduced by a subordinating conjunction (see Titrud 1986:70–72 for further discussion on this and on the "Ascensive και").

Comparing καί with Other Greek Coordinating Particles

I propose that the main difference between the conjunctive καί and the other coordinating particles is the degree of relationship between the propositions being conjoined. When καί is used, it implies that what follows is closely related to what precedes; this is not so when other particles such as δέ, ἀλλά, and τότε[6] are used. With respect to τότε, this is demonstrated by the fact that τότε may introduce a new paragraph (e.g., Matt. 2:7, 16; 3:13; 4:1; 9:14; 24:9, 23; 25:1; Luke 21:10; John 19:1; Acts 1:12); however, the καὶ τότε configuration does not introduce a new paragraph (e.g., Matt. 7:23; 24:10, 30; Mark 13:21,[7] 26,[8] 27). The καί in the καὶ τότε configuration signals

---

[6] Although grammatically τότε is an adverb, it also may serve semantically as a coordinator of propositions, signifying a sequential or simultaneous relationship (e.g., Matt. 24:9, 23).

[7] Interestingly the TEV, JB, NEB, Phillips, and Nestle-Aland introduce a paragraph break here, but more than likely, due to the nature of the καὶ τότε configuration as demonstrated elsewhere, the NIV, RSV, NASB, and KJV are right in not introducing a new paragraph.

[8] Here only the NIV and LB introduce a paragraph break.

that the following clause is still closely related semantically to the preceding one, and therefore still within the same paragraph unit.

Similarly, although καί (not καὶ τότε) may introduce a new paragraph in narrative, it does not do so nearly as often as, for example, δέ does. And when καί does introduce a new paragraph, the paragraphs are more closely linked semantically than when δέ introduces a new paragraph. In other words, there is a greater degree of cohesion between paragraphs linked by καί. A paragraph introduced by καί is very closely related to the preceding paragraph, continuing the same participant(s), setting, and often the same event (e.g., Matt. 4:23; 7:28; 9:1). On the other hand, a paragraph introduced by δέ is likely to be very loosely connected to the previous paragraph, having new participants and setting (e.g., Matt. 2:1, 13; 3:1; 4:12).

It could even be argued that, in the Epistles, καί as a conjunction does not introduce a paragraph break. Paragraphs are often introduced by δέ, οὖν, γάρ, and asyndeton, and, less commonly, by διό,[9] διὰ τοῦτο,[10] ἄρα, and ἄρα οὖν.[11] Although καί introduces a coordinate clause about as often as all the other coordinating particles combined, it is extremely rare to find καί introducing a paragraph as indicated in the Nestle-Aland, 26th edition.[12] Following the paragraph divisions of this edition, I found καί introducing a paragraph only in 1 Corinthians 2:1; 3:1; 12:31; 2 Corinthians 1:15; 7:5; Ephesians 2:1; 6:4; Colossians 1:21; 1 Thessalonians 2:13; Hebrews 7:20; 9:15; 10:11; 11:32; 1 Peter 3:13; 1 John 1:5; 2:3; 3:13, 19; 3:23. This infrequency makes us wonder whether the author really intended a transition at these points. Is it also possible that καί has an adverbial function in some of these instances?

In some of these exceptions where καί is found paragraph-initial, there are alternative textual readings. In 1 Thessalonians 2:13 and 1 John 3:13 and 19, καί is omitted in a number of manuscripts. In 2 Corinthians 7:5, the conjunction is γάρ. Being a postposition particle, it automatically occurs after the καί which here functions as an adverb. It is so translated by TEV, JB, NEB, RSV, and Phillips. In other instances, a personal, relative, or demonstrative pronoun immediately follows the καί (e.g., 1 Cor. 2:1; 3:1; Eph. 2:1; Col. 1:21; Heb. 11:32; 1 Pet. 3:13; 1 John 1:5). In these instances, the καί more than likely is adverbial, emphasizing the pronoun.[13] As for the remaining instances

[9] E.g., Rom. 2:1; 1 Cor. 14:13; Eph. 2:11.

[10] E.g., Rom. 5:12; Eph. 1:15; Col. 1:9.

[11] E.g., Rom. 8:1, 12; 2 Thess. 2:15.

[12] The various English translations in more cases than not concur with Nestle-Aland's paragraph breaks.

[13] See Titrud 1986:75–76 for the support for this statement.

where καί seems to occur at a paragraph break, I suggest that Tischendorf's and/or Souter's *Novum Testamentum Graece*, along with some of the English translations, are correct in not positing a paragraph break.

My conclusion is that, in translating the Epistles, a new paragraph should not be made where a conjunctive καί begins a sentence in the Greek text. A paragraph-initial καί followed by a pronoun or a postpositive particle (e.g., γάρ) should be classified as an adverb. This is a helpful rule when we are not sure where paragraph breaks should be made. This is the case, for example, at Colossians 2:13 and 3:15: the NIV posits a paragraph break at Colossians 2:13 (also LB) and 3:15 (also Callow 1983); however, in these same places, Nestle-Aland and most other English translations do not. I would argue in the light of the above that Nestle-Aland and the other English translations intuitively[14] discerned rightly that there should not be a paragraph break at Colossians 2:13 and 3:15.[15]

The close interrelatedness of propositions coordinated by καί is also shown by the degree of ellipsis[16] that may occur. If two clauses joined by καί have a number of common elements, these elements can be omitted without introducing obscurity or ambiguity into the conjoined structure. One example is 1 Timothy 1:2, "The life was made manifest, καί we saw [it], καί we testify [concerning it to you], καί we proclaim to you the eternal life. . . . " Like "and" in English, καί allows for a great deal of ellipsis, more than most conjunctions.

The close interrelatedness of propositions conjoined by καί is also demonstrated by what Jean Goddard (1977) calls "pairing." Pairing is the coordination of two or more propositions which have a closer relationship to each other than to the other propositions in a series. For example, in Ephesians 6:1–9, "fathers" are paired with "children" and "masters" are paired with "slaves" by the conjunctive καί in verses 4 and 9 respectively. Note that "children" and "fathers" are separated from "slaves" and "masters" by asyndeton (Ø) in verse 5. (Also note that the RSV is more consistent here than Nestle-Aland with the paragraph breaks.)

[14] I say "intuitively" because there are places where Nestle-Aland and the other versions did not adhere to this "rule" that the conjunctive καί never begins a paragraph. Two such places are Heb. 9:15 and 10:1, where only NASB and LB did not posit a paragraph break. (The NASB and LB, however, did not adhere to this rule in other places, as in 1 John 2:3.)

[15] Note that Callow also introduces a new paragraph at Col. 3:17 and at 2 Thess. 2:6 (Callow 1982). However, again it seems that Nestle-Aland and all the English translations discerned correctly that no paragraph break should occur here.

[16] Ellipsis can be regarded as substitution by zero.

Still another example of pairing is 1 Peter 3:3. Why are the constituents "braiding of hair" and "decoration of gold" conjoined by καί, and the following constituent "wearing of robes" conjoined by δέ? Peter may have intended the "braiding of hair" and the "decoration of gold" to have a closer relationship to each other than to the "wearing of robes"—he may have been referring to adorning braided hair with gold. Roman women of means were extraordinarily fond of jewelry and often bedecked their hair with gems and sometimes wore a coronal, or tiara, consisting of a band of gold and precious stones (Tucker 1910:297, 312).

The distinction between καί and δέ. Beginning Greek students are usually taught that δέ means contrast.[17] Zerwick (1963: para. 467), for example, states, "The particle δέ almost always implies some sort of contrast."[18] Turner (1963:332), to the other extreme, in recognizing that δέ does not always mean contrast, states that δέ is usually indistinguishable from καί. The middle ground between Zerwick and Turner can be found in A. T. Robertson (1934). He is correct in claiming that though there is no essential notion of antithesis or contrast in the word δέ itself,[19] "what is true is that the addition is something new and not so closely associated in thought as is true of τέ and καί" (p. 1184).

Thus, although δέ itself is not inherently adversative, yet due to its function of marking what follows as something new and distinct, it readily allows an adversative sense (dependent, of course, on the context). The basic difference between δέ and the conjunctive ἀλλά is that, when δέ implies contrast, it does so depending on the context, whereas the inherent meaning of ἀλλά is contrast. The difference between δέ and καί, on the other hand, seems to be that of distinction versus relative closeness between propositions (or propositional clusters).

The distinction between καί and τέ. One of the obvious differences between καί and τέ is the frequency of their occurrence: καί occurs in the New Testament 9,164 times, τέ only 215 times (De Gruyter 1980). Most of the occurrences of τέ are in Acts (170 times). Another difference is that τέ is a postposition particle, as δέ is.

[17] BAGD (s.v. δέ) states that δέ is "one of the most commonly used Gk. particles, used to connect one clause w. another when it is felt that there is some contrast betw. them, though the contrast is oft. scarcely discernible."

[18] Thrall (1952:50–67) rightly disputes this. She notes that contrasts in Mark are indicated not only by δέ, but by the conjunctive καί as well, and that, in fact, δέ can occur where there is no trace of contradiction at all. Thrall's treatment, unfortunately, is "of a somewhat negative character," as she herself admits, for she is unable to come up with a convincing analysis.

[19] At the very beginning of the New Testament, in Matt. 1:2–16, δέ occurs a number of times without an adversative sense.

Levinsohn (1979:10–14) distinguishes between καί and τέ in terms of the "Union" factor: Union is understood to mean that the elements so linked are viewed as united into a single whole, and the absence of this factor means that they are treated as distinct. He marks καί as [– Union] and τέ as [+ Union]. This is similar to Turner's statement that τέ "joins more closely than simple καί and joins words which have between themselves a close or logical affinity" (Turner 1963:339). However, in the light of the preceding discussion, especially καί's ability to introduce apposition, one cannot conclude that καί links elements that are not to be viewed as a single whole. Καί does unite elements that are to be viewed as one entity. This τέ does not do. Though τέ unites elements that have a close or logical affinity, these elements are still nonetheless distinct. More correctly, one could describe καί as having a wider continuum than τέ as to the degree of closeness or logical affinity: τέ is more specific, conjoining elements having a close or logical but nonetheless distinct affinity. (Another element seemingly inherent in τέ on the interclausal level is its nature to introduce comments of a parenthetical nature, as in Acts 1:15; 2:40; 4:13, 33; 10:22, 33; 11:26.)

It would appear that the construction τὲ καί is synonymous with καί . . . καί "both . . . and." There is a difference, however, as to what is being intensified. In the καί . . . καί construction, the first καί is the adverb intensifying both elements. In the τὲ καί construction, on the other hand, the τέ is the conjoiner of the two elements and the καί is intensifying the second element (e.g., Acts 22:4, "I persecuted the followers of this Way to their death, arresting men and (τέ) even (καί) women"; 1 Cor. 1:24, "Jews and (τέ) even (καί) Gentiles"; Heb. 5:1, "to offer gifts and (τέ) particularly (καί) sacrifices for sins"). Here, τὲ καί is substituting for what would hypothetically be a καί (CC) καί (AB) construction, since καί καί would have been phonetically awkward.[20] The construction καί καί was grammatically possible but phonetically dissonant, and τὲ καί was a viable substitute.

Summary of the Uses of καί

Καί may function grammatically as an adverb or as a conjunction. In most cases in Greek, the grammatical structure signals which of these functions applies. When καί occurs postpositionally in a clause

---

[20] English also has constraints against the juxtaposition of homophones. For example, in response to "I gave her two apples," John could say "I gave her two also" or "I gave her some too" or "I gave her one too." But he would not say "I gave her two too." This sounds awkward and is rejected by most English speakers.

or when it is found between two unlike grammatical units, it is an adverb. This does not mean that καί as an adverb is always restricted to a postposition. It may occur initially when causes are conjoined by asyndeton or by postpositional conjunctions. On the other hand, καί as a conjoiner of clauses is always restricted to initial position. This is an important distinction to make, often overlooked by exegetes.

Καί as an adverb serves basically as a spotlight. It is an intensifier calling special attention to what follows. The nature of the emotive impact, (whether surprise, bewilderment, disbelief, or some other feeling) is contingent on the context. It may be translated in English by such words as "even," "also," "indeed," "very," and "certainly." However, at times, a more ingenious method may be needed in order to elicit the particular emphasis portrayed.

Similar to "and" in English, καί as a conjunction serves both on the intraclausal and on the interclausal level. It is also a coordinating conjunction even though there may be rare instances where logically one proposition is subordinate to the other. When καί does coordinate what is semantically a subordinate clause, it is encoding more prominence upon the subordinate clause than it would have if introduced by the more specific subordinating conjunctions. Throughout the paper we have also posited that there is an element of καί that is unlike "and," namely that it regularly introduces apposition, and that this, too, is often missed by exegetes. Too often a distinction between two elements conjoined by καί is forced. Rather, we have maintained in light of the rule of maximum redundancy that if apposition is a viable option among constituents of propositions conjoined by καί, it should be highly considered.

We have also demonstrated that one of the distinctive features of the conjunction καί when compared with other conjoining particles is that of union. καί informs that the following is to be closely united with the preceding. There is a closer relationship between propositions when coordinated by καί. This is illustrated by the degree of ellipsis that may occur, the regularity of apposition being introduced by καί, and the fact that καί rarely (and in epistle material, it may even be argued never) introduces a paragraph break.

Καί in 2 Peter

Every writer has an "idiolect" of his own. Therefore, as an aid in determining the interpretation of a given passage which contains καί, an analysis of that particular writer's employment of καί throughout his text (or texts) could prove beneficial. In this section we analyze the use of καί in 2 Peter, which in turn will aid us in determining the

Table 1: The Conjoining Particles and their Functions

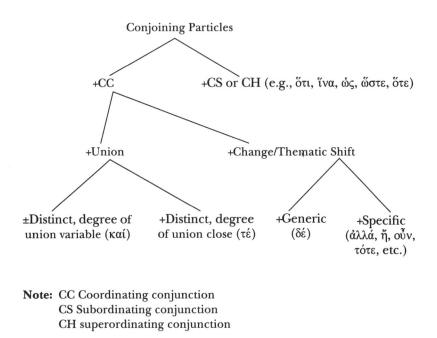

Note: CC Coordinating conjunction
CS Subordinating conjunction
CH superordinating conjunction

meaning of ambiguous or obscure passages (e.g., 2 Pet. 3:10). The reason why 1 Peter is not combined with 2 Peter in the analysis is due to the practically universal doubt as to whether or not 1 Peter and 2 Peter were written by the same writer. More than likely Peter used different amanuenses for the two letters, or possibly Peter himself wrote 2 Peter whereas 1 Peter was written via Silvanus. The use of amanuenses was common. Paul himself used one in Romans (16:22), and probably in all or most of his epistles (Philem. 19; 1 Cor. 16:21; Gal. 6:11; Col. 4:18; 2 Thess. 3:17). The apostles probably did not dictate word by word to their amanuenses, but more than likely the amanuenses were given a free hand with respect to the grammatical construction of the content dictated to them (see also Kelly 1981:26; Titrud 1986:91–92).

Below we have listed all the occurrences of καί in 2 Peter and have commented in each case on its particular function. In the case of καί functioning as a conjunction, we have specified the type of semantic relationship between the propositions being coordinated by it. (See Table 2).

Table 2: Semantic Relationships Indicated by καί

RELATION	OTHER CON-JUNCTIONS	ENGLISH GLOSS	EXAMPLE
COORDINATION			
Sequential (also intraclausal; e.g., 2 Pet. 2:12)	τότε, δέ	"and" (then)	Acts 5:20
Simultaneous	∅	"and," ∅	Mark 1:35–37
Conjoining (also intraclausal; e.g., Mark 3:18)	δέ, τέ	"and," ∅	1 Thess. 2:15b,c,d
Contrast 2:1; Rom. 1:13	ἀλλά, δέ	"but," "however"	Mark 12:12; 1 John (parenthetical)
Contrastive Assertion		"(and) yet"	Matt. 6:26; 11:19; John 1:10; 5:44; 1 Cor. 5:2; 1 Pet. 2:16
Result	ὥστε	"thus," "(and) so"	1 John 2:20b; Matt. 8:15; 1 Pet. 5:4[a]
Apposition[b] (a) Equivalent (also intraclausal) (b) Amplification/ Explicative/ Exegetical (c) Specific (also intraclausal, e.g., Mark 16:7; Acts 22:25[c] (d) Summary		∅ "and," "that is" "in other words" "namely," "(and) specifically," "including" "In summary," ∅	Matt. 7:2; 8:17 Matt. 5:42; 12:32; 1 Pet. 2:25; Col. 1:17a[d] Matt. 5:44; 11:12;[e] 1 John 3:12; 1 Pet. 3:10; Rev. 14:10b Matt. 10:36; Acts 6:7; 1 John 3:23
SUBORDINATION			
Temporal	ὅτε	"when"	Mark 15:25; Luke 19:43; Heb. 8:8

Table 2: *continued*

RELATION	OTHER CON-JUNCTIONS	ENGLISH GLOSS	EXAMPLE
Grounds	γάρ	"for"	1 Pet. 4:18[f]
Reason (causal)	ὅτι	"because"	Mark 8:3; Rev. 12:11
Purpose	ἵνα	"so that"	Matt. 8:8; 26:25; Luke 7:7
(Orienter) - Content	ὅτι, Ø	"that," Ø	Mark 10:26; Rev. 6:12

a. The καί here connects the reward in 5:4b with 5:3b. If you do 5:3b, then you will be rewarded.

b. There is a great deal of overlapping between the subcategories a, b, and c.

c. A Roman citizen, *and* uncondemned *at that.*

d. Verse 17 is reiterating and expounding on verses 15 and 16 (O'Brien 1982:47).

e. Most commentaries see βιασταί as referring to violent men and hence understand βιάζεται as passive.

f. Καιι here introduces a quote as a grounds for the preceding material. The implied link that it makes between the preceding material and the quote is something like "you know I speak truthfully because it is written in God's Word." (Fedukowski n.d.)

1:1 δοῦλος "slave" καὶ ἀπόστολος "apostle"—Generic-Specific

"Slave" expresses the more general and "apostle" the more specific relation. (See Huther 1881:289.)

τοῦ θεοῦ ἡμῶν "our God" καὶ σωτῆρος Ἰησοῦ Χριστοῦ "Savior Jesus Christ"—Conjoining.

The two descriptive phrases are probably referring to the same person since they are both governed by only one article, τοῦ. (See Titrud 1986:60–66 or Titrud 1991:12–15 on the Granville Sharp's rule. Most scholars agree here.) The author is fond of combining Christological titles (cf. 1:11; 2:20; 3:2, 18).

1:2 χάρις ὑμῖν "grace to you" καὶ εἰρήνη "peace"—Semi-Equivalent

The combination of the Greek epistolary greeting (χάρις) with a Hebrew greeting (εἰρήνη) became a new and characteristic development in the formula of greeting (see BAGD, s.v. "εἰρήνη," 2). There is much overlapping between the two expressions. While it may be justified to take these two words in their full theological import, it should be borne in mind that, as in the Pauline corpus, this is a greeting formula which should be considered as a single unit (see Arichea, Jr. and Nida 1975:7).

τοῦ θεοῦ "of God" καὶ Ἰησοῦ τοῦ κυρίου ἡμῶν "of Jesus our Lord"— Generic-Specific

Green (1982:62) remarks that "many MSS read simply 'in knowledge of our Lord', probably correctly . . . it fits the singular *his* of verse 3; and elsewhere in this Epistle it is Jesus alone who is the object of *knowledge* (epignosis)." However, the textual evidence for deleting τοῦ θεοῦ καὶ Ἰησοῦ is slight, and Green's argument for doing so could be handled by analyzing καί here as encoding a generic-specific relationship (cf P[72] where καί is absent and thus the phrase less ambiguously infers a generic-specific relationship; for Jesus Christ alone as the object of knowledge in 2 Peter, see 1:2, 3, 8; 2:20; 3:18).

1:3 ζωὴν "life" καὶ εὐσέβειαν "piety"—Amplification

"Godly life" (cf. TEV, Phillips, LB). There is no need to see a distinction here as is done by most commentators and translators.[21]

δόξῃ καὶ ἀρετῇ—Equivalent

"The pair δόξῃ καὶ ἀρετῇ should be understood, like other pairs of words in 2 Peter, as closely related in meaning" (Bauckham 1983:178). Here is an example where each member of the pair specifies the meaning of its co-member. Both δόξα and ἀρετή have a wide range of meaning (see the various meanings given in the lexicons for these two words, e.g., BAGD). The juxtaposition of these two lexical items linked by καί limit their range of meanings to that of denoting *divine power*.[22]

1:4 τίμια καὶ μέγιστα—Amplification

If this order is original, 2 Peter is amplifying the fact that the promises granted to us are not only of great worth (τίμια) but superlatively of very great (μέγιστα) worth. If the order is the reverse, as in some manuscripts (e.g., C, P), the τίμια would be specifying in what way the promises are very great.

1:5 καὶ αὐτὸ τοῦτο δέ—Adverb

Some have understood the καί here as adding something new to what has gone before (so Huther 1881:298; Johnson 1988:36).

---

[21] "We should probably see the whole expression as hendiadys" (Bauckham 1983:178).

[22] δόξα καὶ ἀρετή was a stock combination in Hellenistic writers, especially Plutarch. See Bauckham (1983:179); BAGD, s.v. "ἀρετή," 2.

However, this is not the function of καί here. The δέ is the coordinating conjunction signifying the addition of something further. The καί is an adverb intensifying αὐτὸ τοῦτο as in the RSV, TEV, and NIV, "For this *very* reason."

1:8 ὑπάρκοντα "being" καὶ πλεονάζοντα "abounding"—Amplification

Not just to possess (ὑπάρκοντα) these qualities but to possess them in (increasing) abundance (see NIV and JB).

1:10 κλῆσιν "calling" καὶ ἐκλογήν "choice"—Semi-Equivalent

"There is probably no great distinction between the two terms intended here" (Bauckham 1983:190).

1:11 τοῦ κυρίου ἡμῶν "our Lord" καὶ σωτῆρος Ἰησοῦ Χριστοῦ "Savior Jesus Christ"—Conjoining

Again the two descriptive phrases are referring to the same person (see 1:1; cf. 1:8).

1:12 εἰδότας καὶ ἐστηριγμένους—Amplification

ἐστηριγμένους further expresses the degree of their *knowing*, knowing in the sense of being "firmly convinced and committed to it" (ἐστηριγμένους ἐν being a dead metaphor. Compare its use in Luke 22:32; Rom. 16:25; 1 Thess. 3:2; 1 Pet. 5:10). οἶδα in the New Testament (as with *yāda*[c] in the Old Testament[23]) does not merely encode a theoretical knowledge about someone or something, but it also often implies an intimate acquaintance and a positive relationship with that which is known, in this case with the truth.[24]

1:14 καθὼς "as" καί—Adverb

The adverb καί here intensifies Peter's certainty concerning his approaching death. Though left untranslated by most translations, it has the sense here of "as *indeed* . . . "/or probably better yet "as *in fact* our Lord Jesus Christ has made clear to me."

1:15 δὲ καί—Adverb

Here καί is textually suspect (not found in P72). Καί does not have the function of connecting this sentence with the foregoing as claimed by Huther (1881:311) and Alford (1866:396), for this is the function of δέ. Rather the meaning seems to be "not only will I refresh your memory as long as I live (v. 13), but *even* after my departure I will see to it that you will always be able to remember these

---

[23] See Brown, Driver, and Briggs (1907), s.v. "*yāda*[c]."
[24] See BAGD, s.v. "οἶδα."

things (v. 15)." However, this adverbial καί is again left untranslated by most translations.

1:16 δύναμιν "power" καὶ παρουσίαν "presence"—Amplification

Again this pair of words should be understood as one entity and not, as is implied by most translations, as two distinct elements concerning our Lord Jesus Christ.[25] TEV has rightly united the two concepts, "the mighty coming." Compare also Bauckham's translation, "the coming of our Lord Jesus Christ in power" (1983:215).

1:17 τιμὴν "honour" καὶ δόξαν "glory"—Equivalent

Again we have a natural pair and the distinction between them should not be forced as is done by most commentators (e.g., Kelly, Green, Mayor). δόξα probably does not specifically point to the ethereal radiance of the transfigured Jesus, about which nothing has been said. Rather the two terms should be seen here as virtually synonymous, both expressions being used to intensify the exalted status received, hence "greatly honored."

1:18 καί . . . —Adverb

Probably here an adverb with the sense of "indeed." "We can verify verse 17 for we *in fact* heard the voice."

1:19 καὶ ἔχομεν "we have" . . . —Result

καί closely conjoins the propositional clusters of verses 16–18 with that of verses 19–21, the relationship being one of result. "We were eyewitnesses . . . so we have confirmation of what was said in prophecies." (JB; cf. also TEV, NEB, LB).

ἡμέρα διαυγάσῃ "day dawns" καὶ φωσφόρος ἀνατείλῃ "morning star rises"—Generic-Specific

"The day dawns" probably refers to the Parousia generally whereas "the morning star" refers to Christ specifically (cf. Rev. 22:16).[26]

2:1 δὲ καί—Adverb

Exactly why Peter is intensifying/emphasizing the following depends on our understanding as to who are the recipients of the letter. If Peter is writing to a Gentile constituency who may not be all that familiar with the Old Testament, he could be evoking an element of surprise. Not only were there true prophets back then

---

[25] δύναμις is often associated with the Parousia. See Matt. 24:30; Mark 9:1; 13:26; Luke 21:27.

[26] Bauckham (1983:225–26); Green (1968:88); and many others.

(v. 19) confirmed by Peter's own experience (vv. 16–18), but there were *even/also* (καί) false prophets. If Peter was presupposing that the recipients of the letter were well versed in the Old Testament, he may be evoking a strong reminder upon them that *even* back then there were false prophets.

ὡς 'as' καί—Adverb

Again evoking surprise and/or the surety of what is being stated, "as *indeed/in fact*," the comparison relationship is reflected only in the ὡς, not the ὡς καί combination as implied by some (e.g., Bigg 1901:273; Johnson 1988:70).

καὶ τὸν ἀγοράσαντα "the one having bought" . . . —Adverb

καί as a coordinating conjunction coordinates like grammatical units which is not the case here since ἀρνούμενοι "denying," a participle, is grammatically (as well as semantically) subordinate to the previous clause. (See Titrud 1991:5–6 for further discussion on this phrase).

2:2 καὶ πολλοὶ "many" . . . —Conjoining

2:3 καὶ ἐν πλεονεξίᾳ "in (their) greed" . . . —Conjoining

καὶ ἡ ἀπώλεια αὐτῶν οὐ νυστάζει "their destruction has not been asleep"—Amplification

As in 1:19, here is another example of poetic parallelism. "Their destruction" is specifically stating what is implied in "their condemnation."

2:5, 6, 7—Conjoining

καί in these verses is introducing coordinate statements with the εἰ of verse 4 implied.

2:8 βλέμματι "in seeing" γὰρ καὶ ἀκοῇ "in hearing"—Conjoining

γάρ is the particle that coordinates this verse with verse 7, a further explanation of Lot's distress (see BAGD, s.v. "γάρ," 2). καί on the other hand coordinates βλέμματι with ἀκοῇ.

2:10 τοὺς . . . πορευομένους "following (after)" καὶ . . . καταφρονοῦντας "despising"—Conjoining or Result

The following of the corrupt desire of their sinful natures and the despising authority are done by the same group, being governed by one article. In fact, the intent here could be that of a logical-result relationship between the two propositions which then would have the sense of "especially those who follow their corrupt bodily lusts and so despise the lordship of Christ."

2:11 ἰσχύϊ καὶ δυνάμει—Equivalent

Again there is no need to try to force a distinction between these two virtually synonymous terms (e.g., ἰσχύς emphasizing the outward, physical manifestation, and δύναμις the inward, spiritual or moral virtue[27]). Rather the doublet emphasizes the totality of their power.

2:12 εἰς ἅλωσιν καὶ φθοράν—Sequential

" . . . born to be caught and (then) killed."[28]

καὶ φθαρήσονται "they will be destroyed"—Adverb

Due to the intensive nature of the adverbial καί, it would seem that the writer is explicitly stressing the fact that they will indeed perish. Phillips expresses the καί here well: "will most *certainly* be destroyed in their own corruption." (Emphasis mine).[29]

2:13 σπίλοι καὶ μῶμοι—Equivalent

JB expresses well the intensity of this reduplication, which especially in their figurative meaning are virtually equivalent: "They are unsightly blots on your society."

2:14 . . . μεστοὺς μοιχαλίδος "full of adulterous (lust)" καὶ ἀκαταπαύστους ἁμαρτίας "not ceasing from sin"—Specific-Generic

Here the two descriptive phrases connected by καί are closer related to each other than the following descriptive phrases introduced by asyndeton (∅). Compare NIV, "with eyes full of adultery, they never stop sinning; . . . "

2:17 πηγαὶ ἄνυδροι "waterless springs" καὶ ὁμίχλαι "mists" . . . —Equivalent

Poetic parallelism emphasizing that they are completely dry. Though they put on a show, they have nothing *at all* to offer.

2:20 τοῦ κυρίου [ἡμῶν] καὶ σωτῆρος Ἰησοῦ Χριστοῦ—Conjoining[30]
2:22 κύων "(the) dog" . . . καὶ ὧς "(the) sow" . . . —Equivalent

Poetic parallelism. Both sayings illustrate the false teachers' apostasy. Having been "cleansed from their past sins" (1:19), they are

---

[27] As claimed by Vincent (1914:696).

[28] Here false teachers are likened to animals that were born to be slaughtered. "The idea that certain animals were born to be slaughtered and eaten was common in the ancient world (Juvenal 1:141; Pliny, *Hist. Nat.* 8:81; *b. B. Mes.* 85a)" (Bauckham 1983:263). Hence φθορά here must mean "destruction" (not "corruption").

[29] It is not true as Bauckham (1983:264) claims that "certainly" is an unnatural sense of καί, and that "also" is its expected sense. On the adverbial function of καί see Titrud 1991:4–8.

[30] See 2 Pet. 1:1, 2, 8, 11.

returning to their past immoral nature (see also Bauckham 1983:280).

3:2 τῶν ... ῥημάτων "words" ... καὶ τῆς ... ἐντολῆς "commandment" ... —Conjoining

Since καί implies a close-interrelatedness among the propositions it conjoins, "the commandment of the Lord and Savior through your apostles" could refer specifically to Peter's (and the other apostles') warnings concerning false teachers upon whom the Old Testament prophets predicted divine judgment (e.g., Amos 9:10; Isa. 5:18–20).

τοῦ κυρίου καὶ σωτῆρος—Conjoining (see 2:20)

3:4 καὶ λέγοντες "saying"—Conjoining

3:5 οὐρανοὶ "heavens" ... καὶ γῆ "earth" ... —Conjoining

ἐξ ὕδατος καὶ δι' ὕδατος—Conjoining, Result, or Apposition

The semantic relationship between these two prepositional phrases would vary depending upon one's understanding of what they are referring to. Does ἐξ ὕδατος refer to "the elemental stuff out of which the universe was made" (Kelly 1969:359), or to the world's emergence out of the watery chaos (Bauckham 1983:297)? Also, what is the understanding of the phrase δι' ὕδατος? Some have understood διά in a local sense, "between, in the midst of the waters" (e.g. JB; Mayor 1907:151) referring to Genesis 1:6–9. Others (e.g., Bauckham), on the other hand, argue that this would be an unusual use of the preposition, especially in light of the fact that in the very next verse the preposition διά clearly is instrumental. (Also it is noted that in Gen. 1:6, the LXX does not read διά, but rather expresses the thought by ἀνὰ μέσον ὕδατος καὶ ὕδατος "in the midst of water"). Therefore it is argued that διά in 2 Peter 3:5 is also instrumental. And yet exactly how the water is instrumental is also understood differently by exegetes. Is it by means of the water that the earth was created, or the means by which it is sustained? The combination chosen on each of these points determines the semantic relationship between the two phrases.

3:7 οἱ ... οὐρανοὶ "the heavens" καὶ ἡ γῆ "the earth"—Conjoining

3:7b κρίσεως "judgment" καὶ ἀπωλείας "destruction"—Amplification

The destruction of the godless further specifies what the day of judgment entails (cf. NEB "until the day of judgment *when* the godless will be destroyed").

3:8 ... ἔτη "years" καὶ χίλια "thousand" ... —Conjoining

3:10 στοιχεῖα "elements" . . . καὶ γῆ "earth" . . . —Amplification

Poetic parallelism, common in the Old Testament, was also a fa-
vored style of the writer of 2 Peter (cf. also 1 Peter 2:8; 3:10). Could
it not be that here in 2 Peter 3:10 καὶ is introducing apposition as
well, making explicit what is meant by the previous obscure term?
Hence, "the elements will be destroyed by fire, that is the earth and
(thereby including) everything in it will disappear/vanish."[31] This is
definitely a possibility, for the author of 2 Peter regularly employs
καί to introduce apposition. When we check this possibility with the
context we find that it makes perfectly good sense. Also grammatically it satisfies the question not addressed by the commentaries
concerning the conjoining particles in this verse. Why is it that δέ
conjoins the clauses "the heavens . . . " and "the element . . . "
whereas καί is the conjoiner for the clauses "the elements . . . " and
"the earth. . . . " If καί is understood as introducing apposition, it
also takes care of the question as to why only here is στοιχεῖα added
when elsewhere in Scripture (including 2 Pet. 3:5, 13) only the
"heavens" and "the earth" are in juxtaposition. (See also Gen. 1:1;
14:19, 22; Matt. 5:18; 11:25; 24:35; Mark 13:31; Luke 10:21; 16:17;
21:33; Acts 4:24; 14:15; 17:24; Rev. 14:7; 20:11). It also answers the
question that has puzzled many commentators as to why γῆ is omitted in verse 12.[32] If understood as apposition, there is no omission.
Also apposition would alleviate all the problems that the proponents of the above three interpretations have with one other. For
example, if the elements refer to earth, air, fire, and water, one
would be speaking of fire destroying fire. And how is it distinct from
"the heavens" and "the earth"? If elements refer to the heavenly
bodies (sun, moon, and stars) then what do the heavens means?
Surely the dwelling place of God will not be dissolved.[33] Likewise, if
they refer to spirits, can spirits be burned and dissolved?[34] Each of
the three suggested interpretations leaves a lot of questions dan-
gling. These all are solved nicely if apposition is posited, that is, if

[31] See Titrud 1986: 110–113 for justification for translating εὑρεθήσεται as "will
disappear/vanish." There we have determined that εὑρεθήσεται "will be discovered" is
the preferred meaning, since it is the oldest reading and the one which best explains
the origin of the others. We also concluded that the clause is a rhetorical question and
could then have the meaning "will not be found" (cf. Rev. 20:11 " . . . earth and sky
fled away, and no place was found for them"). The rhetorical question would then also
be understood as parallel and synonymous with what will happen to the heavens. They
too "will disappear/pass away/come to an end (παρελεύσονται)."

[32] Joseph B. Mayor (1907:162), in response to Spitta's query as to why καὶ γῆ is omitted here, explains that "the *rhythm* of the sentence would have suffered from the addition." (Emphasis mine). This, however, is not a very satisfactory answer.

we understand "the earth . . . " as amplifying the clause "the elements. . . . " στοιχεῖα then in 2 Peter 3:10 would have the sense of the elemental substances of the earth.

γῆ "earth" καὶ τὰ ἐν αὐτῇ ἔργα "the works in it"—Generic-Specific

Special attention is made to the fact that nothing on the earth will escape from disappearing. Lest there be any misunderstanding, the author is emphasising that included in this act will be the disappearing of all creation on earth (probably refering to the works of both God and humans).

3:11 ἐν ἁγίαις ἀναστροφαῖς "in holy conduct" καὶ εὐσεβείαις "piety"—Equivalent

Virtually synonymous expressions placing emphasis on what is to be the proper conduct.

3:12 προσδοκῶντας "awaiting" καὶ σπεύδοντας "hastening"—Amplification

More than likely the relationship here is that of Amplification resulting in the sense that their waiting for the Day of God is not to be a passive waiting but rather actively speeding its coming (e.g., by helping to make the gospel known to all ethnic groups, Mark 13:10; Matt. 24:14; cf. Rev. 7:9).

οὐρανοὶ "heavens" . . . καὶ στοιχεῖα "elements" . . . —Conjoining

Contextually, στοιχεῖα has previously (v. 10) been introduced as distinct (στοιχεῖα δέ) from "the heavens." Hence apposition is not an option here.

3:13 οὐρανοὺς "heavens" καὶ γῆν "earth"—Conjoining

3:14 ἄσπιλοι καὶ ἀμώμητοι—Equivalent

" . . . without any blemish *whatsoever*" (cf. 2:13).

---

[33] We maintain that the plural heavens (οἱ οὐρανοί) here means everything above (or outside) the earth. This would include the heaven of the clouds (atmosphere) and the heaven of the sun and stars. However, the third heaven (2 Cor. 12:2) that is the dwelling place of God would of course be excluded. Also, although in later times there are instances of στοιχεῖα referring to the heavenly bodies (TDNT, s.v. "στοιχεῖον," pp. 681–682), W. L. Liefeld argues that the evidence for this is probably too late to allow its consideration in 2 Pet. 3:10 (*The Zondervan Pictorial Encyclopedia of the Bible*, 1975, s.v. "Element (Elemental Spirit), Elements.")

[34] E. Schweizer also argues that a connection between the term "elements" and stars or spirits (demons) cannot be found before the second century A.D. ("Christianity of the Circumcised and Judaism of the Uncircumcised. The Background of Matthew and Colossians," in *Jews, Greeks and Christians. Religious Cultures in Late Antiquity. Essays in Honour of William David Darries*, ed. R. Hamerton-Kelly and R. Scroggs [Leiden: Brill, 1976], pp. 245–60).

3:15 καὶ τὴν τοῦ κυρίου . . . —Conjoining

καθὼς "as" καί—Adverb ("even/also/indeed")

3:16 ὡς "as" καί—Adverb ("in fact")

οἱ ἀμαθεῖς "unlearned" καὶ ἀστήρικτοι "unsteady"—Conjoining

ὡς "as" καί—Adverb ("also")

3:18 ἐν χάριτι "grace" καὶ γνώσει "knowledge"—Amplification

Second Peter seems to regularly employ καί in order to encode that the following is amplifying the preceding (e.g., 1:3, 4, 8, 12, 16, etc.). Could it not be the case here as well? Thus a proposed translation would be: "On the contrary, continue to grow in grace, and specifically I am referring to knowledge being given by our Lord . . . " (subjective genitive).[35]

καὶ νῦν "now" . . . —Adverb ("both")[36]

νῦν "now" καὶ εἰς ἡμέραν αἰῶνος "for ever"—Conjoining

Summary of the Functions of καί in 2 Peter

Of the fifty-eight occurrences of καί in 2 Peter, twelve function adverbially. Most significant is the fact that in twenty-three of the remaining forty-six occurrences where καί functions as a coordinating conjunction, it is used to introduce apposition (in most cases that of equivalence or amplification, but also generic-specific as, for example in 1:1, 2, 19, and specific-generic as in 2:14). In two more instances a semi-equivalent relationship is coordinated by καί. Thus in 2 Peter when καί is functioning as a coordinating conjunction approximately half the time it is introducing apposition.

References

Alford, Henry. 1866. *The Greek Testament*. vol. 4, 3d ed. London: Gilbert and Rivington.

Arichea, Daniel C. Jr. and Eugene A. Nida. 1975. *A Translator's Handbook on Paul's Letter to the Galatians*. New York: United Bible Societies. P. 7.

---

[35] If γνώσει τοῦ κυρίου is analyzed as an objective genitive, as done by all the translations, there arises the problem of having an awkward construction, that is treating the genitive as simultaneously subjective (in relation to grace) and objective (in relation to knowledge). Note that "grace" and "knowledge" share the same preposition. Not only grammatically but also contextually (cf. vv. 16 and 17) it makes more sense to analyze this construction as a subjective genitive.

[36] See Titrud 1991:7–9 on the construction of καί . . . καί ("both . . . and").

Arndt, William F. and Wilbur F. Gingrich, trans. 1979. *A Greek-English Lexicon of the New Testament and Other Early Christian Literature,* revised and augmented by F. Wilbur Gingrich and Frederick W. Danker from Walter Bauer's fifth edition. Chicago: University of Chicago Press.

Bauckham, Richard J. 1983. *Jude, 2 Peter.* Word Biblical Commentary. Vol. 50. Waco: Word.

Bigg, Charles. 1901. *The Epistles of St. Peter and St. Jude,* ICC. Edinburgh: T & T Clark.

Blass, F. and A. Debrunner. 1961. *A Greek Grammar of the New Testament and Other Early Christian Literature.* A translation and revision of the 9th–10th German edition by Robert W. Funk. Chicago: University of Chicago Press.

Brooks, James A. and Carlton L. Winbery, 1979. *Syntax of New Testament Greek.* Washington, D.C.: University Press of America.

Brown, Francis, S. R. Driver, and Charles A. Briggs. 1907. *A Hebrew and English Lexicon of the Old Testament.* Oxford: Clarendon Press.

Callow, John C. 1982. *A Semantic Structure Analysis of Second Thessalonians.* Ed. by Michael F. Kopesec. Dallas: Summer Institute of Linguistics.

_____. 1983. *A Semantic Structure Analysis of Colossians,* ed. by Michael F. Kopesec. Dallas: Summer Institute of Linguistics.

Denniston, J. D. 1959. *The Greek Particles.* 2d ed. Oxford: Clarendon Press.

Denton, Peter. 1985. "An Analysis of Granville Sharp's Rule: The Use of a Single Article to Govern Several Conjoined Nouns." Unpublished paper done for New Testament 803 with the use of GRAMCORD, a computer retrieval system, at Trinity Evangelical Divinity School.

De Gruyter, Walter. 1980. *Computer Konkordanz zum Novum Testamentum Graece.* New York: Walter De Gruyter.

Fedukowski, Donna. N.d. "Semantic Structure Analysis of 1 Peter." Unpublished draft. Dallas: Summer Institute of Linguistics.

Friberg, Barbara, and Timothy Friberg, eds. 1981. *Analytical Greek New Testament.* Grand Rapids: Baker.

Goddard, Jean. 1977. "Some Thoughts on δέ and καί in Acts 5:1–8:1a." *Translation Department Microfiche Library (SIL's)* 12:79227.

Green, Michael. 1968. *The Second Epistle General of Peter and the General Epistle of Jude.* The Tyndale New Testament Commentaries. Grand Rapids: Eerdmans.

Hendriksen, William. 1957. *New Testament Commentary: Exposition of the Pastoral Epistles.* Grand Rapids: Baker.

Huther, Joh, ed. 1881. *The General Epistles of Peter and Jude.* Meyer's Commentary on the New Testament. Edinburgh: T & T Clark.

Johnson, Edna. 1988. *A Semantic Structure Analysis of 2 Peter.* Dallas: Summer Institute of Linguistics. P. 36.

Jones, Larry Bert. 1983. *Pragmatic Aspects of English Text Structure.* Dallas: Summer Institute of Linguistics and University of Texas at Arlington.

Kelly, J. N. D. 1969. *A Commentary on the Epistles of Peter and Jude.* Harper's New Testament Commentaries. New York: Harper and Row.

Lampe, G. W. H. 1961. *A Patristic Greek Lexicon,* s.v. καί. Oxford: Clarendon Press.

Larson, Mildred. 1984. *Meaning-based Translation.* New York: University Press of America.

Levinsohn, Stephen H. Levinsohn. 1979. "Four Narrative Connectives in the Book of Acts." *Notes on Translation.* January: 1–20.

_____. 1980. "Relationship between Constituents Beyond the Clause in the Acts of the Apostles." Ph.D. thesis. University of Reading.

_____. 1981. "Sentence Conjunctions and Development Units in the Narrative of Acts." *Selected Technical Articles Related to Translation* 5. Dallas: Summer Institute of Linguistics. Pp. 2–39.

_____. 1987. *Textual Connections in Acts.* Atlanta: Scholars Press.

Liddell, H. G. and R. Scott. 1968. *A Greek-English Lexicon.* 9th ed. with supplement, revised by H. S. Jones. Oxford: Oxford University Press.

Mayor, Joseph B. 1907. *The Epistle of Jude and the Second Epistle of Peter.* London: Macmillan.

Milligan, George. 1908. *St. Paul's Epistles to the Thessalonians.* London: Macmillan.

Moore, Bruce. 1972. "Doublets." *Notes on Translation* 43:3–34.

Moule, C. F. D. 1959. *An Idiom Book of New Testament Greek.* 2d ed. Cambridge: Cambridge University Press.

O'Brien, Peter T. 1982. *Colossians, Philemon,* vol. 44, Word Biblical Commentary. Waco, Texas: Word.

Robertson, A. T. 1934. *A Grammar of the Greek New Testament in the Light of Historical Research.* Nashville: Broadman.

Robson, Edward Alfred. 1979. "Kai-Configuration in the Greek New Testament." Ph.D. dissertation, Syracuse University.

Silva, Moises. 1983. *Biblical Words and Their Meaning: An Introduction to Lexical Semantics.* Grand Rapids: Zondervan.

Smyth, Herbert Weir. 1956. *Greek Grammar.* Cambridge: Harvard University Press.

Thrall, Margaret. 1962. *Greek Particles in the New Testament.* Grand Rapids: Eerdmans.

Titrud, Kermit. 1991. "The Overlooked Καί in the Greek New Testament." *Notes on Translation,* vol. 5, 1:1–28.

_____. 1986. "The Abused Kai." M.A. thesis, Trinity Evangelical Divinity School, Deerfield, Illinois.

Tucker, T. G. 1910. *Life in the Roman World of Nero and St. Paul.* New York: Macmillan.

Turner, Nigel. 1963. *Syntax,* vol. 3. A Grammar of New Testament Greek, ed. by James H. Moulton. Edinburgh: T & T Clark.

Vincent, Marvin R. 1914. *Word Studies in the New Testament,* vol. 1. New York: Charles Scribner's Sons.

Zerwick, Maximilian. 1963. *Biblical Greek.* Adapted from the 4th Latin edition by Joseph Smith. Rome: Scripta Pontificii Instituti Biblici.

13

Towards an Exegesis of 1 John Based on the Discourse Analysis of the Greek Text

Robert E. Longacre

Introduction

The First Epistle of John has been notoriously difficult to outline. Every expositor has an outline of the book, and the outlines, although similar at some points of division, for the most part go their own ways. So striking is this difference between the various suggested outlines of the book that it almost amounts to a denial of structure to the book. In this article[1] I raise the possibility that discourse analysis can suggest a natural outline for the book, and beginning with such a natural outline of the book enables us to grasp the fundamental thrust of the whole and to understand better what the book is saying.

I shall, first of all, divide the book into structural paragraphs which I believe are indicated by certain features of the surface structure of the book. Then I am going to discuss the distribution of the verb γράφω ("write") in Greek, and on the basis of the distribution of this and other performative verbs shall argue that the book has its introduction, of a rather long and disproportionate size, a body, and a closure. Third, I shall adopt the point of view that the book is fundamentally not an expository but a hortatory discourse. Accordingly, I shall take the command forms as the basic material around which the rest of the book nucleates. Fourth, using the concept of peak, which I have found useful in discourse analysis in many languages around the world, I shall identify the peaks in the introduction and

---

[1] For a fuller presentation of the analysis assumed in this article, see Longacre (1983). The present article is offered as a sequel to the former on the supposition that a published analysis is often far from explicit as to its underlying methodology. Anyone who wants a copy of the former article can write the author at 7500 W. Camp Wisdom Rd., Dallas, TX 75236. Please enclose $2.00 for photocopying and postage.

the peaks in the body of the book. I shall show that these peaks peculiarly develop the main message of the book. Finally, I shall consider the macrostructure of the book in the van Dykian sense of the word, i.e., the gist of a work, what it is all about. I shall find statements of the macrostructure in the paragraph immediately preceding the dual peak of the main body of the book and in the paragraph immediately following that dual peak. It will be possible to show that with these overt indications of the macrostructure, and the very nature of the points highlighted in the peaks of the introduction and in the body of the book, we can pinpoint accurately what the apostle is saying in this epistle.

Clue One: Distribution of Vocatives

There are structural paragraphs (Longacre 1987, 1980), in most cases indicated by the distribution of vocatives. The first paragraph of the book serves as an introduction both to the introduction of the book itself and to the whole epistle. I indicate its nature here. (1) It is largely expository in structure with behavioral implicates found only in the final purpose clauses of verses three and four. (2) In its array of tense/aspect forms it is somewhat unique compared to the epistle as a whole: (a) the only imperfect tenses in the whole epistle are found here (ἦν, "was"); (b) there is a preponderance of perfects (ἀκηκόαμεν, ἑωράκαμεν; (c) there is a sprinkling of aorist forms, enough to suggest a set of historical contingencies; and (d) there are some performative presents (μαρτυροῦμεν, ἀπαγγέλομεν, γράφομεν). The thrust of the whole thing is somewhat as follows: "The word of life was (imperfect) from the beginning, but was manifested (aorist) in time. We have heard and seen it (perfects, i.e. past events with continuing implications for the present), and we tell (present) you about it, so that you may have fellowship with us so that your joy will be full."

First John 1:5–10 constitutes what can be called an expository, coordinate paragraph. It has covert exhortations but is expository in surface structure. The beginning of the passage, verse 5, sounds like a new departure compared to the four verses of the immediately preceding stretch. "And this is the message which we have heard from him and announce to you, that God is light, and there is no darkness at all in Him." The rest of this paragraph contains conditional sentences to the effect: "If we say 'a' we are on the wrong side with bad consequences. If we say 'b' we are on the right side with good consequences." Notice that this is a kind of highly mitigated exhortation for us to get on the right side of things and line up with the forces with positive consequences.

First John 2:1–6 constitutes a paragraph which is inaugurated with the vocative τεκνία μου, that is, "my little children." Verse 1 of this chapter continues with, "These things I wrote to you so that you will not sin." The concession is added to it, "If we sin we have an advocate," and then the main thesis gives us reasons why we should not sin. The reasons do not go with the word "write," but rather with the part of the verse that says, "Do not sin." This is a hortatory paragraph, but the hortatory component is buried in the purpose clause of verse 1 and takes the form of: "the one saying so and so is wrong and the one saying the opposite is correct"; so again we are exhorted by implication to get on the right side of things.

First John 2:7–11 constitutes another paragraph beginning with a vocative, the word ἀγαπητοί in verse 7. This verse goes on to say, "I am not writing a new commandment but an old commandment that you have had from the beginning," then says that really it is a new commandment. Next the writer mentions the matter of the one who loves his brother versus the one who hates his brother, thus giving us mitigated hortatory forms of a sort we notice in the previous paragraph. The substance of the new command is not told to us in so many words, but the rest of the paragraph, verses 9 through 11, imply that it is connected with love versus hate.

First John 2:12–17 is another paragraph beginning with the words, "I write to you little children" followed by "I write to your fathers; I write to you young men." The whole thing is cast into the aorist instead of the present tense on being repeated, "I wrote to you children; I wrote to you fathers; I wrote to you young men." All these are connected with conditions for writing. This can be considered to be the somewhat elaborate introduction to the paragraph. The exhortation of the main part of the paragraph is, "Don't love the wrong thing." That is, "Don't love the world, because if you do, the love of the Father is not in you." Notice that we come here to overt, albeit negative, imperatives. This feature will be treated below as marking one of the peaks of the introduction.

First John 2:18–27 is marked as a separate paragraph by the clause which begins with παιδία, i.e., "Little children, it is the last hour." The thought of the last hour as an apostasy is developed as a theme in verses 18 through 19. Then the thought that you have a χρίσμα or "anointing from the Holy One" is developed in verses 20 and 21 followed in 22 by what we might paraphrase as "There is a big lie on the loose." The hortatory heart of the paragraph begins in verse 24: "Let that which you have heard from the beginning remain in you." This is a third person imperative form. And all this ends with a climactic wind-up in verse 27: "And as for you, the anointing you received from Him remains in you, and you do not need that anyone should teach you, but just as His anointing teaches you concerning all things and it is true and is not a lie, and just as it taught you, remain in Him." Notice how the emphasis on "remain in Him" or "remain in the teaching" in verse 24 and at the end of verse 27 brackets nicely the hortatory heart of this paragraph. This run-on climatic structure we will consider to mark a peak, when we get around to the detailed study of such matters in section 4.

First John 2:28–29 is a hortatory-reason paragraph which concludes the introduction of the whole book. I will discuss in the section immediately below on what basis I called 1:5–29 the introduction to the book. For the moment notice the paragraph found in 2:28–29: "And now τεκνία (children) remain in Him,"—thus echoing the emphasis in the preceding paragraph. The attached reason is, "And if you know that He is righteous, you know that everyone who does righteousness is born of him." Again we have the structure of the third "ideal" person. The one who does so-and-so is on the right side. The one who does the opposite is on the wrong side.

First John 3:1–6 (beginning the body of the book) is a paragraph heralded with the word ἴδετε ("behold") in verse 1; the vocative which we are accustomed to seeing paragraph-initial is delayed until verse 2. So verse 1 reads, "Behold what love the Father has given us that we should be called sons of God, and we are. On account of this the world does not know us because it did not know Him." Then in verse 2 we find ἀγαπητοί, "Beloved, now are we children of God." In the hortatory body of the paragraph, which I consider to be verses 3 through 6, we have constructions of the variety "everyone who." In verse 3 "everyone who has this hope." In verse 4 "everyone who does sin." In verse 6 "everyone who remains in Him does not sin. Everyone who sins has not seen him nor known Him." Again this third person construction (everyone who does so and so is on the wrong side, while everyone who does the opposite course of action is on the right side) is a highly mitigated form of exhortation making this paragraph a covertly hortatory paragraph.

First John 3:7–12 constitutes another covertly hortatory paragraph heralded by the initial vocative τεκνία: "children, let no one deceive you." Much of the argumentation of this paragraph is expressed in a form already familiar: "one who does this versus the one who does that," and "everyone who." It winds up in verse 10 with the construction, ἐν τούτῳ, that is, "in this" which in 1 John inevitably takes us cataphorically to a clause at the end of the verse, where another "everyone who" statement is found. Comments and appended reasons continue the thought through verses 11 and 12 with a reference to Cain, who was of the evil one and slew his brother.

First John 3:13–18 is clearly a hortatory paragraph. It begins at verse 13 with "Do not marvel, *brothers*, if the world hates you." Again the vocative demarcates the paragraph here. The argument which continues is one with which we are already familiar. The body of the paragraph states in verse 14, "One who does not love abides in death," continuing with, "Everyone who hates his brother is a murderer," ending in verse 18 with the words (the vocative occurring in this case also at the end of the paragraph), τεκνία: "little children, let us not love in word, or in tongue but in deed and in truth"—with what is again probably another negative imperative form.

First John 3:19–24 is, strangely enough, expository in structure. Its thesis is stated in verses 19 and 20 before the vocative onset in verse 21. The thesis in verse 19 states, "And in this we know that we are of the truth and shall assure our hearts before Him." Then, continuing in verse 20, "If our hearts condemn us, God is greater than our hearts and knows everything." The vocative occurs as late as verse 21, but is closely connected in thought to the preceding thesis. "Beloved, if our heart does not condemn us we have boldness before Him." The thought of verse 21 continues through verse 24 in what we will hope to show later on is a chiastic pattern finding its key in verse 23. "And this is His commandment, that we should believe on the name of His Son Jesus Christ and love one another."

First John 4:1–6 starts with the vocative "beloved." I believe it belongs to one of the peaks of the body of the epistle, and the whole thing can be paraphrased as, "Beware of loose teachings which will try to deceive you, because they are not really from God." The ἐν τούτῳ construction is used in verse 2, "In this we know the Spirit of God or the true teaching, namely, every spirit (every teaching) which confesses Jesus Christ came in the flesh is of God." Then the opposite is given: "Every spirit which does not confess Jesus Christ is not of God." Again this is a rather familiar kind of argumentation. The whole paragraph continues with various other arguments ending at the end of verse 6 with a phrase ἐκ τούτου with a genitive which in this case is clearly anaphoric in that it refers to the preceding statement: "In this we know the Spirit of truth and the spirit of error."

First John 4:7–10 again begins with the word "beloved," but now the paragraph is frankly hortatory with overt command forms: "Beloved, let us love each other," followed by the words, "because love is of God." This in turn falls back on the argument, "Everyone who loves is born of God, and everyone who doesn't love is not of God." Again there are ἐν τούτῳ type reasons attached.

First John 4:11–21 in some ways acts like an amplification and paraphrase of the preceding paragraph. It stands out, however, with the vocative "beloved" and continues on to say, "If God so loved us we ought to love one another." It is strongly hortatory as witnessed by the form ὀφείλομεν: "We *ought* to love one another." It repeats the themes from the previous paragraph but amplifies them with considerable addition of new material. We will treat this below in section three as one of the peaks of the body of this discourse.

First John 5:1–12 is a long, run-on paragraph with a loose grammatical structure and a dense lexical structure. It does not begin with a vocative, as we have come to expect in previous paragraphs, but there seems to be a sharp discontinuity between it and the previous sections. In fact, as we will see below in section five, the macrostructure of the book is restated in 5:1 just as it was stated in the final paragraph of chapter 3. The uniqueness of the run-on structure of this paragraph and its lexical density set it apart from all other paragraphs in the book.

First John 5:13–21 is the closure of the book. It abruptly reintroduces the verb "write" (ταῦτα ἔγραψα ὑμῖν), "These things I have written to you."

In verse 21 the finis of the book has τεκνία again: "Little children keep yourselves from idols."

In summary, we can posit a string of *natural* paragraphs. Most are marked with a vocative, either in the initial sentence or in a sentence or two into the body of the paragraph. Other considerations such as ἴδετε in verse 21 and discontinuities of subject matter mark these suggested paragraphs as units of the text. Having isolated these units of the text, we then will not feel free to divide and group their contents according to what we think the subject matter outline should be. As for content, I believe that what we find in these natural units of the text is what the apostles wanted to group together into these units. We shall not try to follow his development of thought from natural paragraph to natural paragraph throughout the epistle.

Clue Two: Distribution of the Verb γράφω

Faced with this string of sixteen paragraphs we will certainly ask ourselves what to do next. Is there any natural grouping of these paragraphs into larger units? I believe that we can see a broad grouping into introduction, body, and conclusion. The verb γράφω occurs in the introduction and the conclusion, but not in the body of the work, which is 3:1 through 5:12. Admittedly this looks like a somewhat oversized introduction compared to the body of the work. So long is the introduction, in fact, that it contains most of the themes of the body of the work. And so long is the introduction that its own peaks parallel to the peaks of the body of the work.

The verb γράφω occurs in 1:4; 2:1; 2:7, 8; six times in 2:12–14; and in 2:26. I believe that in this section, especially 1:5–2:28, the apostle sets out to tell why he is writing to those who are receiving his epistle. In the process he works in most of the themes or emphases of the body of the work itself.

The use of the performative verb γράφω comes to a head (a performative peak of sorts) in 2:12–14, where the performative verb γράφω occurs with vocatives six times. The repetition is a way of reinforcing the message by repeating the verb "write" six times at this place and with the audience partitioned into "children," "fathers," and "young men," with a special challenge given to the "young men" in verses 13c and 14c. It has long fascinated commentators that between verses 13 and 14 there is a shift of tense from the present tense of γράφω to the aorist tense ἔγραψα. Of some interest is the fact that once the verb is changed from γράφω ("I write") to ἔγραψα ("I have written") the aorist remains the tense in which the word "write" occurs in the rest of the epistle. This is true in 2:21, 2:26, and 5:13.

The closure of the book begins in 5:13, where the verb γράφω in the aorist reoccurs. "These things I have written to you that you might know that you have eternal life, to you who believe on the name of the Son of God." I note again that the tense/aspect switch between γράφω and ἔγραψα has its watershed in 2:13–14. It is possible to argue here that the apostle begins with the sense of writing only a letter. After he has gone past a certain point, he is able to view the letter as something of an event that is completed, or at least reasonably sure of being completed. This would then account for the difference between the continuative thrust of the present ("I am writing") and the sense of completion in the aorist ("I have written").

My claim, then, is that the contribution of the verb γράφω ("write") is such that we can claim that the first two chapters are introductory material, despite the heavy weaving in of thematic material that characterizes the body of the book as a whole. Not only is the verb γράφω found but other performatives as well, so that in these two chapters the speech situation ("I am writing to you") is foregrounded.

Clue Three: Counting and Weighing the Kinds of Verbs

This point is somewhat of an aside. Let us stop to look at the book as a whole and ask ourselves what kind of a discourse it might be. I shall argue here that the brute statistics of the book (as far as the type of verbs that occur) are misleading; that the command forms are central; and that the book moves from mitigated (almost disguised) commands to overt commands at the structures which we call the peaks of the book.

Let us look at some of the statistics of the book and ask ourselves if the epistle has an overall expository cast or an overall hortatory cast. We will look, then, at the statistics—even though we will find they are somewhat misleading.

An expository discourse should highlight the most static clauses of the language as its main line, while a hortatory discourse should highlight command forms. Static clauses are relational rather than active. In 1 John there are eighty-three instances of main clauses which have the verb "be," "have," null in place of "be," or the verb "remain/stay." These main clauses are clearly static and relational. Twenty-four clauses of acquaintance or awareness ("know," etc.) occur in main clauses and are also static. Thirteen perfect verbs occur, some of which are clearly static in thrust. Twenty-five presents and futures occur, while eighteen performative verbs ("testify," "announce," "write") occur, but mainly in chapters 1 and 2. Five narrative (aorist) verbs occur, each of which presumably could have begun an embedded narrative. Finally, sixteen command forms occur, that is, imperatives, hortatives ("let us love"), jussives ("let him love his brother also"), and "ought" forms. Of the 184 verbs thus cataloged, the 83 be/have/know clauses and remain/stay clauses account for 45%. Acquaintance/awareness/know verbs constitute an additional 13%, which if added to the above gives a total of 58% of the main forms that are decidedly relational and static. The overt command forms, by contrast, constitute only 9%. Obviously the general cast of the surface structure of 1 John looks decidedly more expository than hortatory. Nevertheless, the matter is not to be so simply settled by appeal to verb classification and counting. The hortatory forms, although only 9% of the book, are basic to the thinking of the entire book and, in fact, dominate the portions of text in which they occur.

The command forms, broadly conceived, range all the way from highly mitigated commands to more overt structures with the imperative and the word "ought" as the most forceful. Looking again at 1:5–10, we find conditional sentences which could be summarized as "If we do x, that is not good. If we do y, that is good." X and y can be considered to stand for antonyms, opposite courses of activity. This is a mitigated way of giving exhortation to the effect that we should do what is good. It conceives of the universe as polarized into good and evil: if we line up on one side we line up with the good; otherwise we line up with the evil. The covert thrust is, "Line up with the good, not with the evil." In 2:7–10 we have the hint of a new commandment given—a new commandment which is still an old commandment—which is inferentially connected with advice to love, given again in the conditional mode. In 3:7–12 another type of mitigated exhortation refers to the third person. The one who does so and so is on the side of the good. The one who does the opposite is on the side of the bad. This is similar in many ways to the conditional structures we find in chapter 1. Finally, in 3:16b we find the verb ὀφείλομεν, "we ought to." Here the verb "ought" is strongly hortatory and is used rather than the imperative, but perhaps it is as strong or stronger than any imperative form. By *count*, expository-type verbs predominate, but as to *weight*, hortatory-type verbs predominate.

Clue Four: Peaks of the Book are Especially Crucial to the Message

Peaks of the book, i.e., points of cumulative development (Longacre 1983a, 1985), are the places where overt imperatives and "ought" forms are characteristically found. Noticing where there peaks occur and what precedes and follows them is an excellent way to arrive at the message of the entire book. The peaks are dual, both in the introduction and in the body of the book. There is an ethical peak, and there is a doctrinal peak. The introduction has in 2:12–17 a strong exhortation not to love the world. This is the ethical peak of the introduction. The doctrinal peak is in 2:18–27 with the warning that it is the last hour, that the believers have an anointing from the Holy One, and that a big lie is on the loose, i.e., a denial that Jesus Christ is the Son of God come in the flesh. Here the apostle deals with the primitive Christological error of his day, something which eventually emerged in full-fledged docetism or gnosticism. These ethical and doctrinal peaks of the introduction precede the conclusion in 2:28, which starts off καὶ νῦν τεκνία ("and now little children remain in him"). I believe we can take the καὶ νῦν as marking a summary and that this is the closure of the introductory section of the book.

In the body of the book the doctrinal peak (4:1–6) occurs first and is shorter than the ethical peak (4:7–21), which occurs following it. There is something peculiar about the development of the second peak, but first let us consider the doctrinal peak. 4:1 starts with an exhortation not to believe every spirit (every type of teaching) but to test the spirits to determine whether they are of God. The test is whether or not the doctrine, or "spirit," confesses Jesus Christ come in the flesh and makes Christ central. There is also a secondary criterion: What kind of company do these teachers keep? They are of the world, and they speak as of the world; but we are of God.

The ethical peak is a peculiar development in that it ranges over two paragraphs, the second of which is a paraphrase of the first; but since paraphrase and recapitulation of various sorts is a very common feature of peak, this should not surprise us. The whole can be regarded as a compound paragraph with two component paragraphs. The first paragraph is 4:7–10, and the second paragraph is 4:11–21. Both component paragraphs are strongly hortatory. 4:7 starts with ἀγαπητοί, ἀγαπῶμεν ἀλλήλους, and 4:11 has ἀγαπητοί . . . ὀφείλομεν ἀλλήλους ἀγαπᾶν. That is, "let us love each other" and "we ought to love each other," respectively.

The thematic clauses in the first paragraph (4:7–10) are "let us love," "love is of God," and "God proved his love by sending his only Son to die for us." The same three thematic clauses are found in the second paragraph (4:11–21) with a lot of additional material. Thus in verse 11 we are told, "Beloved, if God so loved us [referring to God sending His Son], then we ought to love one another." After some material on "no one has seen God, but if we love God, God dwells in us," we are told in verse 14 that "we have seen and bear witness that God sent his Son as savior of the world." The reminder in verse 15 exhorts us to doctrinal commitment to confess that Jesus is the Son of God if we say that God lives in us. Verse 16, again referring to the incarnation, says, "And we have known and believed the love which God has for us." The passage goes on to say, "God is love, and the one who dwells in love dwells in God, and God dwells in him." Then in verses 17 and 18 there is an amplificatory comment about being perfected in love beyond fear. In verse 19 the renewed command comes: "Let us love because he first loved us." (Or, "We love Him because he first loved us.") And we are reminded again in verse 20 that if anyone says that he loves God and hates his brother, he is lying. So we see a certain amount of practical application and comment of various sorts, but the same primary emphases are found: that we ought to love, that God is love, and that God sent His Son as proof of His love.

The two paragraphs together, I believe, constitute the greatest passage in the New Testament on the obligatory nature of Christian love. Suffice it to say, however, that the ethical and doctrinal paragraphs are woven together in both the introduction and in the ethical part to remind us that to be a Christian, to be a believer, involves ethical and doctrinal obligations, and neither one will suffice in the absence of the other. This is more overtly developed in the next point.

Clue Five: Macrostructure as a Control on the Content

The macrostructure of a text (Van Dijk 1977, 1980) is a summary or précis or abstract of a text which is stated so that it gives the central thrust of the whole work. Properly stated, a macrostructure serves as a control on the content of the text. Since everything cannot be included in any one text, a text is selective according to its central thrust. The macrostructure also controls what is developed in detail and what is simply referred to in passing. The peaks of a book are often especially relevant to the macrostructure. A macrostructure can also, on occasion, control the order of presentation of a work. From this standpoint it is interesting that in 1 John the ethical peak precedes the doctrinal peak in the introduction while the doctrinal peak precedes the ethical peak in the body of the work so that the doctrinal peaks are bracketed with ethical peaks.

While it can be inferred that the message of the book is the message of the doctrinal peaks and the ethical peaks combined, i.e., "don't love the world but love God, and above all love our fellow Christians"; and "believe correctly with the center of our belief resting on the fact of the incarnation, God come in human flesh," we might wish that there was some place in the book where the macrostructure was stated in more overt form. It is, however, so stated not once but twice. Furthermore, these overt statements of the macrostructure are found preceding the twin peaks of the body and following the twin peaks of the body, so that statements of the macrostructure reinforce the cumulative developments in chapter 4.

We need to look again, therefore, in detail at 3:19–24, the passage that immediately precedes the first of the dual peaks in the body of the work as given in 1 John chapter 4. There is, to be sure, a grammatical constituent structure of this paragraph as shown in Diagram I. This takes the thesis as stated in 3:19–20 with the antithesis stated in the remainder of the paragraph. There is an intricate layering of constituents so that within the antithesis, verses 22 and 24 can be considered to be a result appended to the thesis of verse 21, "Beloved, if the heart does not condemn us we have confidence before God." Within the result, verse 22 takes as its thesis, "And whatever we ask of Him we receive from Him because we obey His commandments and do those things that are pleasing to Him." There is a comment on this which is a comment paragraph with its own thesis in verse 23 and comment in verse 24. The thesis is, "And this is His commandment, that we should believe in the name of His Son Jesus Christ and love each other as He has given us commandment." The comment on that in verse 24 is, "The one who keeps His commandments abides in Him and He in Him." The comment on that is, "In this we know that we abide in Him because of the Spirit which He has given us."

While this can be considered a reasonable view of the logical structure of the verse, there is an overriding chiastic structure which

Diagram 1: The constituent structure of 1 John 3:19–24

19. *THESIS:* [καὶ] ἐν τούτῳ γνωσόμεθα ὅτι ἐκ τῆς ἀληθείας ἐσμέν, καὶ ἔμπροσθεν αὐτοῦ πείσομεν τὴν καρδίαν ἡμῶν

20. ὅτι ἐὰν καταγινώσκῃ ἡμῶν ἡ καρδία, ὅτι μείζων ἐστὶν ὁ θεὸς τῆς καρδίας ἡμῶν καὶ γινώσκει πάντα.
    ANTI: RESULT PARAGRAPH

21. *THESIS:* ἀγαπητοί, ἐὰν ἡ καρδία [ἡμῶν] μὴ καταγινώσκῃ, παρρησίαν ἔχομεν πρὸς τὸν θεόν.
    RESULT: COMMENT PARAGRAPH

22. *THESIS:* καὶ ὃ ἐὰν αἰτῶμεν λαμβάνομεν ἀπ' αὐτοῦ. ὅτι τὰς ἐντολὰς αὐτοῦ τηροῦμεν καὶ τὰ ἀρεστὰ ἐνώπιον αὐτοῦ ποιοῦμεν.
    COMMENT: COMMENT PARAGRAPH

23. *THESIS:* καὶ αὕτη ἐστὶν ἡ ἐντολὴ αὐτοῦ, ἵνα πιστεύσωμεν τῷ ὀνόματι τοῦ υἱοῦ αὐτοῦ Ἰησοῦ Χριστοῦ καὶ ἀγαπῶμεν ἀλλήλους, καθὼς ἔδωκεν ἐντολὴν ἡμῖν.
    COMMENT: COMMENT PARAGRAPH

24. *THESIS:* καὶ ὁ τηρῶν τὰς ἐντολὰς αὐτοῦ ἐν αὐτῷ μένει καὶ αὐτὸς ἐν αὐτῷ.
    COMMENT: καὶ ἐν τούτῳ γινώσκομεν ὅτι μένει ἐν ἡμῖν, ἐκ τοῦ πνεύματος οὗ ἡμῖν ἔδωκεν.

needs to be considered as well (Diagram II). Thus, verses 19–21 deal with how we are to know that we are of the truth. Verse 22 says, "Whatsoever we ask we receive from Him because we keep His commandments and do those things that are pleasing to Him." This causal clause or reason clause ("because we keep His commandments and do those things that are pleasing to Him") is developed in verse 23 ("And this is His commandment," which is further specified "that we should believe on the name of His Son Jesus Christ and love one another"). Then, verse 23 closes with the words, "As He gave us commandment," which echoes the thought at the beginning of the verse ("This is His commandment"). Then verse 24 echoes the thought of verse 22 ("The one keeping His commandment dwells in Him and He in Him"), which echoes the reason clause in verse 22. Finally, the whole thing winds up with the end of verse 24: "In this we know that He remains in us by the Spirit He has given us." And that echoes again the thought of verses 19 to 21: "How are we to know that we are of the truth?" The whole thing is an A, B, C, D, E, C′, B′, A′ structure. At the center of the chiasmus are these words: "that we should believe on the name of His Son Jesus Christ and love one another" (D, E above). Grammatically, these words are deeply buried in

Diagram 2: The chiastic structure of 1 John 3:19–24

A   Verses 19–21—How to know that we are of the truth.
    B   And whatsoever we ask we receive from Him *because we keep His*
    commandments and do those things that are pleasing to Him. (22)
        C   And this is *His commandment:* (23)
            D   That we should believe on the name of His son I.X,
            E   And love one another,
        C′   As *He gave us commandment.* (23)
    B′   *The one keeping His commandments dwells in Him and He in him.* (24)
A′   In this we know that He remains in us, by the Spirit which he has given us.

the paragraph because they comment on a causal clause. Nevertheless, these clauses give us, buried in this fashion in layers of chiasmus, the macrostructure of the book. What God has commanded of
us, what He wants of us is that we should believe on the name of His
Son Jesus Christ and love one another. Correct belief centers in a
view of the person of Jesus Christ. Correct action centers in Christian love for each other and for God. This, then, is the macrostructure given in a passage which immediately precedes the peaks.

Immediately following the peaks we find a very striking passage,
1 John 5:1–12, which is a run-on paragraph chiefly consisting of thesis and comment in successive imbedded paragraphs. In effect, this
paragraph picks up a word or phrase from the preceding verse and
develops it as a comment, only to have a word of phrase in the comment picked up and developed in the next verse, and so on, in an
amazing chain. It is loose grammatically for this reason. The pattern
of thesis/comment follows on and on and on through the passage. On
the other hand it is dense lexically, referring to many themes and
many emphases of importance to Christians. The important point for
us right now is, however, that the whole thing starts with a restatement of the macrostructure, i.e., 5:1. This reads, "Everyone who believes that Jesus is the Christ is born of God," and the second part of
the verse says, "And everyone who loves the one who begat, loves also
the one who is begotten of Him." That is, if we love God, who has begotten all these children, and if we have the new birth in Christ Jesus,
then we love the ones who are begotten as well. So again, we find here
an echo of the macrostructure, that we should believe in Jesus and
love God and our fellow Christians. Again, we are not left to guess
what the macrostructure is. It is overtly stated in strategically placed
passage immediately before and after the twin peaks of the body
(which, in turn, especially develop the macrostructure).

Summary

I believe, then, that the message of 1 John is very clear. it is overtly
stated and is developed in a masterful way in the peaks of the introduction and especially in the peaks of the body of the work; and the whole
book is brought to bear on it. The strongest command forms are found
in the peaks, and the most extended development of the themes are
found in the peaks. The message, then, is very clear for us. To be a fol-
lower of the Christian way requires doctrinal and ethical commitments.
We must believe in the central fact that God sent His son, that God
came incarnate in human flesh; and we must take this as a central doctrine around which other doctrines of the Christian faith are developed. We must love God and our fellow men, and this requirement is
equally stringent. Throughout church history Christians have tended
to err on one side or the other. We have examples of sterile, even un-
loving orthodoxies, and we have had examples of loving and ethical
systems which play down almost to the vanishing point the distinctives
of Christianity. The second course of action is really quite impossible
without the undergirding belief system. We are told in 1 John that we
love because He first loved us, and the great spring of love in the Christian heart comes from what God has done for us, i.e., being accepted
and loved by Him first of all with His love demonstrated in sending His
Son. So ultimately a merely ethical Christianity without this great doctrinal fact behind it runs out of moral and ethical steam.

Methodological Comments

I come down now from the high ethical plane of the content of
1 John to discuss again how we got to the content, the particular methodology which we employed. To review, I tried to set up, as fairly as I
could, structural paragraphs based on the surface structure of the book
and took these as primary. Consequently, I included in the same paragraph whatever the author put into that paragraph rather than making
my own semantic outline of what in my judgment should belong together. Second, I took the distribution of the performative verbs, especially the verb "write," very seriously, thus giving me a breakdown of the
paragraphs as a linear string into introduction, body, and conclusion.
Third, I looked at the work noting the occurrence of expository and
hortatory verbs and decided that the book was primarily hortatory.

This led to the analysis underlying this paper (Longacre 1983b) and
highlights the position of the hortatory or the command forms in the
book as a whole. This meant that we had to have some kind of constitu-

ent analysis of the book. In fact, every serious student of discourse eventually needs to do such an analysis: How do the various sentences of the text relate locally to each other? There are various catalogs of the relations that characterize local spans or paragraphs. These catalogs are found as far back as the work of Daniel Fuller (1959); the early and later work of Beekman and colleagues on what is now called SSAs; and my own catalog of interpropositional relations which is found in chapter 3 of Longacre (1983a but in earlier editions going back for quite a few years earlier). We also have a catalog of sorts in de Beaugrande and Dressler (1989) and in Van Dijk (1977). More recently, we have the work of Thompson and Mann (1986) doing something of the same sort. The analysis of constituent structure is time-consuming. On the other hand doing the constituent structure of 1 John can help one understand better how the hortatory forms occupy a dominant position over other forms in local spans and how the command forms in general occupy a dominant place with other elements ancillary. One relation frequently encountered in 1 John is the relation of contrast issuing forth in surface-structure antithetical paragraphs.

Fourth, to refer to the immediate context of this paper, we looked at the matter of peaks, attempting to discover where overt imperatives are found and where the thought of the author reaches its most detailed and developed expression. We noticed the peculiar fact that the peaks in 1 John are dual in every case, and herein lies an overt feature of the surface structure which reflects the dual emphases of the book, i.e., the emphases on belief and on love. Finding such peaks is important to understanding the message of the book. Of course, we have had to recognize the importance of Van Dijk's concept of the macrostructure, which gives a top-down control over the book as a whole and which enables us to account for its various parts and their relative development, even at times their relative ordering.

We should start with obvious things about the surface structure and take them very seriously: what the author decides to put into the same paragraph, and how he distributes performative verbs versus verbs of other types. This analysis then can proceed by giving a crucial place to hortatory forms in a hortatory discourse, by taking note of how the peaks especially develop the thought, and by recognizing how the macrostructure acts as a control on the design of the whole.

References

de Beaugrande, R. and J. W. Dressler. 1981. *An Introduction to Text Linguistics*. London: Longmans.

Beekman, J., J. Callow, and M. Kopesec. 1981. *The Semantic Structure of Written Communication.* Dallas: Summer Institute of Linguistics.

van Dijk, T. A. 1977. *Text and Context.* London: Longmans.

_____. 1980. *Macrostructures: An Interdisciplinary Study of Global Structures in Discourse, Interaction, and Cognition.* Hillsdale, NJ: Lawrence Erlbaum.

Fuller, D. P. 1959. *The Inductive Method of Bible Study.* 3d ed. Pasadena, CA: Fuller Theological Seminary. Photocopy.

Longacre, R. E. 1979. "The paragraph as a grammatical unit." In *Discourse and Syntax,* ed. by T. Givon. (Syntax and semantics 12.) New York: Academic.

_____. 1983a. *The grammar of discourse.* New York: Plenum Press.

_____. 1983b. "Exhortation and mitigation in the Greek text of the First Epistle of John." *Selected Technical Articles Related to Translation 9.* Dallas: Summer Institute of Linguistics.

_____. 1985. "Discourse peak as zone of turbulence." In *Beyond the Sentence: Discourse and Sentential Form,* ed. by J. R. Wirth. Ann Arbor: Karoma Publishers. Pp. 81–98.

Mann, W. C. and S. A. Thompson. 1986. "Relational propositions in discourse." *Discourse Processes* 9. Pp. 57–90.

14

Discourse Analysis and Jewish Apocalyptic in the Epistle of Jude*

Carroll D. Osburn

Chaine has aptly noted, "La nature des erreurs combattues est la question principale touchant l'origine de l'épître" (1939:281). It is evident that no analysis of historicity in Jude can proceed apart from the literary question of Jude's midrashic use of Jewish apocalyptic. In traditional exegesis of the Epistle of Jude, the *function* of the several references to unfamiliar accounts in intertestamental Jewish literature is neglected, often resulting in conflicting assessments of Jude's meaning. The exegetical matter of first importance, though, is not merely how to explain certain ambiguous elements in Jude, but how to understand the significant utilization of Jewish apocalyptic in this epistle. It cannot be said that the task of exegesis has been discharged until an adequate analysis of the semantic structure of the text has emerged, indicating clearly how the smaller units of text are grouped into large semantic units, how these facilitate the development of the literary thrust of the document, and finally how the text is related to the historical situation emerging from the literary analysis.[1]

How, then, are we to proceed with our investigation of history and apocalyptic in the Epistle of Jude? Dahl (1967:317–18) suggests:

*This paper originated as "The Epistle of Jude and Heresiological Tradition," presented to the VII International Conference on Patristic Studies at Oxford on 12 Sept. 1975. I am grateful to Prof. R. McL. Wilson for the invitation to serve as Visiting Prof. of New Testament at the Univ. of St. Andrews during the Candlemas and Whitsunday terms of 1980, enabling me to pursue this topic further. This essay was delivered in the present format at Rijksuniversiteit Utrecht, The Netherlands, on 21 Oct. 1986, and with bibliographical update at the Seminar on Discourse Structure at the Summer Institute of Linguistics in Dallas on 30 May 1991.

[1] For general discussion of linguistics and biblical interpretation, see Cotterell and Turner (1989), although for practical application of discourse analysis to biblical materials the suggestions of Beekman and Callow (1974:267–341) remain very useful.

(1) the integrity of the epistle may be assumed as a working hypothesis which is confirmed if it proves possible to understand each section with a definite purpose within the letter as a whole; (2) the reconstruction of the historical background must mainly be based upon information contained within the epistle itself with clear and objective statements forming the primary data and admonitions and warnings included as reflecting possibilities; (3) reconstruction of the historical background will recommend itself to the degree to which it is able to account for the total argument and all details within the epistle with minimal dependence upon hypothetical inferences from extraneous sources or constructs, and will gain probability if it can be integrated without difficulty into a comprehensive picture of the history of early Christianity in its contemporary setting.

There are three discernible types of material in Jude: (1) the admonition (vv. 1–4; 20:25); (2) the description of the opponents; and (3) warning exhortations (intermingled in vv. 5–19). Much of the confusion in the history of the interpretation of the Epistle of Jude is due to failure to distinguish forthright descriptions of the intruders from the apocalyptical warning exhortations in verses 5–19. In fact, only by careful attention to Jude's literary structure can one distinguish accurately between these literary warnings and the actual crisis of Jude's concern.

The Epistolary Framework of the Epistle of Jude

Jude 1–4

In the prologue of verses 1–4, the salutation appears in conventional epistolary form as a greeting (see Doty 1973:27 and Aune 1987:184–86). The normal χαρεῖν of Hellenistic correspondence (Acts 23:6) is supplanted here by the whole of verse 2. Jude's triad is conventional enough, and certainly each of the terms is appropriate to the situation mentioned in verses 20–23. That the readers are "called" and "kept safe" state motifs integral to the letter. Jude's πληθυνθείη likely does not derive from 1 Enoch 5:5, "the years of your destruction shall be multiplied [πληθυνθήσεται] in eternal execration." Van Elderen (1967:46–48) observes this uncommon verb to convey a strong sense of confidence in fulfillment.

The shift from the greeting to the introductory exhortation in verses 3–4 is accomplished by "beloved," which here, as in verses 17 and 20, functions as a discourse marker to highlight transition to different material.

The literary thrust of the document is expressed in verses 3–4 as a literary petition (see Mullins 1962:48–54 and Bjerkelund 1967).

"While making every effort to write to you concerning our common salvation, I felt it necessary to write to you" serves as the background. "Urging you" gives the verbal petition and "to contend for the faith once given to the saints" indicates the desired action. Verse 4, then, denotes the reason for the petition. This vigorous petition finds precise expression in verses 20–23, where the actual exhortation is presented in three imperatival terms, τηρήσατε, σώζετε, and ἐλεᾶτε. It is clear that verses 3–4 and 20–23 constitute the literary thrust of the document. Two subordinate invitations in verses 5–16 and 17–19 that reflected intently upon commonly known matters which Jude thought to have direct bearing upon the immediate historical situation were carefully constructed to focus attention upon the exhortation in verses 20–23. These contours of Jude's discourse are foreshadowed in the prologue, as the writer surfaces the motifs and theological concerns with which he intends to construct this brief letter. Watson (1988:29–72) correctly identifies the main concern of the document as the infiltration of the church by the intruders in verse 4, but his separation of verse 3 as *exordium* from verse 4 as *narratio*, and these from verses 20–23 as an *adfectus*, skews the literary connection between verses 3–4 and 20–23. Sellin (1986:206–225) analyzes Jude in chiastic form, placing undue emphasis upon verses 4–16. The relational function of γάρ in this form renders untenable the suggestion of Reicke (1970:287) that verse 4 is to be separated from verse 3 and placed in the body of the letter rather than in the introduction.

As the παρακαλῶ form suggests, the reason for Jude's concern and his compulsion to intervene literarily becomes explicit in verse 3. While these intruders could have brought their characteristics with them into the church, the focus in verse 4 is not upon their pre-Christian nature but upon their present character. Meecham (1952:285) rightly excludes μετατιθέντες and ἀρνούμενοι here from his list of present participles of antecedent action. The force of παρεισέδυσαν is that the essence of their character was not altogether apparent until well after their admittance, when the damage being done by their aberrance began to evidence itself in certain defections. While maintaining Christian affiliation (v. 12), these intruders remain decidedly secular (vv. 4, 8, 12, 16).

Plumptre (1903:203) and James (1912:37) are correct in observing no sanction in προγεγραμμένοι for the later Calvinistic theory of a Divine decree predestining certain ones to condemnation. Likewise, Kelly (1969:250) is unconvincing that Jude intimates that long ago the names of these opponents were entered in heavenly books dictating the destiny of individuals. The basic question, however, concerning the description of these enigmatic intruders involves specifically which written source Jude had in mind with προγεγραμμένοι in verse 4. Zahn (1909:ii, 80) is surely incorrect in suggesting that τοῦτο refers to παρεισέδυσαν. Jude's κρίμα is one that hangs over the opponents themselves. Spitta (1885:310ff) rightly understands "this [τοῦτο] judgment" to refer to the judgment Jude is about to declare; namely, the condemnation inherent in ἀσεβεῖς "ungodly," as used by some ancient writer. Bigg (1902:326) can hardly be correct in supposing Jude to have been quoting 2 Peter. While πάλαι refers to a relative recent past in Mark 15:44, Schelkle (1970:152–53) and Kelly (1969:249) argue convincingly that the eschatological judgment prominent in 1 Enoch pervades Jude's epistle and provides the essential understanding of this earlier written judgment.

Kelly (1969:249) proposes 1 Enoch 1:9 (Jude 14–15) to be the basic reference, suggesting also possible influence from 1 Enoch 48:10 (p. 252), but that text is oblique in this instance, for the Enochic text to which Jude refers in "written beforehand" is rather 67:10: "For the judgment shall come upon them because they believe in the lust of their body and deny the spirit of the Lord." Wand (1934:199) mentions this possibility without comment. Functioning as the concluding portion of the παρακαλῶ form, the historical aspects of this apocalyptic reference provide the *point d'appui* for Jude's castigation of the opponents, against which the exhortation to faithfulness stands in bold relief. The reference to 1 Enoch 67:10 is neither an explicit quotation nor a mere allusion but an adaptation in which the ancient message is retained while the wording has been adjusted in view of Jude's historical concern and theological understanding. The juxtaposition of "this judgment" and "ungodly" in verse 4 is not accidental; rather, it indicates Jude's reflection upon 1 Enoch 67:10, as well as upon the theophany in 1 Enoch 1:9, which lies behind Jude 14–15, where the repeated use of ἀσεβεῖς ("ungodly") indicates this to be the cause for judgment. Jude's insertion of "ungodly" between "judgment" and the two following participles in verse 4 ("changing" and "denying") evidences his intention to link certain aspects of the character of these intruders with those of the longstanding eschatological enemies of God, which he summarizes with "ungodly," and of denoting a common fate. In the first participial phrase, Jude adapts Enoch's simple statement of lust, noting that the intruders have changed the doctrine of grace to accommodate licentiousness (see also vv. 8, 23), which is coherent with the general picture emerging in the epistle. In the second, Jude alters Enoch's simple denial of the spirit of the Lord to "deny our only master and Lord Jesus Christ."[2]

---

[2] For discussion on why "master" should be taken with reference to Christ here rather than to God, see Osburn (1985:300–302).

The dual mention of God and Christ in the salutation, the exhortation, and the doxology is best maintained here by treating God as the focus of "changing" and Christ as the focus of "denying." Seen in this way, Christ is viewed as μόνον δεσπότην, "only master," not in distinction from God, but from any who would usurp divine mastery over men, especially these intruders. By rejecting Christ, the opponents have forfeited a saving relationship with the Father, much like the eschatological enemies of God mentioned in verses 5–16. Obviously the alteration of God's grace into licentiousness would constitute a practical denial of the Lord. A careful analysis of the epistle unencumbered with preconceived notions of the nature of the opponents leads one to conclude, with Michl (1968:78), that there is no indication in Jude of a denial of Jesus' humanity, as in 1 John 2:22 (cf. Mayor 1907:271) or of His deity. Sidebottom (1967:38) attempts to explain "denying" based upon 1 and 2 John, but the explanation is inappropriate to this context. In view of the structural importance of Jude's accusation of licentiousness, it seems that in this instance poor theology was not merely attended by sordid living but that sensual preferences resulted in nullifying the example of Christ and perverting His true nature and authority (see Wand 1934:119). Certainly, Jude's strong christological response to the situation was not made by force of argument against an open repudiation of Christ, but by speaking from an undaunted position of faith in Jesus as God's agent on behalf of the righteous (vv. 1, 21, 25) and His role in the certain judgment against the ungodly (vv. 14–15). The incongruity involved in attempting to combine Christian piety and lasciviousness invariably involves christological misunderstanding or rejection. Whatever the opponents may have denied, rationalized, or disregarded concerning Christ, there is no reason to suppose that they brought some aberrant christology into the church.

One cannot escape the fact that there is a paucity of doctrinal argument in the epistle. It is only necessary to conclude from Jude's silence that, in view of their propensity for licentiousness, certain aspects of the church's understanding of Jesus did not commend themselves to the intruders, who evidenced an insouciance for Jesus tantamount to rejection. With this adaptation of 1 Enoch 67:10, Jude not only provides initial description of the opponents but specifies the reason for his vigorous exhortation in verses 3, 20–23; he relates the sinfulness and doom of the intruders to that of the long-standing enemies of God in Jewish tradition. Chaine (1939:299) rightly observes Jude to be treating a concrete situation while employing Enochic terminology and concept. The contrast between the faithful recipients and these opponents throughout the document is anticipated in the prologue in terms of "you" (vv. 3, 5, 12, 17, 20, 24) and "these" (vv. 4, 8, 10, 11, 12, 14, 16, 19). The actual content of "contend for the faith" is specified in verses 20–23.

Jude 20–25

Following the admonition in verses 5–16 to regard the character and fate of the opponents as equivalent to that of the eschatological enemies of God and the stern warning in verses 17–19 to regard them as the very ones anticipated as troublemakers by the apostles themselves, Jude makes two basic exhortations in verses 20–23 which actually constitute the exhortation to "contend for the faith" in verse 3.

First, in verses 20–21, the principal exhortation revolves around "keep yourselves in the love of God," in contrast with the preceding examples of ungodliness. Jude appends three participial phrases to "keep," each drawing imperatival function from the finite verb. Certainly, enmeshing themselves in solid Christian perspective, prayer in the spirit, and eschatological hope are included by way of constructive admonition as to how this can best be accomplished.

Second, the exhortation in verses 22–23 is directed toward what the readers can do for those inclined to defect. Although there is textual uncertainty in these verses, the three-clause text in $\aleph^c$ (Nestle-Aland[26]; UBS Greek NT[3]; Jerusalem Bible; NIV; NRSV) is certainly to be preferred. I am honored that Bauckham (1983:110) found my (1972:139–44) study convincing, but stimulating conversations with Harold Greenlee during a Bible translation workshop in Guatemala in the fall of 1980 have led me to view the three-clause text of $\aleph^c$ as correct (see now Kubo 1981:239f). Since verses 20–23 constitute the specific content of the intense exhortation "to contend for the faith" in verses 3–4, these concluding admonitions constitute the *raison d'être* of the epistle.

Whereas in the first instance Jude admonishes the recipients to solidify their own Christian commitment, the second aspect is directed to what the readers can do for those involved in defecting from genuine Christianity. The first clause is a mandate to treat mercifully those who waver and/or doubt. While including the struggle with theoretical matters in verse 4, the participle has specific reference to those within the Christian community who were inclined to defect, yet still weighing their alternatives. With regard to the second clause, Jude admonishes his readers to take overt action to reclaim those ensconced in the ways of the opponents but who may yet be influenced by the genuine Christian alternative. The third clause should be taken to mean that the readers should have patience with those whose life-styles had come to involve licentiousness, yet with the stern caution that they must remain cognizant of the danger involved in helping those in that situation, lest they themselves be tempted by the licentiousness they would inevitably encounter. Lenski (1966:648) is incorrect in taking this second ἐλεᾶτε as "avoid." Jude's admonition is to treat with gentleness and sensitivity any in the church who opt for licentiousness and christological unconcern yet say in some fashion, "Lord, help thou my unbelief!"

Due to centuries of liturgical usage the last two verses of Jude are frequently viewed merely as a *benedictus par excellence* and are rarely read as an integral part of the epistle. There is strong reason to believe, however, that the author intended to accomplish more with these words than to display creative and eloquent praise. Robertson (1934:1199–1200) overstates all evidence in calling verses 24–25 a "primitive Christian song." The doxology in verses 24–25 serves appropriately as a conclusion to the exhortations in verses 20–23 by centering final attention upon the One in verses 1 and 21 in whose love they are to keep themselves and upon Jesus Christ, by whom this is accomplished (vv. 1, 4, 5, 14, 21). The close connection between the opening and closing formulas in early Christian literature has been noted by Roller (1933).[3] "Guard you from falling" refers to avoiding moral lapse to 1 Enoch's preservation from ruin at the judgment. Similarly, "to stand" is to be taken with reference to the shaking of the earth at the advent of God, especially prominent at 1 Enoch 1:5–7 in the context of judgment.[4] By keeping themselves in the love of God, the readers will avoid both moral lapse and the calamity to befall the ungodly at the great "shaking," and be able to "rejoice" [ἀγαλλιάσει] at the judgment.[5] Although there is a textual discrepancy at 1 Enoch 104:4, the Ethiopic text reads in admonition to the righteous, " . . . cast not away your hope, for you shall have ἀγαλλιάσις as the angels in heaven.[6] The LXX usage of "rejoicing" as intense delight based upon a right relationship with God (Isa. 16:10; 22:13; 35:10; 65:18f; Ps. 50:10 [ET 51:8]) continues in the New Testament at Acts 2:46f and resurfaces in Ignatius to Ephesians 9:2, 1 Clement 63:2, and Barnabas 1:6. The use of the term as eschatological rejoicing, however, continues in 1 Peter 4:13; Revelation 19:7; and Martyrdom of Polycarp 19:2, as well as here in Jude 24.

This is to suggest that the judgment theme which dominates Jude from verses 3–4 is expressed in the doxology in apocalyptic terminology

[3] See also Champion (1934:104–5); Jewett (1969:18–34).

[4] See also Judg. 5:4–5; Isa. 64:1; Hab. 3:6; Mic. 1:4; Ass. Mos. 10:1–10; Ps. Sol. 2:40; 1 Enoch 102:3.

[5] See 1 Enoch 5:9; 27:3–4; Test. Levi 18:14; Test. Judah 25:5; Test. Benj. 10:6; as well as Strack and Billerbeck (1956:IV, 851f).

[6] See Flemming (1902:164); Kenyon (1941:f12v); and Bonner (1937:71).

characteristic of the judgment theme from 1 Enoch 67:10 in Jude 4 and of the entire midrashic warning in verses 5–16, yet indubitably expressive of the exhortation constructed around τηρέω ("keep") throughout the epistle (vv. 1, 6, 20, 24). In contrast with the grim depiction of the doom of the intruders of Jude's concern, the masterful doxology reflects great depth of spiritual awareness in denoting the security adhering to those who persist in distinctly Christian ways. The literary function of this lofty doxology, then, is that of a prayer that the faithful may be preserved in their Christian faith rather than be consigned to an inevitable fate due to adopting the decadence of the opponents.

Warning Admonitions and Characterization of Opponents in Jude 5–16

Jude 5–7

To combat the deteriorating situation, the exhortation in verses 20–25 is prefaced by two strongly worded enjoinders to reflect upon pertinent warnings with which they were familiar, but which were not being brought to bear upon the present problem, at least with the force Jude deemed necessary. In the first of these reminders (vv. 5–16), Jude drew from the Old Testament and contemporary Jewish literature a few selections which state in unmistakable terms the dire consequences of pursuing the course of the opponents; these selections invigorate his proposals in verses 20–23 (see Ellis 1978:221–26). In the second reminder (vv. 17–19), Jude appealed to earlier apostolic warnings to these readers that such a situation as this appeared imminent; Jude wanted to identify these intruders as those whom the apostles anticipated and to dissuade anyone inclined to follow them.

Jude wrote verses 5–16 as a midrashic-type commentary on the infamous incident in which the wandering Jews in the desert were destroyed for their unbelief. Obviously, verses 5–6 were intended as the basis for the "reminder." The supplementary midrashic material which follows was drawn from various pseudepigraphical sources and should be taken in a parenetic sense as literary warnings illustrative of the principal historical reference in verse 5 and apocalyptic allusion in verse 6. Woven into this midrashic material, however, are several attempts by Jude to link the rebelliousness and fate of the traditional enemies of God with the rebelliousness and fate of these troublesome intruders and those who opt to defect to their number. The function of these midrashic elaborations is fourfold: (1) verses 5–16 clearly state the terrible fate destined for all who pervert the order intended by God; (2) Jude links the rebelliousness of the intruders with that of classic ungodliness; (3) specifically the coming judgment against the "ungodly" is made to apply to the "certain people" of verse 4 with the 1 Enoch 1:9 quote in which the rejected Christ will reappear in eschatological judgment; and (4) the entire unit warns the readers to take seriously the admonitions in verses 20–23.

Verses 5–7 constitute the opening unit of discourse in this section. The prime example of judgment upon the disobedience of ancient Israel and upon the rebellious angels form the basis of the following castigation of the "ungodly intruders," followed by the Sodom illustration underscoring the motif of disobedience and fate (see Klijn 1984:2.237–44). Considerable disparity exists within the manuscript tradition concerning the text of Jude 5. The preferable reading of the verse is ἅπαξ πάντα, ὅτι Ἰησοῦς with A B 33 2344 it^{ar,dem,div} vulg eth Jerome Cyril, rendered " . . . although you have known all these things formerly, that Jesus . . . " (see Osburn 1981:107–15). Fossum (1987:232, n. 45) wrongly attributes to me espousal of "kyrios" in verse 5 in *NTS* (23 [1977]:337). Wand (1934:201) and Kelly (1969:254), among others, go much too far in detecting in "all things" a deeper Gnosis. At least since Jerome (*contra Jov.* 1), Jesus [Ἰησοῦς] has been viewed here as a reference to Joshua, as in Acts 7:45 and Hebrews 4:8 (see Kellett 1903–4:381).

This view is not without serious defect, though, for while Joshua did lead Israel into the promised land, the actual destruction of Israel to which Jude refers cannot be ascribed to the son of Nun. Alternatively, the view that Jesus had saved the people out of Egypt and subsequently destroyed those who did not remain faithful is frequently observed to be a common feature in second-century literature, such as Justin Martyr (*Dial.* 120.3), which specifically mentions Jesus as "the one who led your fathers out of Egypt" (see Wikgren 1967:148). However, in view of Hebrews 11:26 and 1 Corinthians 10:1–11, there is no reason why Jude could not have written "Jesus" with this understanding in the mid-first century (see Ellis 1957:66–70). It is true, as Harris (1920:II, 52) observed long ago, that one is hardly alien to primitive Christianity who detects Jesus in the events of the history of Israel. Kelly (1969:255) objects that the subject in verse 5 is also the subject in verse 6 and that Christ is nowhere depicted as having imprisoned the evil angels. However, in view of 1 Enoch 69:26–29 where "that Son of Man" sits in judgment upon evil angels imprisoned in chains, and 1 Peter 3:22, there is no substantial reason why Jude could not have understood Jesus as subject of "he has kept" in verse 6 as well.

The ultimate reference in verse 5 can hardly be Numbers 25 or Exodus 32:27–35. Jude's reference is rather to the total experience of the wandering Israelites summarized so succinctly in Numbers 14:26ff. (See, among others, Seethaler 1987:262.) The subsequent illustrative material in verses 6–7, joined to verse 5 by the coordinating particle τε, forms a unit of text, all of which is related to "remind you" in verse 5. This triad of Israelites, fallen angels, and Sodomites occurs in Ecclesiasticus 16:6–14, and it is not at all improbable that this combination was suggested to Jude from that source since it occurs in a context of ethical admonition.

Structurally, verses 5 and 6 both describe and note the downfall of their objects; both verses end in verbs, and both have the same subject from verse 5. The impropriety of the angels consists of a purposeful aberrancy on their part which resulted in their being forcefully subjugated and condemned (1 En. 21).[7]

In their impertinence, they obviously reckoned wrongly on the response of God and on the severity of the judgment against them (1 En. 68). The narrative of the angels who rebelled and subsequently were cast down from heaven, where they then committed sexual intercourse with the daughters of men, derives from Genesis 6:1–4.[8]

Cassuto (1973:17–28) argues convincingly that this narrative is not actually contained in Genesis 6 but that it arose at a later period (see Wickham 1974:135–47). It is found in 1 Enoch 6–16 and 86–88 in rather developed form, and it is of more than passing interest that 1 Enoch 18:15f mentions the rebellion of the stars and that allusion is made to these "wandering stars" in Jude 13. (See also Test. Reub. 5; Test. Napth. 3; see also LXX(mss) on Gen. 6, Josephus, *Antiq.* 1.3.1, and Philo, *de Gigant.* 2.) Early patristic writers evidence the narrative as well, employing it to account for the existence of evil (Justin Martyr, *Apol.* 11:5, Clementine Homilies 8:11, Clement of Alexandria, *Strom.* 5.1.10, and Tertullian, *de Virgin.* 7). In the authoritative Jewish writings of the period, however, great stress was placed upon the fact that nowhere in Scripture is one to find reference to intercourse between angels and women. "Sons of God" in Genesis 6 was taken to refer to "distinguished men" by Sifre Numbers 86 and Bemidhbar Rabbah 27:2–5. Now it is clear that Jude makes no reference in verse 6 to Genesis 6:1–4, but to contemporary Jewish legend, the essential features of which are set out clearly in the opening

[7] See Dubarle 1950:145–48; Bauckham 1983:50; and Bauckham 1985:313–30.

[8] See Ginzberg (1955:I, 148f, and V, 153–58) and the older studies of Heller (1910:202–12), and Lods (1927:295–315), as well as more recent works of Bamberger (1952), Alexander (1972:60–71), Berger (1973:1–1), Nickelsburg (1977:383–405), and Marrs (1980:218–24).

pages of 1 Enoch in the context of eschatological judgment. Jude's literary focus in verse 6, then, is upon the *fate* of these angels who failed to "keep themselves" in the situation to which they had been appointed by God (see 1 En. 54:4–6). Verse 6, therefore, functions as a coordinate illustration of the historical example of disobedience and fate in verse 5 and serves admirably to underscore the importance of taking the exhortation in verses 20–23 with the utmost seriousness.

In verse 7, the subordinating particle ὡς introduces a simile that brings the rebelliousness and fate of the ancient cities of Sodom and Gomorrah into comparison with that of the angels in verse 6. James (1912:38) erroneously takes "these" [τούτοις] in verse 7 to refer to the opponents in verse 4.

While Genesis 19:4–25 would have been familiar to the writer, the reference is rather to the use made of this incident in subsequent Jewish tradition as a proverbial object-lesson of God's retribution for disobedience.[9] First Enoch 67:4–7 also contains the view that these angels were believed to be imprisoned in a perpetual fire beneath the Dead Sea (Eccl. 10:7).

While a similarity with respect to sexual incontinence is evident, the angels in verse 6 cannot be said to have committed homosexuality. The comparison "in a similar manner to these" is the rebellious mind-set which resulted in the judgment of doom against both groups, as is the case in Testament of Napthali 3–4; Jubilees 20:5; and 3 Maccabees 2:4–5, where the angels and Sodomites again serve this illustrative purpose. Thus, verse 7 functions in tandem with verse 6 to illustrate the judgment of doom in verse 5 against ungodliness and to anticipate the call to commitment in verses 20–23.

Verses 6–7, then, are analogous to verse 5 with respect to the dire consequences which result from disobedience of God. Not only δεῖγμα, "warning examples," in verse 7, but the entire unit of verses 5–7 is comprised of warning examples, much like those in 1 Corinthians 10:11, which were noted by Paul to have been "written for our instruction." As Jude mentioned at the beginning of verse 5, he has incorporated nothing significantly innovative; he has simply resurfaced well-known information with which to intensify the aberrance and fate of the opponents mentioned in verse 4 and continued in verses 8–16.

---

[9] See Isa. 1:9; Jer. 23:14; Ezek. 16:48ff; Amos 4:11; Test. Asher 7:1; Test. Benj. 9:1; Jub. 22:22; 36:10; Matt. 10:15; 11:24; Rom. 9:29; and Josephus, *Jewish Wars* 4:483–85, as well as the important reference in Sanhedrin 10:1–3.

Jude 8–10

The relationship of these three examples to the intruders is now made explicit by "similarly" in verse 8. The establishment of a certain continuity between those situations and that of the intruders of Jude's concern is accomplished by "defile," "reject," and "blaspheme," each of which is related to the participle "dreaming." "Filthy dreamers" of KJV, which takes the participle only with the first verb, is a certain mistranslation. It is not to be expected that an exact parallel can be found in each of these three verbs and the aforementioned examples of fate in verses 5–7; however, one can see that while the particulars differ, rejection of God's order and catastrophic fates are had in common (see Bauckham 1983:55). Kelly (1969:221), Windisch (1951:41), and Knopf (1967:226) take "dreaming" to refer to esoteric visions or revelations of some sort (as in Isa. 23:16–32; 27:9f). Balz (*TWNT*, viii, 553) argues convincingly that, due to the brevity of this expression in contrast to the fuller description of the excesses of the opponents and, due to the predicative linking of the participle with the subject, Jude has no reference to ecstatic or visionary experiences. There is no basis for the suggestion of Sidebottom (1967:80, 87) by indiscriminately combining verses 8 and 16, that they take money for these revelations. "Dreaming" must be taken with each of the three following verbs, thus necessitating an understanding of the participle with reference to a spiritual condition.

Spitta (1885:342), quoting Hofmann, notes, "Instead of thinking with clear minds and deliberate thought, they have taken off in a confused, even unreal, notion in which they indulge themselves." He adds that these intruders do as they do, "not from a clearer knowledge of God's will, but from a delusion." Further, in view of the fact that "dreaming," intended to depict the intruders as living under a false impression, serves well to denote the comparison between the delusion of the intruders and that of the deluded characters from Israel's literary heritage, the focus and force of the intended simile become immediately clear. While Bigg (1902:330) expresses difficulty in tracing this metaphorical meaning of the term in Greek literature, one must note its use in Strabo, *Geography* 15.1.59, to mean "deluded assumptions," as well as the fact that deluded or lapsed ones are called "sleepers" in Sirach 22:9, Ephesians 5:14, and 1 Thessalonians 5:5–7. The view that delusion is meant in Jude 8 is traceable as early as Clement of Alexandria, *Thoughts on the Epistle of Jude*.[10]

---

[10] See in critical scholarship, Chase, "Jude," *HDB* (II.805); Schlatter (1950:88); and Reicke (1964:201).

The evident comparison between the groups in verses 5–7 and 8ff, as among the groups within verses 5–7, is that of delusion, lapse, and fate.

While sexual impurity is obviously meant by "defile the flesh," the specific type of sexual misconduct in the fallen angels narrative is inappropriate to the opponents here, and it is not at all certain that homosexuality was intended to carry over from verse 7. The assertion of Kelly (1969:258f) that homosexuality is not meant because "other" [ἕτερος] demands flesh of *another* kind (*viz.*, angels) is unsatisfactory because the term here in reference to homosexuality refers to flesh of another kind *than that appointed by God.* Although this particular impropriety could very well have been one aspect of the "licentiousness" in verse 4, the comparison between verse 8 and verses 6–7 is not often of specific sins, but of disobedience to God and the ultimate fate of such a course of action. Similarly, "reject lordship" is parallel with the preceding examples in general, but in view of verse 4 is also an apt description of the opponents. "Lordship" could be taken, with Reicke (1964:201) and James (1912:38), as a generic singular, or in view of verses 4 and 16 with reference to "authority"; but Wohlenberg (1915:302) is probably correct in detecting here a reference to the rejection of Jesus. Note this usage later in Shepherd of Hermas 5.6.1.

With δόξας βλασφημοῦσιν, however, a fresh element is brought to bear. "Glories" is used with reference to angels, as in Testament of Levi 18:5 and Testament of Judah 25:2 (a notion rooted in Exod. 15:11 [LXX]) (see Schrage 1973:226 and Michl 1968:81–82). However, there is no basis for supposing with Sidebottom (1967:87–88) and Moffatt (1928:234–35) that this blasphemy had anything to do with the angels creating the world in opposition to the will of the true God. Kelly (1969:263–64) notes that there exists no grounds for attributing to these opponents such advanced views as in Irenaeus, *Against Heresies* I.25.1f. The notion that "glories" here refers to church leaders is negated by the observations: (1) that the illustration in verses 9–10 makes sense only if the term refers to angelic beings; and (2) there is no plausible instance of δόξαι with this meaning (see Sickenberger 1911:57–59). Jude's accusation of the opponents is that they vilify the spiritual domain.[11]

The following reference to Michael the Archangel provides a contrast to the "blasphemy" in verse 8 in that Michael, while engaged in hand-to-hand combat with the Devil himself, was not so presumptuous as to speak in a blasphemous manner, but kept within appropriate bounds. I am inclined to agree with Bauckham (1983:61) that Michael

---

[11] See the discussion in Bauckham 1983:57–59.

simply became aware that he was not the judge; all he could do was ask God to condemn Satan. Jude's reference is to a Jewish legend recorded in the Assumption of Moses, but unfortunately not extant in any manuscripts of that work.[12] In Hermas, *Similitudes* 8.3.3, a Michael is said to be superior to the other six most prominent angels and Kelly (1960:95) conjectures that Hermas equated him with the archangel Michael and also saw in him the Son of God, both of whom pronounce judgment upon the righteous (*Similitudes* 9.3.2–7; 9.6.3–6) and deliver up the ungodly (*Similitudes* 8.2.5; 8.4.3; 9.7.1f). However, Jude 8–10 reflects neither that Jude himself nor his readers shared the angel christology of a later period nor that he intended Michael in verse 9 to be symbolic of Christ. This parenthetical literary contrast was intended rather as an a fortiori antithesis to the arrogant, yet naive, mockery of the spiritual realm by the opponents. In verse 10, the intruders are said to do what Michael himself would not. They blaspheme things they do not even comprehend, yet they are enmeshed in a delusion in which what they do know leads to their destruction.

So verses 8–10 serve to underscore Jude's observation that in terms of ungodly living, flouting authority, and disrespect for the spiritual realm, these deluded intruders are very much like the deluded Jews in the desert, the fallen angels, and the Sodomites. Not keeping a proper relationship with God surely results in destruction, a point driven home beginning in verse 11.

Jude 11–13

The Semitic οὐαί, "woe!" begins a unit of discourse that continues through verse 16 and delineates further character of the intruders (vv. 12a, 16) and prescribes their doom (vv. 11, 12b–15).[13] The section is in the literary form of ascription in which "woe" is the ascriptive, "to them" the object, the three clauses of Cain, Balaam, and Korah provide the reason, and "these are . . . " (vv. 12–13) is the commentary (see Mullins 1973:194–205, esp. 197). Boobyer (1958:45–47) has argued convincingly that in intertestamental Jewish literature Cain, Balaam, and Korah were seen as prototypes of evil who met horrible fates, and that the three aorists used here are to provide graphic expression to the inevitable fate awaiting these intruders.[14] The contention of Turner (1976:iv, 140) that ἐπορεύθησαν is merely

[12] See Clement, *Adumb. in epist. Iudae*; Origen, *de Prin.* 3.2.1; Didymus, *In ep. Iud. enarr.*; and Gelasius of Cyzicus, *Church History* 2.20.7.

[13] See fuller discussion of this unit in Osburn (1985:296–303).

[14] See Vermes (1973:127–77) on the various forms of the Balaam tradition. See 1 En. 22:7; Jub. 4:1ff; Test. Benj. 7:4; and Josephus, *Ant. Jud.* 1.2.2 on the Cain legend, as well as McNamara (1966:156–160).

a Hebraism for "behave" is negated by Luke 22:33, where πορεύομαι occurs as a euphemism for "fate." It is irrelevant, then, to search for specific parallels in the behavior of the intruders of Jude's concern to that of these three ancient persons.

By way of commentary upon this ascription of doom, Jude appends several brief statements of which the last four are metaphorical. The punctuation in verse 12 is problematic, but whether one takes οἱ with συνευωχούμενοι, "carousing" (with Westcott-Hort; RV), or with σπιλάδες ("hidden shoals"; with TR; RSV), the essential features of Jude's thinking remain clear. By "carousing," they wreak havoc with the love feasts and by "taking care (only) of themselves" they evidence an exclusivism disrespectful of Christian unity and fellowship. Ἀγάπαις, "love feasts," which is the correct reading of the text, refers to meals of religious significance in which fellowship attended the satisfaction of hunger (as in Acts 2:46) and which were sometimes eucharistic (as in 1 Cor. 11:17ff).[15] "Shepherding themselves" does not refer here to church oversight, but to selfish behavior at these love feasts. Jude's complaint is that the deluded intruders still participate in gatherings of the Christian community where their insidiousness undermines the faith and behavior of sincere Christians.[16]

Following these descriptive assertions, Jude writes four metaphors which drive in the wedge concerning the fate he ascribes to these intruders in verse 11. Apparently Jude was reliant upon 1 Enoch 80:2–8 (see Osburn 1985:299 and Burkitt 1914:70–71). Two principal reasons may be adduced in this regard. First, 1 Enoch 80:2–8 occurs in a section which treats the impending punishment of the ungodly. Second, Jude's first (waterless clouds), second (unfruitful trees), and fourth (wandering stars) metaphors occur in precisely that order in this Enochic text.

Jude's third metaphor is not apparent in the extant text of 1 Enoch 80. Charles (1913:ii, 245) notes the textual problem in the Ethiopic Enoch at 80:4–5. Knibb (1978:ii, 186) notes the attempt of Halévy (1867:389) to explain the difficulty on the basis of an assumed Hebrew *Vorlage*. It is possible that Jude's third metaphor reflects an independent text-form no longer traceable in the Enochic tradition other than in the mention in Lactantius (*Divine Institutions* 7.16) in his reference to 1 Enoch 80:2–8 that the sea will be rendered unnavigable. However, it seems to me that the metaphor of the foam on the violent sea in Jude 13 must be accounted for on some basis other than 1 Enoch 80.

---

[15] See Bigg (1902:333) and Kelly (1969:271) on the alteration of ἀγάπαις to ἀπάταις.
[16] See Mayor (1907:40), *contra* Bigg (1902:333–34) and Wisse (1972:133–43).

Bigg (1902:335) noted terminological parallels in Moschus (*Idyll.* 5.5) and Euripides (*Herc. Fur.* 851), but concluded that the imagery was probably suggested by Isaiah 57:20.[17] Against this is the observation that the imagery of the violent sea has to do with the tumult of the ungodly rather than with their licentiousness. Oleson (1979:492–503) suggested that Jude was consciously alluding to a pagan account of the birth of Aphrodite. (See Plato, *Rep.* 2.377E–378A, and Cicero, *de nat. Deor.* 2.24.63f.) According to the legend, Kronos cut off his father's testicles with a sickle and threw them into the sea, where they gathered foam [ἀφρός]; supposedly, Aphrodite was born from that foam, which is said to have washed up on the south shore of Cyprus. Pseudo-Nonnus states, "because of this he says that she is born and honored shamefully, for thus both the honors and festivals connected with her are performed with shameful deeds and sensuous harlotry" (see Brock (1971:181[64]). While the only direct verbal echo between *Theogony* 190–92 and Jude 13 is the word "foam," Oleson nevertheless postulates: (1) that Jude's intruders are the waves which buoy up the severed sexual organs of Kronos in explicit licentious imagery; (2) that Jude was consciously alluding to this grotesque pagan myth in Hellenizing fashion for the purposes of evangelism and pastoral discipline; and (3) that the specific motivation for the use of this legend lies in the proposal that Jude's epistle was directed to the Cypriot community of Nea Paphos, which was quite near the legendary location of Aphrodite's birth.

Oleson's proposal has in its favor the unmistakable reference to the evident licentiousness among the intruders (Jude 4, 8, 23). In view of Acts 17:28, 1 Corinthians 15:33, and Titus 1:12, it is not permissible to argue that Jude could not have had reference to Hesiod's *Theogony*. However, the presence of such a pagan legend in the midst of a section dominated with quotations of and allusions to intertestamental Jewish apocalyptic literature is decidedly strange and requires more than an apparent verbal echo in order to be acceptable as the textual basis for Jude's third metaphor. Oleson's suggestion must be considered tenuous at best.

In Jude 12–13, the writer is creating his own live metaphors, relying upon the apocalyptical imagery in 1 Enoch 80:2–8. The literary focus of these metaphors is to underscore the rebelliousness and inevitable fate of the intruders of verse 4, providing a decisive denouement to the ascription of doom which begins in verse 11. Accordingly, any assessment of the precise intent of Jude's third

---

[17] See also Windisch (1951:44); Schelkle (1970:163); Leconte (1961:75); and Bauckham (1983:89).

metaphor must accord with that literary thrust. The more appropriate question is why Jude did not use the moon metaphor in 1 Enoch 80:4–5. It may be suggested that while the first two and last metaphors required no alteration, the singular reference to the moon was not immediately applicable to Jude's castigation of the intruders. Reasoning that a reference to the sea would round out a cosmic symbolism (or perhaps because the sea had already been referred to in "hidden shoals"), Jude had only to recall 1 Enoch 67, where verse 10 had already provided the *point d'appui* for his epistle (Jude 4), and observe the "convulsion of the waters" connected with hot lava resulting in an offensive effusion of sulphur (67:5f). Verses 4 and 13 underscore this text as that of judgment upon the imprisoned angels for their evident licentiousness (vv. 8, 10, 13). Further, the delusion of the angels is specified in verse 13, where the same convulsing waters which they hold of value in healing are said to be the very waters of judgment which will change into a sea of eternal fire that will ultimately destroy them.

This suggestion of the origin of Jude's third metaphor has the advantages: (1) of maintaining the metaphorical imagery of the violent sea in a context of eschatological judgment upon imprisoned angels who are sexually aberrant, and (2) originating in a section of 1 Enoch to which Jude had already made reference in verse 4. If, indeed, this is the case, Jude has continued his utilization of Jewish apocalyptic imagery from the text of 1 Enoch, which undoubtedly was open before him. In the convulsion of the sulphuric waters that Enoch so poignantly specified as the waters of judgment upon the imprisoned angels, Jude found the imagery for his castigation continuum. It would have been only natural, then, for Jude to turn back the scroll of 1 Enoch to 1:9 and set out in verses 14–15 his adaptation of that text so as to drive in the wedge that the very Jesus whom these reject, in their delusion preferring licentiousness, is precisely the One who (like the waters of convulsion) will ultimately judge and destroy them.

Jude 14–16

It was the investigation of the theophany of 1 Enoch chapter 1 by Vander Kam (1973:129ff) and Black's (1971:1–14) introduction of Jude 14–15 as evidence in the *maranatha* problem that induced me to undertake a fresh examination of Jude 14–15 (see Osburn 1977:334–41). Whereas earlier Old Testament theophanies (Deut. 33:2; Judg. 5:4–5) refer to former appearances of God, later poetic theophanies (Isa. 63:19ff; Hab. 3:1–19; Mic. 1:2–5) evidence the hope of God's return to assist His people and destroy the ungodly. The expansion of these expectations into a statement of God's final, decisive theophany in 1 Enoch chapter 1 is well suited for adaptation by Jude for christological reasons.

The variations within the manuscript tradition of 1 Enoch chapter 1 and in the text of Jude itself, as well as between the two traditions, are instructive. First Enoch chapter 1 is preserved in an Ethiopic translation (see Knibb 1978), a Greek version (see Black 1970), and an Aramaic fragment from Qumrân (see Milik 1976). The introduction to Jude's citation ("as Enoch the seventh from Adam prophesied, saying") is a direct reference to 1 Enoch. Enoch is not called "seventh from Adam" in the Old Testament (though this may be inferred from Gen. 5:1–24 or 1 Chron. 1:1–3), but He is referred to in this way in 1 Enoch 60:8.

Charles (1913:ii, 189) suggested that ὅτι ("that," introducing a quotation) in the Greek Enoch is a misreading of ἰδού ("behold!") which is found in Jude and the Ethiopic. This is preferable to Milik's reconstructed 4Q² Enoch 1:9, which reads "when" as does a palimpsest copy of 1 Enoch 1:9, which has ὅτει. The Greek text of this Gizeh fragment is in Lods (1892) (see also Bauckham 1981:136–38). The interjection "Behold!" appears at the beginning of several Old Testament theophanies (Mic. 1:3; Isa. 26:21; 40:10; 62:11) and is rendered in the LXX by ἰδού. It is more likely that the lacuna in 4Q Enoch 1:9 should read an interjection, perhaps אֲרוּ, rather than Milik's כְּדִי. אֲרוּ occurs in biblical Aramaic at Daniel 7:2, 5–7, 13. The by-form אֲלוּ occurs in Daniel 2:31; 4:7, 10; and 7:8. This would account for the Ethiopic ᵐ፺ሁ. Thus, "behold" in Jude 14 and the Ethiopic Enoch reflect independent reliance upon an interjection in the Aramaic Enoch, and the "when" of the Greek Enoch is, in fact, a misreading of that text.

Then, interestingly, the Greek Enoch reads ἔρχεται (here a futuristic present, "is coming"), a reading also found in the Ethiopic ᵐአሕ. However, Jude 14 reads ἦλθεν. Wohlenberg (1915:318) observes correctly that, although Jude wrote the aorist form, he makes no reference to a past theophany but to a future coming, reflecting a Semitic prophetic perfect in which an event is viewed as accomplished though it is yet to happen (see Kautzsch 1910:312–13). The assumption of K. G. Kuhn ("μαραναθά," *TWNT* 4.472) that the prophetic perfect does not occur in Aramaic must be revised in view of Daniel 7:27.[18] In this case, Jude translated the Aramaic prophetic perfect literally with the Greek aorist. "Is coming" with reference to the future in the Greek Enoch and the Ethiopic are more idiomatic ren-

---

[18] See Strack (1896:21); Schelkle (1970:164); Black (1971:10–11); Vander Kam (1973:148); Knopf (1912:236).

derings which came about as scribes noted the past tense of the original, related that to the context, and decided upon an idiomatic usage to represent the intended future coming. This underscores the strong probability that Jude was working from an Aramaic text of 1 Enoch.

In this connection, the subject of the prophetic perfect in 1 Enoch 1:9 is "the Holy Great One" of verse 3, so there is no expressed subject of the verb in the Enochic texts. Jude, however, reads "the Lord" as subject, revealing his Christian adaptation of this Enochic theophany with evident reference to "the Lord (Jesus)."[19] Thus, the text becomes an unmistakable prediction of the coming of the Lord Jesus in divine judgment upon the ungodly, continuing the literary thrust rooted in verse 5 and ultimately in verses 3–4.

Next, the Aramaic, Ethiopic, and Jude all read "with myriads of His holy ones," whereas the Greek Enoch reads "with His myriads and His holy ones," one further instance of reliance upon the Aramaic by Jude and the Ethiopic at a point where the Greek Enoch has made an alteration. Jude's reading ἐν ἁγίαις μυριάσιν αὐτοῦ, supported by A B K L 056 0142 and numerous minuscules, has strong claim to be the more ancient text-form (see Weiss 1892:42). Then all the Enochic texts read "all flesh," but Jude omits these words. Why? In verse 15, Jude rendered the Aramaic literally by "to bring judgment upon all," as reflected in the Greek and Ethiopic Enochs. However, whereas next the Enochic texts read two clauses "to destroy [all] the ungodly and to convict all flesh," Jude omits "destroy" of the first and "all flesh" of the second, joining the remaining elements into one clause that suits properly his purpose of emphasizing the coming judgment against the ungodly. I remain unconvinced by B. Dehandschutter's (1986:114–20, esp. 118ff) rejection of an Aramaic *Vorlage* for Jude at this point.

From these analyses, three observations emerge: (1) Jude is not only quoting 1 Enoch 1:9, but specifically from an Aramaic Enoch; (2) Jude has made a decidedly Christian adaptation of the Enochic text by the unique addition of "Lord" as subject; and (3) Jude has altered the Enochic text so as to highlight those elements having to do with his emphasis upon judgment against the ungodly.

Jude's use of this particular pseudepigraphical theophany is not unrelated to the intruders of verse 4. In a conscious adaptation of 1 Enoch 67:10, Jude has specified that these individuals are "ungodly," denying the lordship of Christ and having a propensity for licentiousness, and

---

[19] See among others, Kelly (1969:276); Schelkle (1970:164); and Wohlenberg (1915:318).

who have been marked out for "judgment." The judgment occurs in 1QS 4:9–14, where spirits of evil are excoriated in terminology quite similar to Jude. (See Burrows 1951:II for plates and transcription.) Reicke's (1964:197) view that 1QS 4:9–14 suggests the existence of a certain tradition behind Jude's allusions seems plausible. The judgment certainly forms a prominent aspect of the 1 Enoch theophany at verse 7. The repeated use of ἀσέβεια ("ungodly") and its related forms in 1 Enoch 1:9 clearly indicates this to be the cause for judgment. Note Vander Kam's (1973:150) suggestion that these forms may have been suggested to the writer of 1 Enoch from Micah 1:5 (LXX). The juxtaposition of "judgment" and "ungodly" in Jude 4, then, is not accidental but indicative of Jude's reflection upon the Enochic theophany. Jude's alterations to the Enochic text were made consciously and for the specific theological purpose of emphasizing that it is precisely the Jesus whom these reject who ultimately will triumph over them as eschatological judge. The choice of this text was made in the pre-literary stage of the epistle, as Jude endeavored to grapple with the problem he observed permeating some sector of the early church. Both the literary structure and christological thrust of the epistle were influenced profoundly by Jude's adaptation of this prominent pseudepigraphical theophany in elaboration upon the judgment of 1 Enoch 67:10.

Jude then writes verse 16 in a final effort to relate the intruders of verse 4 unmistakably to the eschatological "ungodly." "Grumbling" and "murmuring," frequently used in Old Testament and intertestamental Jewish literature as the antithesis of "faith," occur only here in the New Testament (see De Vries 1968:51–58). Although there is no reason to view these terms as other than descriptive of the intruders, they serve as a kind of midrashic concluding reference to the principal Old Testament allusion in verse 5. There is certainly no reason to view this terminology with reference to Gnostic discontent over the imprisonment of their spark of light in material bodies (see Kelly 1969:278). Three assertions follow in which the independence, arrogance, and unscrupulousness of the intruders are noted. While many have observed that this language is reminiscent of Assumption of Moses 5:5; 7:7–9; and 1 Enoch 1:9; 5:4, it must be noted that these characteristics are of the same sort mentioned in Jude 4, 8, 10, 12, with the addition of "flattery for profit," and provide apt description of the intruders. Bauckham (1983:100) thinks Jude may have had Assumption of Moses 5:5 in mind, which speaks of teachers of the law who "respect persons" perverting justice by taking bribes. However, there is otherwise no reference in Jude to the intruders being "teachers," and I am inclined to retain "flattery." Sidebottom's (1967:80, 87) attempt to relate this phrase to "dreaming" (v. 8) in the sense of esoteric visions for which they receive money is without foundation.

In verses 5–16, then, Jude has utilized the historical incident in Numbers 14:26ff, supported by several well-known pseudepigraphical selections in contemporary literature as a fundamental warning admonition that the ungodliness of the intruders, specified in verses 4, 8, 10, 12, and 16, would result in certain condemnation when Jesus returns in eschatological judgment.

The Apostolic Warning in Jude 17–19

In antithesis to "these" intruders in verses 4 and 8–16, a second reminder upon which to base the forthcoming exhortation in verses 20–23, "beloved" serves here (as in vv. 3, 20) as a discourse marker. Windisch (1951:45) erroneously takes verses 17–18 as an interruption in the description of the opponents. Wand (1934:216), among others, correctly views verses 17–19 as a reinforcement of the warning in verses 5–16. Watson's (1988:29–79) combination of verses 17–19 as *repetitio* and verses 20–23 as *adfectus* to make a *probatio* is unconvincing. The former is best related to verses 5–16 and the latter to verses 3–4. Sellin (1986:206–25) makes the same mistake as Watson in relating verses 17–19 with verses 20–23, rather than with the preceding material.

The aorist imperative μνήσθητε ("remember") marks the shift to the positive reminder that the apostles had warned these readers earlier of the imminent possibility of such intruders who would scoff, preferring ungodliness. Precisely which apostles are in mind and whether their statements were oral or written remain unknown, although in view of the imperfect ἔλεγον the former is preferable. Among others, Bigg (1902:337) notes Jude to be quoting an apostolic document. Second Peter 3:2–3; 1 Timothy 4:1; 2 Timothy 3:1f; and Acts 20:20f are often mentioned in this regard. James (1912:41) and Wand (1934:216) correctly detect no written document. Importantly, Jude does not refer to himself as an apostle here or in the salutation. Rather his appeal is to the apostolic forecast of these intruders as an incitement to heed the following exhortation in verses 20–23.

Parallel with verses 5–16, verses 17–19 have not only a call to remembrance addressed to the faithful but a warning and a castigation of the opponents. "Conducting themselves according to their own ungodly desires" poses no problem, but a diversity of opinion exists on ἐμπαῖκται ("scoffers"). While it has been advanced that the projected mockery is actualized here with respect to denial of the *parousia*, Reicke (1964:212), Schelkle (1970:167), and Kelly (1969:283) have argued convincingly that there is no second-coming problem evidenced in Jude. Reference to scoffing at this point has to do with the licentiousness of the intruders, which results in derisive umbrage at what they consider to be an astonishing naivete on the part of those who shun licentiousness.

In concert with preceding sections of Jude where "these" is used with present participles to describe the intruders, Jude concludes this second reminder in verse 19 with statements designed to leave no uncertainty that these are precisely the ones anticipated by the apostles. Considerable uncertainty exists within critical scholarship, however, over whether Jude's statement should be taken to refer: (1) to separations, as at love feasts; (2) factions; or (3) Gnostic division of men. Kelly (1969:284f), citing such Gnostic division in Irenaeus (*Adv. haer.* 1.6.1–4) and Epiphanius (*Pan. haer.* 31.7), detects a special Gnostic division in which the opponents classify ordinary church members as "natural" and themselves as "spiritual" (see also Schrage 1973:230, and Leaney 1967:97–98). Seen in this way, "natural" would refer not to licentiousness, but to an incapacity for knowing the deeper mysteries of God, as in Plumptre (1903:212). Similarly, Reicke (1964:213) advances that "spiritual" indicates the opponents who claim special knowledge and wisdom for themselves. Taken thus, verse 19 castigates the opponents as a spiritual aristocracy whose exclusivistic tendencies are exhibited in terms of an arrogant Gnostic separation from ordinary Christians. Green (1968:182–84) goes much too far in trying to relate this "dualism" in Jude with the mystery cults, as in Reitzenstein (1927:184). Jude's retort, then, would be that the opposite of their claim is actually true.

On the other hand, advocates of some sort of Gnostic contour to verse 19 have never been able to marshal sufficient evidence to establish that view beyond doubt. Long ago, Bigg (1902:338–39) observed correctly that, in view of the separation at love feasts (v. 12) and attachment to the rich (v. 16), no evidence can be found that these intruders called the faithful "natural," as did the later Gnostics. Bigg called that argument "quite gratuitous." Further, Schelkle (1970:168), Mayor (1907:48), and even Kelly (1969:285) have argued cogently that "spiritual," rather than referring to the acquisition of esoteric knowledge, is capable of simpler explanation as denoting that the opponents are devoid of the Holy Spirit, as in Romans 8:9, whose presence was the *sine qua non* of early Christian experience.

The danger is in reading verse 19 in the light of later constructs. Admittedly, these two terms were Gnostic *later*, but the central questions are whether they were already Gnostic technical terms in the New Testament period and whether Jude intended that meaning here. Haardt (1968:ii, 374–81) notes that the contrast between these two terms in 1 Corinthians 2:14f may seem to present an apparent analogy with Gnosis, but despite ingenious constructions any such connection remains obscure; the heretics cannot be identified as Gnostic with certainty. It is not legitimate to assume that significance attached to particular terms in the context of developed Gnosticism was already attached to them in an earlier period and in a different context. Indeed, as Wilson (1972:71) observes, "Gnosis in the broader sense is not yet Gnosticism, and to interpret New Testament texts which *may* reflect Gnosis in terms of the later Gnosticism is to run the risk of distorting the whole picture."

Accordingly, with Wohlenberg (1915:324–26), Schlatter (1950:92–93), and Michl (1968:89), it is preferable to take "dividers" without Gnostic reference to refer to dissensions within the churches of Jude's concern resultant from the insidious intruders in verse 4. A divisive effect upon the Christian community would be the inevitable result of such characteristics as Jude has attributed to these intruders, and it would be odd if such division had not been mentioned in the epistle. "Natural," meaning "sensual," and "not having the spirit," with reference to the Holy Spirit, are virtually synonymous and complementary of "dividers." This divisive effect of the ungodly scoffers clearly anticipates the exhortation in verses 20–23 for the faithful to build themselves up in the faith, keep themselves in God's love, and otherwise conduct themselves according to the noblest Christian teaching as they attempt to assist those of their number inclined to defect.

Thus, the overall literary structure of the Epistle of Jude is as follows:

[1–2 Greeting

[3–4 Introduction

    [5–7 Literary warnings: rebellion=fate

    [8–16 Link rebellion=fate of eschatological
       enemies of God to rebellion=fate of intruders

  [17=19 Apostolic warnings

[20–23 Concluding appeal. Specific of "contend" in verse 4.

  [24–25 Doxology

The Epistle of Jude:
History and Heresiological Tradition

Despite the vast erudition expended upon the matter, the identity of the "ungodly intruders" of Jude 4 remains an intriguing uncertainty. Numerous attempts to identify them as Gnostics (see Julicher 1894:146 and Scott 1932:226) by ferreting out certain "distinctive features" in Jude's description of the opponents have been nullified in one way or another by those factors which led Lake (1938:167) to note correctly that "it is not sufficient to identify them with any known body of heretics, and to call them Gnostics is merely *obscurum per obscurius.*" (See also Weiss 1886:410f.) Indeed, the paucity of information in the epistle itself had earlier stimulated considerably diverse postulations: Carpocratians according to Holtzmann (1886:532), Cone (1893:338–41), and Pfleiderer (1902:ii.510); Nicolaitans according to Huther (1867:238–39) and Mansel (1875:70); Archontikoi according to Harnack (1897:465f); Cainites according to Lipsius (1869:ii, 505); ultra-Paulinists according to Spitta (1885:503f); and Jewish-Christian heretics according to Pieper (1938). Pieper postulated the party of Thebuthis (1939:66–71, cf. Eusebius, *Ecclesiastical History* 4.22.4–5); but Von Soden (1889:iii, 203–4) postulates Marcosians; Barns (1905:391–411) and Mayor (1905:569–77) postulate Marcosians. Maier (1906:chap. 11) has induced more recent scholars to speak instead rather cautiously of an "incipient Gnosticism," though Wickenhauser (1972:581) cautions that this *keimhaften* Gnosis must not be connected with the later *ausgebildeten* Gnosis. Nonetheless, Barclay (1960:192) suggests the Ophites, and Gunther (1984:549–62) continues such speculation.

Although it has become increasingly clear that the Epistle of Jude exhibits no trace of the important tenets of mature second-century Gnostic systems,[20] it remains to be proven that the "ungodly intruders" of Jude 4 were in fact *primitive precursors* of those systems. Characteristically, verses 4–19 have been thought to surface prime indicators of some sort of proto-Gnostic background to the epistle, that is, that the libertinism of the intruders was combined with doctrinal error which shortly developed into second-century Gnosticism. However, the early history of Gnosticism remains decidedly uncertain, and the data often adduced in support of this theory amounts to little more than a mass of disorganized parallels to Jude. The verses commonly employed to substantiate "incipient Gnosticism" do not readily lend themselves to such an identification. For instance,

---

[20] See Van Baaren (1970:511–27) on tenets of mature Gnosticism.

Kelly (1969:230–31, 253, 264, 278–79) sees in Jude "the opening shots in the fateful struggle between the church and Gnosticism which was to feature large in the second century." Yet Kelly is forced to conclude: (1) that there are no aeons or other typically second-century Gnostic elements in Jude; (2) that the suggestion that the "ungodly intruders" denied Christ in a theological way is only a "tempting inference"; (3) that verse 8 actually contains no reference to angels as agents of an inferior god; and (4) that it is not at all certain that verse 16 alludes to Gnostic discontent with imprisonment in material bodies. Further, it is not necessary to imply from verse 4 a Gnostic degradation of the Creator God to demonic Demiurge. However plausible it might appear that the "ungodly intruders" of Jude 4 and the second-century Gnostic heresies had some vital connection, the precise nature of any such relationship remains decidedly obscure. The theory of "incipient Gnosticism," despite its widespread currency, is an inadequate *prima facie* description of Jude's adversaries.

Similarly, while there is widespread agreement that Jude and 2 Peter have certain similarities (see Maier 1906:159–67 on differences), no clarity has been reached with regard to the relation between the situations reflected in each epistle.[21] There is no compelling reason to view Jude as dependent upon 2 Peter. Fornberg (1977:33–59) argues well that 2 Peter was dependent upon Jude. Although it is assumed by Kelly (1969:225–31), among others, that the "false teachers" of 2 Peter and the "ungodly intruders" of Jude are sufficiently related to warrant their being treated together, any indiscriminate combination of characteristics is methodologically dubious and certain to distort the picture. Likewise, the traditional penchant for assuming a literary relationship between the two documents fails to account for the fact that the material Jude has in common with 2 Peter occurs in a different context and is deficient of the verbal precision one encounters, for instance, among the Synoptic Gospels. Accordingly, while recognizing a certain similarity, one must question the validity of assuming at the outset that one can reconstruct the ancient walls of Jude by using stones borrowed indiscriminately from 2 Peter.

Earlier the primary question was whether Jude's intruders were merely immoral[22] or were in fact heretical teachers (Dorner 1851:i,

---

[21] On the priority of 2 Peter, see Spitta (1885:381–470). On the priority of Jude, see Mayor (1907:xviff). Reicke (1964:190) has resurfaced the view of dependence upon a common source. See further Soards (1988:3831).

[22] See Schwegler (1846:i, 518f); Bleek (1862:555f); De Wette (1853:95).

104). In recent years it has been asked whether the Epistle of Jude was addressed to a particular historical situation at all. Werdermann (1913) concluded in his classic study of this problem that it is questionable to look for a description of a specific group of heretics in the epistle. Werdermann was followed in this assessment by Spicq (1966:202), who posited that one finds in Jude only a "portrait-robot de l'hérétique."

In a reconceptualization of the matter along those lines, Wisse (1972:133–43) has advocated that the Epistle of Jude, rather than having been written to a specific audience to deal with an actual issue in the early church, was merely a clever *ad hominem* argument in pseudo-epistolary form against unspecified opponents of orthodoxy at the turn of the first century. In holding that the epistle was not written to combat the dangerous influence of opponents within the church, Wisse steps outside the traditional quest to identify these intruders and assumes them only to be part of a developing heresiological tradition which shortly resulted in the traditional picture of what characterized an heretical group that one finds, for instance, in Irenaeus. However, if the case for any of the aforementioned postulations as to the nature of Jude's intruders seems precarious, Wisse has hardly succeeded in posing a more plausible thesis, as failure to distinguish historical assertions from apocalyptical warnings, especially in verses 5–16, and his misconstrual of certain historical data, renders his thesis useless (see Bauckham 1988:3809–12).

Using literary controls rather than inclination or ill-fitting constructs not inherent within the document, this study has found no basis for viewing Jude's epistle as pseudo-epistolary. The reference in 1 Corinthians 9:5 to "brothers of the Lord" conducting itinerant ministries could have included Jude. The extensive use of Jewish apocalyptic in the epistle seems to relate the author and his readers to Jewish background (see Longenecker 1975:193–94). That the epistle was composed in Greek suggests a predominantly Jewish audience in the Graeco-Roman world.

The literary analysis has provided a responsible alternative to the uncontrolled assemblage of purported characteristics of Jude's opponents by separating genuine characteristics from apocalyptical data. The intruders are specified by Jude to be: (1) ungodly; (2) licentious; (3) rejecting Christ; (4) in delusion, sexually improper, rejecting lordship, and mocking the spiritual domain; (5) insidiously attending the love-feasts of the church where they attract Christians to their posture; (6) carousing together unashamedly; (7) taking care only of themselves; (8) disenchanted; (9) obdurate; (10) verbally harsh; (11) flattering others for selfish advantage; (12) divisive; and (13) unspiritual. Indeed, when characteristics are allowed to form the picture that remains after the warning apocalyptical references, characteristics from other documents and traits from hypothetical constructs have been dismissed, the intruders of Jude have every appearance of historicity; and there is no reason why the epistle should not be taken as a genuine attempt to counter their sinister influence.

References

Alexander, P. 1972. "The Targumim and Early Exegesis of 'Sons of God' in Genesis 6." *JJS* 23. Pp. 60–71.

Aune, David. 1987. *The New Testament in Its Literary Environment.* Philadelphia: Westminster.

van Baaren, P. 1970. "Towards a Definition of Gnosticism." *Le Origini dello Gnosticismo: Colloquio de Messina 13–18 Aprile 1966,* ed. by U. Bianchi. Leiden: Brill. Pp. 511–27.

Bamberger, Bernard J. 1952. *Fallen Angels.* Philadelphia: Jewish Pub. Soc. of America.

Barclay, William. 1960. *The Letters of John and Jude.* 2nd ed. Philadelphia: Westminster.

Barns, T. 1905. "The Epistle of Jude: A Study in the Marcosian Heresy." *JTS* 6. Pp. 391–411.

Bauckham, Richard. 1981. "A Note on a Problem in the Greek Version of I Enoch 1.9." *JTS* 32. Pp. 136–38.

_____. 1983. *Jude, 2 Peter.* Waco: Word.

_____. 1985. "The Fall of the Angels as the Source of Philosophy in Hermias and Clement of Alexandria." *VC* 39. Pp. 313–30.

_____. 1988. "The Letter of Jude: An Account of Research." *Aufstieg und Niedergang der Römischen Welt* II.25.5. Berlin: de Gruyter. Pp. 3809–12.

Beekman, John and John Callow. 1974. *Translating the Word of God.* Grand Rapids: Zondervan.

Berger, K. 1973. "Der Streit des guten und des bösen Engels um die Seele: Beobachtungen zu 4Q AMR^b und Judas 9." *JSJ* 4. Pp. 1–18.

Bigg, C. 1902. *The Epistles of St. Peter and St. Jude.* ICC. 2nd ed. Edinburgh: T & T Clark.

Bjerkelund, C. J. 1967. *ΠΑΡΑΚΑΛΩ: Form, Funktion, und Sinn der parakalô-Sätze in den paulinischen Briefen.* Oslo: Universitetsforlaget.

Black, Matthew. 1970. *Apocalypsis Henochi Graeci.* Leiden: Brill.

_____. 1971. "The Christological Use of the Old Testament in the New Testament." *NTS* 18. Pp. 1–14.

Bleek, J. F. 1862. *Einleitung in das Neue Testament.* Berlin: Reimer.

Bonner, Campbell. 1937. *The Last Chapters of Enoch in Greek.* London: Chatto and Windus.

Boobyer, G. H. 1958. "The Verbs in Jude 11." *NTS* 5. Pp. 45–47.

Brock, Sebastian. 1971. *The Syriac Version of the Pseudo-Nonnus Mythological Scholia.* Cambridge: Cambridge University Press.

Burkitt, F. C. 1914. *Jewish and Christian Apocalypses.* London: British Academy.

Burrows, M. 1951. *The Dead Sea Scrolls of St. Mark's Monastery.* New Haven: American School of Oriental Research. II.

Cassuto, U. 1973. *Biblical and Oriental Studies.* Jerusalem: Magnes Press.

Chaine, Joseph. 1939. *Les épîtres catholiques.* EtBib. 2nd ed. Paris: J. Gabalda.

Champion, L. G. 1934. *Benedictions and Doxologies in the Epistles of Paul.* Oxford: Kemp Hall.

Charles, R. H. 1913. *The Apocrypha and Pseudepigrapha of the Old Testament.* Oxford: Clarendon Press. II.

Chase, F. H. "Jude." *Hastings Dictionary of the Bible,* II.805.

Cotterell, Peter and Max Turner. 1989. *Linguistics and Biblical Interpretation.* Downers Grove, IL: InterVarsity Press.

Cone, Orello. 1893. *The Gospel and Its Earliest Interpretations.* London: G. P. Putnam's Sons.

Dahl, Nils. 1967. "Paul and the Church at Corinth according to 1 Corinthians 1:10–4:21." *Christian History and Interpretation. Studies Presented to John Knox,* ed. by W. Farmer, C. F. D. Moule, and R. Niebuhr. Cambridge: Cambridge University Press.

Dehandschutter, B. 1986. "Pseudo-Cyprian, Jude and Enoch: Some Notes on 1 Enoch 1:9." *Tradition and Re-interpretation in Jewish and Early Christian Literature: Essays in Honour of Jürgen C. H. Lebram,* ed. by J. W. van Henten et al. Leiden: E. J. Brill. Pp. 114–20.

de Vries, Simon J. 1968. "The Origin of the Murmuring Tradition." *JBL* 87. Pp. 51–58.

de Wette, W. M. L. 1853. *Kurze Erklärung der Briefe des Petrus, Judas und Jakobus.* 2nd ed., rev. by B. Brückner. Leipzig: S. Hirzel.

Dorner, J. A. 1851. *Entwicklungsgeschichte der Lehre von der Person Christi.* Berlin: G. Schlawitz.

Doty, W. G. 1973. *Letters in Primitive Christianity.* Philadelphia: Fortress.

Dubarle, A. M. 1950. "Le péché des anges dans l'épître de Jude." *Memorial J. Chaine.* Lyon: Facultés catholiques.

Elderen, Bastian van. 1967. "The Verb in the Epistolary Invocation." *Calvin Journal of Theology* 2. Pp. 46–48.

Ellis, E. 1957. *Paul's Use of the Old Testament.* Grand Rapids: Eerdmans.

_____. 1978. *Prophecy and Hermeneutic in Early Christianity.* Grand Rapids: Eerdmans.

Flemming, J. 1902. *Das Buch Henoch.* Leipzig: J. C. Hinrichs.

Fornberg, Tord. 1977. *An Early Church in a Pluralistic Society. A Study of 2 Peter.* ConBib, 9; Lund: Gleerup.

Fossum, Jarl. 1987. "Kyrios Jesus as the Angel of the Lord in Jude 5–7." *NTS* 33. P. 232.

Ginzberg, Louis. 1955. *The Legends of the Jews.* Philadelphia: Jewish Publication Society of America. I.

Green, Michael. 1968. *The Second Epistle General of Peter and General Epistle of Jude.* London: Tyndale.

Gunther, John. 1984. "The Alexandrian Epistle of Jude." *NTS* 30. Pp. 549–62.

Haardt, R. 1968. "Gnosis." *Sacramentum Mundi,* ed. by K. Rahner. New York: Herder and Herder. II. Pp. 374–81.

Halévy, M. J. 1867. "Recherches sur la langue de la rédaction primitive du livre d'Enoch." *JA* 6. P. 389.

Harnack, Adolf von. 1897. *Die Chronologie der altchristlichen Literatur bis Eusebius.* Leipzig: J. C. Hinrichs.

Harris, Rendel. 1920. *Testimonies.* Cambridge: Cambridge University Press.

Hartman, Lars. 1979. *Asking for a Meaning: A Study of 1 Enoch 1–5.* ConBib, 12. Lund: Gleerup.

Heller, B. 1910. "La chute des anges: Schemhazai, Ouzza, et Azaël." *REJ* 60. Pp. 202–12.

Holtzmann, H. J. 1886. *Lehrbuch der historisch-kritischen Einleitung in das Neue Testament.* 2nd ed. Freiburg: J. C. B. Mohr.

Huther, J. E. 1867. *Handbuch über den 1. Brief des Petrus, den Brief des Judas, und den 2. Brief des Petrus.* 3rd ed. Göttingen: Vandenhoeck and Ruprecht.

James, M. R. 1912. *The Second Epistle General of Peter and the General Epistle of Jude.* Cambridge: Cambridge University Press.

Jewett, Robert. 1969. "The Form and Function of the Homiletic Benediction." *Anglican Theological Review* 51. Pp. 18–34.

Jülicher, Adolf. 1894. *Einleitung in das Neue Testament.* Leipzig: J. C. B. Mohr.

Kautzsch, E. 1910. *Gesenius' Hebrew Grammar,* rev. by A. E. Cowley. 2nd Eng. ed. Oxford: Clarendon Press.

Kellett, E. E. 1903–4. "Note on Jude 5." *Expository Times* 15. P. 381.

Kelly, J. N. D. 1960. *Early Christian Doctrines.* 2nd ed. New York: Harper & Bros.

_____. 1969. *The Epistles of Peter and of Jude.* London: A. & C. Black.

Kenyon, F. G. 1941. *The Chester Beatty Biblical Papyri.* London: E. Walker.

Klijn, A. F. J. 1984. "Jude 5 to 7." *The New Testament Age: Essays in Honor of Bo Reicke,* ed. by W. Weinrich. Atlanta: Mercer.

Knibb, Michael. 1978. *The Ethiopic of Book of Enoch*. Oxford: Clarendon Press. II.

Knopf, R. 1912. *Die Briefe Petri und Judä*. KEK. Göttingen: Vandenhoeck and Ruprecht.

Kubo, Sakae. 1981. "Jude 22–23: Two-division form or Three?" *New Testament Textual Criticism: Its Significance for Exegesis: Essays in Honour of Bruce M. Metzger*, ed. by E. Epp and G. Fee. Oxford: Clarendon Press. Pp. 239ff.

Lake, Kirsopp and Sylva. 1938. *An Introduction to the New Testament*. London: Christophers.

Leaney, A. R. C. 1967. *The Letters of Peter and Jude*. Cambridge: Cambridge University Press.

Leconte, R. 1961. *Les épîtres catholiques*. Paris: Editions du Cerf.

Lenski, R. C. H. 1966. *The Epistles of St. Peter, St. John, and St. Jude*. Minneapolis: Augsburg.

Lipsius, R. A. 1869. "Gnosis." *Bibel-Lexikon: Realwörterbuch zum Handgebrauch für Geistliche und Gemeindeglieder*, ed. by D. Schenkel. Leipzig: F. A. Brockhaus.

Lods, A. 1927. "La chute des anges: Origine et portee de cette speculation." *RHPR* 7. Pp. 295–315.

———. 1892. *Le livre d'Hénoch*. Paris: E. Leroux.

Longenecker, Richard. 1975. *Biblical Exegesis in the Apostolic Period*. Grand Rapids: Eerdmans.

Maier, Friedrich. 1906. *Der Judasbrief*. Freiburg: Herder.

Mansel, Henry. 1875. *The Gnostic Heresies of the First and Second Centuries*. London: Murray.

Marrs, Rick. 1980. "The Sons of God (Genesis 6:1–4)." *RO* 23. Pp. 218–24.

Mayor, J. B. 1905. "The Epistle of Jude and the Marcosian Heresy." *JTS* 6. Pp. 569–77.

———. 1907. *The Epistle of St. Jude and the Second Epistle of St. Peter*. London: Macmillan.

McNamara, Martin. 1966. *The New Testament and the Palestinian Targum to the Pentateuch*. AnBib, 27. Rome: Pontifical Biblical Institute.

Meecham, H. G. 1952. "The Present Participle of Antecedent Action—Some NT Instances." *ET* 64. P. 285.

Michl, Johann. 1968. *Die katholischen Briefe*. RNT, 8. 2nd ed. Regensburg: F. Pustet.

Milik, J. T. 1976. *The Books of Enoch: Aramaic Fragments of Qumrân Cave 4*. Oxford: Clarendon.

Moffatt, James. 1928. *The General Epistles: James, Peter, and Judas*. New York: Harper & Bros.

Mullins, T. Y. 1973. "Ascription as a Literary Form." *NTS* 19. Pp. 194–205.

_____. 1962. "Petition as a Literary Form." *NovT* 5. Pp. 48–54.

Nickelsburg, George. 1977. "Apocalyptic and Myth in I Enoch 6–11." *JBL* 96. Pp. 383–405.

Oleson, J. P. 1979. "An Echo of Hesiod's *Theogony* vv. 190–192 in Jude 13." *NTS* 25. Pp. 492–503.

Osburn, Carroll D. 1985. "I Enoch 80:2–8 (67:5–7) and Jude 12–13." *CBQ* 47. Pp. 300–302.

_____. 1977. "The Christological Use of I Enoch 1.9 in Jude 14, 15." *NTS* 23. Pp. 334–41.

_____. 1981. "The Text of Jude 5." *Biblica* 62. Pp. 107–15.

_____. 1972. "The Text of Jude 22–23." *ZNW* 63. Pp. 139–44.

Pfleiderer, O. 1902. *Das Urchristentum: seine Schriften und Lehren in geschichtlichem Zussammenhang.* 2nd ed. Berlin: G. Reimer.

Pieper, Karl. 1938. *Die Kirche Palästinas bis zum Jahre 135.* Köln: Bachem.

_____. 1939. *Neutestamentliche Untersuchungen.* Paderborn: Bonifacius.

Plumptre, E. H. 1903. *The General Epistles of St. Peter and St. Jude.* Cambridge: Cambridge University Press.

Reicke, Bo. 1970. *De Katolska Breven.* Stockholm: Verbum.

_____. 1964. *The Epistles of James, Peter and Jude.* Garden City, NY: Doubleday.

Reitzenstein, R. 1927. *Die hellenistischen Mysterienreligionen.* Stuttgart: B. G. Teubner.

Robertson, A. T. 1934. *A Grammar of the Greek New Testament in the Light of Historical Research.* Nashville: Broadman.

Roller, Otto. 1933. *Das Formular der paulinischen Briefe.* Stuttgart: Kohlhammer.

Schelkle, Karl H. 1970. *Der Petrusbriefe, Der Judasbrief.* HKzNT 13.2. 3rd ed. Freiburg: Herder.

Schlatter, Adolf. 1950. *Die Briefe des Petrus, Judas, Jakobus, der Brief an die Hebräer.* Stuttgart: Calwer.

Schrage, Wolfgang. 1973. "Der Judasbrief." In Horst Balz and W. Schrage, *Die katholischen Briefe.* NTD 10. Göttingen: Vandenhoeck and Ruprecht.

Schwegler, A. 1846. *Das nachapostolische Zeitalter in den Hauptmomenten seiner Entwicklung.* Tübingen: L. F. Fues.

Scott, E. F. 1932. *The Literature of the New Testament.* New York: Columbia University Press.

Seethaler, P. A. 1987. "Kleine Bemerkungen zum Judasbrief." *BZ* 13. P. 262.

Sellin, G. 1986. "Die Häretiker des Judasbriefes." *ZNW* 77. Pp. 206–25.

Sickenberger, J. 1911. "Engels-oder Teufelslästerer im Judasbriefe (8–10) und im 2. Petrusbriefe (2,10–12)?" *Festschrift zur Jahrhundertfeier der Universität zu Breslau. SGV* 13–14. Breslau: M. H. Marcus. Pp. 612–39.

Sidebottom, E. M. 1967. *James, Jude, 2 Peter.* London: T. Nelson.

Soards, Marion L. 1988. "1 Peter, 2 Peter, and Jude as Evidence for a Petrine School." *Aufstieg und Niedergang der Römischen Welt* II.25. Berlin: de Gruyter. P. 3831.

Soden, H. von. 1899. *Hebräerbrief, Briefe des Petrus, Jakobus, Judas.* 3rd ed. Freiburg: J. C. B. Mohr.

Spicq, Ceslas. 1966. *Les épîtres de saint Pierre.* Paris: J. Gabalda.

Spitta, Friedrich. 1885. *Der zweite Brief Petrus und der Brief des Judas.* Halle: Waisenhauses.

Strack, H. L. 1896. *Abriss des biblischen Aramäisch.* Leipzig: J. C. Hinrichs.

_____ and P. Billerbeck. 1956. *Kommentar zum Neuen Testament aus Talmud und Midrash.* 2nd ed. München: C. H. Beck.

Turner, Nigel. 1976. *Grammar of New Testament Greek.* Edinburgh: T & T Clark. IV.

Vander Kam, James. 1973. "The Theophany of Enoch I.3*b*–7, 9." *VT* 23. Pp. 129ff.

Vermes, G. 1973. *Scripture and Tradition in Judaism.* 2nd ed. Leiden: Brill.

Wand, J. W. C. 1934. *The General Epistles of St. Peter and St. Jude.* London: Methuen.

Watson, Duane F. 1988. *Invention, Arrangement, and Style: Rhetorical Criticism of Jude and 2 Peter.* SBLDS, 104. Atlanta: Scholars Press.

Weiss, Bernard. 1892. *Die katholischen Briefe.* TU. Leipzig: J. C. Hinrichs.

_____. 1886. *Lehrbuch der Einleitung in das Neue Testament.* Berlin: Hertz.

Werdermann, H. 1913. *Die Irrlehrer des Judas-und 2. Petrus-briefes.* Gütersloh: Bertelsmann.

Werner, E. 1945–46. "The Doxology in Synagogue and Church: A Liturgico-Musical Study." *HUCA* 19. Pp. 275–351.

Wickenhauser, Alfred. 1972. *Einleitung in das Neue Testament.* 6th ed. Rev. by J. Schmid. Freiburg: Herder.

Wickham, L. R. 1974 "The Sons of God and the Daughters of Men: Genesis VI.2 in Early Christian Exegesis." *Language and Meaning: Studies in Hebrew Language and Biblical Exegesis,* ed. by J. Barr et al. Leiden: Brill. Pp. 135–47.

Wikgren, Allen. 1967. "Some Problems in Jude 5." *Studies in the History and Text of the New Testament in Honor of Kenneth W. Clark.* StudDoc, 29. Ed. by B. Daniels and J. Suggs. Salt Lake City: University of Utah Press.

Wilson, R. McL. 1972. "How Gnostic Were The Corinthians?" *NTS* 19. P. 71.

Windisch, Hans. 1951. *Die katholischen Briefe.* 3rd ed. by H. Preisker. Tübingen: J. C. B. Mohr.

Wisse, Frederik. 1972. "The Epistle of Jude in the History of Heresiology." *Essays on the Nag Hammadi Texts in Honor of Alexander Böhlig,* ed. by M. Krause. Leiden: Brill. Pp. 133–43.

_____. 1981. "The 'Opponents' in the New Testament in Light of the Nag Hammadi Writings." *Colloque international sur les textes de Nag Hammadi,* ed. by B. Barc. Louvain: Peeters. Pp. 99–120.

Wohlenberg, G. 1915. *Der erste und zweite Petrusbriefe und der Judasbrief.* Leipzig: A. Deichert.

Zahn, Theodor. 1909. *Introduction to the New Testament,* trans. by J. Trout. Edinburgh: T & T Clark.